Benjamin Stonham

The Parable of the Ten Virgins Opened

Or, Christ's coming as a bridegroom cleared up, and improved from Matthew XXV.

Benjamin Stonham

The Parable of the Ten Virgins Opened
Or, Christ's coming as a bridegroom cleared up, and improved from Matthew XXV.

ISBN/EAN: 9783744792752

Printed in Europe, USA, Canada, Australia, Japan

Cover: Foto ©Lupo / pixelio.de

More available books at **www.hansebooks.com**

PARABLE
OF THE
TEN VIRGINS
OPENED:
OR,
CHRIST'S Coming as a Bridegroom Cleared up, and Improved from *Matthew* XXV.

By *Benjamin Stonham*.

vide Dr Calamy's Acct. p 646 Cont. 787.

The *Marriage* of the *Lamb* is *Come*, and his *Wife* hath made her self *Ready*, Rev. 19. 7.

LONDON,
Printed in the Year M.DC.LXXVI.

ERRATA.

PAge 11. Line 8. *Tinie* for *Tyme*. p. 20. l. 18. *by* for *be*. p. 21. l. 23. Read *Voles*. p. 21. l. *ult*. r. such. p. 45. l. 14. r. these. p. 76. l. 14. r. tarryeth. p. 69. l. 38. r. 8. p. 121. l. 22. r. Awakened. p. *ibid*. l. 33. r. 18. p. 122. l, 2. r. the. p. 124. l. 32. r. 28 p. 131. l. 24. r. be. p. 138. l. 37. r. might. p. 139. l. 29. r. Complainers. p. 153. l. 28. r. Delatory. p. 175. l. 36. r. every. p. 186. l. 15. r. her. p. 194. l. 33. r. 32. p. 158. l. 39. r. 11*th*. p. 202. l. 21. r. were. p. 204. l. 17. r. 12. p. 214. l. 3. r. were. p. 216. l. 36. r. shewen. p. 216. l. 40. r. 15. p. 218. l. 40. r. *Mat*. 9. 15. p. 221. l. 40. r. 1 *Kings* 1. 41. p. 227. l. 30. r. peculiar. p. 229. l. 19. r. Attired. p. 233. l. 29. after *Salvation* add *should awaken us*, Rom. 13. 11. p. 234. l. 17. r. oft. p. 241. l. 26. r. as. p. 265. l. 2. r. 29. p. 265. l. 35. r. and as if. p. 279. l. 9. r. bare. p. 283. l. 38. r. as. p. 299. l. 24. r. Type. p. 299. l. 35. r. his. p. 96. l. 18. r. *Ezekiel*. p. 96. l. 34. r. *Ezekiel*. p. 96. l. *ult*. r. resented.

To the READER.

AS in all Ages it hath been Satan's Design to Blind the Minds of Men, even from our first Parents, whom he had soon rockt into a dead sleep, with all their Posterity, in which they had lyen till now, had not Christ awakened them: So ever since, and more Eminently in the last Times is he so Employed, all things concurring to the Accomplishment of his Design. The World, which hath Ordinarily been a pricking Bryar, by that means preventing some Mens Sleeping, hath been turned into a Bed of ease; and the Watch-men, by whom Slumberers should have been awakened, have supported them with Pillows; yea, Men have been so disposed to sleep, that they have closed their own Eyes, until the Best have slumbred, and the most are fast asleep; which hath ever been Dangerous, but now more than ever. Therefore the Lord Jesus Christ, who was manifested to Destroy the works of the Devil, hath Knocked at such sleepers Doors, by his awakening Providences, and by his Servants the Prophets, Rising up early, and sending them. But now the danger of sleeping unto Death is so great, that he sends forth a Cryer at Midnight, to prevent the Ruine that would o're-whelm those Sleepers by the Morning.

This is the Critical Hour, and the last Application; those that do not then Recover, perish for ever. Were we sensible of the present Danger of such a Nature, we should not be Offended at plain dealing.

The following Discourse (which the Providence of God gave me with others an Opportunity to Hear) is of such a Nature: The Instrument by whom this Truth was sounded forth, being first sent to awaken others, now sleeps in Jesus; who willing that all Men should come to the knowledge of the Truth, hath by his Providence Ordered the surviving of this Testimony, that so it may come to their hands who had not an Opportunity, nor (possibly) an Heart to Receive it from the Speakers Lips. It was Joy to me to hear of its being Printed, though I do expect as Christ himself did, so his most Material Truths will meet with hard Usage in the World. The Foundation and Corner-stone, which God lays in Sion, becomes a stone of stumbling to the Men of Judah (being Rejected of their Builders) yet nevertheless precious to them that believe. 'Tis Dangerous not to Believe the Truth, much more to be Offended at it. The Good Lord prevent Sorrow upon either Account.

Receive nothing for Truth, without a Touch-stone: We do not onely Tell Gold after a Brother, but heretofore when Men were more Exact, did Weigh it also with Gold Weights, which then were wont to be in Readiness

To the Reader.

with them, differing from those by which baser things were Weighed. So also is utmost Holy Curiosity Commendable in Weighing Truth, onely let us be careful to have the Sanctuary Ballance (viz.) the Scriptures; and not the Traditions of the Elders, or formerly Received Principles.

And if something be hard to be Understood, be not Hasty to Reject it, much less the whole for the sake of it; the Fault may possibly be in thine Eye, and not in the Object; we Live under a Dispensation wherein the fine Gold, or Gospel-Grace is changed, and become Dim, as well as Lamps going out. The Difference between Wise and Foolish Virgins is not so easily discerned, save by searching the Vessels, which this serves unto, and Gold will lose nothing by being Rubbed; nor can Foolish Virgins be damnified by having the Emptiness of their Vessels discovered, whilst Oyl is to be bought: Solomon saith, to every Purpose there is Time and Judgment, therefore the Misery of Man is great, who wanteth Judgment, to know the Time appointed to his purpose. Every Professor will one day know this Truth, which yet will not prevent their Misery, save by the timeliness of such Knowledge. It was the great Aggravation of Jerusalem's sin and sorrow, that she did not know (even in that her Day) the things that did Concern her Peace, which therefore are hid from her eyes ever since; as we may well expect it will be with those Foolish Virgins, against whom (for the same Reason) Christ will shut his Door.

I know not what would be greater Rejoycing to me than to see Christ in his Truths and Interests advanced in mine own and others Hearts, to the silencing of that Ignorance and prejudice that hath with-stood the Receiving of the Truth in Love, wherein we might have been established, and not so Subject to be blown to and fro by the Tempters Wind, as at this Day. Going out at Midnight is attended with many Difficulties, but when once entred into Christ's Bride-Chamber, they will be no more Remembred, nor will there be any cause of Repenting that Labour when they shall hear others Knock, and Cry in vain without, which God prevent being our Portion, by a Timely and effectual Grafting into the true Olive-tree, that so this Oyl of Grace and Light may never fail, so an Entrance shall be Ministred into the Everlasting Kingdom of the Lord Jesus Christ, which is the Marriage-Supper of the Lamb, to which the Called are pronounced Blessed; untill when, Fellowship with this Testimony is Acknowledged a good Heritage, bestowed by the Lord on a very Unworthy Creature,

VV. B.

THE PARABLE

OF THE

Ten VIRGINS Opened.

Math. XXV. 1.

Then shall the Kingdom of Heaven be likened unto Ten Virgins, which took their Lamps, and went forth to meet the Bridegroom.

Christ having Satisfied his Disciples (in the fore-going Chapter) concerning the Signs, both of *Jerusalem*'s Destruction, and of H's own Coming; doth thereupon Exhort them to be Watchful, both from their Ignorance of that Day and Hour, *Mat.* 24. 42. as also from the Temptations which will Accompany such a Time, in point of sensual Security, *Mat.* 24. 38. Backsliding into Voluptuousness and Persecution, *v.* 48, 49. or at least-wise into a sleighty slumbring disposition, *Mat.* 25. 4, 5. Now, this Coming of Christ is either Personal or Precursory. His Second Personal Coming will be at the beginning of *John*'s *Millennium*, *Rev.* 20. 4. or *New Jerusalem*; and therefore we read of the Lamb's being there, *Rev.* 21. 22. and of Gods Tabernacling with Men, *v.* 3. as Christ did at his Incarnation, *John* 1.

14. in which regard he was then called *Immanuel*, or God with us, *Mat.* 1. 23. Which Perfonal Coming of his cannot fo properly be in this place intended; becaufe its fuddennefs, 1 *Cor.* 15. 52. (together with its Deftructivenefs unto the Generality of wicked ones, 2 *Pet.* 3. 10.) will not fo fairly Admit of any fuch Parley (between the Foolifh Virgins and the Wife, or Chrift and the Foolifh Virgins,) as is here fignified, *Mat.* 25. 9. 11, 12. But there is alfo a Precurfory Coming of Chrift, relating to us *Gentiles*, in thefe latter days, before the *Jews* Converfion; who will (at laft) have all their Ancient Priviledges (in a qualified fence) Reftored to them, but not untill the *Gentiles* fulnefs be come in, *Rom.* 11. 25.

Which Difpenfation (Ultimately referring to the Natural *Jews*) doth feem to be intended by That Coming of Chrift, which is diftinguifhed, as from the Deftruction of that Old Material Temple, fo from the proper Ending of this World at laft, *Mat.* 24. 3. (before which End Chrift will not Come in Perfon, 2 *Pet.* 3. 10.) And which Precurfory Coming of his, may poffibly be meant, by that Sign of the Son of Man, Diftinct from his Coming in the Clouds, *Mat.* 24. 30.

And thus we read of Chrifts Coming to Judge the Earth, *Pfal.* 96. 13. as he will do, when the feventh Trumpet foundeth, *Rev.* 11. 15. 18. or when the Ark is (in the Temple Opened) to be feen, *v.* 19. which Temple is not in *John*'s New *Jerufalem*, *Rev.* 21. 22. or at that Time, when Chrift will come in Perfon; and fo by Confequence, the Lord will come to Judge (and in thefe latter days) before his Perfonal or Proper Coming at the laft; or while the Ark and Tabernacle, or Temple (clear Types of Inftituted Worfhip) are in Being; and therefore thofe very words, *Pfal* 96. 13. are a part of that Song, 1 *Chron.* 16. 33. which *David* Compofed that Day, *v.* 7. in which he did remove the Ark, *v.* 1. Efpecially fince in the following *Pfalm*, (or *Pfal.* 97. which is but an Appendix to this former, or *Pfal.* 96.) God biddeth all the gods (or Men and Angels) to worfhip Chrift, *Pfal.* 97. 7. when he fhall bring in *Again* the firft begotten into the World, *Heb.* 1. 6. (for fo the *Greek* there is to be rendred,) which plainly hinteth Chrift's being to come *Again* before his fecond Perfonal Coming; or while the Ark (or Inftituted worfhip) is abiding, and when it fhall be fet in a New Tent, which *David* (or Chrift) hath pitched for it, 1 *Chron.* 16. 1. in his own City, 1 *Chron.* 15. 29.

And which Precurfory Coming (alfo) might be further Argued, from Chrift's being faid to Reign, together with the Seventh Trumpet's founding, *Rev.* 11. 15. who therefore muft needs come, at fuch a time,

and

The Parable of the Ten Virgins Opened.

and in some sence, though not in Person, as at the first, *Luke* 1. 32. and at the last, 2 *Tim.* 4. 1. for such a purpose. An Earnest of which Coming was in the days of *Constantine*, *Rev.* 12. 5. though but an Earnest, in Comparison of this.

Yea, therefore we also read of Christ's Rejoycing as a Bridegroom, (which is more close unto this present Parable of the Virgins) together with the full Redemption of his People, *Isa.* 62. 4, 5. which Prophecy relateth (Lastly) to the Literal *Jews*, and will compleatly be made good unto them at their last Conversion, before Christ's Personal Coming, as all confess: But in the mean time, their Promises will firstly be fulfilled upon us, that so through our Mercy they may obtain Mercy, having lost their Priority through unbelief, *Rom.* 11. 30, 31. From whence it followeth, that Christ will Come (as a Bridegroom) before his Personal Coming. And under that Consideration shall I pursue this Parable; although I dare not wholly exclude Christ's Personal Coming here, so far as it is Applicable thereunto, since every of his Comings are so like each unto other.

This being Premised, the Observation from the first Verse is this.

Observ. In these latter days, (or a little before the Seventh Trumpet's founding) the Kingdom of Heaven shall be likened unto Ten Virgins, which took their Lamps, and went forth to meet the Bridegroom.

In the Prosecution of which Point, some things will need to be enquired into, which are as followeth.

Quest. 1. What's meant by the Kingdom of Heaven here?

Answ. Those words are variously Interpreted in the Scripture.

1. Thereby is sometimes meant, the True Believers future Glory, which is entail'd upon the Poor in Spirit, *Mat.* 5. 3. and such as do the will of God, *Mat.* 7. 21. From all the Quarters of the World, *Mat.* 8. 11. The Perfection of which Glory will be in Heaven, strictly taken; and well may that State be called a Kingdom, because the Saints shall then be Kings, who now are Sufferers, 2 *Tim.* 2. 12. They shall then trample upon Satan, *Rom.* 16. 20. and not be subject any more to sin or sorrow, since they will be thus freed before that time, *Rev.* 21. 4. This Kingdom is now possessed by them, in Christ their Head, *Eph.* 2. 6. but yet they must conflict and wait, before their proper, Personal, and full possession.

2. Thereby is sometimes meant the Lord Jesus Christ himself; as when the Kingdom of Heaven is likened unto Treasure and a precious Pearl,

Pearl, which doth deferve the Sale of all, to Purchafe it, *Mat.* 13.44, 45, 46. This is the Lord from Heaven, 1 *Cor.* 15.47. The giver of his Peoples Crowns, 2 *Tim.* 4. 8. Yea, whofe very Perfon (by whomfoever he is enjoyed) may well be called an Heavenly Kingdom. The Quinteffence of Heaven confifts in being with him, *Phil.* 1.23. who alfo doth make his People to be Kings at prefent, *Rev.* 5. 10. Nor can an Earthly Kingdom give more content than he, in whom the fulnefs of all things dwelleth, *Col.* 1. 19. who alfo is the hope of Glory, *v.* 27.

3. Thereby are fometimes meant, all manner of Gofpel-Truths, together with the Preaching of them. As when the Kingdom of Heaven is likened unto a Grain of Muftard-feed, *Mat.* 13. 31. efpecially fome kind of Truths, *viz.* The Myfteries of the Kingdom of Heaven, *v.* 11. And therefore the *Pharifees* were faid to fhut up the Kingdom of Heaven againft Men, *Mat.* 23.13. becaufe they kept them from the knowledge of fuch Truths, *Luke* 11.52. The Publication whereof is alfo called by that Name; as when the Kingdom of Heaven is likened unto a Net, *Mat.* 13.47. which is moft fitly applicable unto Preaching, *Mat.* 4. 9. And as thefe things lead unto the Kingdom of Heaven, fo is there a Kingly and Heavenly Authority ftampt upon them, when duly managed, which maketh this to be their proper Name.

4. Thereby is fometimes meant a vifible Gofpel-Church; as when Chrift gave to *Peter* (in the Name of others) the Keys of the Kingdom of Heaven, *Mat.* 16. 19. Or all Church-Power, as it is explained, *Mat.* 18. 17, 18. And into which Kingdom of Heaven none have a right to enter, but they whofe Righteoufnefs is more than *Pharifaical*, Mat. 5. 20. And well may Gofpel-Churches have this Name, where Chrift himfelf is prefent, *Mat.* 18. 20. And whofe Inhabitants are onely Saints, 1 *Cor.* 1 2. and Angels, *Rev.* 1. 20.

5. Thereby is fometimes meant, the Difpenfation of the Gofpel, or ftate of things and Perfons (efpecially among Profeffors) in Gofpeltimes; and as in the General, from firft to laft; fo with Refpect to fuch a particular part thereof, *viz.* The Bridegroom's Coming. Thus is that Phrafe moft frequently to be Interpreted; as when the Kingdom of Heaven is likened unto a Sower, *Mat.* 13. 24. And when *John* bids, *Repent, for the Kingdom of Heaven is at hand,* Mat. 3. 2. And when Chrift faith of *John, That the leaft in the Kingdom of Heaven is greater than he,* Mat. 11. 11. Since though *John's* Miniftration was in fome fence above that of *Mofes,* yet was it not properly Evangelical. And in this laft fence, I fhall purfue thefe words, as being the plain meaning of them.

Queft. 2. Why

The Parable of the Ten Virgins Opened.

Quest. 2. Why is the Dispensation of the Gospel called a Kingdom?

Answ. 1. Because it is Governed by a King, as Christ is called, *Mat.* 2.2. whose Ministration that of the Gospel is, *Heb.* 8.6. Christ's Spiritual Government is Monarchical, which doth admit of no Companions; and therefore there is but one Law giver, *James* 4. 12. Nor will true Saints make mention of any other, *Isa.* 26. 13. And therefore Saints (as such) owe no Obedience unto Man, in Gospel-matters, save as this King's Authority is produced. What an Arch-Traitor is the Man of sin, who dareth to Prohibit or Impose, in such a Case, without Christ's leave? The Nations are for a Kingly Form among themselves, who yet therein Oppose the Sons of *Sion*, but all in vain, and to their own Destruction, *Psal.* 2. 5, 6.

2. Because this Kingdom is Distinct from any other, as in all Constitutions of that Nature. *Moses* hath no Command in Christ's own House; and therefore his bare Authority in (Gospel-times) is no sufficient Plea. The Kings of *Judah* were Types of Christ, and therefore in their days, the Temple was within the City, or Temporal and Spiritual Jurisdiction were then confounded: But in *Ezekiel's* last Vision, (relating to the Second Temple in Gospel-times) the Temple or Sanctuary is without the City, *Ezek.* 45. 1, 2. compared with *Ezek.* 48. 15. To hint the difference of those Dominions, which then will be made visible. Men may Create their Civil Rulers, (at least till such a time,) but cannot thereby make them to have Power in another's Kingdom, which all confess, save in Relation to the Right of Christ.

3. Because it is made up of divers Spirits, as every Kingdom is; wherein some Men are Righteous and others Wicked. A Family may be more pure than can be expected in a Kingdom. And therefore this more Refined Kingdom (here) is distributed into Wise and Foolish Virgins. Subjection unto Christ, doth not sufficiently evince a sameness of Disposition; and the Children of this Kingdom may be cast out of that which is to come, *Mat.* 8. 11, 12. There are a sort of base Professors, who yet may carry it fairly, untill a Temptation cometh, and then they shew themselves. They who are counted the best and upright, may yet prove very bad upon a Tryal, *Mic.* 7. 4, 5.

4. Because the same Laws do bind all sorts of Persons, within the Compass of such a Jurisdiction.: There is not one Law for Great Ones, and another for others; in this (no more than in any other) Kingdom. If this were duly weighed, some would not dare to give themselves a Dispensation, whilst they are opening the Law to others. Nor would
some

some others fondly think, that such a Duty is not incumbent upon them, unless they know it, and have it set upon their Hearts. The Foolish Virgins are not excused, though wanting Oyl or Light; because they and the Wise Live in one Kingdom, whose common Laws do equally Oblige them both.

5. Because it is not easily shaken or Removed, which holdeth true, with reference unto any Kingdom; but eminently here, as *Paul* informs us, *Heb.* 12.28. Churches may fail, and many Revolutions may occurr, but yet the Dispensation of the Gospel is abiding. This Kingdom subverted that of Old, *Heb.* 12.27. but never will be subverted by it: And therefore the Restauration of *Moses* his Law, (upon the Jews Conversion) and of an Adamitical State (or Legal Ministration) in *John's* New *Jerusalem*, are but some Men's un Scriptural Fancies. None will be ever saveable, but by a Gospel Faith and Duty, or through an Interest in the Everlasting Covenant.

Quest. 3. Why is this Dispensation called the Kingdom of Heaven?

Answ. 1. Because it is not of this World, but of a more sublimated or Heavenly Rise. *Moses* his Ministration is called worldly, *Heb.* 9. 1. because it was the same (for kind) with *Adam's*, whose Make was Earthly, 1 *Cor.* 15.47. But Christ's Ministration is like himself, who is the Lord from Heaven, 1 *Cor.* 15.47. How sad is their mistake, by whom the Dispensations of Grace and Nature are Confounded. The good of Nature will never prove Gospel-Holiness; nor is the difference between them onely Gradual, but also in point of Kind (as in Relation to God's thoughts and ours, *Isa.* 55.9.) else Earthly and Heavenly Priviledges may also be as well Confounded.

2. Because what is contained under it, is at the present (mostly) of a more Spiritual and invisible Nature, as Heavenly things yet are, 2 *Cor.* 4.18. He must have more than an Eye of Flesh, who can distinguish between the Wise and Foolish Virgins. *Moses* Transgressors were easily to be Convicted, but proper Gospel-sins are of a more Mysterious Nature. The Weapons of *Paul's* warfare were wholly Spiritual, 2 *Cor.* 10.4. which under the Law were mostly Carnal, consisting of Man's coercive power in Religious Matters. Legal Rewards and Threats were (save in shadows) altogether Temporal; but Gospel-Threats and Promises are chiefly Spiritual and Eternal.

3. Because it leadeth unto Heaven strictly taken, which never was, nor will be done by any other Dispensation. *Moses* did onely undertake for Earthly Blessings, but doth not speak one word of Heaven, save

in

in a way of Type and Figure, *Heb.* 9. 24. And sinless *Adam* should onely have Lived alway upon Earth, but not have been Translated thence to Heaven, by vertue of his present Covenant. Whereas this Dispensation of the Gospel doth rebound fallen Man (beyond whence *Adam* fell) into a state of Heavenly Glory. Oh what a Price is put into their hand, who Live there-under! Such may now walk from Earth to Heaven, as from one Room into another, can they but follow Christ, before the Partition-door between those Rooms is shut.

4. Because it is exceeding Glorious, as are all Heavenly things. *Moses* his Ministration was very dark, but here the Veil is done away, 2 *Cor.* 3. 14. That was the Dispensation of a Servant onely, This of a Son, *Heb.* 3. 5, 6. That was to be done away, but This remaineth, which therefore is much more Glorious, 2 *Cor.* 3. 11. That left poor Souls without a change; but This Transforms those under it, from Glory unto Glory, 2 *Cor.* 3. 18. Here are more Glorious Saints, and Institutions, and Priviledges, and Duties, and Discoveries, than generally were of Old. Here is a Spirit of Glory upon Sufferers, 1 *Pet.* 4. 14. *With Joy unspeakable, and full of Glory,* 1 Pet. 1. 8. Under the Ministration of this Glorious Gospel, 2 *Cor.* 4. 4.

5. Because a Fall from hence is most Destructive, as that from Heaven cannot but be. The wicked Angels are most sadly broken, because they fell from Heaven; and *Capernaum* was brought down to Hell, because sometimes exalted unto Heaven, *Mat.* 11. 23. Whilst *Tyre* and *Sidon*'s Torment would be more Tolerable, *v.* 22. The nearer that sinners are unto the God of Heaven, the more provoking is their sin, and suitable will be their Suffering. Therefore the Children of this Kingdom (if thrust out thence) must look for utter Darkness, *Mat.* 8. 12. It would be better for Foolish Virgins, if they had Lived among the *Sodomites,* whose Judgment will be lighter, because though Hell from Heaven fell on them, yet did they not fall to Hell from Heaven.

Quest. 4. Why are the Professors of such a Time, here called Virgins?

Answ. Because of the Resemblance between them and Virgins in the Letter.

1. Virgins are generally a Younger sort of Persons; and such are these, both in a Literal and Mystical sence. This Dispensation relateth unto a turn of things, such as hath been of later Years, in these our Days: Now, Aged Trees will not so easily bend, or bear a Transplantation; and it is God alone, who can perswade the Heart of *Japhet*,

to

8   The Parable of the Ten Virgins Opened.

to dwell in the Tents of *Shem*, *Gen*. 9. 27. his Younger Brother, *Gen*. 10. 21. Yea, therefore such are Mystically Younger also, because of those later Discoveries which are embraced by them. Both which have been abundantly exemplified, in our first goers forth.

2. Virgins are weak enough, the wisest of them, much more the Foolish ones; and such are these Professors. They are apt to be more ashamed of being seen in a dirty dress, than otherwise they would be, in a Corner; 'tis not sins being in them, but its being seen, that is most troublesome. They are Ambitious of going Fine, although unable to maintain that outward bravery, in point of pretending unto Grace and Peace, supposing else it would be to their shame. They will be in the Fashion, because it is the Fashion, and not because 'tis Modest or Convenient; as many did sometimes own Chrilts Kingly Interest, so long as it was in Fashion, who since have laid it quite aside. They will not Actually be defiled, but yet will dally with some less Temptations. They look to be Entreated, with reference unto the most desirable Offer, although its Loss be thereby hazarded.

3. Virgins will be, and do delight in one anothers Company, and so do these, untill there be some violent separation, or grievous discord. Next unto Christ, sincere Professors are most delighted each in other, *Psal*. 16. 3. Yea, such are for Communion with others also, whilst undiscovered; as Sheep will feed with Goats, untill the Shepherd part them, *Mat*. 25. 23. And more refined Hypocrites will leave the World, to walk with wiser Virgins than themselves; especially if five of such to five sincere ones, as in this Parable. Some Foolish Virgins (or uncontracted ones) may have a Love for Christ, *Cant*. 1. 3. much more for Spouses, *Psal*. 45. 14. whose being put asunder, may be with Mutual Tears.

4. Virgins are visibly undefiled, and such are these; at least, with reference unto more gross Pollutions. They may have wanton hearts, and eyes, and habits, but are not commonly called Adulteresses, Compared with others. These are ashamed of an Harlots Company, and cannot bear to be defamed with her Name or filthiness. Whatever they have sometimes been, they now will Covenant against all manner of Whorish Antichristianism. And with Respect unto their Carriage otherways; such are for Purity, both in Communion and Conversation, which maketh them to be accounted Virgins, untill they be out-stript by others, or do degenerate.

5. Virgins are wont at Marriages to be the Bride's Companions, *Psal*. 45. 14. & for her sake they are the Bridegroom's Friends. The wisest have too much Mercenariness in their Affections; but yet they have a true

Respect

respect for Christ upon his own Account; whilst others go out to meet him, meerly in hope to wear his Favours. What Zeal hath been profest for Christ, of later Years, because the Bridegroom's Coming was then expected? Many threw off their Harlots Veil, lest that should hinder their being the expected Brides Attendants; the reality of whose Affections is now come under a Providential Examination, by Reason of the Bridegroom's stay.

Quest. 5. Why is Christ called a Bridegroom, at such a Time?

Answ. 1. Because the Bride is onely his. By which word [*Bride*] the Saints are sometimes meant; but here 'tis meant of such a glorious Dispensation upon Earth, which Saints expect, and shall Live under. And thus Christ's Spiritual Kingdom was called the Bride, in Competition with *John Baptist*'s Ministration, *John* 3. 28, 29. So is the New *Jerusalem* called, when Christ shall come again, *Rev.* 21. 2, 3. And so is that fore-running State here called, which will be under the Seventh Trumpet. Now, if this Bride be Christs, let us acknowledge all that Glory to be his; and let not *John*'s Disciples murmure at *John*'s Decrease: and let us not fall too much in Love with another's Bride, but let our Rejoycing then be chiefly for the Bridegroom's sake, *John* 3. 29.

2. Because this is the time of Marriage, or else one's being onely made sure to such a Woman, is not enough to make an Actual Bridegroom. Christ was of Old Contracted unto this Kingdom, *Psal.* 2. 8, 9. and 93. 2. but is content to wait, untill his Bride be Ready, and then his Marriage cometh, *Rev.* 19. 7. Although his present Marriage will be but by a Proxy (compared with that in *John*'s *Jerusalem*) after the manner of Earthly Princes, when Living in another Kingdom, as Christ now doth; who therefore honoureth his People first, by giving them leave to Marry his Bride, on his behalf, and then he calls himself the Bridegroom, *Isa.* 62. 4, 5.

3. Because the manner of his Coming then, will be like that of a Bridegroom.

1. Very Glorious. A Bridegroom is deck'd with Ornaments, *Isa.* 61. 10. and so are his Friends and Followers. And thus will Christ come at such a Time, the day of whose Espousals was very Glorious, *Cant.* 3. 11. and then much more his Wedding-day. His Chariots will then be Twenty Thousand, even Thousands of Angels, as on Mount *Sinai*, *Psal.* 68. 17. at his first appearing. The Father will then Declare (as he hath partly done already) that Christ is his Son, *Psal.* 2. 7. By the Glorious manner of his Appearing, *Titus* 2. 13. He will

then ride upon the Heavens, by his Name Jah, *Pfal.* 68. 4. which is contracted of *Jehovah*, the Father's Name, *Pfal.* 110. 1. To fignifie that his appearing Glory then, will be fome lefs Abridgment of his Fathers Glory, *Mat.* 16. 27.

2. With utmoſt ſpeed. A Bridegroom is up betimes upon his Wedding-day; accounting each hour a Year, and knowing no Pace but Galloping; in which regard, the fpeedy moving Sun is likened to a Bridegroom, *Pfal.* 19. 5. And thus will Chriſt come quickly, *Rev.* 3. 11. *Leaping upon the Mountains, and skipping upon the Hills,* Cant. 2. 8. That is, when once he is upon his March, his Perfonal appearing will be in the twinkling of an Eye, 1 *Cor.* 15. 52. And his Precurfory Coming will be a Type of that. The Bride will then be Ready, and then his Motion muſt needs be fwift, that being his onely Obſtacle, *Rev.* 19. 7. The cry of his Saints at fuch a Time, will haften his fpeedy Coming, *Luke* 18. 7, 8.

3. With heightned Zeal, or fulnefs of Affection evidenced. Then ſhall the Field be Joyful before the Lord, *Pfal.* 96. 12, 13. *For Corn ſhall make the Young Men chearful, and Wine the Maids,* Zech. 9. 17. when Chriſt ſhall come as King, *v.* 9. Yea, he will then fcatter his Gifts among the worſt, *Pfal.* 68. 18. Turning their Water into Wine upon his Wedding-day. What Tongue can then exprefs, what Heart can apprehend, the Richnefs of this Bridegroom's Favours upon his Friends, at fuch a time? And as to the Bride her felf, her Clothing ſhall be of wrought Gold, *Pfal.* 45. 13. whom Angels ſhall ſhew to others, with Admiration, *Rev.* 21. 9. Yea, and the King himfelf ſhall greatly defire her beauty, *Pfal.* 45, 11. Rejoycing as a Bridegroom, *Ifa.* 62. 5.

Queſt. 6. What's meant by taking Lamps, and going forth to meet him?

Anfw. Lamps are of ufe to Guide one in the dark, and therefore the Word is likened to a Lamp, *Pfal.* 119. 105. So that by [*Taking their Lamps*] is meant the furniſhing of themfelves with what might be of Ufe to lead them in their way at fuch a Time. They did conclude, the Bridegroom's Coming would be with Clouds and Darknefs, which put them upon this Proviſion. Indeed the Day of his Salvation is as a Lamp that burneth, *Ifa.* 62. 1. But yet this Day beginneth with an Evening, *Zech.* 14. 7. At leaſt-wife, in point of clear Difcerning; as hath been to be Obſerved in our Times, when there was firſt a going out, which all our Profeſſing Virgins did feeem to Underſtand at fuch a time. Now, this going forth to meet him, may be Interpreted three ways.

1. As

The Parable of the Ten *Virgins Opened.* 11

1. As an Evidence of Longing to behold him with the firſt; thus did the *Jews* go out to *John,* Mat. 11. 9. And *Balaam* to meet the Lord, *Numb.* 23. 15. Yea, thus God Meeteth him that Rejoyceth, and worketh Righteouſneſs, *Iſa.*64. 5. And thus all ſorts of Virgins were ſometimes very deſirous to ſee the Bridegroom, who therefore could not ſtay untill he came, but muſt go out to meet him. How did the Pulpits, Preſſes, and Occaſional Diſcourſes (then) abound with canvaſſing Timie Truths and Duties, to furniſh themſelves with Light into their way. They who Delight in Chriſt, cannot but ſeek him alſo, *Mal.* 3. 1. with reference unto his Perſon, Truths, and Intereſts ; and happy is that Soul, who is Admitted to behold this Sun at its firſt Riſe. This vehemency of Deſire, is from the wiſer Virgins Judgment, and from the others Ignorance of the Nature of his Appearing; *Amos* 5. 18.

2. As a ſignal of that Reſpect which they have for him. Thus *Lot* went out to meet the Angels, *Gen.* 19. 1. And *Joſeph* to meet his Father, *Gen.* 46. 29. And *Solomon* his Mother, 1 *Kings* 2. 19. Whereas a Perſon's ſtanding till others come to him, doth manifeſt his Diseſteem of them, *Jer.* 15. 19. Chriſt is the deſerving Object of all Honour, eſpecially when he cometh as a Bridegroom, *Rev.* 19. 7. which Virgins know, who therefore then go out to meet him. Wiſe Virgins ſaw the Glory of his firſt Appearance, *John* 1. 14. but all ſhall ſee that of his Second Coming, *Mat.* 24. 30. which at this Time the Fooliſh Virgins had a Glympſe of; and therefore they alſo are gone forth to meet him.

3. As this their going out, doth intimate, what is Required thereunto?

1. As one goeth out of his Private Houſe into the open ſtreets ; or with Reſpect to that more Publick Teſtimony on Chriſts behalf, at ſuch a Time. This was the caſe of all our Virgins, who did of Old bear Witneſ, to the Truths of Chriſt, but onely in their private Houſes; whereas a Spirit of boldneſs appeared in them afterwards ; So as to declare againſt the whole of (then known) Antichriſtian ſm, yea, in the Face of utmoſt Danger. If any then ſhould but have told them, how they would after run into their holes again, (as they have generally done,) their Anſwer would have been like that of *Hazael's* to *Eliſha,* 2 *Kings* 8. 13.

2. With Reference unto their going out of Ancient Myſtical Houſes, which muſt be left behind, by thoſe, who think to meet the Bridegroom. And thus did all our Virgins at. ſuch a Time. Some then went out of

C 2 their

their former way of National Worship, and Church-Government: Others went out of the Ancient National Church-State: And though some of them were fastned by a Rope unto those Houses still, which since hath drawn them back again; yet others were wholly loosened from them, which is their Mercy. Nor were they likely to wear the Bridegroom's Favours (in case he had then come) without these Tokens of their Virginity.

3. With Reference unto one's outward Interest, which must be gone out of also; and whereupon the other two depend. The least Advance Christ-ward, is into Dirty, Deep, and Dangerous ways at first; and the Mother of Harlots will both brawl and fight, when call'd an Whore, or when her Dress hath any dirt cast on it. And in this Sence, there was a going forth by all our Virgins. Some lost their Goods and Lives, and all did run the hazard of a Doubtful Case, with utmost Resolution. They did run well, had they but been as good at Length, as they were at Hand; and half that Self-denying Courage now, might have procured their Admission into the Bridegroom's Chamber, at his Coming. So much for the Explication: The Application followeth. And so

Use 1. From that word [*THEN*] we have hinted to us, both at what time it will be thus, and what will be at such a time. It hath been formerly Declared, what special Time is here referred unto, *viz*. That which is nigh unto the Seventh Trumpets Sounding: And then this Parable of the Virgins (I humbly suppose) will properly be fulfilled. And when the Generality of Professors do thus go forth, we may conclude from thence, what Dispensation we are hastning under. Now, we have plainly seen (in these our days) that going out to meet the Bridegroom, such as hath not been to be seen in former Ages, which giveth us to ghess at least, where we now are, in this dark Season.

2. Poor Foolish Virgins may sometimes possibly go forth (together with the wise) to meet the Bridegroom. So it is here fore-told, and hath been verified, or at the least, exemplified. Nor can I (as some others) think, this going forth was from a sinful hastiness, although there was no voyce of a Cry requiring it, as afterwards; whereof there was not any such need at first, because that Duty was Then more Obvious, the Spirits more couragious, and their encouragements greater, than at the second time. From whence is hinted, what little cause Men had to count those real Saints, who then went forth.

3. Christ thinks none worthy to be called Professors, save onely Virgins; under which Title here he comprehendeth all the Professors of
such

The Parable of the Ten Virgins Opened. 13

such a time. From whence we may be able to judge, concerning the visibility of their Spiritual State, who are not unpolluted Virgins. Some have been apt to call those Brethren, who still continued in their sin or Antichristianism, meerly because of their Parts and Moral Vertues: But Christ calls her the Mother of Harlots, *Rev.* 17. 5. who was Arrayed in Purple, *v.* 4. which was a Tabernacle Colour. Professors may be Hypocrites, but yet they must be Virgins, or undefiled ones. But then

Quest. How may we know a Virgin, and consequently, a visible Professor?

Answ. First, by way of Premise. My present work is not to Distinguish between a Wise and Foolish Virgin, or Characterize a Real Saint: But onely to shew who may be accounted Virgins, or Professors. In Order whereunto, we must be guided by the Times and Dispensations which Men Live under: Since that may have consisted with Virginity in Times of Ignorance, which doth denominate a Whore, in Times of greater Light and Knowledge. Time was, when Polygamy was not accounted Scandalous, nor Prelacy Antichristian; but many such things are now enough to cloud the visibility of Saint-ship, which heretofore have been more gently censured. Nor must I instance now in any of the Virgins Properties, save what are good and Commendable.

Secondly, By way of Resolution. And so Professors may be known by their resembling Virgins in the Letter, in these Respects.

1. Virgins are very Lovely, *Eccl.* 2. 2. And Desirable, *Isa.* 62. 5. Which doth expose them unto Temptations, 2 *Sam.* 13. 2. Such are Christ's Spouses in Reality, *Cant.* 1. 8. and 4. 7. and 6. 10. Such are all visible Saints in outward shew. They have black Hoods or Masks of outward Sufferings, *Cant.* 1. 6. *Isa.* 52. 14. But otherwise the Countenance is very comely, *Cant.* 2. 14. Such are at a further distance from this world's tanning Sun, and have the Advantage of Adorning Garments; yea, even the Foolish Virgins shine through the Reflection of others beams upon them, with whom they do Converse. Sinners are foul *Egyptians*, compared with *Sarah*, who therefore was most sorely Tempted, *Gen.* 12. 14, 15.

2. A Virgin will not be Hyred to play the Harlot, till first she ceaseth to be (in Heart) a Virgin. We Read of the Hyre of an Whore, *Deut.* 23. 18. Yea, there are some Whores without Reward, *Ezek.* 16. 34. But Virgins (both in the Letter and Mystery) prefer this Chastity before the greatest Gifts. 'Tis not the Pleasure or Profit of such a sin that

will

will entice unto so gross an Act; though lesser failings may be too much indulged. Those are abusively Sir-named Professors, who can comply with what hath been confessed to be Antichristianism; or seem to make no Conscience of Lying, Railing, Cheating, and the like; which are against the Light of Nature, and Answer unto gross Adultery.

3. Virgins will do their utmost to withstand defilement: Such will first Argue with the Tempter, as *Joseph* did with his Mistress, *Gen.* 39. 7, 8, 9. If that prevail not, such then will struggle, as *Tamar* did with *Amnon*, but that he was the stronger, 2 *Sam.* 13. 14. And in that case, such will cry out for help, *Deut.* 22. 27. And more especially unto the Lord, as *David* did, when many rose up against him, *Psal.* 3. 1. 4. Those are not visible Saints, who make a faint Resistance, when followed with Temptations of an Whorish Nature. And though poor Literal Virgins may be enforced, yet can there be no Mystical defiling, without the Party's will; yea, God would help, if heartily cryed unto, *Jer.* 29. 13.

4. A Virgin will not yield, in such a case, whatever Loss or Danger may ensue thereon. *Joseph* would rather lose his Garment, *Gen.* 39. 12. and run the hazard of his Place and Liberty, *v.* 20. than give consent unto his Whorish Mistress. As visible Saints will not be won by hopes of Gain, so neither by the fear of Suffering, to turn Adulteresses, in a Spiritual or Moral sence. Those ought not to be called Virgins, who do prefer their Liberty, Estate, or Life before their Chastity; the loss whereof is lookt upon (by Real Virgins) to be the greatest Suffering, and so it is, both in it self, and as it is so great a sin, which is indeed the onely Suffering to be avoided, in Comparison.

5. Virgins are careful to avoid Debauched Company. Such know that wholesome Counsel, *Prov.* 5. 8. Not to come nigh the Door of an Harlots House; and how poor *Dinah* was defloured, *Gen.* 34. 1, 2. And what a pleasing sin unto the Flesh this is, together with the force of Importunity and Opportunity upon a Treacherous Heart; and how it may be just with God, to leave such Dalliers unto themselves: All which are cogent with them, to keep out of the Tempter's Jurisdiction. The foolish Virgins here, Conversed onely with themselves, and with the Wise. Those are not visible Saints, who make no matter of being in the Devil's way, or of unnecessary Communion with Enticers of this Nature, *Gen.* 39. 10.

6. Virgins will not put on an Harlots Dress. We Read of the Attire of an Harlot, *Prov.* 7. 10. which honest Women will not be clothed with,

with, though never so Rich; yea, though it might keep off some pinching Cold. Our late Professors were very Curious in that Respect; not wearing their former Garments of Distinction, nor using the best Set-Form of Prayer that ever was, because these were accounted Whorish Habits: and their return unto such things again, hath very much blemished their Virgin-Reputation. A Gentleman thinks scorn to have an Ivy-bush hung at his Door; and visible Saints will shun appearances of evil, 1 *Thes.* 5. 22. especially when of so gross a Nature, by which they may be known from others.

7. Virgins are very neat, and studious of their Beauty. *Can a Maid forget her Ornaments,* Jer. 2. 32 ? Nor will a Spouse walk out without her Veil, *Cant.* 5. 7. Such are ashamed to be seen undrest; and what they wear is very clean; yea, they are for the finest stuff, and newest Fashion, with Sobriety. Their Looking-Glasses are of daily Use, nor will they be Offended, if Friendly told of any thing amiss about them; and would have every part of their Attire in its due place and Order. Such will wash oft, and carefully avoid what doth defile them; and keep within doors, for fear of being Sun-burnt. Those are no visible Saints, who are not very Accurate, Compared with the Generality.

8. Virgins are in the best Capacity of caring for the things of God, because discharged from other Cares; which is accordingly improved by Spiritual Virgins, 1 *Cor.* 7. 34. Poor Carnal Creatures are Married unto the World, whose care is therefore how to please that Husband, supposing it to be their Duty, because they have no Faith in God, nor Love for ought but *Mammon.* But visible Saints have had a taste of better things, *Heb.* 6. 5. and can Adventure more upon the Promise, which doth a little sublimate their Spirits and Affections. A Covetous Professor should not be kept in others Company, 1 *Cor.* 5. 11. And Virgins are wont to sort together.

9. Virgins are Noted for their comely silence; as being to be seen, but seldom heard: Whereas an Harlots voyce is Loud, *Prov.* 7. 10, 11. They who have least in Heart, are usually most full of Tongue; but deepest Waters make the smallest noyse. And though Saints are not for an Humorous silence, yet is their speech more sparing, especially in such like Cases, as these which follow. Saints will not Prate against the Truth, nor will they Boast of what they are, nor do they place the main of Duty in much speaking, nor do they relish vain Discourse, or love to speak themselves, but are more swift to hear. *A Wise Man spares his words,* Prov. 17. 27. And Foolish Virgins may Learn that piece of
Heavenly

Heavenly Breeding, by being in the others Company. The very speech of over-talkative Professors doth bewray them.

10. Virgins are mighty apt to blush, upon the least Occasion; whereas an Whores Face is Impudent, *Prov.* 7. 13. Refusing to be ashamed, *Jer.* 3. 3. Some cannot Blush, though guilty of Abominations, which is a dreadful Sign, *Jer.* 6. 15. But visible Saints are of a more Ingenuous Temper, most fully sensible of sin's defilement, and of a more tender Conscience, which makes them apt to Blush when any spot is on them, especially when coming before the Lord, *Ezra.* 9. 6. Yea, when they do but hear or speak of o.her's grosser failings, *Eph.* 5. 12. Harlots count this the Virgins weakness, but it is Vertue's Tincture, and from the want whereof Professors are shrewdly to be suspected.

11. Virgins have very strong Affections, and therefore the Lamentation of a Virgin, is put to signifie the depth of sorrow, *Joel* 1. 8. The Generality will never hurt themselves for Christ; but Spouses love him with their Soul, *Cant.* 1. 7. And Tremble at his Word, *Isa.* 66. 2. And Serve him with all their Might, 1 *Chron.* 29. 2. And break with Longing for him, *Psal.* 119. 20. And Joy in him with an Excessive Gladness, *Psal.* 4. 7. And Mourn for sin against him, as for an Onely Son, *Zech.* 12. 10. Those are no Prophets, (as all the Saints are termed, *Psal.* 105. 15.) whose Spirits and Affections are so much at their own Command, in Spiritual Cases, whilst Things and Persons of a Godly sort, are to be known from others by their Zeal and Vehemency, 2 *Cor.* 7. 11.

12. Virgins are forward to go forth, and meet the Bridegroom, though in the dark; yea, though exposed thereby to Loss and Danger, which is the necessary Consequent of going out at such a Time. 'Tis true, some of them (as the Foolish Virgins) may chiefly be drawn out by their Companions; or from an hope of being put among the Bride's Honourable Women, or meerly from a Religious Humour and spirit of Curiosity, to see and to be seen: But upon one account or other, all Virgins are ambitious of this Service, who otherwise are not so much as visible Saints; and therefore Christ knows not those Foolish Virgins, *Mat.* 25. 12. Because they went not forth the second time, *v.* 8. as at the first, *v.* 1.

MATH.

Mat. XXV. 2.

And Five of them were wise, and Five were Foolish.

IN these words we have the Ten fore-named Virgins Distributed, or Distinguished, with reference unto their Wisdom and Folly, which cannot be meant in a Natural sence, as *Eccl.* 2. 19. Or in a Worldly sence, as *Luke* 16. 8. Or in one's own Conceit and Apprehension onely, which is forbidden, *Rom.* 12. 6. But in a Moral sence, and in Reality.

And so the Observation from these words, is this.

Observ. Professors in these latter days, will be, some of them Spiritually wise, and others of them in the same sence Foolish; as Folly is put for sin, and Wisdom for New Covenant-Grace.

Whence several things are offered to be enquired into.

Quest. 1. Why is New Covenant-Grace exprest by Wisdom, &c.

Answ. 1. Wisdom is chiefly seated in the Understanding, or Intellectual Faculty, and doth consist in Light or Knowledge, and so doth Grace, which therefore is Resembled by it. The New Man is renewed in Knowledge, *Col.* 3. 10. And Grace is called the Law of the Mind, *Rom.* 7. 23. Whilst sin is oft-times called Darkness, *Eph.* 4. 18. and 5. 8. Which meerly being Privative, doth therefore need no positive Cause; and consequently there's no Necessity, that either God should be its Author, or that the Soul (which is its Subject) should be by Natural Generation (upon the one of which Rocks many have run, from un-acquaintance with sin's proper Notion) since sin is nothing but the Issue of an Active Spirit, devoid of Light, which then cannot but err or stumble, *John* 11. 10.

2. Wisdom (or Knowledge) is that, wherein the Image of God consisteth, *Col.* 3. 10. A lower kind of wisdom, was that wherein consisted (mainly) God's Essential Image, *Gen.* 1. 26. And highest wisdom (or true Holiness) is that, wherein God's Personal Image doth consist, *Eph.* 4. 24. As Christ who was his Father's wisdom, *Luke* 11. 49. (with *Mat.* 23. 34.) Is therefore called the Image of his Person, *Heb.* 1. 3. Which is the onely Image of God, now owned by him, in a Moral sence; so that a Godly wise Man is now the onely God-like Man, whereas the Foolish sinner is like unto the Devil, *John* 8. 44. who is Resembled by that Foolish Woman, *Prov.* 9. 13. In opposition unto Christ or Wisdom, *v.* 1.

3. Wisdom is to be got with all our getting, as that which is the Principal thing, *Prov.* 4. 7. Above Gold and Silver, *Prov.* 16. 16. More precious than Rubies, *Prov.* 3. 14. 15. Or all that can be else desired, *Prov.* 8. 11. The price whereof Man knoweth not, *Job* 28. 12, 13. All which is true concerning Grace, which therefore is fitly called Wisdom. Grace is that Better part, or One thing Needful, *Luke* 10. 41, 42. and will be generally so accounted, though now contemned. Saints would not lose their Graces for all the World. Godliness is profitable for all things, 1 *Tim.* 4. 8. It maketh a Poor Man Rich, *Rev.* 2. 9 A Needy Man contented, *Phil.* 4. 11, 12. And taketh the upper hand of present Peace, 1 *Thes.* 1. 1. and future Glory, *Psal.* 84. 11.

4. Wisdom is very Rare, and so is Gospel-Grace. Great men are not always wise, nor yet the Aged, *Job* 32. 9. *Job* found not one wise man among his Friends, *Job* 17. 10. And wisdom was far from *Solomon* himself, when he said, *I will be Wise*, *Eccl.* 7. 23. The whole world doth lye in wickedness, 1 *John* 5. 19. And the one half of Professing Virgins are here declared to be Foolish; yea, 'tis but little Grace that's to be found among the best of God's own People. Some call their Vices Vertues; and most Men count that Spiritual, which is but meerly Animal, or Natural, because they judge of Actions and Affections by their Matter onely: according to which Rule, the Sacred Fire upon the *Jewish* Altar might have been counted Common.

5. Wisdom is chiefly self-advantaging, and so is Grace. If thou be wise, thou shalt be wise for thy self, *Prov.* 9. 12. Such may be profitable to themselves, though not to God, *Job* 22. 2. He therefore loveth his own Soul, who getteth wisdom, *Prov.* 19. 8. 'Tis true, good works are also Profitable unto others, *Tit.* 3. 8. But as self-gain is far the greatest, so Grace (as Grace) doth onely benefit the Soul it self. And though one's strength may help another, without his will, yet wisdom is not Effectual to Preserve, or Guide, save him in whom it is. Gifts may more profit others than ones self, but Grace leaves not its Owner destitute of what it gives to others.

6. A little Folly doth prejudice him very much, who is reputed wise; as sweetest Oyntments are most unsavoury, in Case dead Flyes be in them, *Eccl.* 10. 1. And so it is with Gospel-Grace. A dirty Swine is not so much observed as a Dirty Sheep; nor sin in any, so much as in the Saints, because their Linnen is clean and white, *Rev.* 19. 8. which maketh spots to be the more conspicuous. Degenerating Saints are most abominable, as Animal parts and Spirits Putrified (because they are the best) are most Offensive. Let not a wise man therefore utter vanity,

vanity, whatever others do, *Job* 15.2. Remembring how wicked ones Blafphemed when *David* fell; 2 *Sam.* 12. 14. becaufe he had a name for wifdom.

Queft. 2. How fhall we Diftinguifh between a Wife and Foolifh Virgin?

Anfw. 1. By way of Premife. No Man is able (Infallibly) to make it out, wherein this Difference doth confift, fo as to fatisfie himfelf or others fully, from the bare Matter of beft Actions and Aff. &ions; all which are Imitable by fome cunning Hypocrite, who mainly differeth from a Real Saint, in point of Principle, or with Refpect unto that Spiritual Root of Actions and Affections, which chiefly conftituteth their being Gracious; the Nature of which Root is fo Myfterious, as that it cannot well be uttered, much lefs be clearly underftood, without the Spirit's Light and Witnefs. So that man's utmoft work and skill (in matters of this Nature) is, rather to fhew the Negative, or who are not wife Virgins; (fince flefhly Fruits are, of the two, more manifeft, *Gal.* 5. 19.) than to pretend unto the Demonftration of Spirituality; fave by thofe choifer Effects and Properties, wherewith true Gofpel-Grace is conftantly Attended; but yet it is very Cauteloufly to be Concluded by them. And though fome more Diftinguifhing Character (than thofe which follow) might poffibly be produced, in cafe the bufinefs were purfued at large; yet is my prefent enquiry bounded by this Metaphor of Wifdom, and what the Scripture fpeaketh unto the point in hand, under that fpecial and peculiar confideration. Therefore let not the expectations of any be over-large, fince I am now under a double Limitation, *viz.* Firft, Of holding to this fingle word of Wifdom; and Secondly, Of fhewing rather, who are Foolifh, or Gracelefs Perfons, than who may (Peremptorily) be termed Wife; at leaft, with reference unto the Greater part of mine enfuing Characters.

This being Premifed, I now fhall Anfwer unto the fore-named Queftion, by way of fober Refolution, from what the Scripture fpeaks concerning Wifdom, by which the Nature of Gofpel-Grace is fhadowed out unto us. And fo,

1. A Godly wife man departs from Evil, *Prov.* 11. 14. 16. *Job* 28. 28. Sin doth Depart from others, perhaps, together with the Tempter, who fometimes gives his Servants Reft: Or from the want of Natural ftrength, as fome Corruptions may decay with Age; or elfe becaufe one Luft calls for another, as Covetoufnefs will make the Drunkard fober. But otherwife, it is a fport to Fools to be mifchievous, *Prov.* 10. 23. And an abomination to depart from Evil, *Prov.* 13. 19. Where-

as a Gracious Heart runs from a Temptation as from a Bear, and leaveth sin, before it leaveth him; groaning to be delivered, *Rom.* 7. 24. Accepting help offered, as *Jer.* 41. 13, 14. and keeping himself from being touched afterwards, 1 *John* 5. 18.

2. Wise men are for a good Foundation, or Building upon a Rock, *Mat.* 7. 24. whilst Fools are satisfied with a sandy bottom, *v.* 26. If Foolish Virgins be but Reformed, or bear some pleasant Fruit, they never mind the Root or Principal, which is the main of all. Whereas the wiser sort, are for the changing of their Tree, *Mat.* 12. 23. and bearing Fruit in Christ. *John* 15. 2. Or in the newness of the Spirit, *Rom.* 7. 6. Such are for making their Election sure, 2 *Pet.* 1. 10. Proving themselves, 2 *Cor.* 13. 5. and begging of God to search them, *Psal.* 139. 23. because they know, the fairest Super-structure will stand or fall, according to the Nature of its Ground, whereon 'tis raised.

3. Wise men are very circumspect (or Accurate) in their walking, which Fools are not, *Eph.* 5. 15. Poor Foolish Virgins make light of Dallying with Temptations, and mock at something which is a sin, *Prov.* 14. 9. In case their Copy by not blotted, Hair-strokes are not much heeded in their writing. Whereas a Gospel-Saint is very curious, hating vain Thoughts, *Psal.* 119. 113. Abstaining from Appearances of Evil, 1 *Thes.* 5. 22. Proving the Perfect will of God, *Rom.* 12. 2. not venturing unto the utmost of what is Lawful, 1 *Cor.* 10. 23. but walking worthy of the Lord to all well-pleasing, *Col.* 1. 10. and begging to be cleansed from secret faults, *Psal.* 19. 12.

4. Wise ones are for the Building of their House, or for the carrying on of what they have begun; but Foolish Persons are for the plucking down of their own building, with their own Hands, *Prov.* 14. 1. These Foolish Virgins went out at first, but failed the second time, and so lost all their Labour. And therefore with what Face can some men Glory in a former Testimony for that Truth, from whence they have since fallen? Such seem to be Christ's House at present, but do not prove so in the Issue, because they hold not out untill the End, *Heb.* 3. 6. Many come out of *Egypt*, who yet come not to *Canaan*; because their time is spent in walking to and fro, whilst in the Wilderness. Whereas a Gracious Heart goes forward, *Ezek.* 1. 9. forgetting what is behind, *Phil.* 1. 13. And alway adding unto his Spiritual good Beginnings, 2 *Pet.* 1. 5.

5. Wise men will Hear, *Prov.* 1. 5. And Hearken unto Counsel, *Prov.* 12. 15. And will receive Commands, *Prov.* 10. 8. Whereas Fools are not to be spoken unto, because they will despise the Speakers wisdom, *Prov.* 23. 9. How sadly doth some Professor's prating evidence

The Parable of the Ten Virgins Opened.

dence their present Folly, and their future Fall, *Prov.* 10.8. When Truths are not received in Love, (whatever Ignorance may be pretended) 'tis one sad sign of a Professor's state, 2 *Thes.* 2. 10. 12. And this is the saddest time for Cavilling that ever was, as Foolish Virgins will Experience, with whom the wise (at such a time) will not delight to Talk, when sought unto for Oyl or Light, *Mat.* 25. 8, 9. whose Answer intimateth, their being weary of Discoursing with them.

6. A wise man seeketh knowledge, *Prov.* 18. 15, and doth not onely receive it, when brought unto him: Such know its worth, and that it lyeth low, as Silver doth; which putteth them upon a suitable searching for it, *Prov.* 2. 4. Saints can have no Peace, in being Ignorant of their Duty, but are Industrious to understand it. Some things are left more dark in the Scriptures, that studious Saints might be distinguished from sluggish sinners, whose Soul desireth, and hath nothing, *Prov.* 13. 4. How little is some kind of Knowledge searched after by the generality, who rather seem to be afraid of seeing that which hazardeth their worldly Interest, and thereby are evinced to be Foolish Virgins.

7. The wisdom of the Prudent, is, to understand his way, *Prov.* 14. 8. and to look well unto his going, *v.* 15. Such will not see with others Eyes, as to the matters of their Faith and Practice; but Labour for a full perswasion in themselves, *Rom.* 14. 5. They are not under the Command of Major vote, 1 *Kings* 22. 13, 14. but are Redeemed from Traditions, 1 *Pet.* 1. 18. and have no Masters (or Leader of the way) save onely Christ, *Mat.* 23. 10. Whereas the simple believeth every of some mens words, *Prov.* 14. 15. and it sufficeth him, if others can make it out, with reference to what he Doeth, or doth Believe. The greatest part (I fear) of late Professors, may thus be proved to be Foolish Virgins.

8. Wise men are for the Reduction of what they know, unto the Rule of Practice; or for the shewing of their Wisdom by their works and Conversation, *James* 3. 13. The Doer of Christ's sayings, is onely dignified with that name of wise, *Mat.* 7. 24. whereas the simple Hearer is called Foolish, *v.* 26. At what a rate will some men talk? Wherewith themselves are fully satisfied, like silly Fools. Many can hear their sin Reproved, and will Repeat what they have heard, remaining still what formerly they were. But Gospel-Saints are not for empty Speculations, or the Discoursive part of Duty, or an imposing upon others onely; by which their Heavenly wisdom doth appear.

9. *Rebuke a Wise Man and he will love thee*, *Prov.* 9. 8. So far are such from Scorning to be Reproved; yea, a Reproof doth enter into such,

such, more than an hundred stripes into a Fool, *Prov.* 17. 10. Professors are generally grown so Proud, that one had better meet a Bear, than Offer to deal plainly with them, *Prov.* 17. 12. Much less are they Reduced by Reproofs; which doth evince their present Folly, and is a sign of following stripes. But Gospel-Saints would have the Righteous smite them, *Psal.* 141. 5. And sheep will run upon their Shepherd's whistle, before his Dog be sent among them. Indeed some Foolish Virgins may bear to be Rebuked; but wiser ones are by that means Reclaimed also, which others seldom are.

10. Wise men are first for Purity, and then for Peace, *James* 3. 17. whilst others are afraid, lest if Truths windows be too big, the House of Peace will by that means be weakned; whereas it is a Duty to throw that House out of Truth's window, rather than that its Light should be Obscured. The general out-cry at this day for Civil Peace, whatever becomes of Truth, doth but declare men to be Foolish. Whilst *Hezekiah* was for Peace and Truth, *Isa.* 39. 8. And all are bid to be for Truth and Peace, *Zech.* 8. 16. Most men endeavour onely to preserve an Outward Union; but *Paul* was meerly for keeping the Spirit's Unity in the Bond of Peace, *Eph.* 4. 3. Sinners would fain have Peace of Conscience: but as there is no Peace unto the wicked, so Gospel-Saints are for no Peace with sin; but are for Purity of Conscience first, and in the second place, for Peace. Yea, this holds true, with reference unto the Peace of God; which though it be highly prized by the Godly wise, yet is Grace first desired by them, and Peace in the second place, *Eph.* 1. 2.

11. Wise men do very much Observe God's dealings with themselves and others, which helps their Understanding, *Psal.* 107. 43. Such are Instructed, when others Suffer, *Prov.* 21. 11. because they wisely consider of God's doing, *Psal.* 64. 9. And in Relation to themselves; such earnestly desire to know, why God contendeth with them, *Job* 10. 2. and what he would have them do, at such a time, *Acts* 9. 6. Such also take notice of their Mercy, and its Circumstances; how it is within the Time prefixed, *Exod.* 12. 41. when in a low Estate, *Psal.* 136. 23. when destitute of other help, 2 *Tim.* 4. 16, 17. when in a Dream, or not expecting it, *Psal.* 126. 1. and when prepared for it, *Psal.* 10. 17.

12. *The Heart of the Wise is in the House of Mourning, whilst Fools are in the House of Mirth,* Eccl. 7. 4. Mourning and Mirth were wont to Live in several Houses, though later times have much confounded Funerals, and Festivals; but Saints are to be known by their abiding in a serious Frame, as in their constant Habitation. There is a

Sober

Sober pleasantness, which (in its season) is allowed, *Eccl.* 9. 7. and an Affected sadness is both Ridiculous and Sinful, *Mat.* 6. 16. But **Sorrow** is better than Laughter, *Eccl.* 7. 3. And as the Levity of some Professors (at this Day especially) will end in Heaviness, *Prov.* 14. 13. So doth it sadly witness (at the present) their want of Spiritual Wisdom.

13. Wisdom doth much appear in men's Discourse. *A Fool is full of Words*, Eccl. 10. 14. *which he that hath Knowledge spareth*, Prov. 17. 27. A Saint's Spiritual Fruits prevent his being over-full of Leaves, which Barren Trees do most abound with. And though a wise man is not for an Affected (much less a sinful) silence; yet when he speaketh, the words of his Mouth are Gracious, *Ecc.* 10. 12. Because his Heart doth teach his Mouth, *Prov.* 16. 23. And therefore his Tongue is Health, *Prov.* 12. 18. Now, if in the bare multitude of words, there wants not sin, *Prov.* 10. 19. much more doth super-added frothiness declare mens. Spiritual Folly, and then too many of our Professors cannot avoid the Name of Foolish Virgins.

14. A wise man's Heart discerneth both Time and Judgment, *Eccl.* 8. 5. and so his Misery is prevented, *v.* 6. Wise Virgins are Instructed to go forth in Time, *Mat.* 25. 10. To Pray in a Time of finding; *Psal*, 32. 6. To bring forth Fruit in its proper Season, *Psal.* 1. 3. which makes it Beautiful, *Eccl.* 3. 11. All *Sion's* Sons are Taught of God, *Isa.* 54. 13. And therefore they know the fittest Time of Mourning and Rejoycing, (whereof the *Pharisees* were Ignorant, *Mat.* 9. 14, 15.) Of minding worldly matters, (which poor *Gehazi* did not, 2 *Kings* 5. 26,) When they should be Importunate with God for sparing Mercy, *Joel* 2. 17. And when they should hold their Peace before him in an evil Time, *Amos* 5. 13. and 6. 10.

15. Much of men's Wisdom and Understanding appeareth in the Coolness of their Spirit, *Prov.* 17. 27. as the Margin hath it; or In the Moderation of their Inordinate Affections, which they that are Christ's have Crucified, *Gal.* 5. 24. Such can Converse about these Lower things, in a way of Holy Carelesness, 1 *Cor.* 7. 29, 30, 31. When others mind with all their might. And in particular, wisdom doth much appear in Meekness, *James* 3. 13. by which *a Prudent man doth cover shame*, Prov. 12. 16. unto his Honour, *Prov.* 20. 3. whereas *a Fools Wrath is presently known*, Prov. 12. 16. *His Lips do enter into Contention*, Prov. 18. 6. *And Anger resteth in his Bosom*, Eccl. 7. 9. Unbridled Passions are one sad sign of Foolish Virgins.

16. A *Wise Man's Eyes are in his Head*, Eccl. 2. 14. or such are to be known by Prudent fore-sight, and by their suitable Actings. Such looks

to be Besieged; and therefore they store themselves before hand with Grace sufficient for those Encounters. Such see, that Riches are uncertain, and therefore they make provision for Eternity. Such know, how sin will gall upon a dying Bed; and therefore they shun it whilst alive. Such do fore-see, the shutting of Christ's Door upon late comers; and therefore they strive to enter, whilst it stands open. Such apprehend Christ's Coming may be delayed, and therefore their Vessels are also fill'd w th Oyl, for fear their Lamps should fail, when fresh Recruits cannot be had, untill it be too late to buy them.

17. Wise men are to be known by their Acquaintance with hidden Mysteries. *Daniel* was noted for his wisdom, because no secret thing was hid from him, *Ezek.* 28. 3. who had a Gift of Resolving doubts, and of shewing Hard Sentences, *Dan.* 5. 11,12. Answerable to which, in Gospel-times, are those more immediate, and peculiar Discoveries of Christ's mind, which therefore are called, the wisdom of God in a Mystery, 1 *Cor.* 2. 7. and which are not perceived (save as they are seen with others Eyes) by him who is meerly Natural, *v.* 14. Such are Time, Truths, and Duties, which are Discoveries of a later date, most bitterly opposed by the world, and rarely received among Professors; and by Acquaintance wherewith, men of that other Spirit have ever been Distinguished from the Generality; nor hath a Real Saint (in all the Scripture) been finally known to fail therein; though *Joshua* and *Zerubbabel* did for a time surcease the Temple work, or chief Duty of that time, who were not yet owned, till their Return, *Hag.* 1. 4. and 2. 20. 23.

18. Wise men (in Evil Times) are subject to be Poor, and therefore to be Despised, with reference unto their singularly useful wisdom; as that Poor man Experienced, who by his wisdom did Deliver a Besieged City, *Eccl.* 9. 14, 15. Indeed the Saints shall one day be Supreme, *Dan.* 7. 27. and then their wisdom will be Admired, as *Solomon's* was, because residing in so Great a Person: But in the mean time, (by reason o a wicked Ruler's Errour) Folly is set in great Dignity, and the R ch, (*viz.* in wisdom, as the Antithesis plainly sheweth) sit in low place, *Eccl.* 10. 5, 6. Thus Christ was thought unworthy to be heard, *John* 10. 20. whilst Hypocrites were had in great esteem, *Luke* 16. 15. And self-denying *Paul* was branded for a Fool, whilst those of a Complying Spirit were called wise in Christ, 1 *Cor.* 4. 10. The Generality of Professors are too Rich, too much Regarded, to be Right: Therefore let no man's Popularity (which is the Badge of Fools, till Christ shall sit upon his Temporal Throne) become the Object of a wise man's Envy.

19. Wis-

The Parable of the Ten Virgins Opened. 25

19. Wisdom Directeth unto the Exercise of greatest strength in greatest Difficulties; as when the Iron is blunt, or when its edge is not whetted, *Eccl.* 10. 10. Jades will draw down-hill, or when a work is easie; but the tryal of Heavenly Metal, is up-hill, or when the wheel is clogged. When Christ was in his Agony, he Prayed most earnestly, *Luke* 22. 44. When *David* was most Derided, he was most Resolute, 2 *Sam.* 6. 20. 22. And when *Paul* was in Bonds, the Godly Brethren maintained his Suffering-cause with much more Holy boldness, *Phil.* 1. 14. whilst others plead, the Time is not yet come, *Hag.* 1. 2. so long as Danger doth attend the Temple-work. Yea, a wise Man doth Scale the City of the Mighty, and casteth down the strength of the confidence thereof, *Prov.* 21. 22. that is, he overcometh in his most sharp Encounters. *Saul* slew his Thousands, but *David* his Ten thousands, 1 *Sam.* 18. 7. because he slew that great *Goliath*, 1 *Sam.* 17. 51. whom *Saul* fled from, *v.* 24. 'Tis one sad sign of a Foolish Virgin, not to prevail in forest Conflicts, but to indulge ones fear and weakness, with reference unto the Power of some Temptations.

20. Lowliness and Wisdom are constant Twins, *Prov.* 11. 2. As Pride is generally the Fools Companion, both in the Letter and mystery. *The Mouth of Fools doth pour out Foolishness*, *Prov.* 15. 2. whereas *the prudent Man concealeth knowledge*, *Prov.* 12. 23. Or is not overforward to Declare what maketh for his Glory. Fools judge themselves to be exceeding wise, *Prov.* 12. 15. But a wise Man thinks that wisdom is far from him, *Eccl.* 7. 23. Poor *Laodiceans* are apt to boast, *Rev.* 3. 17. but he that increaseth knowledge, increaseth sorrow, *Eccl.* 1. 18. It sadly signifieth, when knowledge puffeth up; when God is upbraided with the Creature's Duty; or when one Duty doth not make way for more. Humility is the varnisher of other Graces, but Pride is the Professor's stain, which spoileth all his other Beauty. An humble sinner is better to be liked, than he who Glorieth in his being better, *Luke* 18. 11. 13, 14. The best are Tempted to be Proud. But this Temptation is stoutliest resisted by them; yea, God resists it, *and giveth Grace unto the Humble*, 1 *Pet.* 5. 5.

21. *Wise Men will lay up knowledge*, *Prov.* 10. 14. or Labour to secure it for the time to come. There may be much Hearing, Reading, and Conferring, and yet no wisdom, for lack of laying up what is by such means gained. We Read of Hearing for the time to come, *Isa.* 42. 23. *Mary* was much an Hearer, who kept and pondered in her Heart, what others onely heard with present wondring, *Luke* 2. 18, 19. How Rich might some Professors be, in case their Faculty of

E Laying

The Parable of the Ten Virgins Opened.

Laying up, were suitable to that of getting; by which a Spouse is to be known, at whose Gates are laid up for her Beloved, all manner of pleasant Fruits, both New and Old, *Cant.* 7. 13. Thence is it that a Godly Hearer is said to keep the Word, *Luke* 8. 15. which else is subject to be catcht away, though in some sence it be sown in the Heart, *Mat* 13. 19. An Holy Man doth therefore Meditate in the Law of God, *Psal.* 1. 2. by which he is Distinguished from others, as Clean Beasts were of Old, by chewing the Cud, *Lev.* 11. 7. According to which Rule of Judging, there are (in many Flocks) more Swine than Sheep, because they who divide the Hoof, (or have a double Calling, *viz.* as Men, and as Professors) do not yet chew the Cud, or lay up knowledge; which is one Character of Foolish Virgins.

22. Another property of wise men, is, to use aright that knowledge which they have, *Prov.* 15. 2. A Foolish Virgin may have good store of knowledge, but doth not rightly use it, as do the wise. *Paul* had no want of parts, 2 *Cor.* 11. 5, 6. yet could he do nothing against the Truth, 2 *Cor.* 13. 8. nor set the Tree of Knowledge against the Tree of Life, as others did, 2 *Tim.* 3. 8. with their Perverse Disputings, 1 *Tim.* 6. 5. which did evince their Folly, 2 *Tim.* 3. 9. though such Disputers were called wise, 1 *Cor.* 1. 20. He knew that all things (and consequently sin it self) should work for good to every true Believer, *Rom.* 8. 28. but yet he durst not therefore sin, though Grace thereby should be the more abundant, *Rom.* 6. 1. He knew, that some might weakly be Offended with his Lawful Liberty; yet would he not therefore indulge himself, but seek anothers wealth, in such a Case, 1 *Cor.* 10. 23, 24. He profited in the Jews Religion above his equals, *Gal.* 1. 14. yet was he under the Law to Christ, 1 *Cor.* 9. 21. and counted all other knowledge loss, compared with the Excellency of the knowledge of Jesus Christ, *Phil.* 3. 8. Nor durst he dissemble his Light, as others did, for fear of Persecution, *Gal.* 6. 12, 13. but did improve his knowledge for the Truth, 2 *Cor.* 13. 8. though to the ruine of his Personal Interest, *Gal.* 5. 11. From an habitual contradicting of which Rule, too many at this day are clearly proved to be Foolish Virgins.

Use 1. How sadly are Saints mis-understood by sinners, as if they were the veriest Fools, who are indeed the onely wise. Poor Carnal Creatures, in some Respects, are wiser than the Saints, *Luke* 16. 8. So may a silly Fellow (in trivial matters) out-strip the wisest Statesman. Were we to Judge of Men, by skill in Bodily concernments, or by their Natural Accomplishments, the Righteous would be Condemned: But Men shall be Judged by the Scriptures, *John* 12. 48 and those speak in another Dialect: Let sinners therefore be well Advised, before they

they say unto a Saint, Thou Fool; confidering the Danger of fo fpeaking unto ones Brother, *Mat.* 5.22. And that fad woe againft mif-callers in fuch a cafe, *Ifa.* 5. 20.

Ufe 2. It doth behove the Saints, to be in the Demonftration of that wifdom, for which they have a Name, Poor Spiritual Fools are apt to think all like themfelves, *Eccl.* 10. 3. And indifcreet Profeffors give caufe for fuch an Apprehenfion *But Wifdom is Juftified of her Children,* Mat. 11. 19. And therefore none but Baftards will practically condemn her. Pretenders unto wifdom had need be Circumfpect, fince Grace's Reputation lies at Stake, if they mifcarry. Walk wifely towards them without, *Col.* 4. 5. So will you put to filence their Foolifh Ignorance, 1 *Pet.* 2. 15. Or elfe they will Blafpheme, though greater Folly in themfelves be over-looked by them.

Ufe 3. There is no caufe to wonder, if half the Profeffors of thefe latter Times prove Foolifh Virgins, or void of Grace. Yea, Chrift here fpeaketh with the leaft; for two third parts (at fuch a time) muft be cut off and die, *Zech.* 13. 5. Things really differing in point of kind, can hardly be Diftinguifhed; when the higheft degree of a lower kind, is in Conjunction with the Loweft appearance of an Higher. There are fome Plants endued with a feeming fenfe, there are fome Brutes exceeding like to Men; and there are many Natural Men, who are concluded to be Saints. Now, if the Difciples were fo ftartled, when onely one of them was hinted to be a Traitor, *Mat.* 26. 21, 22. much more ought we to be affected, fince half our number will prove notorious Hypocrites.

Ufe 4. Let all be exhorted to get this wifdom, or Gofpel-Grace; fince wifdom is the Principal thing, which therefore fhould be got with all our getting, *Prov.* 4. 7. And fo much the rather, becaufe it is fo great a Rarity, as is here hinted. Which Exhortation doth chiefly concern thofe Virgins or Profeffors, who have been Convicted to be void of wifdom, by any of thofe fore-going Characters; but may be of ufe to others alfo, to grow in Grace, as is their Duty, 2 *Pet.* 3. 18. or to be yet wifer, as is their Difpofition, *Prov.* 9. 9, with reference to both which forts of Perfons, I fhall endeavour to fet this Exhortation home, by feveral Motives, taken from what the Scripture fpeaks concerning wifdom.

Mot. 1. Wifdom is the way to Honour, as *David* did Experience, whofe Name was much fet by, (among *Saul's* Servants) becaufe of his wife behaviour, 1 *Sam.* 18. 30. And therefore *Solomon* was fought unto, from all the Kings about him, which had heard of his wifdom, 1 *Kings* 4. 34, *The Wife fhall Inherit Glory, whilft fhame fhall be the Fools*

The Parable of the Ten Virgins Opened.

Fools promotion, Prov. 3. 35. Men hitherto have been admired, because of their Natural or worldly wisdom; but the time now draweth nigh, when God (or the appearance of his Grace) shall be for a Crown of Glory, *Isa.* 28. 5. Yea, even at the present, he is Sir-named Reverend, whose other Name is Holy, *Psal.* 111. 9. *And Wisdom makes the Face to shine*, Eccl. 8. 1.

2. Wisdom is that which is most likely to Advance a Man into the Highest Place of Rule and Trust. *Joseph* was seen to be Discreet and Wise, and therefore *Pharaoh* set him over all his House, *Gen.* 41. 39, 40. Fools have been uppermost, but shall be Servants to the wise, *Prov.* 11. 29. because the King's Favour is towards a wise Servant, *Prov.* 14. 35. and he shall Rule over a Foolish Son, *Prov.* 17. 2. Grace hath the Promise of this Life also, 1 *Tim.* 4. 8. which shall be performed in due time, when wickedness shall be de-throned, *Ezek.* 21. 25, 26. And Saints shall have the Kingdom, *Dan.* 7. 27. Judging the World and Angels, 1 *Cor.* 6. 2, 3. The Beast hath Crown'd his Horns, *Rev.* 17. 12. But *David* will cut them off, and then the Saints Horn shall be exalted, *Psal.* 75. 10.

3. A wise Man knoweth hidden Mysteries, or the Interpretation of a thing, *Eccl.* 8. 1. which is a great Advantage. Such Men shall see the Name (or Mind) of God, when he is crying to the City, by some signal Judgment, *Mic.* 6. 9. The Godly wise shall understand God's Loving kindness, in all his dealings with them, *Psal.* 107. 43. which sweetneth Mercies, and makes the Cross more easie. Such Men shall understand the Reason of a Publick Scourge, *Jer.* 9. 12. The Truth and Application of the Promises, *Hos.* 14. 9. together with the time of their Accomplishment, *Dan.* 12. 10. As we would be most knowing men, so let us Labour to be most Holy; since these have that Revealed to them, which is not known to others, *Eph.* 3. 5.

4. *Wisdom is better than strength*, Eccl. 9. 16. or *Weapons of War*, v. 18. both in a Defensive and Offensive way, *Eccl.* 7. 12. 19. and 9. 15. Justice will be too many for the most United force of sinners, *Prov.* 11. 21. but cannot hurt the weakest Saint for ever. Satan knew Christ and *Paul*, who were too hard for him; but he could overcome those wicked Jews, when offering to adjure him, though in the Name of Jesus, *Acts* 19. 13, 14, 15, 16. The words of the Wise are heard in quiet, more than the Cry (or utmost endeavours) of him that Ruleth among Fools, *Eccl.* 9. 17. Some put their trust in Moral Virtues, or Natural Tempers and Resolutions; but Satan's fiery Darts will not be quenched with such Scarfs and Feathers. Saints are the onely Conquerours, *Rom.* 8. 37. because they keep themselves from being touch'd

The Parable of the Ten Virgins Opened.

touch'd by him, 1 *John* 5. 18. Who leadeth others Captive, 1 *Tim.* 2. 26.

5. Many may (in some cases) be a Defence, as well as Wisdom; but the Excellency of Knowledge is, that wisdom giveth Life to them that have it, *Eccl.* 7. 12. A Foolish Man is dead, as to his better part, *viz.* his Understanding; and Graceless Persons are called Idols, *Zech.* 11. 17. in whom there is no Breath (or sign of Life) at all, *Hab.* 2. 19. Yea, sin is the saddest kind of Death that is, because it is both Spiritual, and likely to be Eternal, and yet consistent with the quickest sense of highest Misery. And if such were not Dead indeed, this consideration would make them take fast hold of Grace or Heavenly wisdom, and not to let it go, but keep it, because it is their Life, *Prov.* 4. 13.

6. Wisdom is of most use to others also; because it makes most willing and most successful, *Prov.* 15. 7. Men of a Lower Spirit are sparing in their Communications, lest others should be as knowing as themselves: But Grace is free to light a Greater Candle, though its own lesser Lamp should thereby be Eclipsed. Such also are likely to be most Successful, because they are most careful, and have the promise of Christ's Presence with them. The words of the wise are Goads, and such are careful to fasten their Nails, for fear of dropping out, *Eccl.* 12. 11. And though a wicked man may possibly Convert another, yet is there no Promise for it, save unto those, who do themselves stand in God's Counsel, *Jer.* 23. 22. and winning Souls, or turning Men unto Righteousness, is chiefly Attributed to the Godly wise, *Prov.* 11. 30. *Dan.* 12. 3.

7. Wisdom is that which sets out other things, and without which there's nothing that doth become. Wisdom is good with an Inheritance, *Eccl.* 7. 11. not but that wisdom (it self) is good without it; onely an Inheritance is not else seemly: whereas the wise man's Riches are his Crown, because of that Conjunction, *Prov.* 14. 24. Wherever the Branch (or Christ) doth grow, the Fruit of the Earth will there be Excellent and comely, *Isa.* 4. 2. as Earthen Vessels are, when Tipt with Silver; wether we take that Earthly Fruit, for outward Blessings, or Moral Vertues, and Common Actions, or for a mean Descent relating to a Gracious Soul, whom every thing becometh, as Ordinary Garments do an handsom Body.

8. Folly doth Incapacitate a Man for that which he is apt to be ambitious of, and which nought else can fit him for, save onely wisdom. All would have Joy, but yet delight doth not become a Fool, *Prov.* 19. 10. No more than Laughter doth a Malefactor, when going to Execution.

Execution. *Saul* was defirous of being Honoured, 1 *Sam.* 15. 30. but Honour doth not become a Fool, no more than Snow doth Summer, *Prov.* 26. 1. Men would be profperous; but the Profperity of Fools is their Deftruction, for then they turn away, *Prov.* 1. 32. Men would take in the Creature; but when a Fool is fill'd, the Earth is then Difquieted, *Prov.* 30. 21, 22. Some would be fometimes fpeaking of good things; but Excellent fpeech doth not become a Fool, *Prov.* 17. 7. becaufe it is too High for him, *Prov.* 24. 7.

9. There be many that fay, *Who will fhew us any good?* Pfal. 4. 6. Yea, all would be glad of Earthly Riches; the very fancying whereof is unto fome poor Creatures an over-pleafing Vanity. Now, Riches are entailed upon wifdom, as *Solomon* did Experience, 1 *Kings* 3. 11. 13. And as Chrift promifeth, when Grace, or the Kingdom of God is firft fought after, *Mat.* 6. 33. This hath been alway vertually made good unto the Saints, becaufe Contentment is the Fruit of Godlinefs, which anfwereth unto Gain, 1 *Tim.* 6. 6. But as fuch have the Promifes of this Life alfo, 1 *Tim.* 4. 8. So we are now haftning unto the Time of their Accomplifhment; when Meek ones fhall Inherit the Earth, *Pfal.* 37. 11. Flowing together for Wheat, and Wine, and Oyl, *Jer.* 31. 12. And when their Brafs and Iron fhall be turned into Gold and Silver, *Ifa.* 60. 17. And in a way of Reparation for all their former Loffes, receiving double for their fhame, *Ifa.* 61. 7. Yea, in this Life an hundred fold for that which they have fometimes lent to Chrift, *Mat.* 19. 29. Then fhall their Riches alfo be their Crown, *Prov.* 14. 24. becaufe they will be taught to Confecrate their Gain unto the Lord, *Mic.* 4. 13. and to the Duties of his Worfhip, *Ifa.* 61. 5, 6.

10. Wifdom, or Underftanding doth make the words of Chrift to be exceeding plain, *Prov.* 8, 9. and eafie, *Prov.* 14. 6. which otherwife cannot be Apprehended. *Saints have the mind of Chrift, 1 *Cor.* 2. 16. chiefly becaufe they have the Spirit's Guidance, *John* 16. 13. but partly from an innate fagacity, by which a Man of Underftanding will draw that out which lyeth deep, *Prov.* 20. 5 Now, we muft be Judged by the words of Chrift, *John* 12. 48. And therefore woe be to that Soul who doth not underftand them, and fo cannot receive them. And if fome Children would give any thing, to have their Leffons rendered eafie; what Fools are thofe, by whom Facilitating Wifdom is Defpifed? This Grace is worth the feeking after, were it onely but to remove that Labour of Duty and fweating at it, which Poor fallen Man is fubject unto. Chrift's Yoak is therefore eafie to his Difciples, *Mat.* 11. 30. and his Commandments are not Grievous, 1 *John* 5. 3. which

others

The Parable of the Ten Virgins Opened. 31

others long to be Discharged from, *Amos* 8. 5. because of weariness, *Mal.* 1. 13. With what Delight would sinners mind God's Book, had they but that which would endue them with an Holy Ingenuity, whereby they might be able to Run and Read what is contained in it.

11. When wisdom entreth into thine Heart, *Prov.* 2. 10. it will Preserve and keep thee, *v.* 11. To Deliver thee from the way of evil men, *v.* 12. Which must be meant of Gospel-Grace, else utmost wisdom will not prevent ones Fall, as *Solomon* did Experience; yea, whilst his wisdom (of a lower kind) remained with him, *Eccl.* 2. 8, 9. Vertue may Apprehend, Imprison, Condemn, and Torture sin, but nothing short of Grace, will ever prove its proper Executioner, or absolute Suppressor. Grace is Man Rallied, or Re-inforced with a greater strength than ever *Adam* had; which therefore doth subdue its Adversaries, as *David* did those *Philistines*, 2 *Sam.* 8. 1. whom *Saul* did onely vex, 1 *Sam.* 14. 47. but was at last subdued by them, 1 *Sam.* 31. 4. Now, is not that Balm worth seeking after, which is the onely Healer of a deadly wound, *Jer.* 51. 8? Is not that Armour worth the putting on, which onely will enable to withstand, and having done all to stand, *Eph.* 6. 13? They who now Mock at sin, will one day wish they had been wiser, than to Despise that Grace or Wisdom, by which they might have been preserved from its Mortal sting, although its present stain were not to be regarded.

12. This wisdom had need be speedily endeavoured after, because there is no wisdom in the Grave, which Men are going into, *Eccl.* 9. 10. The Door of Grace is sometimes shut on Earth, as Foolish Virgins will Experience, *Mat.* 25. 10. much more when Hell hath shut its mouth upon the Sinners Soul. Oh how Industrious would the Damned be, had they but any hope of getting that which formerly they have Despised. And no Man hath a Lease of Life, as *Hezekiah* had, *Isa.* 38. 5. which is enough to startle slumbring Fools, for fear of sleeping unto Death; especially since Fools are threatned with the shortest warning, *Luke* 12. 20. Nor will men plainly say, that wisdom is not the principal thing; why then do they delay to get it with all their getting? Which Ordinary wisdom will direct unto, in such momentous and uncertain cases. How careful are Prudent men to expedite the setting of their House in Order, before they dye, which is a Duty, *Isa.* 38. 1. But nothing in Comparison of setting the Heart in Order, and getting ready that Land-Lord's Rent, whose Coming may be before to morrow, and who will then give no longer Day. Whilst men are walking to the Grave, (which every step they take is tending unto) let them remember, there is no wisdom there, and let them Act accordingly.

13. Fools

13. Fools cannot improve the best Advantages, and therefore a Price put into their Hands, is to no purpose, *Prov.* 17. 16. Wise men are for the multiplying of what they have, but Fools are onely good at spending, *Prov.* 21. 20.* Good Company is a precious Talent, but yet the Foolish Virgins were not bettered by being in Communion with the wise. Fools may be oft Instructed, but silly Men and Women are ever Learning, and never come unto the knowledge of the Truth, 2 *Tim.* 3. 6, 7. A Foolish People will badly requite their Gracious Benefactor, *Deut.* 32. 6. or are not the better for Favours shewn them, *Isa.* 26. 10. *And though a Fool be brayed in a Mortar* (or be more hardly used) *yet will not his Foolishness depart from him*, Prov. 27. 22.

14. Fools are unacceptable to God and Man. God hath no pleasure in them, *Eccl.* 5. 4. but doth abominate their very Sacrifices, *Prov.* 15. 8. (they are such sorry things, *Eccl.* 5. 1.) although not brought with a wicked mind, *Prov.* 21. 27. Nor any Man (in his right wits) can take Delight in Mad men, no more than *Achish* did in *David*, when seeming to be such a one, 1 *Sam.* 21. 13, 14, 15. Who can Delight in wicked Fools? Considering their more than Brutish Rage, *Prov.* 17. 12. Their crackling Laughter, *Eccl.* 7. 6. Their vain Voluminous Talk, *Eccl.* 5. 3. Their making a sport of mischief, *Prov.* 10. 23. And their intolerable self-conceit, *Prov.* 12. 15. Therefore good *David* did bewail his being made to dwell in *Mesech*, Psal. 120. 5.

15. *As a Dog returneth to his Vomit, so will a Fool unto his Folly*, Prov. 26. 11. Such may begin to walk in the Spirit, as the Foolish *Galatians* did, *Gal.* 3. 3. but alas, their wisdom is apt to fail them by the way, *Eccl.* 10. 3. as did the Foolish Virgins Oyl, *Mat.* 25. 8. Such may be pretty Sober for a while, but Midsummer Temptations will make these Mad men rage as much as ever. They can do nothing with Discretion; and without Judgment there is no certainty of Perseverance: Such Build upon the Sand, and therefore their House must fall in a Tempestuous day, *Mat.* 7. 26, 27. As any would secure their present standing, so let them seek for wisdom, which onely will preserve them, *Prov.* 4. 5, 6.

16. Let the Portion of such be duly weighed. Fools must expect to be Afflicted, because of their Transgressions, *Psal.* 107. 17. The People that doth not Understand, shall fall, or be severely punished, *Hos.* 4. 14. and therefore he that made them, will not have Mercy on them, *Isa.* 27. 11. This kind of Folly will not Excuse Men, however Natural madness may be indulged. *As a Whip is for the Horse, and*

a Bridle for the Ass; so is a Rod for the Back of Fools, properly relating to them, *Prov.* 26. 3. Stripes are prepared for them, *Prov.* 19. 29. although they do not at the present feel them. Yea, the Great God himself, that formed all things, will both reward the Fool, and will reward Transgressors, *Prov.* 26. 10.

Now, as Men would be Interested in this Gospel-Grace, or Spiritual Wisdom, let them Observe these following Helps.

Helps. 1. Labour to be sensible of its want. *There is more hope of a Fool, than of one wise in his own Conceit,* Prov. 26. 12. because this self-conceited man, must first become a Fool, before he can be wise, 1 *Cor.* 3. 18. *A Soul that's full loatheth an Hony-comb,* Prov. 27. 7. And such will never seek for Grace, who do but think they have no need thereof, *Rev.* 3. 17. Let the fore-going Characters be faithfully improved, whose Light will not Create, but onely manifest mens hidden Folly, before it be too late to purchase Wisdom. The Ruine of these Foolish Virgins arose from hence, because they did not make a timely search into their empty Vessels, through sleightiness, or self-conceit.

2. Make sure of Christ, who is the Head, *Col.* 2. 19. and therefore wisdom cannot be had without him. Grace is by Christ, *John* 1. 17. In whom are hid all wisdom's Treasures, *Col.* 2. 3. From whom we therefore must receive, and as in point of Imputation, 1 *Cor.* 1. 30. So also of Inhesion, *John* 1. 16. And what he hath, is to be had, yea, by the sillest Souls that are. List, how Essential wisdom Cryeth, *Prov.* 9. 3. *Who so is simple, let him turn in hither,* v. 4. *How long will ye love simplicity,* Prov. 1. 22. *When will ye be Wise?* Psal. 94. 8. *Forsake the Foolish, and Live,* Prov. 9. 6. *Unto you, O Men, I call, and my Voyce is unto the Sons of Men,* Prov. 8. 4. *With whom are my Delights,* v. 31. *and those that seek me early shall find me,* v. 17.

3. Next unto Christ, Converse much with his Law or Scriptures; whose use is, to make wise the simple, *Psal.* 19. 7. Yea, which are able to make men wise unto Salvation, 2 *Tim.* 3. 15. Could men but be Admonished by these, instead of their unprofitable Studies, *Eccl.* 12. 12. How might those Conduit-pipes convey this water of Life into their Thirsty Souls! But yet the Scriptures are but the Mines of wisdom, which do require deep digging into, as for Silver, *Prov.* 2. 4. or being In them, as the *Greek* word hath it, 1 *Tim.* 4. 15. Else one may have the Field, and yet not be the better for those Treasures which lye hid therein, and are not sought for. One may both Hear and Read, and yet not rightly Understand, and so not be the wiser, *Acts* 8. 28. 30.

4. *If any man lack Wisdom, let him ask of God, who giveth Liberally,*

and upbraideth not, James 1. 5. But Offer not the Sacrifice of Fools, *Eccl.* 5. 1. whilst you pretend to be at Prayer for Wisdom. Seek for it with all your Heart; else is there no Promise of Success, *Jer.* 29. 13. And be importunate, since Knowledge must be cryed after, *Prov.* 2. 3. And Persevere therein, since he alone is Blessed, who watcheth daily at Wisdom's Gates, *Prov.* 8. 34. But ask in Faith, believing that God is able and willing to bestow this Grace, *Jam.* 1. 5, 6. And alway bear in mind, that early seekers are the surest finders, *Prov.* 8. 17. Which when it is thus asked and obtained, hath other Blessings added to it, 1 *Kings* 3. 11, 12, 13.

5. Have a care with whom you walk; since, though the Company of Wise Virgins cannot insure the Foolish Virgins Change, yet such Companions are a special Help; and he that walketh with Wise men is likeliest to be wise; but the Companion of Fools shall be destroyed, *Prov.* 13. 20. Communion is a Conduit-pipe, through which both Sweet and Bitter Water is conveyed; and such a derivation oft-times doth much assimulate. The Foolish *Galatians* were bewitched with the Eye, as the *Greek* word signifieth, *Gal.* 3. 1. And the beholding of Gospel-Glory in another, is of a Changing Nature, 2 *Cor.* 3. 18. Yea, such as are not altered by their Company, may yet be very much restrained, as *David* was from good, whilst in the presence of the wicked, *Psal.* 39. 1, 2. And as these Foolish Virgins were from Evil, whilst with the Wise.

6. Compare not your selves with your selves, or with such as you are; which was the cause why those poor Creatures were not Wise, 2 *Cor.* 10. 12. Some eminent Professors are seen to be Voluptuous, Dissembling, Proud, Passionate, or Vain; and therefore others make light of such Distempers in themselves. Had there been but one Foolish Virgin amongst these Ten, that One might have been sooner wrought upon; but if there be any Saint, for a Foolish man to turn unto, he will not easily be convinced, as seemeth to be hinted, *Job* 5. 1, 2. Yea, therefore a Scorner will not go unto the Wise, because he loveth not to be Reproved by them, as being better than himself, *Prov.* 15. 12. Whereas we ought to walk according to the choicest Pattern, *Phil.* 3. 17. and onely to follow the Faith of such, but not their failings, *Heb.* 13. 7. Or rather to look at Jesus, *Heb.* 12. 1, 2. and to be perfect as God is perfect, *Mat.* 5. 48.

7. Labour to keep up the Price of Wisdom in your esteem, since none will Buy that which he doth think is naught, whatever he may say, *Prov.* 20. 14. *Eve* was not tempted by the Tree of Knowledge, untill she saw its being to be Desired, *Gen.* 3. 6. Nor will this Tree of Life

(or

The Parable of the Ten Virgins Opened. 35

(or Spiritual Wifdom) be otherwife regarded, or prove Tempting, in an Holy way. Stand in the viewing of thofe fore-going Motives, untill you be in Love with Wifdom; remembring alfo, that all other things to be Defired, are not to be compared to it, *Prov.* 8. 11. *Wifdom Excelleth Folly as far as Light Excelleth Darkneſs*, Eccl. 2. 13. Yea, Death and Deſtruction ſay, *We have heard the Fame thereof*, Job 28. 22. which will not be Exchanged (by its wife Poſſeſſors) for Jewels of fineſt Gold, *v.* 17.

8. Be careful to Improve that Meafure which you have received; ſince unto him that hath (or well improveth) it ſhall be given, *Mat.* 25. 29. Which Promife appertaineth to the truly Gracious, who might have more, did they but Labour as *David* did, who by that means was wifer than his Enemies, or Teachers, or than the Ancients, *Pfal.* 119. 98, 99, 100. Nor can it be denyed, but that a Natural man might do more than he doth, in Order to his Spiritual good; and though I find no Promife of fpecial Grace annext unto the beſt improvement of Nature's ſtrength, yet who doth know what God might do (in way of Arbitrary goodneſs) if fuch did carefully improve their ſingle Talent? And if they turn at his Reproof, he then will pour out his Spirit unto them, *Prov.* 1. 23.

9. Refufe not any good Inſtruction, but Hear it, and be wife, *Prov.* 8. 33. or that thou mayeſt be wife (at leaſt-wife) in thy Latter end, *Prov.* 19. 20. Whereas a Scorner feeketh wifdom, but doth not find it, *Prov.* 14. 6. But he is wife who hearkeneth unto Counfel, *Prov.* 12. 15. Faith comes by Hearing, *Rom.* 10. 17. As Sin firſt entred by the Ear, 2 *Cor.* 11. 3. which when it is not opened to the wife man's Charming, that Poyfon of ſin cannot be changed, *Pfal.* 58. 4, 5. Nor will the Serpent's fubtilty be turned into Heavenly wifdom. Moſt Men are therefore Graceleſs, becauſe they will not Hear, at leaſt, not Hearken to that Counfel which wifdom giveth; & which giveth wifdom the Hearing whereof is both one ſign of wifdom, and one chief means whereby to gain it, which every wife Man will therefore do, *Prov.* 1. 5.

10. Take heed of Satan's Bribes, ſince Gifts will blind the wife, *Exod.* 23. 8. Satan will caſt his Golden Balls before you, whilſt running after wifdom, to ſtop your Purfuit. He tempts to make the Conſcience Drunk with worldly Pleafures, as poor Arreſted Debtors do the Bailiff, thinking thereby to Cheat the Creditor: But Conſcience will awake, and follow fuch felf-deceiving Fools into their everlaſting Chains. Yea, he hath wifdom's Counterfeit, and maketh many think that Notional Knowledge, or Spiritual Gifts, together with the Matter of good Actions, is Gofpel-Grace and wifdom. He alfo calls the ſimple

F 2   to

to him, *Prov.* 9. 13, 16. but not to make them wife, as wifdom doth, *v.* 4.

11. Be Humble, fince wifdom is with the Lowly, both as Humilty is a fign of wifdom, *Prov.* 11. 2. and as it is a means to gain it, *Prov.* 3. 34. Thofe have no Grace, who think they have it, becaufe of their Improving Nature. Know not the Grace you have Received, in Point of Pleading (upon that Account) for more. Thofe are not likely to prefs forward, who do not, in fome fence forget what is behind, *Phil.* 3. 13, 14. Whereas he was the wifeft Man on Earth, 1 *Kings* 13. 12. who Humbly thought that wifdom was far from him, *Eccl.* 7. 23. Scorn not to be Reproved or Corrected; fince the Rod and Reproof give wifdom, *Prov.* 29. 15. And fince meer Natural wifdom is not Reftored to men Diftracted, without big words, and fometimes blows. Scorn not to be Inftructed by an Inferiour, or by an Adverfary; fince we are bid go to the Ant for wifdom, *Prov.* 6. 6. Yea, unto Serpents, *Mat.* 10. 16. This ftanding upon Terms in Spiritual Cafes, proceeds from want of wifdom, and doth Obftruct its being gained. And let not the wife Man Glory in his wifdom, *Jer.* 9. 23. Since Pride fore-runs a Fall, *Prov.* 16. 18

12. The right Numbring of one's Days will much Advance the Application of Men's Hearts to wifdom, *Pfal.* 90. 12. All will confefs their Days cannot be many; but this affects not, fave as they are fo Taught to Number them, *viz.* In a Serious way. Could Men but fee into the fhortnefs of this Life, (wherewith their Outward Comforts will Expire) and that Eternity depends upon this Moment, they would be wifer than they are. Yea, all other kind of wifdom (fave what is Spiritual) will perifh in the Grave, *Eccl.* 9. 10. As did wife *Solomon's* Philofophy, whofe Sacred Writings are onely Extant, 1 *Kings* 4. 32, 33. Death Refprefents the worth of Saving Grace.

Mat. XXV. 3, 4.

They that were Foolifh took their Lamps, and took no Oyl with them: But the Wife took Oyl in their Veffels, with their Lamps.

IN thefe two Verfes we have a Particular Inftance of the fore-named Virgins Folly and Wifdom, with Reference unto that Oyl which the Wife took with them, and which the Foolifh left behind. From whence the Obfervation Offered, is this,

Obferv. Pro-

The Parable of the Ten Virgins Opened. 37

Obſerv. Profeſſors Evidence themſelves to be Wiſe or Fooliſh, by Taking, or not taking Oyl in their Veſſels, together with their Lamps.

In the purſuance whereof, theſe few things may be Quæried.

Queſt. 1. What are we to Underſtand by Oyl? Such as the Wiſe Virgins had?

Anſw. Metaphorical Oyl (which needs muſt be here meant) moſt commonly denoteth the Special Gifts or Graces of the Spirit, and Spiritual Light or Knowledge among the reſt; which therefore are ofttimes called Oyntment, *Cant.*1.3. Unction, 1 *John* 2.20. or Anointing, *v.*27. And becauſe of the full Reſemblance that is between them and Oyl in the Letter; as in theſe following Reſpects.

1. Oyl is very Beautifying; it maketh the Face to ſhine, *Pſal.* 104. 15. Therefore did *Naomi* bid *Ruth* to annoint her ſelf, when going unto *Boaz*, Ruth 3. 3. Such are theſe Gifts and Graces. Grace made Chriſt fairer than the Sons of Men, *Pſal.* 45. 2. The chiefeſt of Ten Thouſand, *Cant.* 5. 10. Yea, therefore his Glory was like the Fathers, becauſe he was ſo full of Grace, *John* 1. 14. Grace makes the Spouſe all Fair and Raviſhing, *Cant.* 4. 7. 9. Whoſe Comelineſs is not deſtroyed by Holy Terror, *Cant.* 6. 4. Nor by the Blackneſs of outward Suffering, *Cant.* 1. 5. This is more Obvious unto a Spiritual Eye, *Acts* 11. 23. But yet Ingenuous Virgins can alſo witneſs hereunto, both in Relation to the Spouſe, *Cant.* 5. 9. and Chriſt, *Cant.* 6. 1.

2. Oyl is of a Regal Nature, and will be uppermoſt; whatever other Liquors it is mingled with; and therefore to be annointed with freſh Oyl, is put to ſignifie, the Exaltation of one's Horn, *Pſal.* 92. 10. Of ſuch a Nature is ſpecial Grace. This Oyl may for a while be under water, when ſhaken by the Tempter's Hand; but ſin ſhall never have Dominion over Saints, becauſe they are under Grace, *Rom.* 6. 14. Such may be ſometimes Foiled, but they will be up again, *Prov.* 24. 16. And every Yoak in time ſhall be deſtroyed from off their Neck, becauſe of the Annointing, *Iſa.* 10. 27. which hath been alway Spiritually made good, and will at laſt appear, with reference unto a Temporal Supremacy there intended.

3. Oyl makes any kind of Motion quick; therefore are Wheels and Locks annointed, together with their Shields of Old, *Iſa.* 21. 5. which made the Enemies Darts to glide off quickly; yea, therefore Men's Bodies alſo were wont to be annointed, to make them nimble. And herein Grace is like to Oyl. Therefore the Saints can run and not be weary, *Iſa.* 40. 31. as were theſe Fooliſh Virgins, for lack of Oyl.

This

The Parable of the Ten Virgins Opened.

This keepeth Satan's shafts from fastening upon their Shields, and makes them go with lesser Weights (or fewer Motives) and with less creaking noise, because their Wheels are Oyled. And though Christ's Mediation be the onely Key, yet must that Key be Oyled with Grace, which much availeth in the work of Opening the Door of Mercy, *James* 5. 16. Not that it works with Christ in point of Impetration; but as it is required by him, unto the Believer's being benifited by his Intercession.

4. Oyl is Embalming; therefore Christ's Body was annointed to the Burying, *Mark* 14. 8. And others came afterwards, on purpose to annoint him, *Mark* 16. 1. Grace also keeps from Putrefaction. The Saints very Bodies shall be made Incorruptible, 1 *Cor.* 15. 53. When Grace is perfected in them, as it was in Christ, who therefore might not see Corruption, because he was God's Holy One, *Acts* 2. 27. Yea, Holy *David* had (in some sence) this Priviledge made good to him, *Psal.* 16. 10. However, in a Spiritual sence, this Oyl of Grace wears off sins fretting Rust, and doth secure its Owner's Name from Rotting, *Prov.* 10. 7. And keeps the Soul from entring into those Degrees of Moral Putrefaction, which others cannot prevent.

5. Oyl is of an Healing Nature, which therefore is applied to wounds, *Luke* 10. 34. and was Symbolically used by those who had the Gift of Healing, *James* 5. 14. *Mark* 6. 13. Such an All-heal is Grace. What noisom Ulcers are upon sinners Hearts, *Isa.* 1. 5, 6. which Grace keeps sweet at present, and is in the way of an Effectual Cure. The best of Nature's Medicines are onely Skinning, or Repercussive, Imprisoning Rebellious Humours, which makes them rage the more, and break out otherwhere with greater fierceness. But Grace Designs the altering of one's Constitution, beginning with the Heart or Mind, and thence expelling into the Members, that which it will not leave there neither, *Rom.* 7. 23, 24.

6. Oyl doth not break the Head. *Psal.* 141. 5. But is of a Mollifying Nature, *Isa.* 1. 6. The Emblem of soft words, *Psal.* 55. 21. And that which gently doth insinuate it self into a Part or Member. Such also is the Property of Grace. A bare Command is very Irritating, *Rom.* 7. 8. And Slavish fear begets an Angry kind of Duty, *Exod.* 4. 25, 26. Which is Tormenting, 1 *John* 4. 18. But Grace doth soften a stony Heart, *Ezek.* 36. 26. And soaks into the Will, *Mat.* 26. 41. Gently dispersing peccant Humours, and making the Soul to Act from Love, so that Commandments are not grievous, 1 *John* 5. 3. And when there's most of Grace in any man, there's most of sweetness, both in Relation to himself and others, proceeding from the Nature of this Oyl.

7. Oyl

The Parable of the Ten Virgins Opened. 39

7. Oyl is not apt to Freeze, like other Liquid things. No more is Grace. Nature is very fluid in the Summer Season, and Hypocrites are Active, while they are in the midst of warm encouragements; but when that Sun declines, how stiff are such, how Cold for Christ, and like dead Flies, untill the Spring returneth? Whereas a truly Gracious Soul, though sensible of such with-drawings, yet is as fit for present use as ever, because of that Native warmth wherewith he is endued. Saints can endure Hardship, 2 *Tim.* 2. 3. 2 *Cor.* 11. 27. Partly because they are inured to it, *Luke* 9. 29. But chiefly from the Grace or Fatness of that Olive-Tree which they are Graffed into, *Rom.* 11. 17.

8. Oyl is not apt to wast, but is the Preserver of other things; and therefore Colours are laid in Oyl. A Carnal Man's Goodness is like the Dew, *Hof.* 6. 4. Or of a waterish Nature, which quickly dryeth up: And Moral Vertues are of a pretty Colour, but apt to fade, because not laid in Grace. How quickly did that Lovely Young Man look pale, for lack of following Christ, *Mark.* 10. 20, 21, 22. Or meerly because his Vertue was not added unto Faith, as it should have been, 2 *Pet.* 1. 5. But Grace is of an Everlasting Nature, not waxing lean with Age, *Psal.* 92. 14. But springing up to Everlasting Life, *John* 4. 14. According to the Nature of its Covenant, *Jer.* 32. 40.

9. Oyl is of a Chearing Fragrant Nature. We read of the smell of Oyntments, *Cant.* 4. 10. whereby they do bewray themselves, *Prov.* 27. 16. Filling the House with Odour, *John* 12. 3. which stirs up Love, *Cant.* 1. 3. and is Heart-chearing, *Prov.* 27. 9. Therefore 'tis called the Oyl of Joy, *Isa.* 61. 3. and Gladness, *Psal.* 45. 7. which was not to be used in the Times of Mourning, 2 *Sam* 14. 2. Nor with a Sin-Offering, *Lev.* 5. 11. Or Jealousie-Offering, *Numb.* 5. 15. which call'd for sadness. All which agrees to Grace, in point of Savour and Refreshing, confest by all who have their Senses Exercised. Christ had Grace poured into his Lips, *Psal.* 45. 2. whose Lips were therefore like to Lillies, dropping sweet smelling Myrrh, *Cant.* 5. 13. Yea, and how Odoriferous might Professors be, did they but Open their Box of Oyntment, or were but in the Exercise of Gospel-Graces.

10. Oyl is a very stately, satisfying, and Pleasant Nourisher. Much of the *Israelites* Food was Oyl, 1 *Kings* 17. 12. whose pleasantness was that by which their Manna was resembled, *Numb.* 11. 8. Yea, Oyl is very satisfying, by reason of its Fatness, and very stately also, which therefore is coupled with fine Flower and Honey, *Ezek.* 16. 13. and Wine, which he that Loveth over-much, will not be Rich, *Prov.* 21. 17. To signifie the equal Costliness of Oyl and Wine. And such a kind of Nourisher is Grace; Heart-strengthning, Soul-satisfying, and very

pleasant

The Parable of the Ten Virgins Opened.

pleafant unto a Spiritual Palate: Yea, when that Stately Feaft of Oyls (as the *Hebrew* hath it) is made upon Mount *Sion*, Ifa. 25. 6. Its firft Courfe will be Grace, as Glory will be the Second, *Pfal.* 84. 11.

11. Oyl is of a diffufive Nature, foaking into the Bones, *Pfal.* 109. 18. And that by which a running River is Refembled, *Ezek.* 32. 14. An Inftance whereof we have in *Aaron's* Oyntment, which ran down from his Head unto his Beard, and thence unto the Skirts of his Garment, *Pfal.* 133. 2. Sin is felf-propagating, and fo is Grace; which is not able to contain it felf, fave as it is enforced. A worldly prudent Man can ftop the current of his Teftimony when he pleafeth, becaufe his Prophecying Spirit is of an Ordinary Nature, which therefore is Subject to fuch kind of Prophets, 1 *Cor.* 14. 32. But good *John Baptift* could not hold his Tongue, although he thereby loft his Head, *Mat.* 14. 3, 4. 10. whofe Life and Liberty might elfe have been preferved.

12. Oyl was abundant in the Land of *Canaan*, which therefore was called a Land of Oyl, 2 *Kings* 18. 32. Efpecially fome part thereof; and therefore *Afher* was bid to dip his Foot in Oyl, *Deut.* 32. 24. wherein much of their Treafure did confift, *Prov.* 21. 20. And wherewith they Traded with them of *Tyre*, *Ezek.* 27. 17. The *Affyrian* boafted of his Natural Oyl, 2 *Kings* 18. 32. But Grace is no where to be found, fave in, and among God's *Ifrael*, and there it is abundant; efpecially with thofe who have the Name for Happinefs, which *Afher* fignifieth, *Gen.* 30. 13. Although their outward Lot (like his) be ftony, yet do they fuck this Oyl out of the Flinty Rock, *Deut.* 32. 13. which is the Richeft Treafure, *Ifa.* 33. 6. and wherewith fuch do Trade, *Rom.* 1. 11.

13. Oyl was of an Ancient Ufe in the Defignation of Perfons unto fome more than Ordinary work or Office, wherewith the High-Prieft was Annointed, *Numb.* 35. 25. So were the Prophets, 1 *Kings* 19. 16. *Pful.* 105. 15. And alfo Kings, 1 *Sam.* 16. 13. As thefe were Types of Chrift, who was both Prophet, Prieft, and King, and was accordingly Annointed, *Ifa.* 61. 1. *Acts* 4. 27. *Pfal.* 45. 7. Thus alfo Grace refembleth Oyl, becaufe the Saints are thereby both Defign'd and fitted for fuch Offices; for he which hath Annointed them is God, 2 *Cor.* 1. 21. Poor Carnal Creatures are Defign'd for Lower Ufes, whilft Higher Places are referv'd for Saints; who as they are at prefent Kings and Priefts to God, fo they fhall Reign on Earth, *Rev.* 5. 10. as *David* did foon after his Annointing; and then will Foolifh Virgins wifh they had their Veffels filled with this Oyl.

The Parable of the Ten Virgins Opened. 41

14. Oyl was of Use in Sacrifices, which *Jacob* therefore poured twice upon his Pillar, *Gen.* 28. 18. and 35. 14. Whereby to Testifie his Thankfulness, and gain some further Mercy from the Lord; Whereof that Typical Meat-Offering did consist, *Numb.* 15. 4. which was as Sauce unto their Sacrifices, to make them Savoury and Compleat; as Grace doth Gospel-Sacrifices, which therefore is Required in Prayer, 1 *Tim.* 2. 8. and Praises, *Col.* 3. 16. But therefore it was Their grievous sin, who set God's Oyl before the Heathen, *Ezek.* 23. 41. And sent their Oyntments unto *Ashur*, *Isa.* 57. 9. meerly to get their Favour. And thus Grace is an Acceptable Sacrifice, when Offered up by Christ, the Altar, 1 *Pet.* 2. 5. Yea, though there be nothing but this Oyl, or Grace appearing in the will, 2 *Cor.* 8. 12. But woe be to those *Israelites*, who prostitute this Sacred Oyl at the Feet of Men, or give up their Light and Duty unto the wills of others, (as many Professors in our days have done) meerly to curry Favour with them.

15. Oyl may be spoyled very much, as Ointment is apt to be, by some dead Flies got into it, *Eccl.* 10. 1. And as Oyl (Typically) was of Old, when touch'd by one that was unclean by having touched a dead Body, *Hag.* 2. 12, 13. And thus, even Saints themselves (yea, and their very Graces) are apt to be unsavoury, by reason of some strong Corruption laboured under. Yea, that which some Men count a sorry Flie, may be sufficient to breed this Putrefaction, untill it be taken away, which cannot be without some kind of loss. And in particular, one's touching (or compliance with) Man's Prohibition of Temple-work, or Open worship (which is the onely thing intended by that Prophet *Haggai*) is apt to make this Oyl unclean, or to obstruct Communion with any so polluted.

16. Oyl is of special Use for Light (which is the Resemblance chiefly here intended:) And so is Grace, which also doth much resemble Light, as sin doth Darkness. Darkness is meerly privative, and so is sin: But Grace is of a positive Nature, which therefore hath its Author, *Heb.* 12. 2. as Light had its Creator, *Gen.* 1. 3. Grace is from Christ, *John* 1. 16. as Light is from the Sun; and sin from Satan, *John* 8. 44. that Prince of Darkness, *Acts* 26. 18. The Light is sweet, *Eccl.* 11. 7. And Grace is a gladsome sight, *Acts* 11. 23. whilst none but Night-Birds can delight in Darkness. The Light makes manifest, *Eph.* 5. 13. And so doth Grace, the Nature of sin and Duty, which poor dark sinners do not understand. There's no Communion between the Light and Darkness, 2 *Cor.* 6. 14. And as not in a Natural, so neither in this Moral sence. Darkness is staining, *Job* 3. 5. and so is sin: But Light and Grace do give a shining lustre, *Eccl.* 8. 1. Darkness and

G Sin

The Parable of the Ten Virgins Opened.

Sin (both of them) are exceeding Cold, *Mat.* 24. 12. whereas Grace (like the Sun) doth set the Heart on burning, *Luke* 24. 32. Darkness Occasions Terror, *Psal.* 91. 5. and so doth Sin, *Lev.* 26. 16. But Grace and Light are equally rejoycing. Darkness and Sin expose unto mistakes and Dangers, both which are happily prevented through the Light of Grace. Darkness unfits for Action, as these poor Foolish Virgins did Experience ; whereas the others Lightsome Oyl kept them in a walking posture (after their being once awakened) untill the Bridegroom came.

These are the Principal of those respects, wherein New Covenant-Grace resembleth Oyl; the last of which (*viz.* Its being of special use for Light) is chiefly here intended. In which regard, I now shall a little further clear up the Nature of this Oyl, or Grace, with reference unto that Light, for which it serveth. And so,

1. This Oyl of Grace (together with its Light) is meerly Spiritual, and no way Natural. There is a Natural Oyl, and there is also a Light of Nature, in a Moral sence, *Rom.* 2. 14. proceeding from a Mystical (yet Naturally Moral) Oyl. But now, this Oyl and Light of Grace is wholly of another Nature. The first *Adam's* Paradise was Richly stored with Natural Olive-Trees, both in the Letter and Mystery ; but Gospel-Grace cannot be had, save by a fresh engrafting into that super-natural Olive-Tree, *Rom.* 11. 24. or Second *Adam*, who is from Heaven, 1 *Cor.* 15. 47. Nature's Wild Olive will never yield this Oyl, which those are therefore strangers unto, who have not in them any thing, save what is Natural.

2. This Oyl and Light of Grace is alway Accompanied with some good Measure of Spiritual Heat. There is a shining Light, which is not burning; as that of the Moon, which fitly answers unto Nature: But that of the Sun (which is an undoubted Type of Christ, *Mal.* 4. 2.) doth set the Heart on burning, *Luke* 24. 32. as well as open the Disciples Eyes, *v.* 31. The Light of Grace is therefore troublesome unto the most, because it is so hot ; whereas a Carnal Jew can Joy (at least-wise) in *John Baptist's* Light, Abstracted from its burning Heat, *John* 5. 35. Christ's Oyl doth scald the Old Man out of Doors; and his very Light or Brightness is Destructive unto wickedness, 2 *Thes.* 2. 8. by which 'tis to be known from that more Carnal Light, which hath no burning Influence upon its Owner's Dross, no more than *Balaam's* had upon his Covetousness.

3. This Oyl of Grace (as that in the Letter also) must first be fired before it yieldeth any Heat or Light, whatever immediate use it may be of, in other regards. Grace doth depend on Christ, not onely as

its

The Parable of the Ten Virgins Opened. 43

its Author, but also as he must Actuate it; or else that Habit must sleep in Cold and Darkness. Those two Disciples had of this Oyl within their Vessels; but till Christ came and kindled it, they neither saw, nor were they warmed, *Luke* 24. 31, 32. Saints never will be Independents, with reference unto Christ's renewing Influences; but he that works the Disposition, must also draw it forth to Exercise; else though they be something, yet can they do nothing, *John* 15. 5. because they Move, as well as Live in him, *Acts* 17. 28. 'Tis to be feared, those men have sought a Wind of Satan, who think they have the Spirit's Wind at their Command.

4. The Light of this Oyl is of no use unto a Natural Eye, but is Offensive to it. Saints have Discoveries thereby made, which others do not understand; both in Relation unto Christ, *Cant.* 5. 9, 10. and things of a Spiritual Nature, 1 *Cor.* 2. 14. Christ was that Light, *John* 1. 9. whom yet the Common Jews received not, *v.* 11. but their very Seers were offended with it, *Mat.* 12. 12. partly because it was too Manifesting, *John* 3. 20. and partly, because it was too Great, or like unto the Sun it self, when looked on; this Object being Light, as well as that by which 'tis seen, *Psal.* 36. 9. Yea, therefore was *John Baptist's* Light rejoyced in but for a Season, *John* 5. 35. though his was far Inferiour unto Christ's, *John* 1. 8. That Light which Natural Men can bear without Offence, (in point of Doctrine or Conversation) is much to be suspected.

This Light of Grace is very clear (compared with any other) or that which makes the Object very plain. Poor Heathens do rather feel than see, *Acts* 17. 27. and common *Israelites* could not look very far, 2 *Cor.* 3. 13. but Gospel-Saints behold with open Face, (compared with others) though in a Glass compared with their Future Sight, 2 *Cor.* 3. 18. Faith gives the clearest Evidence, *Heb.* 11. 1. And therefore True Believers are best Resolved, in point of Sin and Duty, which others stick at, through want of full Conviction. O how is Grace to be desired then, since Answerable to the Measure of our Light! So is the safeness of our Walking, *John* 11. 9, 10. and Satisfaction that our way is Right, *John* 12. 35.

6. This Light is of a Growing Nature, which shineth more and more unto the Perfect Day, *Prov.* 4. 18. A Natural Eye (both in the Letter and Mystery) is apt to wax dim with Age; but though such as Christ doth enlighten, may at the first see Men as Trees, yet do they afterwards see clearly, *Mark* 8. 23, 24, 25. The way of the wicked is as Darkness, *Prov.* 4. 19. but Saints walk in a Beam unto the Sun, Journeying as *Abraham* did unto the Southward, *Gen.* 20. 1. Therefore

fore their Light must needs increase. And when the Moon (or Light of Nature) shall equalize the present Sun, then shall the Sun (or Light of Grace) be as seven Suns United into one, *Isa.* 30. 26. untill Saints know as they are known, 1 *Cor.* 13. 12.

7. The Measure of this Light (as that of a Lamp in the Letter also) is Answerable to the Weik, or that wherein it is subjected. Some Men have larger Hearts, 1 *Kings* 4. 29. or more Receptive Weiks, therefore their Light is greater, *v.* 30. All Saints have Grace, but some have more, according to the Measure of the Gift of Christ, *Eph.* 4. 7. and as Occasion doth require. The Wind of Temptations blusters in some places more; therefore the Light had need be stronger. Some have more Curious work in hand, whose Light had therefore need be clearer. Some Men have work in several places, as had *Paul*, 2 *Cor.* 11. 28. who therefore needed Extraordinary Knowledge, *v.* 26. Or many Lights set up at once, as *Acts* 20. 8. I may not offer to un-Saint another, simply because his Light is less, in case it be sufficient for the Present work, as this, of going forth.

8. This Lightsom Oyl is separable from its Lamp and Vessel; as these poor Foolish Virgins Evidenced, *Mat.* 25. 3. and did Experience, *v.* 8. 'Tis but a common Adjunct, and no Proper Accident, save as it is so made by Grace. When those bad Angels fell from Grace, yet did they keep their Essence still: Nor is it from a Natural Necessity, that Gospel-Saints shall never fall from Grace, but meerly from an Adventitious undertaking on their benalf, *Jer.* 32. 40. When such are Tempted to Presume or Vapour, let them remember the Root bears Them, not They the Root, *Rom.* 11. 18. And therefore let Mens Lamps and Vessels be throughly searched in due time.

9. This Light is in-extinguishable and Everlasting. The Prince of the Air can never blow it out, *Luke* 22. 31, 32. The Waters of Persecution shall never wholly quench it, *Cant.* 8. 7. Nor will it ever of it self go out, as did these Foolish Virgins Lamps, *Mat.* 25. 8. which Argueth their having never (Spiritually) been enlightned, 1 *John* 3. 6. This Oyl is like that Widdow's, 1 *Kings* 17. 16. And this Light is like *David's*, 1 *Kings* 11. 36. whereas the Lamp of the wicked shall be put out, *Prov.* 13. 9. It is with Grace, as with the Sun, whose Light is subject to be Clouded, Eclipsed, and oft-times hidden for a Night; yet it is alway shining, although not alway seen.

10. This Light must yet be carefully looked after, for fear of running in Arrears through want of constant watchfulness; as these wise (slumbring) Virgins did Experience. Those Sacred Lamps were daily to be Dressed, *Exod.* 30. 7. and so must these be Trimmed, else un-removed

The Parable of the Ten Virgins Opened.

un-removed snuffs will prejudice their shining lustre. And though New Covenant-Grace shall never wholly fail, yet is there room for the use of means, which are as necessary, as the End is certain. And that's the Happiness of all wise Virgins, that Christ hath undertaken to rouze them up, as well as to secure their Oyl.

Quest. 2. What's meant by Lamps, distinct from Vessels? And what is further meant by Oyl in the Vessels, together with the Lamps? And by the Foolish Virgins taking no Oyl with them?

Answ. I. By Lamps (distinct from Vessels here) do seem to be chiefly meant, the Souls Affections, in competition with its Judgment, as all these Metaphors do joyntly evidence. Oyl is undoubtedly here put for Light: And Vessels are the subject of that Oyl, from whence the Lamps are fed, or kept from going out. Now, a Mans Judgment is the seat of Light, which therefore fitly Answers unto the Vessels, from whence the working of Affections is maintained; and therefore these Lamps do fully Answer unto those Affections. And this Interpretation (unto me) doth seem to be more fully worded, than that of Practice and Profession, which though it be more commonly received, yet is it not unto the present purpose; since Practice can no way Answer unto Vessels, or Seat of Light, although Profession is somewhat like to Lamps: And since false hearts may Practise much, as well as make a great Profession; and so the difference between a Wise and Foolish Virgin (chiefly intended here) would be destroyed.

II. Oyl taken in the Vessel, doth Naturally import these two things further.

1. That it was not now to Buy, but ready at Hand, yea, in Possession also; and in the surest part of Man, *viz.* The Heart or Judgment. Each Gospel-Saint is Actually blessed with all Spiritual Blessings, *Eph.* 1. 3. And though his Grace be hid, yet it is hidden in the Heart, 1 *Pet.* 3. 4. which is a Castle that Satan cannot Storm, nor shall it be ever taken from him, *Luke* 10. 42. as was that single Talent, *Mat.* 25. 28. which was hid else-where, *v.* 25. Things in the Heart are safer than in the Head or Hand; and of more present use upon Occasion, than if in the nearest shop that is. Therefore wise Virgins will have Oyl in their Vessels, on purpose to prevent that double Danger.

2. Oyl in the Vessel intimateth store thereof; or such a Competent measure of it, as will maintain the Lamp so long as its Light is needful. Indeed the least drop of Grace's Oyl is of the same lasting Nature with abundance; but yet a Competency of its Measure is also requisite unto its lastingness, by virtue of a Divine Appointment, which hath so Ordered its Preservation. Therefore we read of a sufficient Grace, 2 *Cor.*

The Parable of the Ten Virgins Opened.

12. 9. and putting on the whole Armour of God, *Eph.* 6. 13. and of abounding, 2 *Pet.* 1. 8 in one Grace added to another, *v.* 5. that so we might not fall, *v.* 10. nor can there be true Grace without it, *v.* 9.

III. These Foolish Virgins may here be said to take no Oyl.

1. Because they had not the Oyl of Grace, but onely that of Nature; as is most evident, because their Oyl did wholly fail, *Mat.* 25. 8. which that of Grace will never do, but springeth up to Everlasting Life, *John* 4. 14. Now, that which is not of the Noblest kind, is oft-times represented as if it had no Being. Thus Rational Creatures are called the World, *John* 3. 16. and True Believers all Things, *Col.* 1. 20. and Idols (or false gods) Nothing, 1 *Cor.* 8. 4. And thus may Nature's Oyl (or Light) be termed, None at all. This quells their Pride who Glory in a thing of Nought; and shews their sin, who Nullifie true Grace, by making it the same (for Kind) with Nature.

2. Because this very Common Oyl was onely in their Lamps, not in their Vessels. They had some good Affections, but were not Acted by a solid Principle in their first going forth, for then their Light would have continued: Since the Command (had that been eyed) was every whit as clear, (or rather more) the second time. Now, injudicious Acts are counted none; and therefore, although the Jews did oft-times Pray with much self-humbling, yet it is said, they Prayed not, *Dan.* 9. 13. nor were they Humbled to that day, *Jer.* 44. 10. because they onely did such things from flashy Affections, and not from Judgment. How sadly Fools will sometimes weep, which yet among the Wise is counted Nothing.

3. Because this Oyl was spent (at least, they would not use it) when there was most Occasion for its Light; or when the Cry was made at Mid-night. Now, useless things are said to have No Being; as *Job*'s un-useful Friends are called Nothing, *Job* 6. 21. nor ever had such things some kind of Being; in which regard, that onely seemeth to be had, which proves unprofitable (in the Issue) unto its Owner, *Luke* 8. 18. Well therefore may Professors go for workers of Iniquity, *Mat.* 7. 23. when they back-slide, because their Zeal is gone, when Christ and they stand most in need thereof; which therefore is (in such a case) as if it had not been at all. Christ Represents these Foolish Virgins, as those who took no Oyl at first.

Quest. 3. Why were Lamps taken by these Virgins, who took no Oyl?

Answ. 1. Because they needs must have a Form of Godliness, else
all

all Wise Virgins would cast them off, and not be for Communion with them; therefore so small a matter shall not part them. *Saul* was desirous of *Samuel*'s Continuance with him, which made him do more than otherwise he would have done, 1 *Sam.* 15. 30. Formal Professors wou'd gladly shine with others Beams, especially if empty Lamps (put into a common stock) will make them Partners. Yea, Conscience it self will not be quiet without the stirring of some Affections; but if those Lamps be to be seen, poor Fools are satisfied. Those are not worthy to be called Virgins, whose Outside is not very Neat and Trim.

2. Because these Lamps are Light (Compared with Vessels full of Oyl) which therefore lazy Hypocrites will rather chuse to bear. Oyl in a Gracious Heart, is like to Water in its Element, which is not Ponderous; but unto others, 'tis Grievous to be born, who therefore have no delight to carry it. The Light of this Sacred Oyl is like that of the Sun, Discovering Moats as well as Dirt; both which an Hypocrite can bear the Presence, but not the Sight of, in such a Reproving way, who therefore hateth it, *John* 3. 20. This Oyl is also thought too Dear, because the Heart or Vessel must be emptied of other things; which, none but Fools will either wonder at, or grudge: But yet such, therefore are, content to be without it.

3. Such possibly may think, they have this Oyl of Grace, or that it is not now to take; and upon that Account it may be left behind, through self-undoing self-conceit. There have been self-deceivers in all Ages, who yet do most abound in these last days of ours, or in the Declining State of Churches and Professors, Typified by those self conceited *Laodiceans*, who were the last of those Typical *Asian* Churches. Which sad mistake ariseth, partly from lothness to enquire, left Conscience should be disquieted, or lest the Soul should suffer loss; as when Brass Money is become one's own, its Owner will not therefore let another rub it. Partly, because they might think Oyl inseparable from a Lamp, (or that Affections are always Spiritually Judicious) and having Lamps, did thence conclude their having Oyl, Partly, from Spiritual Pride, because Hypocrites would not be thought to want so main a business: And partly, from the Resemblance that is between Special and Common Oyl, or Grace and Nature; as is between Tin and Silver, which therefore (at least, by Fools) are oft Confounded.

4. These Foolish Virgins thought they had enough to serve their present turn; and Hypocrites are for no more, in matters of a Spiritual Nature. As is the work, such is the need of suitable Instruments; a wooden Needle may serve to stitch some coarser Cloth together: And their first going forth was Manifestly of a Lower Nature. I will not say,

say, that Gospel-Grace is absolutely necessary unto the Second going forth; for then, all of that sort must be concluded to be Real Saints, from that very Act of going out; (which I dare not affirm, unless the whole of that Duty be performed, which I shall clear up afterwards:) but something far short of Grace, might carry these out at first; as is apparent, both from the Issue, and from the Nature of that fore-named work, which might Occasion this neglect.

5. Such might, at least-wise think this Special Oyl was to be had in Time, although they had it not at present: And Hypocrites are not for being over-hasty in looking out for Christ's Commodities. They might presume to borrow Oyl of their Companions, in case of need, or that they should have time enough to buy it, as may be gathered from their attempting afterwards, in both these ways to be supplied. Such are acquainted with Christ's tender Bowels, and readiness to help poor sinners, which is abused by them to indulge their present carelesness, and to delay their closing with a present Offer, though to the hazarding of their Eternal State, by dallying with such Opportunities.

Quest. 4. How came they to go forth at first, not having this Light or Oyl? And not (as well) the Second Time?

Answ. 1. At their first going out they were in the Prime of their Affections, and Zeal for Duties of such a Nature. There was some kind of another Heart (like that of *Saul*'s, 1 *Sam.* 10. 9.) bestowed upon all Professors at that time, which raised them unto an higher pitch than Ordinary. They were then like to Ground which had been long un-occupied; and therefore that first Crop was Extraordinary. That was the first resistance made, which usually is very violent, especially among the Ruder sort, although not lasting. An Ordinary Spirit will Act to Admiration, when raised up; and upon that account, these Foolish Virgins might thus out-act themselves at first, untill their Youthful heat was cooled.

2. Their way was not so dark (at their first going out) but that it might be hit, with empty Lamps, at least, without this special Light. It might be some kind of Evening then, but not a Mid-night Darkness, as when the Cry is made, *Mat.* 25. 6. It was an easie matter Then, to bear an open Testimony, because they had some colour of Authority (at that time) to bear them out. And though they ran the hazard of their Estates, yet had they then good store of Company, which will provoke a Worldly minded Man to spend more freely, than else he would do. Nor was there any need of Special Light, to shew the grossness of that Church-state, which then was gone out of.

3. At their first going out, their All was laid at Stake; and in that
Case

The Parable of the Ten Virgins Opened. 49

Case Men will run out at Mid-night without a Lamp or Candle. Their utter Extirpation then was strongly feared, which was enough to draw Men out, who onely had the Light of Nature: But when the Cry is made, the greatest apprehended Danger is in going forth, which may Occasion their pretending Then a want of Light. Men are not so likely to leave their Beds at Mid-night, when Liberty may be secured by keeping in; or whilst there is any hope of being Indulged by some less Complyance.

4. There was a greater probability of present Recompence at their first going out, than at the second time; which is a great Inducement unto Gracelefs Persons. Poor Carnal Professors may help to pluck down Antichristian Officers, if likely to enjoy their Lands and Benefices: And Mercenary Souldiers will Fight most Desperately, in hope of more than Ordinary Pay: Yea, very Hypocrites (or such as *Judas* was) may bear an open Testimony on Christ's behalf, so long as Providence doth seem to favour it, though onely with the Applause of People. But when the Cry is made, these Livings, Spoils, and general Approbations may be more likely to be lost by going forth, which makes the Second time more Difficult.

5. The Truth is, at their first going out, these Foolish Virgins went they knew not whither, and meerly becaufe their Vessels were not stored with Oyl; which made them to attempt at first, what afterwards they were not free to profecute, as might be instanced in abundantly. Did not some Act and Speak, as *Balaam* Bleffed *Ifrael*, not being themfelves at such a time, and as their contrary after-Practice hath evinced? Would many so much have cried some things up, and others down, had they fore-seen what followed afterwards? This was the Fruit of their not being Acted by a Principle, or want of Oyl in Vessels.

Queft. 5. How doth Not-Taking, or Taking Oyl, so Eminently evince Mens Folly or Wifdom, as seemeth to be hinted here?

Anfw. 1. Becaufe the Taking of this Oyl is Principally pretended unto, by all forts of Spiritual Virgins. Would not all Professors be counted Gracious? Would they not be thought to be endued with Saving Light? Yea, will they not grant themfelves to be notorious Fools, in case this Holy Oyl were wholly wanting? All will count him a very Fool, who having none but empty Vessels, doth style himself an Oyl-Merchant, which is the Virgins case: Yea, will not he call himfelf a Fool, who having but one thing needful to remember, doth yet forget to take it? This Oyl is Wifdom, under another Name; he therefore needs must be a Fool, who leaves this Oyl behind him; as he is call'd, whofe Wifdom fails him by the way, *Eccl.* 10. 3.

H

2. Becaufe

2. Becaufe their is no Light or Guidance, without this Oyl. 'Tis not in Man (as he is Naturally confidered) to Direct his fteps, *Jer.* 10. 23. at leaft-wife not in Sp.ritual cafes, 1 *Cor.* 2. 14. or with Refpect unto the Bridegroom's way. And though the Scriptures are a fhining Light, 2 *Pet.* 1. 19. yet are they onely as a Lamp, *Pfal.* 119. 105. which muft be fed with Grace's Oyl, elfe it will be of little ufe, in point of fafe Direction, 2 *Pet.* 1. 16. Now, is it not a very Foolifh part, to walk in unknown Paths without a Light? How may fuch Wander, for ought they know, yea, meet with harm, at leaft-wife go in continual fear, and meerly through their carelefs Folly.

3. Becaufe there elfe will be no Perfevering to the end, which is a point of high Concernment. Nature may Foot it for a while, without this lightfome Oyl, but foon grows weary, as did thefe Foolifh Virgins, and upon that Account. Now, to begin, and not to Perfevere, doth Argue Folly, *Gal.* 3. 3. and that upon a double fcore. Partly, becaufe all former Labour is thereby loft; and is not he juftly mocked, who doth defift from what he hath begun to Build, *Luke* 14. 29, 30? But efpecially, becaufe he onely fhall be faved, who doth endure unto the End, *Mat.* 24. 13. and there can be no higher Folly, than not to think of Soul-Concernments.

4. Becaufe the Trimmed Lamps will not Advantage, but onely Difgrace the Bearer of an empty Veffel. Poor Foolifh Virgins muft have their Lamps, as in my Text; yea, they will Trim them alfo, *Mat.* 25. 7. but to no purpofe, in cafe there be no Oyl. Lamps are no Lightfome Bodies of themfelves, and in the Dark their Trimming is not feen, which therefore needs muft be unprofitable Burdens; yea, very Ridiculous alfo: As when a Man is feen to carry fome curious Lanthorn (in the Night) without a Candle. What are the moft Raifed Affections, if man-feitly void of Truth and Judgment, but a piece of Neat, well-worded Non-fence? Which *Solomon* calls the Sacrifice of Fools, *Eccl.* 5. 1. It were far better to make no fhew at all, than thus to fhame one's felf, by offering to deceive another's raifed Expectation; and therefore Hypocrites are moft egregious Fools.

5. Becaufe Another's Oyl or Light will no way benefit a Foolifh Virgin, at fuch a time. Indeed one Lamp, or Candle (in the Letter) may fhew the way to feveral Walkers, but not in a Myftical fence. And though fome formerly have feen with others Eyes, yet is it not fo likely now, or in an hour of Temptation. Wife Virgins are not unwilling to lend what Light they can afford, upon a ferious Motion made, but Fools cannot receive it, at leaft-wife will not; and then the cleareft Sun-beam will not Advantage him whofe Eye is either out, or fhut.

The Parable of the Ten Virgins Opened.

shut. And though a Blind man may be (and oft-times is) Directed by anothers Guidance, yet Foolish Virgins (in such a case and time as this) will not believe the Wise, the Danger of going out is now so Visible.

6. Because this Oyl or Light might easily have been procured by them, if sought for in due time. Silver and Gold are deeply hidden under Ground, which yet Men are content to dig for, whilst Heaven is dis-regarded, although it may be seen with looking upwards. The choicest good things are proffered upon the cheapest terms, *viz.* for Asking, *Mat.* 7. 7. and without Price, *Isa.* 55. 1. Yet most Men rather chuse to Labour (and spend their Mony also) for that which doth not satisfie, *Isa.* 55. 2. Nor is this Oyl a Burden, save unto those who have it not. Now, this is the highest Aggravation of Man's Folly, to Perish for want of that which would have cost him nothing.

Use 1. Upon the whole, we may Observe from hence, that Hypocrites (or Foolish Virgins) will have their Lamps with them, whatever else is left behind. Those may be suspected to be no Virgins, or Visible Saints, who have not had some good Affections stirring in them, and with Respect unto Time Truths, and Duties, such as the Coming of this Bridegroom is, and going forth to meet him. But yet Hell's mouth is full of good Desires; and flashy Affections are nothing like unto a Spouse's Love; yea, those full Sails (without the Ballast of a Solid Judgment) may onely hasten the over-turning of an empty Vessel. What shall we then think of Persons dis-affected to the things of Christ? Who needs must be Prophane, if naked good Affections may be in those, who are but Formalists, or Foolish Virgins.

Use 2. Poor Foolish Virgins are to be known, as by their want of Oyl, so by their want of Care to take it with them, at least-wise in their Vessels, together with their Lamps. The dis-regarding of a Principle doth Argue Mens Natural Foolishness; much more in Spiritual cases, because these are of greatest Consequence: And then, how many Foolish Virgins are there to be seen, in this Professing Generation. The Generality of Professors follow Christ, as those did *Absalom*, in their simplicity, 2 *Sam.* 15. 11. Nor are they careful to Inform the Judgment, so as to hold unto a Righteous Principle. Thence are such sad Apostacies, and shameful self-contradicting Practices, which make their Folly manifest beyond dispute.

Use 3. Wise Virgins are for making sure, by taking Oyl with them, and in their Vessels also. A Soul and Christ are mutually betroth'd in Judgment, *Hos.* 2. 19. and by that means in Faithfulness, *v.* 20. And as Christ's Person is fully known by such, unto an hair, *Cant.* 5. 11. So are they well acquainted with his Interests, before they do Espouse them; which Knowledge and Wisdom is said to be the ground of their Stability, *Isa.* 33.6. So that the Difference between a Wise and Foolish Virgin is very great, in case their Vessels be but looked into, by means whereof most Hypocrites might be Discovered. Away with that Soul-ruining Opinion, That Grace and Nature do onely Differ in Degree; since Christ saith plainly, the Foolish Virgins had no Oyl, that is, no Grace at all; as had the Wise, and in their Vessels also: or as was Evidenced by their Principled good Affections, and Acting from a Spiritually enlightned Judgment.

Use 4. If Wisdom and Folly be thus Discovered, it highly concerneth all Professors to get their Vessels furnish'd with this Oyl; as they would be (and be Reputed) Wise. In Order whereunto let these Directions be Observed.

1. Search your Vessels well. Professors perish for want of self-examination. I like not some mens Boasting; since empty Vessels are wont to yield the greatest sound: A Wise Man seareth, whil'st raging Fools are Confident, *Prov.* 14. 16. Trust not unto another's good Opinion; it was the Ruine of these Foolish Virgins, because they had Communion with the Wise. Be not deceived with the Matter of Religious Duties; Christ calls them workers of Iniquity, who could say much in that Respect, *Mat.* 7. 22, 23. Presume not upon your having Done and Suffered, with reference unto Time Truths, and Duties Heretofore; the Foolish Virgins did go out at first to meet the Bridegroom, *Mat.* 25. 1,2. Nor may we gather Satisfaction from being awakened with the Cry, or from a Trimmed Lamp, and seeming willingness to borrow Light, with reference unto the Last, or Second going out; for so far went these Foolish Virgins.

2. Study the Nature of this Oyl, in Order to your being made in love therewith. How Nimble will it make you for that Race, which giveth an Incorruptible Crown unto the swiftest Runner, 1 *Cor.* 9. 24, 25! How will it Heal those Wounds which sin hath made, in point of Being, though not in point of Guilt! How will its favour chear your Spirits; and not yours onely, but others also, both God's and Man's! How will it make your Faces shine, so as that Graceless Persons shall witness unto your Beauty! How will it feed your Lamps, and Lead you in the Darkest way of most Mysterious Truths and Duties! And is not this Oyl worth carrying with you? Or will you not Exchange your Puddle-water for it?

3. Take heed of being cheated with Nature's Oyl, wherewith (perhaps) these Foolish Virgins Lamps were for a while maintained. This
Oyl

The Parable of the Ten Virgins Opened. 53

Oyl of Grace was Typified by that Holy Oyl of Old, *Exod.* 30. 25. peculiarly belonging unto the Priests, *v.* 30. who were the Types of Gospel-Saints, 1 *Pet.* 2. 9. Which did consist of so much Oyl and Principal Spices, *Exod.* 30. 23, 24. *viz.* Five hundred Shekels of Purifying Myrrh, and Healing Cassia, and half so much of Comforting Cynamon and sweet Calamus, to signifie unto us, that Gospel-Grace is sweetly Comforting, but much more of a Purifying and Healing Nature. Yet as this Holy Oyl was Subject to be sinfully applyed to others besides the Priests, (as Hypocrites may flatteringly be called Saints:) So was it apt to have its like or Counterfeit; both which are evident from that strict Prohibition, *Exod.* 30. 33. And from the Latter of which (*viz.* its being Imitable) doth seem to be hinted to us, that it requireth abundant Knowledge and all Judgment, in way of Tryal to Approve, those things which Differ in point of Excellency, *Phil.* 1. 9, 10.

4. Labour to be Engrafted therefore into Christ, that good Olive-Tree, as he is called, *Rom.* 11. 24. from whom this Special Oyl must be Derived. Christ's Faithful Witnesses are sometimes called Olive-Trees, *Zech.* 4. 11. *Rev.* 11. 4. because the Candlesticks (or Saints and Churches) are maintained with their Oyl or Light, *Zech.* 4. 12. But yet these very Trees (Compared with Christ) are onely Olive-Branches, *Zech.* 4. 12. because Christ is the Root of all their Fatness, *Rom.* 11. 17. There is indeed another Root, or a Wild Olive-Tree, *Rom.* 11. 24. which is the first *Adam*'s Nature: But Souls must be cut off from that, and Graffed (contrary unto Nature) into the other, *viz.* Christ, as is there signified, before they can partake of his good Oyl, *v.* 17. Earth will as soon grow up to Heaven, as will the First *Adam*'s Nature into the Second's, 1 *Cor.* 15. 47. without this Supernatural Transplantation.

5. Be sure to have enough. Improve your Fears of having no Oyl at all, unto the Multiplying of your hidden store. Christ calls for widened Mouths, *Psal.* 81. 10. Who giveth Liberally without upbraiding, *James* 1. 5. save where his Offers are not Accepted, *Mat.* 11. 20. In times of Danger, (such as these are) no man repenteth of buying necessary Arms, although he may not have Occasion for them. However, Godliness is Profitable unto all things, 1 *Tim.* 4. 8. which therefore will be our mony at any time, especially at Christ's Appearing, 2 *Pet.* 1. 10, 11. Yea, this Expensive hour of Temptation doth need a more than Ordinary stock; and these wise Virgins therefore slumbred, because they had not Oyl, or Light enough to keep them waking. Empty your Vessels therefore, and get them Multiplyed, or Enlarged,

so

so will this Oyl increase, especially when it is poured out (or in continual Exercise,) and with the Door shut upon you, or without Ostentation, 2 *Kings* 4. 3, 4, 5, 6.

6. Look after these things betimes. Christ calls for being heard *To Day*, Heb. 3. 7. and would not have you to delay your Neighbour (much less your selves) untill to Morrow, *Prov.* 3. 28. In Times of bad Trading (such as these are) who knows how soon Christ may shut up his shop; especially since we are now looking for that Lord's-day, 2 *Pet.* 3. 10. (in a fore-running sence, explained formerly,) on which he will not work, *Rev.* 22. 10, 11. However, what Fools are they, who think their Spiritual and Eternal state can be too speedily secured? Especially since Christ doth here fore-tell their doleful Portion who took no Oyl with them at first. The Time is hasting, when it will be sufficient to keep Men out for ever, meerly because they come too late, or when the Door is shut; which will not be Opened, unto the loudest Knock, or Cry, *Luke* 13. 25, 26, 27.

Use 5. Let the Professor's Acting from a Principle of Solid Judgment, in every of his Spiritual Undertakings, evince the having of this Oyl in Vessels, together with the Lamps of good Affections. Unto the setting home of which Exhortation, let these few Motives be duly weighed.

1. Our God is a God of Judgment, *Isa.* 30. 18. whose Predestination followeth his fore-knowledge, *Rom.* 8. 29. Who weigheth the Just man's Path, *Isa.* 26. 7. Who worketh all things after Counsel, *Eph.* 1. 11. and all whose ways are Judgment, 4. 37. His Spirit also is a Spirit of Judgment, *Isa.* 4. 4. which therefore is shadowed out by those seven Eyes engraven upon Christ, that Corner-stone, *Zech.* 3. 9. because Christ hath the seven Spirits of God, *Rev.* 3. 1. by which is meant the Holy Ghost, *Rev.* 1. 4. And Christ himself (or Wisdom) dwells with Prudence, *Prov.* 8. 12. betrothing Souls unto himself in Judgment, *Hos.* 2. 19. and who is called the Discretion of his Father, *Jer.* 10. 12. by whom the Heavens were prepared, *Prov.* 8. 27. Now, what a shame it is to Christians, in case their Acts be in-judicious; since they pretend to be the Children of that God of Judgment, endued with his Spirit of Judgment; and to have put that New Man on, which is renewed in Knowledge, after his Image, (*viz.* Christ's) who hath Created them, *Col.* 3. 10.

2. Else Actions are not Rational, and so beneath a Man, much more a Christian; which is a great Reproach, both to a Christian's Person and Profession. Insensible Creatures are Acted by their Natural qualities; Brutes by Instinct, and Fools (or Men Distracted) by sudden

Fancies:

The Parable of the Ten Virgins Opened.

Fancies: But Sober Persons walk by a Rule of Judgment. Now, what a shame it is for Christians to come short of Men, who should be more, *1 Cor.* 3. 3. at least-wise Rational, since onely those are called unreasonable, who have not Faith, *2 Thes.* 3. 2. Though Natural Reason will never grow up to Gospel-Faith, yet Grace is so far from Destroying Reason, as that it self is nothing else but Holy Understanding, *Prov.* 9. 10. or Good Judgment, *Psal.* 119. 66. And therefore some Men count Religion a meer Humour, because Professors are not seen to be duly Rational; as when such manifestly contradict their own Professed Righteous Principles.

3. We call for the Exercise of utmost Judgment in another, especially if we our selves are any way concerned in their Actings; which should Oblige our walking by that Rule our selves. How apt are we to censure Another's In-advertency, and to Mock that Foolish Builder, who did not first set down, *Luke* 14. 28, 29, 30. *Thou therefore which Teachest another, Teachest thou not thy self,* Rom. 2. 21? How sharply do we Rebuke a Friend or Servant, who doth endammage himself or us, through want of being well Advised? And shall we indulge that Giddiness in our selves, which is injurious to our Souls, or Christ? We beg, that God would not Correct us in his Anger, but with Judgment, for fear of being brought to nothing, *Jer.* 10. 24. And shall we Offer unto him a Sacrifice without an Head, or not do unto him, as we would have him do to us, *Luke* 6. 31? Yea, therefore Christians should be ashamed of not Considering what they do for him, *Eccl.* 5. 1. because the Riches of his Grace hath so abounded towards them, in all Wisdom and Prudence, *Eph.* 1. 7, 8. as might be cleared up at large.

4. We use to be Preponderate in other Matters, and Christianity is the Highest Calling, *Phil.* 3. 14. which therefore doth require the constant Exercise of our Maturest Judgment. Shall we consider what is spoken by us before Judicious Men, and yet be hasty to utter any thing in Prayer to God, *Eccl.* 5. 2? Shall we first count the Cost, before we begin an Earthly Building, and not much more, with reference to our Engaging in the ways of Christ, *Luke* 14. 27, 28.? Are we content to Learn the Mystery of a Common Trade, before we Set it up; and shall we rush into a Gospel-Temple, before we know the Pattern of that House, *Ezek.* 43. 10? A Man will tell Gold, after his Father; and shall we not tell Truth after a Brother, but pin our Faith upon a Teachers sleeve? And if we are wont to hear both Parties speak, before we Judge in Humane Causes; shall Christ (in any of his Truths, or Members) be Condemned, before he hath been heard

to

to speak, *John* 7. 51 ? How may poor Carnal Creatures thence conclude, that such irrational Professors are meerly Humorous?

5. It may provoke us hereunto, because this Oyl in Vessels (or walking by a Principle of Solid Judgment) is so exceeding Rare, which some Men think is not a Duty, and fewer Evidence it by their Practice, among Professors. Good *Agur* humbly thought himself Inferiour unto an Ordinary Man, *Prov.* 30.2. and yet his Reasonableness (in point of worldly Riches, *v.* 8.) did prove him to be above the most: But God doth bid Idolaters to shew themselves Men, *Isa.* 46.8. And *Solomon* in his Time could not find two among a Thousand, *Eccl.* 7. 28. Yea, it should seem, that One could not be found in Populous *Jerusalem, Jer.* 5. 1. Our Lot is cast into those Times, wherein a Man is precious, above the Gold of *Ophir, Isa.* 13. 12. at least, wherein there are Seven Women unto One Man, *Isa.* 4. 1. And as appeareth by Mens injudicious Actings. Thence is it, that many are so tossed to and fro, and Principles so frequently contradicted ; nor can men give a Reason of their Faith or Practice, because they are guided mostly by Affections, as Ships are by their Stern, and not their Head.

6. We else shall want the benefit of that Satisfaction in a Duty, which otherwise might be enjoyed. How chearfully both Horse and Man will Travel in a way that's known, compared with another, though possibly an unknown path may be as right and better. And though poor Brutes are pleased, if onely Sense be in its Exercise; yet Men (and much more Christians) are like to Fishes upon the Land, out of their proper Element, save as their Judgment also is employed. The Sinners mis-guided Understanding doth yield him more imagined content, than doth the Upright Walker's Ignorance. What Pleasure can any take in Hearing the most precious Truths, save as he grasps them ? Nor is the Conscience satisfied with the fairest Shews, save as Affections are enlivened with an Intelligent Heart or Soul. 'Tis not a Real (but Rational) Act of Faith, which giveth Comfort ; or as a Direct Act of Believing is Reflected on: Nor can we Joy in any kind of Duty or Obedience, in a solid way, save as it is perform'd with Understanding; since, else its Graciousness cannot be known, which groundeth Joy.

7. Acts unadvisedly performed (or without Judgment) are never Lasting. As is the Root or Fountain, so is the durableness of streams and Branches. Some little Rivulets (fed by a Living Spring) will hold their Course, when greater Land-Floods are wholly dryed up: And Ivy (about the Oak) will dye, when Natural Oak-Branches Live; because that Ivy hath not these Branches Root. He onely believeth for

The Parable of the Ten Virgins Opened. 57

a while, who hath no Root, *Luke* 8. 13. for want of Hearing with Underftanding, *Mat.* 13. 23. Thence is it, that an Hypocrite will not Pray alway, *Job* 27. 10. Nor will a Fool pay that which he hath rafhly Vowed, *Eccl.* 5. 4. No more than Foolifh Virgins will ever perfevere, who take not Oyl in Veffels at their firft fetting out. But that which is done in Judgment, is done for ever, *Hof.* 2. 19. Its Nature hath been duly weighed, and therefore it will not lightly be Repented of; Effects and Confequents have been confidered, which therefore will not hinder its Purfuance; and that which is begun with good Advice, will never fail, through want of being furnifhed with what is needful for its Accomplifhment. Judicious Saints will perfevere.

8. Elfe can we look for no Acceptance, much lefs a Receco npence; fave as our Actings and Affections proceed from Judgment. The Head (among all other Parts) was firft required, in Legal Sacrifices, *Lev.* 1. 8. becaufe that is the Seat of Knowledge: But if we Offer the blind for Sacrifice, will God be pleafed with us, or Accept us, *Mal.* 1. 8? He therefore hears not Sinners, *John* 9. 31. for he hath no pleafure in fuch Fools, *Eccl.* 5. 4. whofe Heart is fo far diftant from himfelf, *Ifa.* 29. 13. and from their Duty, *Ezek.* 33. 31. And what Reward can Men expect from God, in cafe their Work be of a Brutifh Nature? Man's Underftanding is that Male, which God hath Bleft him with, chiefly for Sacrifices to himfelf; and without which no Bleffing (but a Curfe) is to be looked for from this great King, *Mal.* 1. 14. Such may go wrong, as well as right, for ought they know, who know not what they do: And Duty performed by Accident, may Peradventure be Rewarded, or if it fo falls out. Such act not with Refpect to a Divine Command; for then Obedience would be Univerfal, *John* 6. 38, 39. And if the Command fets not on work, the Promife is at Liberty in point of Pay. Such do but half their work at beft, leaving the better half undone: And no Inheritance can be expected, unlefs the Lord befollowed whelly, *Jofh.* 14. 9.

9. Difcretion will Preferve thee, *Prov.* 2. 11. but there is he that is Deftroyed for want of Judgment, *Prov.* 13. 23. both in refpect of Sin and Suffering. How fadly (in his hafte) did *David* fpeak, *Pfal.* 116. 11. And there is more hope of of a Fool (in point of being Reclaimed from Sin) than of one hafty in his words or matters, *Prov.* 29. 20. And as to Sufferings, Judgments are prepared for him that fcorneth Judgment, *Prov.* 19. 28, 29. Yea, it went ill with *Mofes*, for fpeaking unadvifedly, *Pfal.* 106. 33. And *Nadab* and *Abihu* dyed, for Offering ftrange Fire before the Lord, *Lev.* 10. 1, 2. being fomewhat Diftempered in their Heads, as feemeth to be hinted by that

I *immediate*

immediate following Prohibition, of Drinking Wine or Strong drink, when going into the Tabernacle, *v.* 9. And if the bare Carnality of Affections (Typified by that strange Fire) be of so sad a Nature, how do they take God's Name in vain, (for which he will not hold them guiltless, *Exod.* 20. 7.) who Sleep, or Wander in a Religious Duty? And what if he then should cut them off, as he did those Priests?

10. How just is it with God, to give those up unto an in-judicious mind, who do not serve him with their Mind or Judgment? As that unprofitable Servant's Talent was taken from him, *Mat.* 25. 28. And as their Vineyard is Let out to others, who do deny its Fruits unto the chief Proprietor, *Mat.* 21. 24. Yea, customary sleightiness doth Naturally beget an Habit of that kind, which soon will leaven the whole lump of Actions: As one may be so Giddy with frequent Turning, as not to Command his standing when he would. Now, a Reprobate Mind (or void of Judgment, as the *Greek* word signifieth) is one of the saddest Characters, and sorest Judgments threatned, *Rom.* 1. 28. the fear whereof made *Paul* to mind (himself) that which he Preach'd to others, 1 *Cor.* 9. 27. How sad would it be, if Hearts should grow wild through wandring; and silly, through multiplyed Acts of In-advertency; and Carnal, for want of Exercising Spiritual Infused Habits, which else may fall into a great Decay! A Closed Eye is justly blinded, *Mat.* 13. 14, 15.

11. If Vessels be not filled with Oyl, they will abound with something else unto our Dis-advantage: There being no absolute vacuity or utter emptiness; and as not in a Natural, so neither in this Moral Sence. Hence it is, that sleighty Professors are of an Airy Spirit at the best; yea, even their Mind and Conscience is Defiled also, *Titus* 1. 15. who do profess to know God, but in their Works deny him, to every good work being Reprobate, or void of Judgment, *v.* 16. An empty Vessel is apt to have Puddle-water cast into it by some mischievous Person: And empty Houses (though never so Neatly Garnished) are subject to be haunted, or possess'd by Evil Spirits, *Mat.* 12. 44, 45. Since while Men sleep, the Enemy will sow his Tares, *Mat.* 13. 25. And therefore if the Heart be not Engaged in a Religious Duty, it is not onely vain, but wicked also, *Ezek.* 33. 31. Now, what a sad thing it is, if we shall deny that unto Christ, which if he hath not, the Devil will have; and at the worst time that is, or while we are pretending to be most Holily employed, and in Christ's Service.

12. There is no Oyl at all, unless it be in Vessels, together with the Virgins Lamps, as may be gathered from this Text: To signifie
that

The Parable of the Ten Virgins Opened. 59

that there can be no Grace at all, where good Affections do not proceed from Spiritual Judgment; as there can be no proper Vertue, when Actings and Affections are Morally in-judicious; nor yet right Reason, when Words and Actions are wholly destitute of Natural Judgment. One part of a wicked Man's Description, is, his not understanding Judgment, *Prov.* 28. 5. and that there is no Judgment in his goings, *Isa.* 59. 8. and without which Discretion, all other fairness whatsoever, is but as a Jewel of Gold in the Snout of a Brutish Swine, *Prov.* 11. 22. Whereas the Wise Man's Eyes are in his Head, *Eccl.* 2. 14. who swears in Judgment, *Jer.* 4. 2. and whose Affairs are Ordered with Discretion, *Psal.* 112. 5. So that it doth concern Professors to have Oyl in their Vessels, and to evince it by the Judiciousness of their proceedings in Religious Duties, as they would not be numbred among Transgressors or Graceless Persons.

13. We border upon those Times, wherein our Principles will be enquired after, as well as Practices; which therefore had need be minded by us, for fear of what may follow. Time was, when *Paul* himself was but a Child, who then was satisfied with Lower things, as Children are with Brutes and Babies: But when he became a Man, he put away those Childish things, 1 *Cor.* 13. 11. Judging himself and others, not by the Zeal of an Affection, save as it was according unto Knowledge, *Rom.* 10. 2. And we have ground to hope, that wiser Virgins will for the future be well Advised, with whom they walk; searching the Vessels of their Companions, and trusting no more to Trimmed Lamps. In the Time of *Ezekiel*'s Second Temple, the Sons of *Zadock*, Ezek. 44. 15. shall stand in Judgment, *v.* 24. causing the People to Discern, between the unclean, and the clean, *v.* 23. not bringing into the Sanctuary Strangers uncircumcised in Heart, as did their Predecessors, *v.* 7. who will be then Degraded, *v.* 13. As we would therefore stand in God's Holy place, when *David*'s Tabernacle shall be reared up; so let there be a suitableness between our Hearts and Hands, or Principles and Practices, *Psal.* 24. 3, 4.

14. We cannot shun appearing before Christ's Seat of Judgment, 2 *Cor.* 5. 10. who then will separate the Sheep and Goats, *Mat.* 25. 32. both which divide the Hoof, and chew the Cud alike; onely they differ, as to the Spirit or Principle, from whence those Actions do proceed. God searcheth Hearts (or Vessels) to give unto every Man according to his ways, *Jer.* 17. 10. as all the Churches shall one day know, *Rev.* 2. 23. Christ will not Judge by Sight or Hearing, *Psal.* 11. 13. who doth Accept a willing Mind, 2 *Cor.* 8. 12. more than the work of him, whose Heart or Meaning is not engaged in it, *Isa.*

10. 6, 7. Now, what will it advantage us, if wisest Virgins should be satisfied with our naked Lamps, since that great Judge will also pierce our Vessels, passing his final Sentence on our Eternal state accordingly. As we wou'd therefore not come under the Foolish Virgins Condemnation, so let us take heed of their miscarriage, or trusting to good Affections.

In Order whereunto, these Helps may be of Use.

1. Habituate your selves to be considerate, in every of your Common undertakings: Since he that is a rash or hasty Man, will scarcely ever prove a Solid Christian. There is an unruly Spirit, which some Men are possessed with, *Prov.* 25. 28. whose Customary In-advertency in Ordinary Matters, doth much more easily beset them in Religious Exercises. As a Bodily Temper doth much affect the Natural Spirit; so doth a Christian's Duty favour of his Natural Disposition: Since Nature is both therein a fellow-worker, and Grace's Elder Brother. A wise Man's Heart is wont to teach his Mouth, *Prov.* 16. 23. therefore his words are Gracious, *Eccl.* 10. 12. And if a constant Watch were set before our Lips, Saints would not want the benefit of Ordinary helps in Extraordinary cases. But he that is not careful in the least, (such as our Natural concernments are, wherein both Grace and Nature joyn) will much less be so in the greatest, *Luke* 16. 10. Such as Religious Matters are, wherein (as to the point of Care) Grace usually is left alone.

2. Indulge not your Affections over-much, whose proper place is, to be Servants unto the Understanding's Dictates;but he that Delicately bringeth up his Servant from a Child, shall have him to become his Son at last, *Prov.* 29. 21. As *Hagar* did Despise her Mistress soon after her being taken into her Master's Bosom, *Gen.* 16. 4. Wine takes away the Heart, *Hos.* 4. 11. Or Judgment, *Prov.* 31. 4, 5. And one may Eat unto Intoxication, *Eccl.* 10. 7. Therefore Christ biddeth to take heed of Surfeiting and Drunkenness, as Men would not be unawares surprised, *Luke* 21. 34. And if in Natural Respects, then much more in a Moral sense, Men of Inordinate Affections, are generally injudicious, because of the Members warring against the Mind, *Rom.* 7. 23. which we are therefore bid to Mortifie, *Col.* 3. 5. And as Affections are termed Lusts, when fixt upon a sinful Object; so when they are not duly bounded, with reference to what is Good, which yet is alway of a Lower Nature; and partly, upon that Account, the Foolish Virgins might forget to fill their Vessels, because they did so violently Affect the Bridegroom's Coming, upon a Carnal Score.

3. Behold the Beauty of Judiciousness in Other's Actings, how comely

comely such are in going! Men of a sleighty Spirit themselves, wil yet bear witness unto the seemly carriage of another who walks by Judgment. Heart answereth unto Heart, as doth the Face (in water) to it self, *Prov.* 27. 19. That is, there is an Harmony or sweet Agreement between the Hearts of Men, as is between a Face and its Reflection. How Grateful is Consistency in a Discourse, when one thing correspondeth with another, and every Expression with the speaker's Understanding: Yea, we are apt to be in Love with seriousness, although appearing onely in the Countenance, much more in Words or Actions; and such especially as are of high concernment. Man's Beauty is chiefly seated in his Eye, the Rolling whereof (both in a Natural and Moral sence) disfigureth the fairest Face; especially when they who seem to be Religious, are least attentive unto the matters of their God. How justly do we loath that man, whose Heart (we know) agrees not with his Tongue; especially when such egregious Nonsence is confidently uttered with strong Affections. This we can see in others, which should provoke its greater detestation in our selves.

4. Let us Reflect upon our own Experiences, which are the very Life of Reasons, and Proof of Demonstrations. Have we not been oft-times ashamed of making Enquiry after Vows, by Reason of a Rash Engagement? Have not our Hearts oft smitten us, for leaving them behind, in a Religious Duty? And shall we yet feed that Worm of sleightiness, which hath so gnawn our Consciences? Whereas on the other side, what inward satisfaction hath been the consequent, of pondering what we hear; and pouring out the Soul in Prayer; and of our being in that Duty, which we at any time have been employed about? Indeed how can it be expected, that the Spirit in man should be well pleased, save as it self is Exercised in a Service? Which else will sharply chide, as did those *Ephramites* with *Gideon*, because they were not called to Accompany him in such an Expedition, *Judg.* 8. 1. And as the Judgment is more Spiritual, so are the Senses better Exercised, *Heb.* 5. 14. To smell the sweetness of that Spikenard, which Christ exciteth, whilst he is sitting at the Spouse's Table, *Cant.* 1. 12. And if the present Taste hath so Refresh'd us, much more should we remember the benefit of that Digestion, which hath attended the calling of our Spirits in, as such a Feast; compared with that Leanness, which always is the consequent of having our Heads employed other ways, in Spiritual meal-times, as in a Bodily Respect.

5. Be earnest with the Lord in Prayer, who is the Father of our Spirits, *Heb.* 12. 9. both as he is the Former of them, *Zech.* 12. 1. and

as he hath them under his Command, *Prov.* 16. 1. Prayer is too heavy a work for us (and so is every other Duty) unless the Spirit helpeth our Infirmities, *Rom.* 8. 26. which Heavenly Monitor is to be had when seriously asked by us, *Luke* 11. 11, 12, 13. *David* was purposed, that his Mouth should not Transgress, *Psal.* 17. 3. yet did he also beg, that God would set his Watch before it, *Psal.* 141. 3. And if Christ be withdrawn, though but a little way, his poor Disciples will fall asleep, when bid to Watch and Pray, *Mat.* 26. 38, 39. 41. 'Tis not in clearest Arguments, or Observations, or Experiences, to Rule that Heart which must improve them, save as it self is over-ruled by the God of Spirits, to Understand, and Mind, and Follow such Directions; whose onely work it is, to Keep such things for ever in the imagination of his People's thoughts, and to prepare their Heart unto himself, 1 *Chron.* 29. 18. Onely this Spirit must earnestly be desired by us, as Food is by an hungry Child, *Luke* 11. 11, 12, 13. Nor will it wholly take the work out of our Hand, but as it witnesseth together with our Spirits, *Rom.* 8. 16. So doth it help Infirmities, *v.*26. by lifting together, over against us, as the *Greek* importeth.

Use 6. It doth behove the Virgins to Search and Try whether they Act from Judgment; and from a Judgment Spiritually enlightned.

Now, the Judiciousness of our proceedings, may be Discerned by these Signs.

1. That which is done in Judgment, is duely weighed before-hand, as to its Nature, Grounds, Effects, and Requisites. As to its Nature, they know the Lord, (*Hos.* 2. 20.) who are in Judgment betrothed to him, *v.* 19. whereas he is a Foolish Vower, (*Eccl.* 5. 4.) who afterwards doth say (before this Angel) it was an Error, *v.* 6. Such also know, what Grounds they do proceed upon, and therefore it is incumbent upon Christians, first to Believe, and then to Speak, 2 *Cor.* 4. 13. Yea, and to give a Reason of their Hope, 1 *Pet.* 3. 15. and fully to be perswaded in their Mind before they Practise, *Rom.* 14. 5. And such will first sit down (or mind Effects) before they begin to Build, *Luke* 14. 28. In which regard, Christ bids him weigh the Consequents of being his Follower, *Mat.* 8. 20. who was so forward in his Offer, *v.* 19. Nor will such make Attempts, till their Ability for such a work be understood, *Luke* 14. 31. or what is requisite for such an undertaking, and till it is first fitted, *Prov.* 24. 27.

2. That which is done in Judgment, is carefully attended unto, in the Doing of it, as need requireth. The words of such, are with Heart-Meditation, before the Lord, *Psal.* 5. 1. The Consideration of

of whose being so far above them, makes their words few (or well Digested) and not Rash or Hasty, *Eccl.* 5. 2. Such diligently mind what is Confess'd or Promised, or Prayed for, in Order unto a suitable Pursuance; whilst others Lay such kind of Eggs, and then leave them, as doth the Ostritch, (*Job* 39.13,14.) who is hardned against her Young ones, as though they were not hers, *v.* 16. because she is deprived of Understanding, *v.* 17. Hence is that clashing disagreement between an injudicious Person's Speech and Practice, *Mat.* 23.3. there being so great a Distance between his Heart and Lips, *Mat.* 15.8. as is between the sleighty Hearer's Ear and Heart, who therefore soon forgetteth what manner of Man he was, whilst his Affections were sometimes stirred in him, *James* 1. 23, 24. but not his Judgment.

3. That which is done in Judgment, is firmly persisted in, and gaineth strength by Opposition. Judgment is as the Eye, and what a man hath seen, he will not question, though all the World should differ from him, in that particular. Judgment is the Root of Actions, which shooteth deeper into its ground, when shaken with the wind of Persecution. *Paul* Acted from a Principle of Judgment, who knew in whom he had Believed, 2 *Tim.* 1. 12. and therefore kept the Faith, 2 *Tim.* 4. 7. when all forsook him, *v.* 16. Whilst *Peter* ran, for Company, *Mark* 14. 50. from under the most strong Affectionate pre-obligation, *Mat.* 26. 33. But therefore *Peter* (afterwards) could not but speak what he had seen, *Acts* 4. 20. though Man forbad him, *v.* 18. whose Boldness made his Persecutors to perceive, that he had been with Jesus, *v.* 13. His Heart was never right with God, who is not stedfast in his Covenant, *Psal.* 78. 37. Nor had such ever any depth of Root, who finally fall away in times of Tribulation, *Mat.* 13 21. Whereas his way shall be established, whose Path is Pondered, *Prov* 3. 26.

4. That which is done with Judgment, is also Ordered with Discretion; according to the Nature, Time, and other Circumstances of a Duty. As there are Songs, 1 *Kings* 4. 32. Songs of Degrees, *Psal.* 120. Title; and a Song of Songs, *Cant.* 1. 1. So there are lesser and more Weighty Matters, *Mat.* 23. 23. the latter of which are principally attended unto, by Judicious Practisers. Such are for Real Truths at any Time, but yet predominant Time-Truths, are chiefly insisted on by a Judicious Preacher. If there be any Vertue, it will be thought upon by such, *Phil.* 4. 8. but yet Faith is the Prime Object of a Judicious Christian's Diligence, 2 *Pet.* 1. 5. If Civil Subjection to Antichristian Powers, (which is more dark) be bogled at by such, much less will Man's Commands, or Prohibitions (in Religious Matters) be complied with, by a Judicious Scrupler; because this latter is more
clear.

&c. r. Such will do good to all, but more especially where need doth most require; or else their Love doth not abound in Knowledge and all Judgment, *Phil.* 1. 9.

5. That which is done with Judgment, is done with due Affections also; the Judgment being alway so Accompanied, as Princes are with their Attendants, although Affections oft-times go alone. They who judiciously confess a failing, (especially some kind of sins) are suitably Affected with inward bitterness, *Zech.* 12. 10. else do they not seem to know that kind of Plague, 1 *Kings* 8. 38. which must be driven out with Holy Violence. Such will pour out their Heart in Prayer, *Psal.* 62. 8. especially for Spiritual Blessings: Else do they not pray with Understanding; since cold Petitioners (in such Cases) do onely Teach another to deny them. Such will draw out their Soul (together with their Bread) unto the Hungry, *Isa.* 58. 10. else may they give much Alms, as did the *Pharisees*, *Mat.* 6. 2. who yet omitted Mercy, *Mat.* 23. 23. because they did it not with Bowels of Compassion. And such who do judiciously return unto an open Testimony (in Times of Danger) as their Duty, cannot but be ashamed of their former failing in that Respect; and so in any other case whatever.

6. That which Men do with Judgment, they will endeavour to Accomplish, by the diligent use of most effectual Means conducing thereunto. Such are no Idle Beggars, but he that Cryeth after Knowledge (with Understanding) will seek her also, and search for her, as for hid Treasure, *Prov.* 2. 3, 4. Temptations Cordially groaned under, are striven against, and watched over, else do not men judge them very burdensome, what-ever may be deceitfully pretended unto. Such also study what to render, for all those Benefits, which are judiciously acknowledged by them, *Psal.* 116. 12. or how to take in their Bonds, and Pay their Vows, which have been made with Understanding, *v.* 18. Whereas men guided by meer Affections, are to be known by their remissness of their Endeavours, and sluggishness of their Desires, and the In-activity of their Acknowledgments. Nor can we better Judge of Heartless Hypocrites, than by Observing the Dis-proportion that is between their Practice and Profession, *Mat.* 23. 3.

These are the Signs of Acting from Judgment, in the General. The Signs of being Spiritually Judicious (in our Religious Actings) are briefly these which follow.

1. The Light of Spiritual Judgment, is also Universal; at least, with reference unto the Main of whatsoever is a Duty. Men Naturally Judicious, are Uniform, as to the whole of a Particular Action: But that which is truly Spiritual, doth suitably appear, in every of a Judicious

The Parable of the Ten Virgins Opened. 65

dicious Profeffor's ways. Nature deals by Retail (in Spiritual Matters) but Grace by whole Sale: And therefore he is guided into All Truth, who by the Spirit of Truth is guided into Any one, *John* 16.13. Grace doth renew the Mind, and casteth Salt (as did *Elisha*) into that Spring which healeth every of its Streams or Actions; as Natural Understanding doth in Ordinary Cases, but not Religious. No Verdict can rightly pass upon a man, but by Accumulation, or taking him altogether, No more than Parrots can be concluded Rational, or Drunkards Sober, from some few words which they may utter; And therefore Saints are oft-times called Vines, whose Fruit is Clustered, as *Phil.* 1. 11.

2. True Spiritual Light is of a self-evidencing Nature ; like that of the Sun, which needeth no Forreign help, nor can be Discern'd by any other, save its own Beams ; and which the strongest Arguments cannot prevail against, in his Opinion whose Eye is therewith Lightned. Such call for no Reason, save what is Scriptural ; nor can they see with Nature's Spectacles in Spiritual Cases; nor are they shaken in their Faith, by meer Prudential Arguments, or Man's Authority. Those are not Spiritually Judicious, who plead for Nature's Negative Voice upon Divine Commands; or Argue from thence the Warrant of self-preservation, when Christ (who is the Lord of all, *Acts* 10. 36.) expresly calls for self-denyal. Prophets were therefore counted Mad, 2 *Kings* 9. 11. and so was *Paul*, 2 *Cor.* 5. 13. because so confident, against all Rules of Ordinary Demonstration ; not knowing Christ after the Flesh, as heretofore, *v.* 16. And every Man in Christ is thus Renewed, *v.* 17.

3. True Spiritual Light is throughly Purifying; And therefore the Spirit of Judgment is also called the Spirit of Burning, *Isa.* 4. 4. with reference unto that Dross and Filth, which it Discovereth and consumeth, both at once. Those men who are but Naturally Judicious, may alter their Opinion or former evil Practice, yea, with Affection also ; and yet without the utter Extirpation of a contrary Principle, As is to be Observed in some Moralists, who yet without the Spirit of Christ can never Mortifie a sinful Lust, *Rom.* 1. 13. But Duty proceeding from Spiritual Judgment, destroys the Root of Disobedience; as doth the Love of Truth, what is Erroneous: Yea, the Confession of a sin (when it is Spiritually Judicious) doth secretly Eradicate that which is so acknowledged. Let us Observe what Execution is done upon our Spiritual Adversaries, by every one of our Religious Exercises, as we would Argue our being therein Acted by a Spiritually enlightned Judgment: Since Christ's Peculiar Baptism (with the Holy Ghost)

K　　　　　　　　　　　　　　is

is, of a fiery Nature, and so appeareth, by its consuming what-ever is combustible, *Mal.* 3. 11, 12.

4. True Spiritual Light Transforms a Soul into the Nature of what is thereby seen or done; it being the Spirit's property to change Beholders into the Image of what it doth Discover, 2 *Cor.*3.18. *Balaam* did Naturally Understand what he denounced upon *Israels* Cursers, *Numb.* 24. 9. which yet did not prevent his cursed following Practice, *Rev.* 2. 14. No more than Notional Acquaintance with Gospel-Mysteries, can change a Carnal Heart, who yet may Naturally understand them, 1 *Cor.* 13. 2. But he that Spiritually (or by the Spirit of Faith, 2 *Cor.* 4. 13.) believeth in Christ, is thereby turned into a New Creature; all things are New, as well as Old things done away, 2 *Cor.* 5. 17. Such are Transfigured, as Christ was in Prayer, *Luke* 9. 29. and are Delivered into what they Hear, as it is in the *Greek*, *Rom.* 6. 17. because this Spiritual Digestion doth Convert a Feeder into the Nature of his Meat, which Natural Understanding doth not, but leaves the Heart as void of Spirituality, to be sure (though not, perhaps, so grosly vicious) as it was before.

5. Men Naturally Judicious, are alway Sober; but Spiritual Judgment doth also keep them very Humble, and of a Lowly Heart, with reference to what they either Know or Do. That Knowledge is but Natural at the best, which Puffeth up, 1 *Cor.*8. 1. And Elevating Duty is not Evangelical, which some are apt to Glory in, because they know not wherein true Spirituality doth consist, and how far short they come thereof. But the work of the Spirit is to Mortifie all Fleshly Lusts,*Rom.*8. 13. and Pride among the rest, by convincing the Soul of more Mysterious failings,*John* 16.8,9.comparing Spiritual things with Spiritual, 1 *Cor.* 2. 13. by pressing forward, so as to make us forgetful of what is behind, *Phil.* 3. 13, 14. and by affording its super-added help in Holy Exercises, *Rom.* 8. 26. all which are of an Humbling Nature. How can he Boast, whose work is seen (by the Spirit's Light) to be imperfect, and full of Blemishes? Yet, who doth see, he worketh not, as unto that wherein the Glory of his work consisteth. They who are apt to be Transported, do not appear to be Judicious, at least, not Spiritually.

MAT.

MATTHEW XXV. 5.

While the Bridegroom tarried they all slumbred and slept.

IN this Verse, we have an Account of the fore-named Bridegroom's tarrying, together with what followed thereupon, *viz.* The slumbring and sleeping of all these Virgins.

Observ. After these Virgins going forth at first, the Bridegroom tareth; which doth Occasion their General sleep and slumber.

Quest. I. In what sence doth the Bridegroom Tarry, after such a Time?

Answ. I. Negatively; Christ is not slack as Men count slackness, 2 *Pet.* 3. 9. nor doth he pass the time appointed, as *Pharaoh* did, *Jer.* 16. 17. but as the Day of his Coming is known to him, *Zech.* 14. 7. So will it be Observed by him, unto a self-same Day, as when he brought *Israel* out of *Egypt*, Exod. 12. 41. which must be Acted over a Second time, *Isa.* 11. 11. And as the Agreement may be in other respects, so doubtlessly in this, that Christ will hasten this latter in his Time, *Isa.* 50. 20. and beyond which he will not tarry, no, not an hour.

II. But then Affirmatively; Christ may be said to Tarry, (or to Prolong his Time, as the *Greek* word signifieth) in these Respects.

1. With Respect to the seeming Need of his more speedy Coming; as when he tarried two days still, after the News of *Lazarus* his Sickness, *John* 11. 6. whose Death else might have been prevented, *v.* 21. And thus the Virgins thought (at their first going forth) that there was need enough, why Christ should then have come; in which regard, he might be said to Linger. The Witnesses had then already Prophesied (as some yet hope) 1260 Years in Sackcloth; and was it not then High time to Perfect their Redemption? Especially when Christ himself did sometimes plead for those Poor Jews, who had been then but 70 Years in Literal *Babylon*, *Zech.* 1. 12. And since Relapses are likely to be most Dangerous. Had Christ come then, his People's Faith would not have failed, his own Beloved Interest would not have Dyed, nor would some others have so Blasphemed, as whilst he doth Delay his Coming, *Mat.* 24. 48.

2. With reference unto the Virgins Longing for him; and therefore

Sisera's Chariot-wheels were said to *Tarry*, becaufe his Mother did fo long to fee him, *Judg.* 5. 28. as all the Virgins fometimes did, (with reference unto Chrift) and may do ftill; which did invite their firft going out to meet him, and hath Occafioned their fad Complaining of his ftay. Some wifh for this Day of Chrift in way of Scoffing, 2 *Pet.* 3. 3, 4. but others do more ferioufly feek after him, *Mal.* 3. 1. yea, Foolifh Virgins alfo, or fuch as will not ftand when he appeareth, *v.* 2. Now, a Soul that longs to fee the Face of Chrift is apt to fay, *God hath forgotten*, *Ifa.* 49. 14. Yea, *that his Promife faileth for evermore*, Pfal. 77. 8. At leaft, to cry, *How long, O Lord*, Rev. 6. 10. *make hafte and make no Tarrying*, Pfal. 70. 5.

3. With reference unto their General Expectation of his Coming, at their firft going out: In which refpect, he may be faid to *Tarry*, as *Zacharias* did, becaufe he came not fo foon as was expected by the People, *Luke* 1. 21. Which confident Expectation of him (at fuch a Time) we know to have been True, and may conjecture at its Rife.

1. Partly; from an Impatient hafte, proceeding from the weaknefs of Mens Faith, *Ifa.* 28. 16. but yet Occafioning their being Confounded or Afhamed, as the Apoftle hinteth, *Rom.* 9. 33. becaufe they hope for that which is fo vehemently defired, *Job* 6. 19, 20. As Confident fpeaking doth follow True Believing, 2 *Cor.* 4. 13. So Confident Expecting is equally (oft-times) the Fruit of Fancy, fince Men are apt to pre-conclude (with utmoft confidence) what is Importunately defired by them; as did, not onely *Sifera*'s Mother, concerning her Son's Victory, *Judg.* 5. 29, 30. but *David* alfo, concerning his Sons Life, 2 *Sam.* 18. 27. Now, all thefe Virgins did earneftly wifh for the Bridegroom's Coming, at their firft going out; from whence their Expectation of him might arife, and confequently their fuppofal of his Tarrying beyond the Time.

2. Partly from probable Grounds, both Scriptural and Providential. His Coming (at their firft going out) was Generally the Object of their Faith and Prayer, with whom God's fecret is, who therefore might conclude his fpeedy Coming *Then*, from *Pfal.* 25. 14. *Luke* 18. 7, 8. His Servants (at that time) took Pleafure in *Sion*'s Stones, as was apparent from their Endeavouring *Then* to Build them up, with greateft Hazard, Induftry and Alacrity: who therefore might fuppofe, the Time (yea, the fet Time) was come, from *Pfal.* 102. 13, 14. The many wondrous works of God (relating unto the Time before mentioned) did much encourage to believe the near approaching of Chrift's Name or Difpenfation; from *Pfal.* 75. 1, 2. The falling

The Parable of the Ten Virgins Opened. 69

Stars (at such a Time,) did comfortably evidence, that the Son of Man, was even at the Doors, from *Mat.* 24.

The Witnesses have been signally warred with, as *Rev.* War doth properly import their being uppermost, or upon ; and therefore it might be Then presumed, the Kingdom e left to other People, from *Dan.* 2. 44. No wonder then ions were so high.

pally, because they were not aware of Christ's fore-runner, ice unto his Coming as a Bridegroom, which is sufficiently re Scriptures: And after which Harbinger, his Proper ll be ushered in, by such a sad state of things, as we have Thus Christ himself was slain, after his being Proclaimed is Disciples, *Luke* 19. 37, 38. As *David* was pursued by his having been Annointed King by *Samuel*, 1 *Sam.* 16. 13. the Saints being called Earthly Kings, *Isa.* 24. 21. they hered together as Prisoners in the Pit, *v.* 22. as *Joseph* was, . After that his Supremacy was first Declared, *v.* 9. And *ion*'s set time is come, *Psal.* 102. 13. there will be a fore *v.* 8. Drink mingled with weeping, *v.* 9. a Casting down, 3 lifted up, *v.* 10. groaning Prisoners, and some Condem-, *v.* 20. Yea, after the fourth Beast's being slain in the lit-he rest of the Beasts (or a grosser interest) will in some e, though they have no Dominion (or proper settlement) -phrase, *Dan.* 7. 11, 12. And when the Witnesses are Ri-ended, or have Received their Kingdom, as Christ did upon on, *Luke* 19. 12. then comes that dreadful Earthquake, *t*, 13. which Terminateth upon their Enemies, but will Be-hers, as seemeth to be hinted by that Harvest, *Rev.* 14. 15. Vintage, *v.* 18. just as God's *Israel* met with that check in of *Achor*, after their being Actually possess'd of *Canaan*, 6, 7, 8, 9. And as poor *David* had long War with the *aul*, 2 *Sam.* 3. 1. after being made King in *Hebron*, 2 *Sam.* is the Jews were troubled, *Ezra* 4. 4. after the return of vity, *v.* 1. All which (with reference unto the latter days) gnified, by that Prophetical praying for a Turn, *Psal.* 85:4. aptivity is brought back, *v.* 1. and by the *Assyrian*'s inrode *el*'s Land, *Isa.* 8. 7, 8. Or that of *Gog* and *Magog*, into a ; brought forth out of the Nations, *Ezek* 38. 18. and by s coming against *Jerusalem*, when Re-Inhabited, *Zech.* 12. the bringing again of their Captivity, *Joel* 3. 1, 2. Then Time of *Jacob*'s greatest Trouble, *Jer.* 30. 3. 7. of *Sion*'s
Second

Second Travail, *Mic.* 4. 10. and of Satan's refitting *Joshua*, after his having been a Brand pluckt out of the *Babylonish* Fire, *Zech.* 3. 1, 2.

These things the Scriptures have fore-told, but they have not been generally understood; and therefore Christ hath been conceiv'd to tarry, or prolong his Time, meerly through our mis-apprehension.

Quest. 2. Why doth Christ Tarry beyond the Expected Time?

Answ. Not from his being forgetful, or asleep, as *Baal* was tauntingly said to be, 1 *Kings* 18. 27. Since Christ is alway mindful of his Covenant, *Psal.* 111. 5. and doth not sleep or slumber, *Psal.* 121. 4. however wrongfully he may be Judged of, *Psal.* 44. 23, 24. Nor from any want of Power; whence *Amasa*'s tarrying beyond his time might possibly arise, 2 *Sam.* 20. 5. Since Christ is Almighty, *Rev.* 1. 5. who therefore is improperly said to have been hindred, or withstood by the Prince of *Persia*, *Dan.* 10. 13. --- Much less from want of Will, or good Affection; from whence *Lot*'s lingring in *Sodom* did proceed, *Gen.* 19. 16. but not Christ's Tarrying here, no more than in that case of *Lazarus*, John 11. 6. whom he yet Loved, *v.* 3. and whose sad Death, *v.* 14. (together with his own, *v.* 34. and his beloved Sisters Weeping, *v.* 33.) had been prevented by his coming sooner, *v.* 32. especially since Christ now cometh as a Bridegroom, whose stay cannot be therefore thought to be from want of Love or any good Affection.

But he now Tarrieth for other Reasons, such as these are:

1. To proclaim his Sovereignty; as when he would not Gratifie his Mother just at her Time, to let her know, his God-head was not in Subjection to her, *John* 2. 3, 4. God sometimes bids his People to Command him, *Isa.* 45. 11. but lest they should abuse his Condescention, he therefore would not heal *Miriam* now, as *Moses* did too boldly move, *Numb.* 12. 13, 14. Must he needs therefore come at such a Time, for fear of frustrating his Creatures Expectation? Or lest their Labour should be lost, in going out to meet him? Christ may set Man his Time, the Disputing whereof was their great sin, *Hag.* 1, 2. But it becomes a Spouse not to awake her Love, or stir him up, untill he pleaseth, *Cant.* 8. 4. The Temple-work will be revived, but so, as that it shall appear to be an Act of Grace, and not of proper Debt, *Zech.* 4. 7.

2. To make his Coming the more desired, which is a chief part of his Design, and thus Accomplished. Christ will not come as King of Nations, untill he be Desired by them, *Hag.* 2. 7. no more than *David* would be King of *Israel*, 2 *Sam.* 2. till such a Time, 2 *Sam.* 5. 1. He will be enquired of, *Ezek.* . 37. and they shall seek him, *Hos.*

Hof. 3. 5. with all their Heart, *Jer.* 29. 13. resolving to make mention of his Name alone, *Isa.* 26. 13. And thus, when both the Bride, and he that Heareth, shall say, *Come*, *Rev.* 22. 17. then, *I come quickly*, saith the Bridegroom, *v.* 20. Now, though an Hypocrite will not pray alway, *Job.* 27. 10. yet tarrying is an Incentive to a Cordial seeker, who is not silent in the Night, although his Cry (the Day before) hath not been heard, *Psal.* 22. 2. Yea, therefore such will pray more earnestly, *Luke* 22. 44. And as Christ's Satisfaction is thus consulted for, so is his People's also; since a Return of Prayer is then most Acceptable, *Psal.* 69. 13. when Eyes are apt to fail with waiting, or when one's Throat is dryed through weary Crying, *v.* 3.

3. Christ therefore Tarrieth at such a Time, because his own set Time is not Then come: Which Time (in such a Case) is not for us to know, *Acts* 1. 7. Our Time is (in such Cases) always ready, so is not his, *John* 7. 6. who will not come, untill the fulness of his Time be come, *Gal.* 4. 4. till when, a Thousand Years (with him) are as one Day; but when that Time is come, one Day is as a Thousand Years, 2 *Pet.* 3. 8. That is, he will not Tarry, *Heb.* 10. 37. Nor is it any just matter of Grief to us, that Christ thus tarryeth, since Fruits are sweetest, when fully Ripe: However it is no cause of Wonder, since Mercy must give place to Truth, *Psal.* 138. 2. and therefore those Days of Tribulation are no whit shorter, than as was fore-determined, *Mat.* 24. 21, 22.

4. That so his Coming might be with greater State, after the manner of Earthly Kings, whose Motion therefore is not too quick, and who are therefore wont to have an Harbinger, as Christ hath also, which cannot but Occasion some kind of tarrying. Christ's Spiritual Kingdom was thus Ushered in, *Mat.* 3. 3. much more (then) must his Temporal Kingdom be so Attended, because the Glory of this latter will be more Visible. And though Christ's Coming (in this Parable) will be but such an Harbinger, compared with his Personal Coming, yet this fore-runner (compared with it self) will also have its Messenger, when Christ shall come into his Temple, *Mal.* 3. 1. which Temple is not in being at his Personal Coming, *Rev.* 21. 22. And thus *Elias* must first come, *Mark* 9. 12. untill the ending of whose Ministration, the Bridegroom tarrieth. Poor Virgins would fain have had him come forthwith, but that would not so well have suited his designed Kingly State.

5. That so the Foolish Virgins might be Discovered. Christ alway cometh with his Fan, *Mat.* 3. 12. and Fullers Soap and Fire, *Mal.* 3. 2. which they must be brought under, who are not absolutely cut off,

as others, *Zech.* 13. 8, 9. *John Baptist* laid his Ax unto the Root of Fruitless Trees, *Mat.* 3. 7, 8, 9, 10. much more will Christ himself unmask all sorts of Hypocrites. This Coming will much resemble that at Last, *Mat.* 24. 30. and therefore Sheep and Goats will now be severed, *Mat.* 25. 32. or such as formerly have been accounted clean, *Deut.* 14. 4. Now, had Christ come at first, these Foolish Virgins had not been known, no more than Carnal *Israelites* would have been if *Moses* had not delayed his coming, *Exod.* 32. 1. Therefore Christ Tarryeth to make his Jewels up, or that Men might Discern between the Righteous and the Wicked, *Mal.* 3. 17, 18. We should not else have known who of Christ's Followers would have denyed him.

6. That so his Coming might be upon a New Covenant-score, or meerly for his own Names sake, which is consulted for, *Ezek.* 36. 22. And which had not been so Apparent, in Case he had come Then. All sorts of Virgins (at their first going out) were in their Prime, their Lamps were very Trim, and their Affections much let out in way of Prayer and Zeal for Christ. So that his Coming then might have been thought to be Deserved, Men are so apt to Magnifie their Duty; and therefore (possibly) his Coming in that Nick of Time was verily Expected by them with so much Confidence. But he doth choose to tarry till all those Virgins be asleep, that so it might appear to be an Act of double Grace, *Zech.* 4. 7. *viz.* with reference to their unworthiness at the present, as well as with respect to any Natural Tye that was upon him at the first.

7. To try the Faith and Patience of the Best. Christs Coming is Ushered in by a trying hour, and with respect to all, *Rev.* 3. 10. The tryal of whose Faith is much more precious than that of Gold, 1 *Pet.* 1. 7. Now, had Christ come at first, this tryal had not been made: Whereas his tarrying doth Experiment what they will say, as to the Promise of his Coming; whether they will Repent of former Duty, because their Recompence is not so speedy; how they can wait one hour beyond the utmost of their Expectation, how they can bear to be Derided, because Events are not according to their Hopes; whether their Faith was grounded upon the Scriptures, or mainly upon uncertain Providences; what they will say, when *Israel* falls before the King of *Ai*, in their own Land of Promise? What they will do, when Tempted to deny their Ancient Master? Whether they can believe the Resurrection of a Dying cause? Or how they can Return (with *David*) into a former low Condition, after their having been Advanced? And how the Valley of *Achor* (in these latter days) can be a Door of Hope.

8. Tha

The Parable of the Ten Virgins Opened. 73

8. That Servants (of a Lower Rank) might have that Opportunity, both for their Work and Wages, diftinct from that of Sons, which otherwife could not have been effected. As in a Great Houfe, there are fome Veffels to Honour, and fome to Difhonour, 2 *Tim.* 2. 20. So Chrift hath both his Saints and Sanctified ones, whofe Work and Wages are Diftinct, both in Refpect of Worth and Time. The Lord will give a Banner to them that fear him, *Pfal.* 60. 4. And *Judah* alfo fhall be employed at *Jerufalem*, *Zech.* 14. 14. Such Honour have all the Saints, *Pfal.* 149. 9. But he will firft Command his Sanctified Ones, fuch as the *Medes* and *Perfians* were, *Ifa.* 13. 3. 17. till when, the Men of *Judah* cannot be at *Jerufalem*. And as his Saints fhall be Rewarded at his Coming, *Rev.* 11.18. So meaner Servants muft have their Temporary Gifts before that Year of Liberty, *Ezek.* 46.17. Therefore he Cometh not at their firft going forth, that fo this Difference between his Sons and Hired Servants might be confulted for, whom he will have to be Diftinguifhed.

9. That fo the Sufferings of other Fellow-Servants might alfo be fulfilled; in which regard, thofe former Sufferers, (who cryed, *How long*) were bid to Reft yet for a little feafon, *Rev.* 6. 10, 11. Chrift hath a great Refpect for Paffive Duty, and till that be Accomplifhed, he will not enter into his Glory, *Luke* 24. 26. though fome Men's Expectations be thereby Difappointed, *v.* 21. Yea, thofe Difciples of a choifer Spirit will alfo Rejoyce in their Prolonged Sufferings, till that which is behind (of Chrift's Afflictions, in their flefh) be filled up, *Col.* 1. 24. Now, had Chrift come at firft, *John Baptift* had not been a Prifoner; and many Late Sufferers would not have come upon the Stage, fince groffer Perfecutions (or Deftructions) will come to a Perpetual end, when Chrift fhall have prepared his Throne for Judgment, *Pfal.* 9. 6, 7. There would not elfe have been thofe Hopeful Prifoners for him to fend forth, and render double unto, *Zech.* 9. 11, 12. when he fhall come as King, *v* 9.

10. The Lord is therefore *Slack*, (or rather long-fuffering) becaufe he is not willing that any fhould perifh, but would have all come to Repentance, 2 *Pet.* 3. 9. as *Paul* came not (as yet) to thofe *Corinthians*, from a Defign to fpare them, 2 *Cor.* 1. 23. and not from any Lightnefs, *v.* 17. The faving of thofe *Samaritans* did countervail his Tarrying, *John* 4. 40, 41. Yea, therefore *Paul* endured much for the Elects fake, that they might alfo obtain Salvation, 2 *Tim.* 2. 10. And thofe Old Saints might not receive the Promife in their Days, God having provided fome better thing for us, that they without us fhould not be made Perfect, *Heb.* 11. 39, 40. Now, had Chrift come at firft,

L the

the Hearts of some Fathers (then) had not been turned to the Children, unless *John Baptist* had gone Before him, *Luke* 1. 17. Nor had his Patience been so apparent, as now it is, unto the utter silencing of those who have not sued out their Pardon in this Respite.

11. To Prove the Spirit of Ancient Persecutors, whether they will be Warned by his Affrighting Messenger, or go on still, unto their utter Extirpation. God's Method is to Usher in Rejection by an immediately fore-going Admonition, *Titus* 3. 10. Since the Beginning of a Judgment is apt to Promise a Souls Return, which Christ is willing to Improve, to shew the Riches of his Mercy. Thus *Pharaoh* had his Respite, *Exod.* 8. 15. to try the Nature of his Relenting, *v.* 8. And *Zedekiah*'s threatning Adversary was Removed, *Jer.* 34. 21. To try the Performance of that Liberty which he had Promised in his Distress, *v.* 8. 11. And therefore Christ's Ministration was after *John*'s, Acts 10. 37. to try what Operation his Harbinger's Rebuke would have upon the *Pharisees* and *Herodians*, Mark 9. 12, 13. Nor would it else have been so manifest, that Envious *Edom* would have so looked upon his poor Distressed Brother, *Obad.* 12. Or that the *Assyrian* would have got the Men of *Judah*'s Money, 2 *Kings* 18. 13, 14, 15, 16. and then Engage against them, *v.* 17. Or that all sorts of Interests would have Combin'd with *Ashur* against God's hidden Ones, *Psal.* 83. 3. 8. who else might have been Built up in the midst of *Israel*, had they walk'd worthy of their Restauration after an Affrightment, *Jer.* 12. 15, 16.

12. To shame his own unworthy People, 1. *John* 2. 28 by frustrating their Expectation, *Job* 6. 20. and to Correct them, by bringing Trouble and no Good, when they did look for Peace and Healing, *Jer.* 14. 19, 20. He had been oft-times made to Tarry for their Duty, who therefore justly makes them Stay for their Deliverance. They quickly waxed Wan on with a little Liberty, who therefore were remanded into Bonds, till better able to bear Enlargement. They were not Thankful for what they had, which therefore was thought meet to be withdrawn. A Toleration was sometimes called Monstrous, therefore it is Recalled, till it shall have a better Appellation, and duly General Distribution. They had a mind to spare some Goodly *Babylonish* Garment; therefore though *Jericho* was fallen before, yet *Ai* must check them in their own Land. They were exceeding Hypocritical, *Isa.* 10. 6. therefore they must fall under the Slain; and it is well, if that be all that is to be inflicted, *v.* 4.

13. To make the Revelation of himself (at last) more Ravishing, and his Continuance Grateful by Reason of his present Tarrying, as

warmth

The Parable of the Ten Virgins Opened.

warmth is after a tedious Winter, and Meat unto an hunger-bitten Soul. Christ (or the Head-stone) must be brought forth with shoutings, *Zech.* 4. 7. And when he Comes, he means to tarry by it; for though *John* must Decrease, *John* 3. 30. yet will there be no End of Christ's increasing Government, *Isa.* 9. 7. therefore he will consult for more than Ordinary Welcom. Now, that which hath been long desired, is most Affectionately Entertained, and like to be most Lastingly Delighted in: Since waiting doth enlarge one's Receptivity, and gathereth up the Souls Affections into the Bosom of its Beloved Object, untill that Object doth become the sole Inheriter of its Love. Therefore the Saints shall not grow weary of being ever with the Lord, 1 *Thef.* 4. 17. because they have been made to wait for his Appearing, 1 *Thef.* 1. 10. with so much earnest Expectation, 2 *Cor.* 5. 2.

14. To Fit and Prepare all sorts of Persons for their respective future Portions at his Coming. Christ waiteth to be Gracious to his People, *Isa.* 30. 18. and the Damnation of others doth not slumber, 2 *Pet.* 2. 3. yet doth he tarry till These be fitted to Destruction, and till Those be prepared unto Glory, *Rom.* 9. 22,23. *Israel's* Redemption must therefore be delayed, because the *Amorites* sins were not yet full, *Gen.* 15. 16. Nor will Christ Bury those Dead, untill some competent Waiting hath evinced that they are 'Dead indeed. Yea, God's own People were too Hot to Drink at their first going out; they were not fine enough to be then Married; they were too Young to Sway the Scepter, too Private Spirited to be entrusted with a Publick Stock; too High to be Exalted, too Sensual to eat their fill, too Low of Stature to wear Long Robes, too Cholerick to eat Christ's Sweetmeats; indeed too Many to be Feasted, and too too Carnal for a Spiritualized Kingdom. But when the Grapes are fully Ripe the Vintage will be Gathered, *Rev.* 14. 18, 19. And when the Bride is Ready the Bridegroom will not tarry, as till that time he doth, *Rev.* 19. 7.

15. To shew the Greatness of his Power, in scattering his Re-inforc'd Adversaries, and in Reviving that Work which had been given up for Dead and Buried. As he abode still where he was, *John* 11. 6. till *Lazarus* was Dead, *v.* 14. and had been four Days Buried, *v.* 39. that his Disciples might Believe, *v.* 15. and that his Enemies might bear Witness to such a Miracle, *v.* 46, 47. The Virgins Party was too Potent at their first going out, as *Gideon's* was, who Therefore were not then Delivered, lest *Israel* should vauntingly impute their being saved to their own Hand, *Judg.* 7. 2. Therefore Christ tarrieth untill their Power be wholly scattered, *Dan.* 12. 7. to make them sing, *His Holy Arm hath gotten him the Victory*, Psal. 98. 1. and not their Sword, *Psal.*

44.

The Parable of the Ten Virgins Opened.

44. 3. Nor would the Faith of some have been so strengthned by healing what was onely Sick, as by one's being Raised from the Dead; which latter *Dives* thought (in Hell) sufficient to Convince the greatest Unbeliever upon Earth, *Luke* 16. 30. Nor doth Christ judge the Beast to be an Adversary strong enough untill the Dragon doth succeed him, whom *Pharaoh* Typified, and whom God raised up to shew his Power, *Exod.* 9. 16. Christ sleepeth till the Ship be full of Water, *Mark* 4. 37, 38. But when *Senacherib* (or *Babylon*'s Assistant) doth threaten *Lebanon* and *Carmel*, 2 *Kings* 19. 23. *Now will I Rise, saith the Lord,* Isa. 33. 9, 10. And when all Nations are United against *Jerusalem*, Then shall the Lord go forth and fight against them, as in the day of Battel, *Zech.* 14. 2, 3.

16. To Aggravate both *Sions* Mercy, and her Opposers Judgment by their joynt-suddennefs at his Appearing thus unawares. At their first going out the Virgins Generally did Expect him, and so did others, as their Amazing fear did then Evince: therefore Christ tarrieth, designing to surprize them all, as they are either Watching, *Luke* 12. 37. or Sleeping, *Mark* 13. 36. or Revelling, *Mat.* 24. 49. at least-wise minding other Matters, *Luke* 17. 28. and not thinking of him, *Mat.* 24. 44. Which suddennefs doth marvelloufly Affect (according to the Nature of a Difpenfation) both in a way of Paining at the very Heart, *Jer.* 4. 19, 20. and of Rejoycing, 2 *Chron.* 29. 36. How will the Saints Mouth be filled with Laughter when their Captivity is Returned, whilst they are in a Dream, *Pfal.* 126. 1, 2. And how will others be confounded when their inevitable Destruction cometh, whilst they are saying, Peace and Safety, 1 *Thef.* 5. 3! Therefore Christ doth prolong his Time, that so his unexpected Coming might fill his Peoples Hearts with Wondring, and others with Consternation.

Quest. 3. What are we to Understand by *Slumbring* and by *Sleeping*, here? Both as to the Difference that is between them, and as to the Particular Cases which they refer unto.

Answ. 1. As to the Difference between these two, it may be considered two ways. Either first, with Respect unto their Nature; and so all know that Slumbring is less than Sleeping, as being but an Entry into the Sleeper's House. A Slumberers Senses are not so fast bound up, but that he can hear some greater Noise, and understand what is said or done, and give some kind of Answer; yea, have some stirring of Affections, and be awakened sooner than he that's fast asleep: Witness the Spouse, whose Heart was then awake, therefore her Sleep was but a Slumber, *Cant.* 5. 2. because she then could hear the Knock of her Beloved, and understand his Voyce, *v.* 2. and gave some kind of

Answer,

The Parable of the Ten Virgins Opened. 77

Anfwer, *v.* 3. Yea, had fome Moving in her Bowels for him, *v.* 4. and prefently awakened fo, as that fhe arofe and Opened to him, *v.* 5, 6. This fhews the Difference that is between them, as to their Nature. Secondly, this Difference may be confidered, as to their Ufe or Application here, unto thofe Virgins; which may be double.

* 1. In a way of Diftribution, or fo, as that the Foolifh Virgins flept, whereas the Wife did onely flumber. And fuch a Diftinction may eafily be fuppofed, fince Folly *(* or Weaknefs *)* doth much incline unto a Deeper kind of Sleep, as is to be Obferved in filly Aged People and little Children. Saints are not wont to be fo altogether heavy Headed as others are who want their rouzing Heat, and many other Soul-awakening Helps, which Grace affordeth. Saints are (all of them) Children of the Day, 1 *Thef.* 5. 5. but they that Sleep, Sleep in the Night, *v.* 7. Chrift keepeth his Difciples waking with frequent Jogs, *Luke* 22. 46. Yea, their own Confcience is an Alarm to them. Slothfulnefs cafts finners into a deep Sleep, *Prov.* 19. 15. But Saints have fomething elfe to do, *Pfal.* 132. 4. Nor will their Riches fuffer them to fleep, like other poor Creatures, *Eccl.* 5. 12. Therefore this fleep and flumber may be thus Diftributed among the Virgins here; which is one way of Underftanding them.

2. It may be taken in a way of fhewing how fleep at laft did feize upon them all, *viz.* by flumbring at the firft, or that they all firft flumbred, and fo at laft fell faft afleep. As we would not give fleep unto our Eyes, fo we fhould not give flumber to our Eye-lids, *Prov.* 6. 4. The latter of which is but a Needle, which will foon ftitch our Eyes together. Therefore Chrift bad his Difciples Watch, for fear of entring into Temptation, *viz.* by giving way unto their flumbrings, *Mat.* 26. 41. Sluggards (both in the Letter and Myftery) plead onely for a little fleep, a little flumber, a little folding of the Hands together, *Prov.* 6. 10. But we are taught (from what the Virgins have Experienced) to be more Wife, than to crave Liberty of Leaping up unto the Knees in the Ocean. And thus the Difference between thefe two is brifly Opened, both as to their Nature, and Application.

II. As to the Particular Cafes here referred unto, thefe Virgins may be faid to flumber and fleep, as followeth.

1. With Refpect to common Principles of Truth and Righteoufnefs, which formerly have been avouched. Time was, when Reafon and Scripture-proof have been demanded inftead of Major Vote, or meer Humane Authority. A Fundamental Publick Good hath been preferred before the moft Ancient Cuftom, Higheft Worldly Form, or Perfonal Intereft of any Man whatever. Right Gofpel-Churches, Truths, and

and Ordinances, have not been sometime Judged of according to the Flesh, or by the Numerousness of their Abettors, but by Agreement with the Rule. It heretofore hath been Accounted sin to fail in Duty, though Ignorant thereof; or though (at least) one be not Spirited thereunto, but now the Case is altered. There was a general Cry (at first) for Liberty of Conscience in Matters of a Religious Nature; which when some Men had gained for themselves, how did they vilifie those very Arguments (in others Mouths) and break that Sword in pieces by which themselves had been Defended.

2. With reference unto their sometime Zeal for Christ, and against the Man of sin; subjection unto Commands and Prohibitions in Religious Matters hath been Accounted onely due to Christ, which yet of later Years hath been thought yieldable unto Man without his being Deified. Some Men have separated from those supposed Churches, whose Acts of Office (and consequently their Essence) have been confessed *valid*, which since hath been denyed by them to others, untill the Essence (as well as Purity) of their own Churches be Destroyed. Did some Men ever think they should have been free to swear (by necessary consequence) the Preservation of that Hierarchy which they had formerly Declared to be Antichristian? Time was when such were loth to use Christ's Form of Prayer, who since could hear Humane Imposed Liturgies; And they who sometimes pressed hard for Purity in Communion, could since endure to walk with those who have returned to their Ancient Vomit, and have not cast them out.

3. With reference unto their Entertainment of Christ's Little ones, such as Time-Truths, and Duties are. Some have been bold (of later Years) to Question the Being of Time-Truths at all, who yet doubt not the Truth of something which scarce had any Being before their Time. Others would grant that Name to be abiding still, but not its Application, save unto what was Fansied and Approved by themselves. Others would yield that Application also, which some contended for, who yet thought other common Truths more Profitable to be insisted on, though little else (but such as these) was sometimes urged by themselves, and such Discourses then were counted Edifying; yea, very great stress was laid thereon by all the Virgins at their first going out. But since that time succeeding Infants of this Nature have much been over-looked (if not over-layed) by our Sleepers, and their poor Nurses have been Offended sadly.

4. With reference unto their former Courage and self-denyal in the way of Duty. How boldly did these Virgins sometime Talk and Write, unto the Hazard of their All, who since have quarrelled with the

The Parable of the Ten Virgins Opened. 79

the very Name of Self-adventuring. Time was when Suffering Service was thought most Honourable, but since that time, if Active Duty be more safe, it hath been set before the other. Christ's In Ltu:ed Worship hath been thought worth the loss of Life, but that (of late) was counted Lawful to be Dispensed with, if but Estate or Liberty were by that means endangered. How will some (one day) be ashamed of fearing the Oppressor's Fury, when it shall (tauntingly) be said unto them, *Where is the Fury of the Oppressor*, Isa. 51. 13? Yea, they who sometimes have not feared many Deaths in the Open Field, have since been frighted from their Duty by a Prison. Nor is it to be wondred at, if waking Little Children be in the Exercise of greater strength than Giants that are fast asleep.

5. With reference unto their sometime Faith and Hope, as to the Bridegroom's Coming. At their first going out how did the Pulpits ring with *Babylon*'s Funeral Sermons! Yea, Civil Constitutions were also threatned with being shaken in pieces, as some then Witnessed; nor was there so much striving (then) against the fifth Monarchy-Principle,—as who should be the Men; Christ's Coming was (at that time) so generally expected. But since that time, where is (said some) the Promise of his Coming, 2 *Pet*. 3. 4? It is Delayed, saith another. *Mat*. 24. 48. We had great Hopes (said some of his Disciples) we Trusted it had been He, *Luke* 24. 21. But that Expected Child (said others) hath proved a false Conception, *Isa*. 26. 18. Not so, I hope, (saith *Hezekiah*) onely there is not Strength to bring it forth, *Isa*. 37. 3. No, no, (saith *Sion*) the Lord hath forsaken me, my God hath quite forgotten, *Isa*. 49. 14. Thus hath there been a Mighty Cry, but yet no Faith on Earth, *Luke* 18. 7, 8. whilst others of a more Believing Spirit have been for Signs and Wonders, *Isa*. 8. 18. And if it now be otherwise, 'tis either from some present Dream, or from the Virgins late awaking.

6. With reference unto their former Accurateness, or walking closely with the Lord, as doth become the Gospel. Time was when all our Virgins were very Sober, seeming to be of a serious Spirit, not swallowed up in Worldly businesses, willing to hear what might be Offered, Diligent in Religious Exercises, and trembling to think of grosser failings, in point of Practice or Opinion. But since that time how have they flinted it in Worldly Fashions, making Provision for the Flesh: What Levity hath appeared in their Spirits, and Frothiness in their Discourse? How hath their Cloven Foot United, having Buried their General in their Particular Calling? How have they scorn'd Instruction, at least, to be Reproved? How yawningly hath God been

Wor-

Worshipped, whilst *Mammon* hath had the Male? Yea, how have Dangerous Errors been Indulged, and Grosser breach of Duty made light of? Thus have the Wiser Virgins slumbred, whilst others have fallen fast asleep.

Quest. 4. What are the Distinct or Proper Signs of slumbring and sleeping?

Answ. 1. The Signs of slumbring (suitable to what is in the Letter) are these.

1. The slumberers Eyes are closed, who therefore cannot see, unless it be some little glimmering of a greater Light that's just before them: Whereas the wakers Eye is Open, who therefore seeth at a distance, and can discern what is more darkly hinted, by sending forth to meet the Object, and in a way of Prying Observation. But slumberers cannot understand some kind of Truths and Duties which formerly were very plain, save as their present Lustre can penetrate a shut Eye-lid, or not without some more than Necessary Demonstration. Time was when all our Virgins were fully satisfied concerning several things, which since they say are not so clear; the Reason whereof is more to be Lamented, than to be wondred at, *viz.* The Heaviness of their Eyes, which must be throughly first awakened before they can see the Glory of Christ's altered Countenance, or of those Men who talk of Sufferings, *Luke* 29. 30, 31, 32.

2. The slumberer's Posture is very much wavering, this and the other way, untill such either be awakened, or else laid down to sleep. Watchmen can stand whole Days and Nights, *Isa.* 21. 8. but others are tossing to and fro ; one while enclining to Prophaneness on the Left hand, another while to Right-hand Superstitions ; sometimes too forward, and presently fallen back as much behind. Seers may be for Going on unto Perfection, *Heb.* 6. 1. therefore all kind of Alterations are not to be Condemned: But one may easily Distinguish between the Watchman's walking and the Slumberer's Nodding ; between a Judicious variation and Childish instability. When Persons do thus Multiply self-contradicting Motions, or when their Head hath lost its due consistency in Matters of Faith or Duty, we may conclude them to be slumbring, especially if they have formerly been more Discreet and Fixed.

3. The slumberer's Hand is easily apt to let things go or fall, who thereupon awakeneth, unto his Fruitless sorrow. A watchful Christian is to be known by holding fast that which he hath Received, *Rev.* 3. 2, 3. especially what is of worth, and of a Brittle Nature, such as are the stedfast Profession of our Faith, *Heb.* 10. 23. the Confidence of our Hope unto the End, *Heb.* 3. 6. the Form of sound words, or Scripture-Language,

The Parable of the Ten Virgins Opened. 81

Language, 2 *Tim.* 1.13. the word of Chrift's Patience, *Rev.* 3. 10, 11. and every Gofpel-Inftitution, *Rev.* 2.25. yea, whatfoever is good and true, 1 *Thef.* 5.21. or that good thing (be it what it will be) which is Committed to his care, 2 *Tim.* 1. 14. But flumberers may foon have fuch things wrefted from them; yea, of themfelves (by little and little) they will let fall what hath been fomet'mes highly prized, and then awaken, when in fome fence it is too late. How fadly Remifs (of later Years) have the moft of Virgins been, as to their Ancient Teftimony, the Purity of their Communion, the Savourinefs of their Difcourfe, their fearching after Knowledge, and the like; all which evinceth their having entred into this fad Temptation.

4. Slumberers may Hear, and underftand a little, but fuch are not Affected duly with what is faid or done. Such can endure to hear their fcruples Anfwered, their Duty Opened, their Sin Reproved, and yet have no Impreffion (to any purpofe) upon their Spirits. They may have fluggifh good defires, and yet have nothing, *Prov.* 13.4. becaufe their hands are folded, *Prov.* 6.10. there way is as an Hedge of Thorns, *Prov.* 15.19. there is (fay fuch) a Lion in the way of Action, *Prov.* 26. 13. and therefore their defire kills them, *Prov.* 21.25. Such may be heard to groan in Prayer, with reference unto fome Corruptions, but take no further courfe to be Delivered : They like fuch kind of Spiritual Food, but that it grieves them to bring their Hand and Mouth together, *Prov.* 26. 15. therefore fuch Roaft not what they have feemed to take in Hunting, *Prov.* 12.27. *Lord evermore give us this Bread*, fay fuch, *John* 6. 34. but do not eat it, when fet before them, *v.* 35, 36. Whereas a watchful Chriftian hath his Affections ftirring, and is in an immediate fit Capacity for fuitable Actings, as in that cafe of Opening, *Luke* 12. 36.

5. Slumberers may fometimes fpeak, but very fimply ; witnefs the flumbring Spoufe, whofe Anfwer to her Beloved's Voice was like that of a Child, as if fhe knew not how to Drefs her felf, or how to put that on, which was put off, *Cant.* 5. 2, 3. They feem to Pray in the Spirit, but not with Underftanding, not knowing what they fay, no more than *Peter* did, *Luke* 9. 33. when half afleep, *v.* 32. They will confefs, if fuch a Rule were followed, God would be Glorified more, yet will they not grant it to be their Duty. Another's Ruining of himfelf and Family, (in a common cafe) will be acknowledged to be his Liberty, but not his bounden Duty, for fear themfelves fhould then be made to Suffer with him. They heartily could wifh that all were free to Suffer in fuch a caufe ; till when, they Judge it not incumbent upon

M

particu'ar Pcifons, as if anothers failing might warrant mine. They will Declare compliances with Man's Commands or Prohibitions to be unlawful, and yet themfelves perfift in fuch a way. Whereas a watchful Chriftian is to be known by that confiftency which is between his Heart and Tongue, his Practice and Profeffion.

6. Slumberers will oft-times waken, and yet immediately will Nod again, both in the Letter and Myftery. A fudden Light may rouze fuch up a little, as did *John Baptift*'s Light thofe flumbring Jews, which made them Skip or Dance a Galliard, though onely for an hour, as the *Greek* there hath it, *John* 5.35. and as his Difpenfation (in our Days) hath wrought upon fome others, who fince that time have flept again. Much more will fuch be ftartled with a fudden Noife, fuch as is that of a Terrible Word, or louder Providential Knocks: All which were foon forgotten by Ancient *Ifrael*, *Pfal*. 78.11. though God had flain fome of them, and had Redeemed the reft, *v*. 34, 35, 36, 37. But moft of all, fuch may be made to look about them when they are ftruck, or nipt, or Perfonally (although more gently) touched; as *Pharaoh* did, when ftruck with God's own Hand, *Exod*. 8.8. but was at his old work again, *v*. 15. as *Abab* did, when forely nipt with that Denunciation, 1 *Kings* 20. 42, 43. but prefently Nodded into a greater fin, 1 *Kings* 21.2.4.13.16. and as the Difciples did, when touch'd by Chrift, *Mat*. 17.7, 8. whom he then kept awake, elfe had they flept again, as at another time they did, fo foon as his back was turned upon them, *Mat*. 26.43.

7. Slumberers cannot endure fome kind of fudden, loud, or difmal Noifes. One muft begin with fuch, a great way off, as *Nathan* did with flumbring *David*, who elfe would not have born too fudden a Rebuke, 2 *Sam*. 12. 1. 7. Such muft be gently dealt with at the firft, elfe droufie Carnal *Ifraelites* will be Difturbed, in cafe the Trumpet's Voice be very loud, *Exod*. 19.16. They muft have fmooth things fpoken to them, *Ifa*. 30. 10. elfe will they be Offended, as were the *Pharifees* when Chrift fpake harfhly to them, *Mat*. 15.7. 12. Whereas a watchful Cnriftian is not furprifed with Chrift's fudden Knock, *Luke* 12. 36. but can immediately then fay, *Loe, this is he*, becaufe they have waited for him, *Ifa*. 25. 9. Nor are fuch Paffionately affected with the Loudnefs of his Voice, becaufe they fain would hear and underftand it. Nor is their Head Difquieted with fmiting reprehenfions, becaufe it is according to their Expectation and Defire, if need requireth, *Pfal*. 141.5.

8. Slumberers cannot endure the Light, efpecially in cafe it be too nigh, too Glorious, or uncertain in its fhining. Such will Approve an
Open

Open Testimony in Others, or in the General, but not with Respect unto Their Times or Persons; 'tis not the Nature (so much as Nearness) of that Light which doth Offend them. Such will confess Church-Members should be Saints, but that they should be more than Babes in Christ, is somewhat too Glorious a Discovery for some awakened ones, much more for Slumberers. Such are for Hoping to the End, so long as Providential Grounds are steady; but if those waver, the Light of this Duty is so uncertain, as that it doth Disquiet them, who fain would slumber untill the Day break, without Dispute. Therefore such gladly would have that Light removed till such a Time, and then it will be Acceptable, as Christ was to the Converted Jews, though it was still a burden unto others, who Laboured under a Spirit of Slumber, *Rom.* 11. 8.

These are the Signs of *Slumbering*. The Signs of *Sleeping* are as followeth.

1. Men fast asleep can hardly Hear, and to be sure, not See at all; Sleep being that which bindeth up the Outward Senses altogether; as in this Moral sence it was with those on whom the Spirit of a Deep sleep was poured out, *Isa.* 29. 10. Such must be loudly cryed unto, else can they Hear no more than *Baal* did, because (as *Elijah* said, by way of Holy taunt) *He, peradventure, was asleep,* 1 Kings 18. 27. Such do not see those Angels who Observe unseemly Gestures in Religious Exercises, 1 *Cor.* 11. 10. nor how Christ walketh among the Golden Candlesticks, *Rev.* 2. 1. nor how their shame is seen by others, else would they watch, and keep their Garments, *Rev.* 16. 15. *John* saw Christ's Glory, *John* 1. 14. but so did not the Jews, who therefore slept whilst this Sun shone full in their Faces, *Mat.* 13. 13. 15. and so it is still, with reference unto his Interests, though one would wonder that People do not perceive the easiness of his Yoak, (compared with that of Satan and the Man of sin) both in Relation to his Spiritual, Ecclesiastical, and Temporal Kingdom, but onely that their Faces are, as it were, hid from him, *Isa.* 53. 3. and Eyes are closed.

2. Men fast asleep are apt to Dream, and thereupon to Laugh or Weep, when many times there is no cause, but what is of a quite contrary Nature, unto the Aggravating of their Grief and Shame when once they come to be awakened. We may conclude those Men to be asleep, who Dream of Eating when they are faint, *Isa.* 29 8. who call their Lying Dreams the Word of God, *Jer.* 23. 28. or who are filthy Dreamers, *Jude* 8. pretending unto an Interest in Christ, and yet will turn his Grace into Lasciviousness, *v.* 4. So on the other side, they who were in a Dream when *Babylon's* Captivity was returned, *Psal.* 126.

The Parable of the Ten Virgins Opened.

126. 1. and did evince it by their Weeping, when there was Ground for Joy, or when the Foundation of the Second House was laid, *Ezra* 3. 12. as in a way suitable to that Type, some Old Professors in our days have done, whose very Age disposeth (as in the Letter) to Sleep and Dream. But whilst such sleep at Prayer, they are not wont to Dream of Hell, or how poor *Eutychus* was likely to have never wakened more, *Acts* 20. 10. Nor are their Affections Exercised according to Substantial Grounds, or as the Case indeed requireth.

3. Sleep makes the Greatest Giant as unactive, and as unable to help himself or others, as is the Weakest Child: Therefore Men of an Active Spirit are described by their not sleeping, *Isa.* 5. 27. Yea, God himself (when Active for his People) is said to be Awaked, *Psal.* 78. 65. Till when, Christ's Presence with his Disciples did not profit them, *Mat.* 8. 24, 25, 26. Nor can his Poverty be prevented who loveth sleep, *Prov.* 20. 13. Some are as Lions, in point of Strength, provided they be awake; but when the Horse and Chariot are cast into a sleep, *Psal.* 76. 6. then are the stout-hearted spoyled, and none of the Men of Might can find their Hands, *v.* 5. Such cannot prevent their Falling down from a Third Loft, though taken up Dead, *Acts* 20. 9. and never likely to be Recovered but by a Miracle, *v.* 10. Those Men are fast asleep, whose Arms are folded, *Prov.* 6. 10. whose Field is over-grown with Thorns, *Prov.* 24. 30, 31. 33. who do not rise up from the Dead, *Eph.* 5. 14. who put not their Beautiful Garments on, *Isa.* 52. 1. or do not awake to Righteousness, 1 *Cor.* 15. 34. especially at such a Time as this, *Rom.* 13. 12, 13.

4. Men fast asleep know not what doth befall them, or is done unto them, although in never so Material a Respect. Such may be Robbed of a Rib, as *Adam* was, (or of their strength) and yet without any apprehended pain, *Gen.* 2. 21. Yea, such may be deprived of all their former strength, as *Sampson* was (together with his Locks) whilst *Delilah* made him sleep upon her Knees, *Judg.* 16. 19. The Enemy may come and sow his Tares among their Wheat who are asleep, *Mat.* 13. 25. which will not be rooted again, *v.* 30. so long as this World continueth, *v.* 39. Yea, such may have a Dead Child (or one of *Satan's* Brats) laid in their Bosom instead of one alive; as had that Woman while she slept, 1 *Kings* 3. 20. Such may be in Danger of being Slain, as *Saul* was, when fast asleep, 1 *Sam.* 26. 7, 8. who lost his Spear, and yet he knew it not, *v.* 21. Yea, such (being softly gone unto) may have a Nail driven into their very Temples, as *Sisera* had when he was fast asleep, *Judg.* 4. 21. Those Men are more than Slumberers, who are not deeply sensible (at that

very

The Parable of the Ten Virgins Opened.

very inftant) of fuch like Spiritual Loffes and Hazards run.

5. Men faft afleep are apt to be fecure, though in the midft of utmoft Dangers; as fleeping Drunkards are upon a top-Maft, and in the midft of the Sea, *Prov.* 23. 30. 34, and as poor fleeping *Jonah* was, when the Ship was almoft broken, and Heathen Mariners cryed every Man unto his God, *Jonah* 1. 4, 5. Such have Gray hairs upon them here and there, and yet they know it not, *Hof.* 7. 9. Feafting and making Merry, when at the very Gates of Death, *Ifa.* 22. 13. The Day of the Lord is Darknefs, and not Light to them, yet do they Ignorantly defire it, *Amos* 6. 18. although not likely to ftand at his Appearing, *Mal.* 3. 1, 2. Yea, fuch will Eat and Drink, and Buy and Sell, and Plant and Build, untill the Son of Man doth Come, (as in the days of *Lot* and *Noah*) unto their utter overthrow, *Luke* 17. 26. 28. 30. Whereas a watchful Chriftian is conftantly at work with Holy Fear, *Phil.* 2. 12. not being fecure, though in no vifible Danger, *Job* 3. 25, 26. but Trembling in himfelf when fpeaking of God's Salvation for his Annointed People, *Hab.* 3. 13. 16. How would it ftartle fome afleep, could they but fee how daily Induftrious, and felf-fufpitious others are, whofe work is yet already done, as to the Main thereof.

6. Men faft afleep are apt to be awakened with much Affrightment, upon fome rouzing Noife or Accidents; as that poor Jaylor was, who being awakened with an Earthquake, and feeing the prifon-doors open, drew out his Sword, and would have killed himfelf, fuppofing the Prifoners had been fled, *Acts* 16. 26. 27. Such being pricked at the Heart, are fubject to cry, with fhrieking, *What fhall we do*, Acts 2. 37? Yea, to lay violent Hands upon themfelves, as *Judas* did, *Mat.* 27. 5. or at leaft, Defperately to fay, with *Cain*, My fin is greater than that it may be forgiven, *Gen.* 4. 13. as the Margin there hath it, and as the fame *Hebrew* words are elfewhere rendred, *Pfal.* 51. 5. *Gen.* 50. 17. *Exod.* 10. 17. And if Judge *Felix* Trembled when *Paul*, a Prifoner, did but Reafon at his Bar concerning the future Day of Judgment, *Acts* 24. 25. much more will fuch be ftartled, when awakened out of their prefent fleep, *Dan.* 12. 2. and made to appear before Chrift's Judgment-Seat, 2 *Cor.* 5. 10. to receive their dreadful Sentence, *Mat.* 25. 41. And in the mean time Chrift's Coming (as a Brdegroom) in the Night, will be (in fuch Men's Apprehenfions) like that of a Thief, *Rev.* 3. 3. or as if he came onely to fteal and kill, and to deftroy, *John* 10. 10. Whereas a watchful Chriftian can bear Convictions without Aftonifhment, *Ezra* 10. 2. and will have Confidence at Chrift's Appearing, 1 *John* 2. 28. being able immediately to Open to him when he fhall come and knock, *Luke* 12. 36. Queft. 5. How

Quest. 5. How are we to Interpret that word [All] with reference unto the Virgins, & their being over-taken with this Temptation?

Answ. This word [All] is of a Diverse Acceptation, of use to be Observed.

1. It sometimes signifieth some of All sorts, where there is any Distribution made, as of these Virgins into Wise and Foolish. Thus Christ is said to have tasted Death (with reference to its special Benefits) for All or Every Man, *Heb.* 2. 9. as he did sometimes heal All Sicknesses, and Every Disease among the People, *Mat.* 4. 23. That is, some of All sorts, or all Manner thereof, as it is there Translated, which is the same *Greek* word as in the other place. Thus also [All the World] is sometimes used; as when *John* (Writing to the Jews) calls Christ a Propitiation, not onely for Their sins, but also for the sins of the whole World, 1 *John* 2. 2. *viz.* for some of All sorts, both Jews and Gentiles; which Gentiles (Distinct from Jews) are sometimes called the World, *Rom.* 11. 12.) and not with respect to Every individual in the World, since Christ is onely a Propitiation through Faith, *Rom.* 3. 25. which Faith All Men have not, 2 *Thes.* 3. 2. In which sence also Christ lightneth every Man, *John* 1. 9. if meant of Spiritual Light, since some have not the Spirit, *Jude* 19. But [All the Virgins] in my Text, is meant of more than some of All sorts.

2. By this word [All] sometimes the whole (or Every Individual) is intended, without the least Restriction or Limitation. Thus *All* (as in the *Greek*) or whosoever believeth in Christ, shall not perish, *John* 3. 15. and thus the Promise is sure to All the Seed which is of the Faith of *Abraham*, *Rom.* 4. 16. And thus All *Israel* (in the Letter) shall at last be saved, *Rom.* 12. 26. Thus also is Marriage Honourable in All, without excepting any, in competition with Fornication, *Heb.* 13. 4. And thus All Scripture (and every part thereof, unto a word or syllable) is given by Holy Inspiration, 2 *Tim.* 3. 16. But as the former sence was too Restrictive, so is this Second too Comprehensive to be intended in my Text; as if All Virgins or Professors (not any one excepted) are then asleep, or slumbring, since there would else be no room for any Watchers, nor consequently such whom Christ will then serve, which yet is intimated, *Luke* 12. 37. and by such Watchers this very Cry at Mid-night seemeth to be made; therefore All will not be asleep, in that sence.

3. The word [All] is oft-times put to signifie the Generality; as All *Judea* went out to *John*, *Mat.* 3. 5. And as those walked in All God's Ordinances, *Luke* 1. 6. and as the Gospel went into All the Earth, *Rom.* 10. 18 &c. In which last sence, these Virgins (All of them) are said to sleep and slumber.

The Parable of the Ten Virgins Opened. 87

The Ground and Reason of which General sleep may be, as unto God, That so the Lord might thereby Humble the Generality of Professors, at such a Time. And thus was *David*'s Covenant (partly) Ordered, 2 *Sam.* 23. 5. that none should then seek after God, *Psal.* 14. 2. as his Dispensation was a Type of Christ's, *Rom.* 3. 11. and as with reference unto Christ's Spiritual Kingdom, so with Respect unto his Temporal Redemption also, *Ezra.* 20. 44. by turning their Captivity, who then were sleeping, or in a Dream, *Psal.* 126. 1. as it is with sinners when Christ first gives them Light, *Eph.* 5. 14. Nor can his People's Pride be more effectually prevented, than by their slumbring at such a time; since by that means there is no visible Difference between the Wise and Foolish, and since they fail in the Predominant Duty of such a Time, and which they have been so eminently forewarned of by Christ himself, *Mark* 13. 35, 36, 37. And thus, when All have sinned, the freeness of their Redemption is consulted for, *Rom.* 3. 23, 24. or when the Deliverer of *Sion* shall turn away ungodliness from *Jacob*, *Rom.* 11. 26. finding them (at that time) in Blindness, *v.* 25. or Labouring under that Spirit of slumber which he hath therefore given them, *v.* 8. But as to Means, or Second Causes, the Reason of this General sleep, is, because,

1. Christ Cometh in the Night, 2 *Pet.* 3. 10. and the Cry is made at Mid-night, *Mat.* 25. 6. As Typically of Old in *Egypt*, *Exod.* 12. 29. which Night is thought to be no Time for work, *John* 9. 4. but General sleeping, 1 *Thes.* 5. 7. and though some Rise up early, and others sit up late, *Psal.* 127. 2. yet All are wont to be asleep at Midnight: So that the very Season is one Reason why this Temptation is so Epidemical. Now, who would have imagined (according unto common Rules of Judging) that such a Friend, a Saviour, and much more a Bridegroom, should Order his Coming at such a Time? Especially since he was confidently Expected the Day before? Yea, one might be apt to think that Work or Labour, should onely be expected (from Man) untill the Evening, *Psal.* 104. 23. by vertue of God's Appointment, and that his sleep might then be warrantable, since, when the Night cometh, no Man can Work, *John* 9. 4. 'Tis true indeed, this holdeth not in Moral Cases, or when a Particular Exception is expresly made; but drouzy Heads are easily thus made to sleep when Satan rocks them.

2. Because of so many bad Examples set, the force whereof is greater than that of Precepts, since these do onely Teach, whereas the other, (*viz.* Examples) Draw, especially in sinful Cases. Most Men will rather go out of their way than lose their Company; as *Joash* did (with

reference

reference unto his evil way) so long as good *Jehoiada* Lived, 2 *Chron.* 24. 2. And as more do out of Christ's way on that Account, since Solitariness doth more Afflict (the Generality) than Disobedience. Now, here is no want of sleepy Presidents, with reference unto all sorts of Virgins: and if a little Leaven be so dangerous, 1 *Cor.* 5. 6. much more will half Mankind (*viz.* the Woman) encourage the other half (*viz.* the Man) to follow that Example, *Gen.* 3. 6. and when All go astray, the Priests themselves will hardly stay behind, *Ezek.* 44. 10. 'Tis like, these Virgins fell not All asleep at once, but Nodded one after another, untill the last was over-taken also, because she had not one Companion left to keep her waking; as poor *Elijah* ran for Company, when fansying himself to be alone.

3. Sleep is the Natural Effect of certain Causes, which Antecedents being General, the Consequent must needs be so, according to the Ordinary course of Nature; and this is Principally the Reason why this Temptation doth Generally so prevail (at such a time) upon these Virgins. Sleep is Occasioned (as in the Letter, so in the Mystery) sometimes from Weariness, *Judg.* 4. 21. Sometimes from having nought to do, *Prov.* 19. 15. Sometimes from Fansied security, *Luke* 12. 39. Sometimes from having Nought to lose, *Eccl.* 5. 12. Sometimes from Sensuality, *Joel* 1. 5. And sometimes from a Swoon, *Mat.* 9. 24. All which meet here, with reference unto these Virgins. They have been lately wearied with the greatness of their way, from *Canaan* to *Assyria*, *Isa.* 57. 9, 10. They have been Slothful, in hiding that Talent, which should have Publickly been improved, *Mat.* 25. 25, 26, 27. They were Secure, as in the Days of *Lot* and *Noah*, *Luke* 17. 26. 28. 30. Yea, they were Spiritually poor, which made them careless, *Rev.* 3. 17. They have been very Sensual, *Mat.* 24. 38, 39. Yea, they have fallen into a Spiritual Swoon, and must be awakened from some kind of Death by the sound of the Seventh Trumpet, *Rev.* 11. 15. 18. No wonder then, if Sleep hath been so General, the Causes of it having been so too.

Quest. 6. What Influence doth Christ's Tarrying lend unto the Virgins Slumbring?

Answ. 1. Because Sleep is very Natural, yea, unto Christ's own Disciples in his Absence, especially in Spiritual Respects, as sometimes in the Letter, *Mat.* 26. 40. Whilst *Adam* was alone, his sinless Nature was inclined to Sleep, *Gen.* 2. 20, 21. And much more is the Old Man subject thereunto, save as the Second *Adam* bids that sleeper to awake, *Eph.* 5. 14. Christ is that Sun, upon whose Setting, or with-drawing, Man Naturally falls into a slumber, and is apt to sleep

The Parable of the Ten Virgins Opened.

the sleep of Death, save as his Eyes are so enlightened, *Psal.* 13. 3. Christ sets the Soul on work, who else is Idle, *Mat.* 20. 1. 6, 7. And slothfulness will quickly cast one into a Deep sleep, *Prov.* 19. 15. Now, whilst the Bridegroom tarrieth, his quickning Influences are withheld more than before they were; and if he abideth still, though but two days, *John* 11. 6. his very Friend sleepeth, untill he goeth to awake him, *v.* 11.

2. Because Satan is then most busie, who hath the greatest Skill (next unto God himself) of casting poor Creatures into a slumbring Frame. He knows what is intailed upon Watchers at such a time, *Luke* 12. 37. 42. who therefore will Then be sure to be at *Joshua*'s Right hand, resisting him, *Zech.* 3. 1. when likely to be cloathed with Change of Raiment, and with a fair Mitre upon his Head, *v.* 4, 5. He also knoweth how sadly the Sleeper's House will then be broken through, *Luke* 12. 39. and what Temptations such will be exposed unto, both in respect of Sin, *v.* 45. and Suffering, *v.* 46. especially Professors, or such as know Christ's will, and yet are careless, *v.* 47. He also hath his Songs and Cradles, and Soporiferous Applications, wherewith to make men sleep, as *Delilah* did her *Sampson*, Judg. 16. 19. And though Christ doth prolong his Time, yet Satan then knows his Time is short, which makes him Rage the more, *Rev.* 12. 12.

3. Christ's Tarrying Occasions Grief, and Grief Occasions Drousiness; therefore the Virgins slumber, if Christ be absent, especially when he Tarrieth. It is so in a Spiritual case as it was with *Israel*, who were for the making of other gods, when *Moses* (who was a Type of Christ) Delayed his coming down out of the Mount, *Exod.* 32. 1. It was so in the Letter, when sorrow made these Disciples sleepy while Christ was absent, and with respect unto his sad expected absence afterward, *Luke* 22. 45. And if his going from them (for the Comforter) so fill'd their Hearts with sorrow, *John* 16. 6, 7. much more the Hope of his Return, when it is deferred, will make the Heart sick, *Prov.* 13. 12. and consequently, the Head exceeding heavy. Many of our Virgins eyes were ditted up with dirty Tears, and they have Cryed themselves asleep, as Children oft-times do, when left alone in some dark Room, and partly from Vexation.

4. No Man Precisely knoweth when he will Come, or whether some awakening intimations of it be not meer Delusions, which addeth weight unto the former Heaviness, and doth encourage slumberers to be secure. Some ask, How long, *Rev.* 6. 10? but none can absolutely tell, *Psal.* 74. 9. whether it will be at Even, or at Mid-night, or at the Cock Crowing, or in the Morning, *Mark* 13. 35. This Day and Hour being

The Parable of the Ten Virgins Opened.

being hid from Angels, *Mat.* 24: 36. and from the Son himself, *Mark.* 13. 32. as he is Man. Yea many false Alarms also are fore-signified, which we are bid to take heed of, *Mark.* 13. 21, 22, 23. And to be Sober as well as Vigilant, with reference unto the end of all things being at hand, 1 *Pet.* 4. 7. Now, when poor *Samuel* (in the Night) is wakened with an uncertain Call, he may be easily perswaded to lye down again, 1 *Sam.* 3. 4, 5. And Passionate *Jehoram* (in such a Case), will roundly say, *What should I wait for any longer*, 2 Kings 6. 33.

5. Such onely think (at first) to slumber, but not to sleep; or onely to sleep a little, but hope to waken before his Coming; or that they shall awaken presently, and soon be ready, upon some timely presumed Notice of his Coming: All which help forward this Temptation while he tarrieth. Sin is Deceitful, stealing upon some (as sleep doth) by degrees, who onely meant to slumber or dally with its Temptations: Others Design a down-right sleep, but onely of so long continuance, trusting that Conscience will awaken them at such an hour of the Night: But he that saith in his Heart, *My Lord delayeth his Coming* (the same *Greek* word that is in my Text) will take his fill of sinful sleep, *Mat.* 24. 48, 49. especially when such are furnish'd, as these Virgins are, some of them with Oyl in Vessels, and all with Trimmed Lamps, who therefore doubt not of being Ready. So that the Bridegroom's tarrying must needs Occasion the Virgins slumbring.

Use 1. From the Bridegroom's tarrying we may Observe, that Christ's Affections (the strongest of them, *viz.* his Conjugal Affections) are absolutely under his own Command; though he now cometh also to Execute his Vengeance, *Isa.* 61. 2. which is another very strong Affection. He is the Lord of Anger, as the *Hebrew* hath it, which is Translated Furious, *Nahum* 1. 2. and doth evince it by his slowness thereunto, though great in Power, and of an Holy Nature, and much provoked by his Enemies, *v.* 3. He also loves the Dispensation of his Coming, which therefore is oft-times called his Bride: Yet is he not thereby Transported to out-run his Father's Time, though strongly urged by all his Paranymphs, or Bride-maids earnest Expectations. True Holy Zeal is no way inconsistent with due Sobriety, whatever some may Fansy; but turbulency in Affections is one sad sign of their being Carnal, though fixt upon a Spiritual Object. When Tempted to be Impetuous, let us remember Christ, and that they who are his, have Crucified such Affections, *Gal.* 5. 24. as is their Duty, *Col.* 3. 5.

2. If all the Virgins be asleep (at least-wise slumbring) at such a time, we then may hence conjecture at the Reason of what hath been

to

to be Observed among the Churches and Professors of later Times, unto some Men's Amazement, supposing this Parable to have such a reference, as hath been with Sobriety suggested. Some have admired that Men pretending unto Light and Conscience should be so Blind, so wavering, so apt to let their Duty fall, so little Affected with what they Understood, so Childish in their Reasonings, so oft Relapsing into the same Temptation, so utterly unable to bear plain dealing, and so Offended with some kind of Light. Whilst others have been stark Deaf, affected strangely with ungrounded Pansies; unable to Resist the Weakest Adversary, not knowing what did befal them, yea, very secure in greatest Dangers, and marvellously affrighted with what in its self hath been a Mercy. The Reason whereof hath been their being all asleep, which is not so obvious in a Spiritual sence, as in the Letter; else should we not so much have wondred at these Appearances.

3. We now may see what little cause we had to be Offended with the Dis-appointment of our sometime Expectation; since Christ had told us of his tarrying, after the Virgins first going forth to meet him. Some have been therefore apt to Question wholly, whether that was He, because they trusted he would have then Redeemed *Israel* altogether, *Luke* 24. 21. But oh we Fools, and slow of Heart, to believe all that the Prophets have spoken, *v.* 25. Ought not Christ to have suffered these things (after his being Proclaimed King) and then to enter into his Glory, *v.* 26? Our failing at this Day is sadly Aggravated by that Record, and by Christ's own Prediction here (added to those of Old) according to what hath come to pass. Let us with shame acknowledge our former Inadvertency; and not persist to Question the Next Approaching of his Name, because of that; which is indeed one Promising Sign thereof; *viz.* his Tarrying beyond the Time Expected.

And since the Bridegroom's tarrying Occasions sleep, by those forenamed Influences thereby Ministred, these following Considerations may be of some Preventive Use, by way of Counterpoise.

1. Let us Remember; that all this while we have been meerly Exercised with the want (or rather the Delaying) of a Priviledge, and of a Lower Nature onely. Christ's Spiritual Presence (and our Communion with his Grace or Peace) hath not been necessarily denyed unto us, by Reason of this late Dis-appointment: Yea, such Communications might have thereby abounded, had we been Watchful in such a Trying Hour, since in his absence, the Comforter is promised to supply his place, to our Advantage, *John* 16. 7. 'Tis not Christ's fault, but ours, if the Quintessence of Outward Liberty be not enjoyed by us in Soul-Enlargements; since, if the Father was to be seen in Christ, *John*

14. 9. much more Chrift's Quickning Prefence is in the Spirit, and without which his Flefh would profit nothing, *John* 6. 62, 63. Now, fhall we caft away thefe choifer Influences (as Sleepers do) meerly becaufe we yet have not what is of far lefs worth? What clearer Evidence can there be of Childifh Folly and Mercenarinefs in our Profeffion, than to Defpife Chrift's Peace becaufe of Worldly Tribulations, and to defift from bounden Duty for want of Prefent, or immediate Pay?

2. It feems Chrift waiteth alfo, as this his Tarrying doth import; Expecting, till his Enemies be made his Foot-ftool, *Heb.* 10. 13. And fhall not we then Watch with him one Hour, *Mat.* 26. 40. efpecially when bid to do fo, *v.* 38? His bare Command fhould fatisfie a Friend, *John* 15. 14. a Lover of him, *John* 14. 15. much more his Practice, *John* 13. 14. efpecially with reference unto the fame Time, as well as Thing; as n this cafe it is. Shall we not take that Yoak upon us, (and count it eafie alfo) wherein himfelf is willing to be a Partner, *Mat.* 11. 29. 30? Thofe are Proud Servants, who will not Help their Lord, by lifting at the Other (and Lighter) end of any Burden. Yea, he is Suffering all this while; and is it not a fhame for his Difciples to fall afleep, whilft he is fweating, as it were, great drops of Blood, *Luke* 22. 45? Efpecially fince he hath fignified his being then at Prayer for *Peter* alfo, and the reft, *v.* 31,32. who formerly had continued with him in his Temptations, *v.* 28. but now could neither Pray for him, nor for themfelves, being faft afleep, *v.* 46.

3. Chrift alfo tarrieth, for our Advantage, as hath been fhewn: And fhall we then fo ill requite him, as at that very Time to Grieve him by our fleeping? He thereby doth defign the Actuating of our Graces; fhall we then let thofe Habits fleep, as if we had a mind to crofs him? This Refpite is vouchfafed for our Dreffing; and fhall we onely then improve it in putting off our Cloaths for fleep? How fadly did it aggravate the cafe of *Saul* and *Eli*, that they fhould fin juft when God was Eftablifhing the one Man's Houfe, 1 *Sam.* 2. 30. and the other's Kingdom, 1 *Sam.* 13. 13. How will it vex awakened Virgins, to think how ill they have Rewarded Chrift and their own Souls by flumbering at fuch a Time, as doubtlefsly it did King *Joafh*, who ftayed his own Hand, when God had given him leave to fmite his Enemies untill they were confumed, 2 *Kings* 13. 18, 19. This Trying Hour is that wherein more work might have been done than all the Day before; and trifling now, may prove more Dif-advantaging than any of thefe fleepers Dream of, whofe utmoft Diligence afterwards will not Redeem what Now is Loft.

4. He

The Parable of the Ten Virgins Opened. 93

4. He will Come certainly at laſt, *Hab.* 2. 3. and unawares on them who are not Watchful, *Luke* 12. 45, 46. and this all are fore-warned of, on purpoſe to prevent their ſleeping. In caſe the Lord were not to come, that ſlothful Servant would be the Happieſt Man: Or if one might be ſure to be awakened in due Time: Yea, ſleep might be more Pleaſant (though no whit ſafer) if this had not been ſounded in our Ears, which one would think, ſhould make the Virgins ſtartle, however others may ſleep ſecurely who know it not. Now, it might break poor *Sampſon*'s Heart, that he ſhould ſleep till his Hair was cut, and then awaken with that ſad word, *The Philiſtines be upon thee*, Judg. 16. 19, 20. eſpecially he having Twice been warned before, *v.* 9. 12. When apt to ſlumber, let that be founded in our Ear, *The Bridegroom is upon you*; whoſe ſudden coming unto Sleepers may be of ſadder conſequence than that of the *Philiſtines* was to *Sampſon*. And if this were of Ancient Uſe, *Mark* 13. 35, 36, 37. much more to us, on whom the End is near approaching.

5. We may be ſure (upon Subſtantial grounds) that Chriſt will come as ſoon as may be, or that he will tarry no longer than he needs muſt. There are ſome Watch-men upon *Jeruſalem*'s Walls which never hold their Peace, and who are bid to keep no ſilence, nor give him Reſt, till he Eſtabliſh her, *Iſa.* 62. 6, 7. And his Elect do Generally make an heavy Cry, whom he will therefore ſpeedily avenge, although their Faith is gone, by his long bearing with them, *Luke* 18. 7, 8. Yea, his own Intereſt doth put him on upon a three-fold ſcore; Partly, becauſe that Diſpenſation is his Bride, whom none can Love more than the Bridegroom doth; and therefore he onely tarrieth till all things are made ready for the Marriage, *Mat.* 22. 4. Partly, becauſe he cometh as an Avenger upon his Wicked Adverſaries, which is an caſe unto his Heart, *Iſa.* 1. 24. And therefore he will not long be burthened. And Partly, becauſe he all this while is in a Suffering ſtate, as to his Name and Intereſts, and ſuch a blot will ſuddenly be wip'd away. Therefore we may conclude his Coming with utmoſt ſpeed, and ſo keep Waking.

6. His Coming as a Bridegroom, (in theſe our Days,) cannot but be exceeding near, from all thoſe Plauſible fore-named Grounds, (both Scriptural and Providential,) by which the Virgins were all encouraged to Expect him at their firſt going forth. And unto which I now ſhall add One more, which is (to me) a Demonſtration; *viz.* Becauſe that Diſpenſation (with reference unto its Preſent ſetting up) was manifeſtly (of later Years) The Truth of ſuch a Time; ſince it Then was the Onely Truth oppoſed by Worldly Powers, and meerly

in

in regard of its being then to be set up. Now, Worldly Powers will alway Persecute some Glorious Truth of Christ or other; such as (by way of Eminency) Time-Truths are: Therefore this having been the Only But of Persecution, (and with Respect unto its Present Exaltation) 'tis thereby evidenced to have been The Truth of such a Time, and consequently to have been speedily to be Advanced, since else (in such a Respect) it cou'd not be a Truth. Which might have kept us Waking.

MATTHEW XXV. 6.

And at Mid-night there was a Cry made, Behold the Bridegroom Cometh; Go ye out to meet him.

IN this Verse we have a Notification of the Bridegroom's Coming; wherein we may Observe, 1. The Thing Notified, He Cometh. 2. The Note of Attention added, [Behold] he Cometh. 3. The Means or Manner of this Notification, by a Cry. 4. The Time when this Cry is made, viz. At Mid-night. 5. The Duty thereupon Exhorted unto, Go out to meet him. From all which the Observation is this.

Observ. After the Bridegroom's Tarrying for a certain time, a Cry is made at Mid-night to the Virgins, *Behold he Cometh, Go ye out to meet him.*

Quest. 1. How will the Bridegroom come, both as to the Kind and Manner of his Coming?

Answ. As to the Kind thereof (and meerly with Respect unto his Temporal Kingdom) there is a Diverse Coming mentioned in the Scripture.

1. There was a Typical Coming in *David*'s Time, *Psal.* 40. 7. in whom Christ came to Do and Suffer his Father's Will, *Heb.* 10. 7, 8, 9. and doth now Reign accordingly, though more invisibly at the present, *Heb.* 2. 8. and with Respect unto his Father *David*'s Throne. To which may be referred what of that Typical Nature was Before, when Christ did first set up his Temporal (as well as Spiritual) Kingdom in the World, *Deut.* 33. 2. and when that Kingdom was Restored afterwards, *Zech.* 2. 10.

2. There was a Coming (afterwards) by way of Shew or Emblem,

The Parable of the Ten Virgins Opened.

when Chrift was Transfigured upon the Mount, *Mat.* 17. 1, 2 which feemeth to be that Coming in his Kingdom, which fome there ftanding fhould not tafte of Death untill they faw, *Mat.* 16. 27, 28.

3. There alfo was a Coming in the days of *Conftantine*, when Chrift did firft Erect his Temporal Kingdom, *Rev.* 12. 5. to Recompenfe his Faithful Servants, *Rev.* 7. 17. and Execute his vengeance upon others, *Rev.* 6. 16, 17.

4. There will be alfo his Coming as a Thief, *Rev.* 16. 15. when *Ifrael* (or the Eaftern Kings) fhall be Converted, *v.* 12. to whom fhall come the firft (or chief Dominion that ever yet was, *Mic.* 4. 8. who fhall be All Righteous, *Ifa.* 60. 21. but yet not Perfect, therefore that alfo will be but for a Time.

5. There will be his Second Appearing at the laft, without fin, *Heb.* 9. 28. which therefore muft needs be Perfonal, or in his Humane Nature, wherein he fometimes bare the fins of his Elect; *1 Pet.* 2. 24.

6. But then there alfo is a Precurfory Coming, which laft is Principally intended in this Parable, as hath before been hinted.

Thus will Chrift's Temporal Throne have fix fteps up into it, as *Solomon's* had of Old, *1 Kings* 10. 19.

The Manner of which Precurfory Coming will much Refemble that of his Perfonal Coming, and the reft, as in thefe following Particulars will appear.

1. His Coming will be very fudden. When his Enemies will be fecure, *1 Thef.* 5. 2, 3. *Mat.* 24. 49. 50. *Luke* 17. 28, 29, 30. When the Foolifh Virgins think there's time enough to Buy Oyl in, *Mat.* 25. 10. When former Signs will not be feen, by Reafon of their Difcontinuance, *Pfal.* 74. 9. *2 Pet.* 3. 4. When his Elect abound with unbelieving Cries, *Luke* 18. 7, 8. When there will be great Mountains in his way, *Zech.* 4. 7. the Mount of Olives to be divided, *Zech.* 14. 4. and none fhut up or left in *Ifrael*, *Deut.* 32. 36. This rotten Old Houfe will fal' in a Calm, defpifed fore-warnings will thus be punifhed, his former tarrying will thus be recompenfed; he then hath nothing elfe to do, but juft to come; thus will he amaze the World, and thus hath he confulted for the need of Daily Watching, *Mark* 13. 36.

2. His Coming will be with a dreadful Earthquake, *Zech.* 14. 5. Valleys will be Exalted, and Mountains Level'd; *Ifa.* 40. 4, 5. The Old Heavens will pafs away, and the Earth be burnt up, *2 Pet.* 3. 10. and New Created, *Ifa.* 65. 17. The ftate of things will be diffolved, and yet not Ruined, *Pfal.* 75. 2, 3. He then will tread the Wine-prefs of the Almighty's wrath and fiercenefs, *Rev.* 19. 15. till blood come unto the Horfe Bridles, *Rev.* 14. 20. *Michael* and the Dragon will then

then try their utmost; the Trouble then must needs be great, *Dan.* 12. 1. And if the Beast's Fall (before) was shaking, much more will Satan's be so, *Rev.* 12. 8, 9. Christ will then come to Judgment, *Rev.* 11. 1 S. the Name whereof made *Felix* tremble. And this will be a Time of Restitution, *Acts* 3. 21. and therefore of much Commotion. Yea, all must be done in a little time, which cannot be without a mighty noise. See therefore to your standing, *Luke* 21. 36. and flee away from *Babylon*, *Jer.* 51. 45. as far as *Azal*, or separation, *Zech.* 14. 4, 5.

3. His Coming will be with Clouds and Darkness, *Psal.* 97. 2. as to the Justifiableness of several things, according to a common Rule of Judging. *Israel* will then be as the Dew which tarrieth not for Man, *Mich.* 5. 7. but readily will Publish that word which God himself gives forth, *Psal.* 68. 11. The Temple and City Walls will not depend upon a fresh Humane Command, *Ezra* 5. 3. but will be pleaded by an Ancient Order, *v.* 11. 13. which was Divine, *Ezra* 1. 1. That Day of the Lord will be upon every one that is Lofty, *Isa.* 2. 12. the spoilers will then be spoyled, *Ezra* 39. 10. the Judge will pull down and set up at pleasure, *Psal.* 75. 7. the Solitary shall be set in Families, *Psal.* 68. 6. and out of *Judah* shall come every (so called) Oppressor, *Zech.* 10. 4. This King's High-way will not be Common, but where there none was wont to be, for his Redeemed, *Isa.* 35. 8, 9. as it was of old, *Psal.* 77. 19, 20.

4. Yet Righteousness will be his Habitation, *Psal.* 97. 2. which will sustain him, *Isa.* 59. 16. As to his making war with some, *Rev.* 19. 11. and his Redeeming others, *Isa.* 1. 27. *Israel's* Nobles shall be of Themselves, *Jer.* 30. 21. which is but Righteous, according to the *Chaldeans* Principles, *Hab.* 1. 7. They shall be Righteously Redeemed for Nought, because they were so Sold, *Isa.* 52. 3. No Weapon shall prosper any more against the Just, the Servants of the Lord, which will be both their Heritage and Righteousness, *Isa.* 54. 17. Christ shall then Reign, *Rev.* 11. 15. and he in that respect will then be called a Righteous Branch, *Jer.* 23. 5. for unto him it appertaineth, *Jer.* 10. 7. whose Right it is, *Ezra* 21. 27. God's Law (viz. the Light of Nature and the Scriptures) will be the Rule; for he will then Magnifie his Law, and for his Righteousness sake, *Isa.* 42. 21. Saints then will walk in the Name of the Lord their God, which is but Just, since others Judge it to be their Right, *Mic.* 4. 5. *Babylon* shall be Rewarded, as she hath Rewarded others, *Rev.* 18. 6. and Saints shall have double for their shame, *Isa.* 61. 7. both which are Righteous, 2 *Thes.* 1. 6, 7.

5. His Coming will be variously Represented by Men of Differing

The Parable of the Ten Virgins Opened. 97

Spirits. Some will suppose him to be *John the Baptist*, Mat. 16. 14. But others will more confidently say, *Loe, this is He*, *Isa.* 25. 9. And Blessed is the People that know the (Seventh Trumpets) joyful sound, *Psal.* 89. 15. Some will be Angry, *Rev.* 11. 18. and oppose him, *Psal.* 2. 1, 2. as the *Philistines* did *David*, 2 *Sam.* 5. 17. but others will desire him, *Hag.* 2. 7. Some will then stumble, and thereby be ensnared, *Isa.* 8. 14. but others will call his saddest Executions Righteous, *Rev.* 16. 5. and blessed is he that is not Offended in him, *Rev.* 15. 3. Some will then Sing, whilst others shall Cry for sorrow of Heart, *Isa.* 65. 14. Some will give Glory unto God, *Rev.* 11. 13. Indeed who shall not fear him, and Worship before him, *Rev.* 15. 4? Yet others will not Repent to give him Glory, *Rev.* 16. 9.

6. His Coming will be with Glory, Riding in the Heavens, by his Name *Jah*, *Psal.* 68. 4. and being thereby Declared to be the Son of God, *Psal.* 2. 7. His Harbinger hath been astonishing, as *Luke* 3. 15. much more himself will be so, as of Old, *John* 10. 41. Kings will then shut their Mouths at him, *Isa.* 52. 15. and Heathens will bow unto his Scepter, *Isa.* 19. 18. A New Earth and Heavens (or Glorious Dispensation) will be Created, *Isa.* 65. 17. wherein all sorts of Persons shall then share, *v.* 20. The Lustre whereof will be set out by that sad state of things immediately before, *Psal.* 32. 5. The Spirit also will then be poured forth, *Isa.* 32. 15. whose Fruits will be unto his Praise and Glory, *Phil.* 1. 11. He will then come with all his Saints, *Zech.* 14. 5. most Gloriously attired, *Zech.* 3. 4, 5.

7. The Glory of this Coming will be Low at first. *Babylon* will then be taken at one end, *Jer.* 51. 31. *Israel's* last Enemies will first be Ruined in some Isles, *Ezek.* 39. 6. Glory to the Righteous will first be heard from the utmost parts of the [then] known Earth, *Isa.* 24. 15, 16. The first Ruler in *Israel* will be from *Bethlehem Ephratah*, or Fruitful House of Bread, *Mic.* 5. 2. when the *Assyrian* is in that Land, *v.* 5. The Tents of *Judah* (in competition with the Glory of *David's* House) will first be saved, *Zech.* 12. 7. The Sanctuary waters will first be to the Ankles, *Ezek.* 47. 3. The Tenth of the City will onely fall at first, *Rev.* 11. 13. and more will follow after, *Rev.* 16. 19. But the Stone will become a Mountain, *Dan.* 2. 35. The Grain of Mustard-seed will grow Exceedingly, *Mat.* 13. 31, 32. His Temporal Kingdom will increase, as did, and doth his Spiritual.

8. His Coming will (in some sense) be Once for All, though with some kind of Circumstantial variation, as to the Measure, Place, and Manner of his Appearing. The Seventh Trumpet will continue untill the Last Trump shall sound, *Rev.* 16. 17. The Gentiles Glory will
increase

increase untill their Fulness be come in; upon whose Degeneration (then) Christ's will Translate that Kingdom to the Jews, *Rom.* 11. 24. untill his Coming to Reign in Person, when Jews and Gentiles shall have fulfilled their Course. But Antichristianism will have its deadly blow at first, for all the last Plagues are killing. And Grosser Persecutions or Destructions will come to a Perpetual End, wherever Christ hath once set up this kind of Throne, *Psal.* 9. 6, 7. And thus the Saints Dominion (once begun) will be for Ever, *Dan.* 7. 27. passing from them to Christ himself, and thence at last unto the Father, 1 *Cor.* 15. 28.

Quest. 2. What's meant by this Word, *Behold*, with reference to his Coming?

Answ. 1. *Behold* sometimes imports Presentiality, as *John* 1. 29. And thus he Cometh when the Cry is made, *viz.* soon after; therefore 'tis said, he Cometh; not that he Will Come. The Time of this Cry doth clearliest hint his near Approach, which therefore is to be Studied and Observed. Time was, when it was Dangerous to reckon his Day at Hand, 2 *Thes.* 2. 2. And when the Seventh Angel begins to sound there will be Time no longer, *Rev.* 10. 6, 7. But a little before that Time it will be said, *Behold he Cometh*. There will be Time After that for all the Virgins to Trim their Lamps, for some Discourse between them concerning Oyl, and for the Foolish Virgins going out to Buy it; but not for their Return before his Coming, *Mat.* 25. 6, 7, 8, 9, 10. And if (as some conceive) this Cry hath been already made, 'tis near indeed.

2. It sometimes hinteth Obviousness or Easiness to be Discerned, *John* 11. 36. Of such a Nature is his speedy Coming then unto an Open and Observing Eye. Christ here affirms it, whose Name is True, *Rev.* 3. 7. and therefore he hath bid it should be Written, *Rev.* 21. 5. His Harbinger is come already at their first going forth; therefore himself cannot be now long after. The Signs hereof had been before, *Luke* 21. 25, 26. whose very beginning called for our looking up, *v.* 28. His previous work is then Dispatch'd; and he is not slack as Men count slackness, 2 *Pet.* 3. 9. This Cry concludes the Second Woe; and then the Third comes quickly, *Rev.* 11. 14. Some will not yet see, but they shall see unto their shame, *Isa.* 26. 11. being willingly Ignorant, 2 *Pet.* 3. 5.

3. It also hinteth In-advertency, as *Mat.* 7. 4. And therefore these Virgins are bid, *Behold*. Some have no mind to see that Object, it so Affrights them to hear of Judgment, *Acts* 24. 35. Others do not believe for Joy, *Luke* 24. 41. nor can they hearken for present Anguish and cruel Bondage,

The Parable of the Ten Virgins Opened. 99

Bondage, *Exod.* 6. 9. especially when this increaseth, *Exod.* 5. 21. after the raising of their Expectations, *Exod.* 4. 31. Others are so engaged in the World, as that they would not have this Earth and Heavens to be yet Destroyed, which makes them in-observant of such Intimations. Some are unwilling to believe untill they See and Feel, *John* 20. 25, especially since some have been mistaken, who rashly have determined the very time. And all are sleepy, who therefore need being bid, *Behold*.

4. It noteth Marveloufness, or Matter of Wonder, as *Isa.* 7. 14. And such a Dispensation is Amazing, upon a manifold score. Its like hath not been seen these many hundred Years, or not since *Constantine's* Time, *Rev.* 12. 5. and with respect to Rarities, Men use to say, Behold. The Lord will then do a New thing in the Earth, by making a way in the Wilderness, and Rivers in the Desert; which therefore may well be bid to be Beheld, *Isa.* 43. 19. Truth is now fallen in the street, and Equity cannot enter, *Isa.* 59. 14. Therefore it may be then well said (by way of Admiration) Behold, a King shall Reign in Righteoufness, *Isa.* 32. 1. The Gentiles shall carry the Saints upon their shoulders, which is a Wonder worthy to be Beheld, *Isa.* 49. 22. There is none that sheweth, yea, there is none that Heareth this; therefore the first Informer may well say, *Behold, behold them*, Isa. 41. 26, 27.

5. It sometimes noteth of what Use and Consequence it is, to take especial Notice of what is so Accompanied, as *Rev.* 3. 20. In which last sence 'tis chiefly here intended. He cometh now to Judgment, *Rev.* 11. 18. and all the Churches shall then know 'tis he that searcheth the Reins and Hearts, *Rev.* 2. 23. He now will give no longer day unto the Virgins to buy that Oyl, which formerly hath been neglected, but onely to Trim their Lamps, and so go forth, or be shut out for ever. The Manner of his Appearing (from first to last) will countervail the glad Beholder's want of sleep, unto Their after-grief who do not mind it. He then will make so great a Change, as that Old Objects will not be worth the looking after, so as to take the Eye off from him. Yea, this very Notice of his Coming will startle all the Virgins; which shews how fitly this word, *Behold*, is set before it.

6. It sometimes doth denote Intreaty or Beseeching; and therefore that word, Loe, or Behold, 1 *Chron.* 17. 1. is else-where rendred, see, I pray, 2 *Sam.* 7. 2. as the *Hebrew* word there used for [Now] is oftimes rendred, *Numb.* 12. 13. *&c.* Nor is it strange, for God (by others) to beseech poor Man; or for his Cryers and Embassadors to Pray Men in Christ's stead, 2 *Cor.* 5. 10. especially in such Momentous

O 2 Cases.

The Parable of the Ten Virgins Opened.

Cases. Christ knows of what concernment it is, to be aware of him, and of his Day, *Luke* 21. 34. who therefore Prayeth them, for their own good. He knows the Judgment wants not Light; who therefore thus applies himself to their Affections by such a Pathetical Exhortation. He knows the Virgins love to slumber, who therefore earnestly beseecheth their awakening. He might Enjoyn what is Convenient, but for Love's sake he rather doth Beseech, *Philem.* 8.9. His Fatherly Compassions are stirred in him for the Wiser Virgins, who therefore speaks thus Affectionately unto them all. Thus doth Christ sometimes condescend to gain our Duty, and to set us a Copy.

Quest. 3. How may we know the Cry which is then made?

Answ. This Cry must either be conceived to be Ordinary, or Extraordinary.

If Extraordinary, it then must be Prophetical, which some may be in the Expectation of, but not upon substantial Grounds. We may not be Wise above that which is Written, 1 *Cor.* 4. 6. Now, the Scripture doth no where plainly hint such Extraordinary Gifts, with reference to these our days; since, if that Prophecy, *Joel* 2.28. be strictly now to be fulfilled again, we may as well expect Christ's Personal Coming Now, which that Place firstly did refer unto, *Acts* 2. 16. Nor is it needful, since the Perfecting of those Scriptures, by which the Man of God is throughly furnished unto all good works, 2 *Tim.* 3. 17. Yea, with Respect unto these Latter days; those have no Light in them, who go not to that Law and Testimony, *Isa.* 8. 20. which are a surer word of Prophecy than is a Voice from Heaven, 2 *Pet.* 1. 18, 19. or one sent from the Dead, *Luke* 16. 30, 31. He also is sadly Threatned, who shall add ought (as Extraordinary pretended Prophets needs must do) unto that finishing Book of Revelations, *Rev.* 22.18. And though God is at Liberty to give forth such a Gift, yet are we not required to Believe on that Account before hand, though Men pretending thereunto may sometimes have hit right. Nay, 'tis expressly said (with reference to such a time) there is no more any Prophet among us that knoweth how long, *Psal.* 74. 9.

I therefore judge this Cry to be more Ordinary, or something which doth occurre (according to the Scripture) after the Bridegroom's having Tarried; and as the next, or more immediate Antecedents of his Coming. As for Example.

1. When the Inhabitants of Mount *Seir* shall be destroyed by *Moab* and *Ammon*, who were Confederates against the Men of *Judah*, 2 *Chron.* 20. 10. which was the Beginning of that Salvation, *v.* 22, 23. in the Valley of *Berachah*, *v.* 26. for poor unworthy good *Jehoshaphat*, 2 *Chron.* 19.

The Parable of the Ten Virgins Opened. 101

19. 2, 3. As that fore-told Chrift's Coming (in *Jehoshaphat's* Valley) to Judge his People's Enemies, after the Return of their Captivity, *Joel* 3. 1, 2. Which said Inhabitants of Mount *Seir* were *Esau's* Off-spring, *Gen.* 36. 8. who was (a very little) *Jacob's* Elder Brother, *Gen.* 25. 25. but Sold his Birth-right or Priority, (and thereby loft his much defired Bleffing of Supremacy) for a Trifle, *Gen.* 25. 33. and 27. 35. whereupon he hated his Brother *Jacob*, v. 41. though *Israel* did not dif-poffefs him of his Inheritance, 2 *Chron.* 20. 10, 11. Thefe Men will joyn (again't *Judah*) with *Moab* and *Ammon*, and yet be Deftroyed by their own Confederates: Soon after which Chrift Cometh.

2. When *Israel's* Adverfaries fhall Unite, to cut them off from being a Nation, *Psal.* 83. 4, 5. Defigning to take God's Houfes into their Poffeffion, v. 12. and burning up his Synagogues in the Land, *Psal.* 74. 8. Then will Chrift evidence his being King of Old, *Psal.* 74. 12. by doing to thefe bold Enemies as to the *Midianites*, *Psal.* 83. 9. and in a very little while his Anger fhall ceafe in their Deftruction, *Isa.* 10. 25, 26. as it was with *Ahafuerus*, upon *Haman's* being Executed, *Esth.* 7. 10. who fought to Deftroy all *Mordecai's* People, *Esth.* 3. 6. Thus when the Heathen help forward their Affliction who are but lately come out of *Babylon*, God will return with Mercy to *Jerufalem*, *Zech.* 1. 12. 15. 16. and make the *Chaldean's* Daughter filent, who had no Mercy for her Captives, *Isa.* 47. 5, 6.

3. When *Israel's* fad Cafe will be (unto the Eye of Reafon) Defperate. One Sign of *Sion's* Reftauration, is, the feeming Incurable-nefs of her Sorrow, and her being called an Out-caft, *Jer.* 30. 15. 17. after the Return of her Captivity, v. 3. When God fhall have Accomplifhed to fcatter the Holy People's Power, then will thefe things be finifhed, *Dan.* 12. 7. after the Time, and Times, and Part of Time, or after the Little Horn's deceafe, who did fo long continue, *Dan.* 7. 25. and confequently after their being poffeffed of the fourth Beaft's Kingdom, v. 21, 22. Their expectations muft mifcarry, who look for deliverance from themfelves, *Isa.* 26. 18. But when the Eyes of Man, as of all the Tribes of *Israel*, are towards the Lord, then will his Burden reft upon the Land of *Hadrach* and *Damafcus*, *Zech.* 9. 1. And thus, No Faith on Earth will Ufher in the Bridegroom's Coming, *Luke* 18. 8. And when there is no Humane interceffor vifible, then Chrift's own Arm will bring Salvation, *Isa.* 59. 16. repaying Recompenfe unto his Enemies in the Iflands, v. 18.

4. When God hath performed his whole work upon Mount *Sion*, he then will punifh that *Affyrian*, *Isa.* 10. 12. the ftretching out of whofe Wings hath fill'd the breadth of *Immanuel's* Land, *Isa.* 8. 8. An Hy-

pocritical Nation muſt firſt be ſoundly whipt, then will that Rod be caſt into the Fire, *Iſa.* 10. 5, 6. 16, 17. *Achan* muſt firſt be fully ſto'ed, and all his ill-gotten Goods conſumed, then will the fierceneſs of God's Anger be turned away, *Joh.* 7. 25, 26. It muſt appear who count God's Service vain, (becauſe the wicked are Delivered) and who yet think upon his Name, *Mal.* 3.14,15, 16. Then ſhall a Providential difference be put between the Righteous and the Wicked, *v.* 18. Two Thirds of *Iſrael* muſt be cut off and die; and the Remaining Third Part muſt be Refined; then ſhall they call upon the Lord and he will hear them, *Zech.* 13. 8, 9.

5. When long endurance (both on God's part and Man's) ſhall fix the Generality in their Reſpective Wandrings. A willing Ignorance is one Gray Hair upon the Old World's Head, 2 *Pet.* 3. 5. or Sign of its Laſt days, *v.* 3. as dying at the Root doth evidence the Harveſt to be fully Ripe. When Controverſies cannot be determined by Ordinary means, then comes the Judge into his Valley of Deciſion, *Joel* 3. 14. When *Daniel* underſtood not the Time of the End, from what Chriſt told the Angel, *Dan.* 12. 6, 7, 8. Chriſt giveth him a plainer Sign, *viz.* the fixedneſs of Men in wicked ways, *v.* 10. Some will debaſe themſelves, even unto Hell, *Iſa.* 57. 9. without being grieved for it, *v.* 10. but go on forwardly in their own way, *v.* 17. then comes the Time of Reſtauration, *v.* 18. and Prince of Peace, *v.* 19. And when theſe Virgins part from inability to Give or to Receive any further Oyl and Light, the Bridegroom cometh before it can be Bought, *Mat.* 25. 8, 9, 10.

6. When *Aſhur* and *Eber* are both of them Afflicted by Ships from the Coaſt of *Chittim*, which *Balaam* makes to be the immediate forerunner of *Aſhur's* Periſhing, *Numb.* 24. 24. and of Chriſt's having the Dominion, *v.* 19. or of his Coming out of *Jacob*, as a Star, to deſtroy the Generality, or all the Children of *Sheth*, *v.* 17. who was the onely Hopeful Remaining Son of *Adam*, *Gen.* 4. 25. put for the Generality of Profeſſors. Now, *Aſhur* came of *Shem*, *Gen.* 10. 22. who was the firſt Devourer of God's *Iſrael*, *Jer.* 50. 17. and their laſt Troubler afterwards, *Ezra* 4. 2. who therefore fitly anſwers unto Satan or the Dragon, who was before the *Babyloniſh* Beaſt, *Rev.* 12. 3. and doth reſiſt *Joſhua* afterwards, *Zech.* 3. 1, 2. *Eber* came of *Shem* alſo, *Gen.* 10. 21. from whom the *Hebrews* (or Profeſſors) had their Name, which was firſt given to *Abraham*, *Gen.* 14. 13. This *Aſhur* (in the latter days) ſhall be United with thoſe *Hebrews*; both which ſhall joyntly be Afflicted (though not Deſtroyed) by Ships from *Chittim*, which was a place eminent for Trade and Shipping, *Ezek.* 27. 6. *Dan.* 11.

The Parable of the Ten Virgins Opened. 103

11. 30. Soon after which, this *Ashur* sh..ll perish for ever, and Christ shall come as King, or as a Bridegroom.

7. When the Harvest is Reaped, as being fully Ripe, *Rev.* 14. 15, 16. then comes the Vintage, *v.* 18. or wrath of God upon his Enemies, *v.* 19. (*Joel* 3. 12, 13.) by the space of two hundred Miles, *v.* 20. Soon after which, seven Angels, *Rev.* 15. 1. come out of the Temple Opened, *v.* 6. Upon the Seventh Trumpets sounding, wherewith Christ comes to Reign, *Rev.* 11. 15. 17, 18, 19. Which Harvest may thus be known. It is an Harvest, *Rev.* 14. 15. which eminently doth consist of Wheat, *Mat.* 13. 29, 30. or Men of a choicer Spirit, who then must be cut down, as to some kind of former standing, Natural, or Mystical. 'Tis Reaped by one like the Son of Man, *Rev.* 14. 14, 15. or by the Son of Man himself, *Rev.* 1. 13. or by a more immediate hand of God, which is a sad Dispensation to the Godly, and therefore it is Accompanied with a Cordial Prologue unto such, *Rev.* 14. 13. 'Tis Reaped upon the Prayer of one out of the Temple, *Rev.* 14. 15. *viz.* an High Priest, or a Priest, at least, who Typified Saints of greater Spiritual Strength, because no other can bear to joyn in such a kind of Prayer, but rather pray against it. 'Tis after the Return of *Babylon's* Captivity, or when the Lamb and his Party are on Mount *Sion*, *Rev.* 14. 1. 'Tis also after that loud Denunciation against Complyers with the Man of Sin, at such a Time, *Rev.* 14. 9, 10, 11, 12.

8. When God shall have made, of a City an Heap, of a Defenced City a Ruine: A Palace of Strangers to be No City, *Isa.* 25. 2. Then will he be a strength to the Poor, *v.* 4. and the Branch of the Terrible ones shall be brought low, *v.* 5. in Order unto his Marriage-Feast, *v.* 6. at his Expected Coming, *v.* 9. Which Dispensation may thus be known: It must be a Metropolis, because there is a Palace in it, which therefore is applyed by some to *Babylon*. It is a Defenced City, and therefore its Ruines must chiefly be within its Walls. It is a Palace of Strangers; as Strangers and *Israelites* are contra-distinct, *Jer.* 5. 19. Such as the *Assyrian* is in *Israel's* Land, *Mic.* 5. 5. Its Ruines must be very Great, because it Never shall be re-built, or not of a long time, at least, as *Exod.* 21. 6. where the same *Hebrew* words are so intended. And this sad Judgment will much Affect; since Therefore shall the strong People Glorifie God, and the City of the Terrible Nations shall fear him, *Isa.* 25. 3.

9. When God shall make his Enemies like a Wheel, *Psal.* 83. 13. in Order to Their being troubled for ever, *v.* 17. who have consulted against his hidden ones, *v.* 3. that Men may know *Jehovah* is most High,

High, over all the Earth, *v.*18. Which Wheel denoteth Reſtleſsneſs, or ſelf-deſtroying Variations; and thus the Lord brings to Nought the Heathens Counſel, *Pſal.*33.10. whereas his Counſel ſtands for ever,*v.*11. becauſe he ſpeaketh and it is done, he doth Command, and it ſtands faſt, *v.*9. Thus *Pharaoh* (that *Egyptian* Dragon) did firſt increaſe his Cruel Perſecutions, *Exod.*5.7, 8. and then abated of his Rigor, *Exod.*8.8. untill he roſe again, *Exod.*14.5. unto his utter overthrow, *v.*28. Thus did the *Aſſyrian* Adverſaries firſt make the Jews to ceaſe by Force and Power, *Ezra*4.23. who afterwards did onely take the Builders Names, *Ezra* 5.4. untill they made a freſh Complaint,*v.*17. unto the Reverſing of that Prohibition,*Ezra* 6.6.11.Thus alſo did the Martyrs Cry, *Rev.* 6.10. becauſe of *Galienus* his increaſing Perſecution, which then abated till the Nineteenth Year of *Dioclẽſian*, *v.*11. who afterwards Revived it, *v.* 11, 12, 13, 14. unto the extirpation of that *Roman* Dragon, *v.* 15. And thus it was with Typical *Sennacherib*, 2 *Kings* 18.13.17. *Iſa.* 37.8, 9.36.

10. When the Worſhip of God is openly Blaſphemed by his Enemies at ſuch a time. The Adverſary's Blaſpheming the Name of God is pleaded as an Argument with him, to pluck his Hand out of his Boſom, *Pſal.* 74.10, 11. and was effectual in that Typical Valley of *Achor, Joſh.* 7.9. though long endured, when firſt the Man of ſin aroſe, *Rev.* 13.5. If *Pharaoh* did profeſs himſelf to be an Atheiſt, *Exod.* 5.2. calling thoſe Idle, who onely would have Liberty to Sacrifice,*v.*17. God will ſoon make him know there is none like himſelf, by ſending all his Plagues upon the others Heart, *Exod.* 9.14. And if the *Aſſyrian* doth Blaſpheme the Holy One of *Iſrael*, *Iſa.* 37.23. calling High places and Idolatrous Altars God's required Worſhip, *Iſa.* 36.7. and likening the true God to Idols, *v.* 20. the Lord will ſoon turn him back, *Iſa.* 37.29. and ſignally deſtroy him, *v.* 36. It alſo much diſpleaſeth God, *Iſa.* 59.15. ſo as to make him Furious, *v.* 18. when he that departs from evil is counted Mad, as the Margin hath it, *v.* 15. and as the *Hebrew* word is by ſome Jewiſh Writers rendred. Yea, Chriſt will ſoon caſt off thoſe Old Profeſſing Jews, who do Blaſpheme the truth of ſuch a Time, which was firſt Preached to them, *Acts* 18.5,6.

11. When *Tyre* and *Sidon* ſhall have Sold the Children of *Judah* unto the *Grecians*, Joel 3.4.6. after the Return of *Babylon*'s Captivity, *v.* 1. then will God plead the cauſe of *Iſrael*, *v.* 2. and raiſe them out of that place again, *v.* 7. caſting their Sellers into that Condition, *v.* 8. in a way of juſt Recompence, *v.* 7. Which *Tyrians* and *Sidonians* of Old, were very like the preſent *Hollanders*, in point of Strength at Sea, *Zech.* 9.3, 4. all manner of Trading, *Ezek.* 27.3. Oppreſſion, *Ezek*.
.28.

The Parable of the Ten Virgins Opened. 97

28. 16. 18. Pride, *Ezek.* 28. 2. 6. Policy, *Ezek.* 28. 3, 4, 5. *Zech.* 9, 2. and falling in with *Ifrael* in their Profperity, 1 *Kings* 5. 1. for a felf end, 2 *Chron.* 2. 15. but elfe a pricking Briar, *Ezek.* 28. 22. 24. Confederating with *Afhur* againft them, *Pfal.* 83. 7. and Selling them unto the *Grecians, Joel* 3. 4, 5, 6. Which *Grecians* here do feem to be the laft of *Ifrael's* groffer Adverfaries, *Zech.* 9. 13. chiefly fo called becaufe of their Refembling the Ancient *Grecian* Monarch, in point of Speedy Conqueft, *Dan.* 8. 5. or filling the breadth of *Immanuel's* Land, *Ifa.* 8. 8.

12. When the Angel out of the Temple, *Rev.* 14. 17. (or Saints of an Higher Rank, fuch as the Priefts were of Old, who onely might enter into the Temple) when fuch are loudly cryed unto by another Angel from the Altar, who had Power over Fire, *v.* 18. or Saints of a Lower Rank, fuch as the Ancient *Levites* were, who Miniftred at the Altar, although not in the Temple: Then will the Vintage of the Earth be Reaped, *v.* 19. by the fpace of two hundred Miles, *v.* 20. And then the Viols are poured out, *Rev.* 15. 1. And when the Watch-men upon Mount *Ephraim* (or Perfons of a Lower Spirit) fhall Cry, *Arife ye, and let us go up to Sion,* Jer. 31. 6. The Lord will then bring them from the North, *v.* 8. and they fhall Tremble from the Weft, *Hof.* 11. 9, 10. Uniting with *Judah* againft the *Philiftines, Ifa.* 11. 13, 14. and againft the Sons of *Greece, Zech.* 9. 13. feeking the Lord, and *David* their King, *Hof.* 3. 5. and being encouraged thereunto by *Abner,* or fome chief Leader, who fometimes was for *Ifhbofheth,* 2 *Sam.* 3. 17, 18. Thus when the Elect fhall cry (or they whofe Actual Saint-fhip is not fo clear) Chrift will avenge them fpeedily, *Luke* 18. 7, 8.

13. When the Priefts (or choifeft Saints) do weep between the Porch and Altar, as not being in the Temple (which yet they had a Right to enter into) but now are come out from thence, *Joel* 2. 17. then will the Lord be Jealous for his Land, *v.* 18. and remove far off from them his Northern Army, *v.* 20. when the Old Heavens (or Prefent ftate of vifible Churches) fhall feem departed, as a fcrowl when it is Rolled together, *Rev.* 6. 14. or when their Beauty is defaced, in Order unto a Change, then will the Great Day of Chrift's wrath come, *v.* 17. And when the four Beafts (or former Church-Officers) are not mentioned as before, but ohely Twenty four Elders, or Saints- at large, *Rev.* 11. 16. The Temple of God in Heaven will foon be Opened, *v.* 19. Nor will that fmoak Offend mine Eyes, wherewith the Temple will be fo filled, as that no Man will be able to enter into it; that being one Sign immediately fore-going the feven laft Plagues, *Rev.* 15. 8. or Seventh Trumpet's Sounding. When fuch as fear the

P Lord

106   *The Parable of the Ten Virgins Opened.*

Lord (in a way of Diſtinction from Ordinary Church-members at ſuch a time) ſpeak oft each to other, *Mal.* 3. 16. God's Day is near, *Mal.* 4. 1, 2.

14. When *Iſrael's* Adverſaries ſhall Divide, each one being ſet againſt his fellow, then is Salvation near at hand. Thus *David's* Kingdom over all *Iſrael* was Uſhered in by *Abner's* falling out with *Iſhboſheth*. Thus *Ammon* and *Moab* (having joyntly ſlain the *Edomites*) did help to Deſtroy each other in that Valley of *Jehoſhaphat*, 2 *Chron.* 20. 13. who were diſtinguiſhed by their reſpective Idols, viz. *Chemoſh* and *Milcom* or *Molech*, 1 *Kings* 11. 7. which latter ſignifies a King, and the former is ſuppoſed to be *Bacchus*. Thus ſhall *Lot's* Children (whom *Aſhur* helpeth) be done unto, as were the *Midianites*, *Pſal.* 83. 8, 9. when every Man's Sword was ſet againſt his fellow, *Judg.* 7. 22. Thus ſhall it be with *Gog* and *Magog*, *Ezek.* 38. 21. or with the People that fight againſt *Jeruſalem*, *Zech.* 14. 12, 13. which is the cleaving of Mount *Olivet* in the midſt, *v.* 4. and then the Lord ſhall come, and all the Saints with him, *v.* 5. This will conclude that Earthquake, *Rev.* 11. 13. which Uſhereth in the Third Woe (or laſt Trumpet of ſeven) quickly, *v.* 14.

15. When Tidings out of the Eaſt or North ſhall Trouble the laſt Northern King, *Dan.* 11. 44. then will be the time of the End, *v.* 40. both of that Northern King, *v.* 45. and *Iſrael's* Trouble, *Dan.* 12. 1. by reaſon of their Prince's interpoſing on their behalf. Which King is there Deſcribed, Partly, by his being from the North (as the *Aſſyrian* was, *Iſa.* 14. 31.) or at a further Diſtance from the Sun, *viz.* a groſſer Intereſt than his Confederates were: Partly, by his entring into the Glorious Land, *Dan.* 11. 41. which fairly hints his being the ſame with that *Aſſyrian*, *Iſa.* 8, 7, 8. Partly, by his Uniting with the King of the South, againſt the former King there, *Dan.* 11. 40. which King of the South may be a more Refined Intereſt, (or ſomewhat nearer to the Sun,) and poſſibly may be *Ezekiel's Gog* (whoſe Name in *Hebrew* ſignifieth *Covered* or *Diſguiſed*,) and with whom *Magog* is United, whoſe Name doth ſignifie *Uncovered*, *Ezek.* 38. 2. both which are Tartar'd, *v.* 21. as is the *Aſſyrian* and his Confederates, *Iſa.* 10. 26. Partly, by *Edom's* eſcaping out of his hand, together with *Moab*, and the chief of the Children of *Ammon*, *Dan.* 11. 41. or not being dealt ſo Rigorouſly with by him, as others may: And Partly, by his having Power over the Treaſures of Gold and Silver, *Dan.* 11. 43. juſt as the *Aſſyrian* boaſteth, *Iſa.* 10. 14. But tidings out of the Eaſt and North will Trouble him, and make him Furious, *Dan.* 11. 44. and ſoon after that comes *Iſrael's* full Redemption, *Dan.* 12. 1. All which (I grant) doth ultimately relate unto the Literal Jews, in their own Land, as

Zech.

Zech. 12. 9. but do believe, we Gentiles (firſt) ſhall meet with Their Temptations and Deliverances. Theſe are the more immediate (Providential) Antecedents of Chriſt's Coming in the Latter days. To which I will but add one more, as followeth.

16. When there ſhall be a General warning given, not to Comply with the Beaſt at ſuch a time, for fear of being thereby brought into a preſent ſtate of viſible Reprobation, *Rev.* 14. 9, 10, 11. then comes that dreadful Judgment, which firſt beginneth at God's Houſe, or with the Harveſt, *v.* 14, 15, 16. and Ends with others, *viz.* the Vintage, *v.* 19. This ſeemeth chiefly to be the Cry here made. VVhich warning is thus Deſcribed there. 'Tis after the Return of *Babylon*'s Captivity, *Rev.* 14. 1. and ſinging thereupon, *v.* 2, 3. as the beginning of *Babylon*'s Judgment, *v.* 7, 8. 'Tis alſo after the Revival of that Beſtial intereſt once more; elſe would there be no need of ſuch a preſent warning. 'Tis a little before the Harveſt, or Chriſt's Viſitation of his own Houſe, *Rev.* 14. 15. It doth not thus ſadly threaten ſuch, who onely have the Number of that Beaſts Name upon them, or his Name; *viz.* ſome more Remote (though Natural) Relation thereunto, ſuch as the Owning of their Acts of Office is; which conſequently doth own their Church; yet may not this viſibly unſaint a Man, as being not overcome till after the Vintage, *Rev.* 15. 2. But thoſe are now ſadly threatned, who worſhip the Beaſt and his Image, or who receive his Mark in their Hand or Fore-head, *Rev.* 14. 9. who do more plainly own him by VVords or Practices, *viz.* either with their Fore-head, the Emblem of a Bold Profeſſion; or with their Hand, the Inſtrument of Action, which Hand is alſo capable of being *Covered*. And ſuch a kind of warning may be this *Cry*, which *Cry* is further Deſcribed in my Text, by ſeveral Arguments or Qualifications. And ſo,

It is exceeding Loud, as that word [*Cry*] importeth; and therefore it needs muſt be ſome General or Publick Notification.

It alſo is a Voice as well as Cry, as that which ſaith, B*ehold*, &c. therefore it is not barely of a Providential Nature.

It alſo is relating to a former Practice, or onely putteth upon going out again to meet the Bridegroom, which hath been done before.

Yet it is not Impetuous or Confuſed, as the *Greek* word ſometimes ſignifieth; but is onely made up of Demonſtration and Beſeeching.

It alſo ſtartleth, or is ſome way Effectual; ſince thereupon the Virgins are Awakened, and do Ariſe.

And it is made at Midnight, after the Bridegroom's tarrying; VVhich Circumſtance of Time doth lead me to the next Enquiry.

Queſt. 4. VVhat

The Parable of the Ten Virgins Opened.

Quest. 4. VVhat are we to understand by Midnight, as being that by which this *Cry* is partly to be known?

Answ. 1. Midnight is a time of thickest Darkness, in which no Man can clearly see or know, but onely Deem or Feel, as did those Mariners at such a time, *Acts* 27. 27, 28. Therefore did not the *Egyptians* stir so long as such Darkness was upon them, *Exod.* 10. 22, 23. And such a Darkness have we felt. He that could sometimes say, *Loe, this is He*, *John* 1. 29, 30. could not so clearly see him afterward, when he was in Prison, *Mat.* 11. 2, 3. *Peter* knew Christ at Liberty more than the Common People did, *Mat.* 16. 14, 15, 16. till Christ was Apprehended, and then he knew him not, *Mat.* 26. 74. it being then about that time of the Night with him, both in the Letter and Mystery. How have Professors been Feeling after God (like those poor Heathens, *Acts* 17. 27.) with reference unto some Truths and Duties which yet have not been far from every of them. And at that time this *Cry* is made.

2. Midnight is therefore also a time of greatest Terror, or being Troubled, *Job* 34. 20. which Aggravated *Pharaoh*'s last Plague, because it was at Midnight, *Exod,* 12. 29. Yea, *Boaz* was then afraid of *Ruth,* *Ruth* 3. 8. who afterwards became his Wife. And such a Midnight have we seen. How have some been afraid, so as to Lie, *Isa.* 57. 11. as if the Enemy were ready to Destroy, and where is the Fury of the Oppressor, *Isa.* 51. 13? when *Ashur* did but onely Threaten, how did poor *Hezekiah* rend his Cloaths, *Isa.* 37. 1. who might have Laugh'ed him to scorn, *v.* 22. Yea, Christ himself at such a time was thought to be an Evil Spirit, *Mat.* 14. 25, 26. and such a call to Duty as now is Owned, was then Affrighting. There was no Lion in the way of Duty, but onely Satan, who would have fled, *James* 4. 7. if stedfastly Resisted, 1 *Pet.* 5. 8, 9. But if the Earth shall quake at Midnight, *Acts* 16. 25, 26. some unbelieving ones are almost frighted out of their wits, as was that Jaylor then, *v.* 27. I wish they may resemble him, *v.* 34.

3. Midnight is a time of Deep and General sleep; therefore that Harlot arose at Midnight to lay her Dead Child in the others Bosom, 1 *Kings* 3. 20. which was not perceived till the Morning, *v.* 21. which Depth of sleep hath Generally been upon our Virgins, and in like manner it hath appeared. How have the VVise been cheated (by their Companions) of Living Truths and former Quickning influences? How have the Living embraced the Dead, *Isa.* 8. 19. because there was no Light (no Morning) in them, *v.* 20. Nor will the Matter be Decided easily, there being no witness, 1 *Kings* 3. 18. or common

Reason

The Parable of the Ten Virgins Opened.

Reason by which to Judge. But if the Living Child (upon a fresh Temptation) shall be in danger of being slain, 1 *Kings* 3. 25. then will its Natural Mother be discerned by the Yerning of her Bowels, *v.* 26. and scarcely otherways; no rbut by such as *Solomon*.

4. Midnight is a time of Lothness to arise, *Luke* 11. 7. unto a Friend, *v.* 5. though one be then awake, till more than Friendship shall constrain it, *v.* 8. And such a Time our Eyes have seen. How meltingly have some of Christ's professed Spouses been moved by him to Open to him, *Cant.* 5. 2. whom they call Friend, *v.* 16. But they have put him off, with telling him, that they were all undrest, in Bed, and should defile their lately washen Feet, (or Dirty themselves by outward Sufferings) by Opening to him at such a Time, *Cant.* 5. 3. They were so far awakened, as to Hear and Parley with him: They were not absolutely Benummed or Disabled by Bonds or Sickness, but that they could have Risen then: Nor did they deny the thing, onely the Time was not Yet come, *Hag.* 1. 2. *Is this your Kindness to your Friend,* 2 Sam. 16. 17? But they impute it to his unseasonableness. Nor will ought but a *Cry* make them Arise; who then, perhaps, may Open to him when he is gone, and may not find him, till greater Sufferings have made them sick of Love, *Cant.* 8. 6, 7, 8.

5. Midnight is a Time for *Sampson* (before his Hair was cut) to Rise and do Exploits, *Judg.* 16. 3. For *David* (or Men after God's own Heart) to Rise, and to give thanks, *Psal.* 119. 62. For *Paul* (a Prisoner of Jesus Christ) to Pray and Sing, *Acts* 16. 25. who (when he was at Liberty) continued his Discourse till Midnight, *Acts* 20. 7. whilst one of his sleepy Hearers had like to have never wakened more, *v.* 9. This also hath been to be Observed by us, in our late Midnight. Some have been strengthened (as *Sampson* was) to quit themselves of those Temptations, which others thought insuperable. Some have been able (in a time of saddest Darkness), to give thanks (with *David*) at the remembrance of God's Holiness, as is their Duty, *Psal.* 30. 4. Some have Lift up their Voice and Sung, when there was no other Light, save that of God's Majesty in the Fires, *Isa.* 24. 14, 15. Some also have thought it meet to continue their Speech (with *Paul*) till such a time, so long as Liberty hath been afforded: Oh that such also could Revive that *Eutychus*, who being sleepy at such a Time, hath fallen into a seeming state of Death out of a Window (or means of Light) three Stories High.

6. Midnight is no time to look for any Notice of a Friend's or Bridegroom's Coming, but rather for such a *Cry* as then was made in *Egypt*, Exod. 12. 29, 30. And such a surcease of Expectations, or such a

Midnight,

Midnight, hath manifestly been upon us. The Bridegroom's near approach hath not been Credited by those who formerly went out to meet him. That Witness hath been wholly waved, as being thought unedifying. It hath Offended some, when but encouraged unto a Sober hope, till Providence should cast the Scale. We have been cast behind in some Men's Apprehensions, as *Israel* in Reality was through others unbelief. Yea, Sober intimations of the Bridegroom's Coming have been (like Thieves) cryed out against, as being Dangerous, or tending to Rob Men of Estate and Liberty. Thus hath a Midnight been Apparent in our Times; and such a Dispensation is that by which the *Cry* is partly to be known, as having been already made.

Quest. 5. Why is a *Cry* Now made, more than at their first going forth?

Answ. 1. Because the Virgins Now are fast asleep, who formerly had been awake. They do not stir, as heretofore, therefore Christ Calls them; they cannot stir untill awakened, therefore Christ Cryeth to them. 'Tis not an Ordinary Voice that can be heard by one asleep; And thus Christ suits his Notice unto their Necessity. He might indeed have bid them now sleep on, as *Mat.* 26. 45. but their Condition Cryeth unto him, to which his Crying Notice Ecchoeth. He knoweth that the Wiser Virgins Spirit is willing, therefore he gives them one awakening more, *Mat.* 26. 41. He knew this Cry would have some rouzing Efficacy; and whilst there is any hope, he is for the use of means, *Luke* 13. 8, 9. Some would have thought it hard, if he had taken them at this Advantage; therefore he takes this course to stop their mouths, *Rom.* 3. 19. His Tarrying was a great Temptation to them, which is removed by his *Cry*. How sadly is the straining of his Voice requited by others snorting!

2. Because they now are put upon the Repetition of a former Practice; which in a Case of this Nature needs a *Cry*. One may do something once, in way of Frolick, which is not Seconded, because it was not thought to be a Duty: And thus some serve the Lord, in way of real Humour, or apprehended Supererogation, who therefore counts its expected Repetition to be unreasonable. One may do that at first, which is recalled upon Second thoughts, till quickned up by fresh instructing Opportunity. However being wearied by their former walk, and having found that Rest is good, they might be somewhat stiff, and loth to Rise, unless some Louder *Cry* doth force them to it. Yea, having once gone out before, they might suppose it needless to go forth again; so sparing we are of Multiplyed pains, save in a way of our own choosing, especially since Christ here takes no Notice of their former

Action,

Action, and since it hath been dis-continued: Both which are strong inducements to sit still at present, *Isa.* 58.3. *Cant.* 5. 3. unless a Call be of a *Crying* Nature.

3. The Season wherein this *Cry* is made doth make it Necessary.

1. As the Midnight is a time of greatest Deadness or Inactivity, both in respect of Inward Liveliness, and Outward Motives thereunto. At Man's awakening (in the Morning) he is most like to God, *Psal.* 17. 15. as to his being Active; but Night (especially Midnight) is Man's time of Rest, *Psal.* 104. 23. Though Beasts of Prey are then at work, *v.* 20, 21. whom in the Morning the Righteous shall have Dominion over, *Psal.* 49. 14. Time also was, when all the Virgins (at their first going forth) were much Encouraged from without. Their Governours began to say, *Jerusalem's Inhabitants shall be our strength,* Zech. 12. 5. they walked then from strength to strength, (increasing in their Number) as they went to *Sion*, *Psal.* 84. 7. God did then own them by his Providence, as Heathens did Confess, *Psal.* 126.2. enough to make the Old Man Lively. But it hath since been otherwise; therefore a *Cry* is Needful.

2. As Midnight is a time of greatest Darkness, especially in Tempestuous Seasons, such as that is, wherein this *Cry* is made. These Virgins (at the first) did seem to have no want of Light, but then were fully Satisfied, as to their Present Work and Duty: Their Loins were girt, and their Lamps burning, which made their way exceeding plain, to what it hath been, since the failing of those Affections by which the Judgment of most Men is guided. How easily then were all Objections Answered; which would not since have been thought strong again, but that the former Light (of General Harmony) is now Eclipsed, which then was clear? Nor can it be denyed, but that the Work (at first) was in it self more Obvious, as will appear upon the Opening of this Latter going out; In which regard, a *Cry* is needful, to clear that Eye, which hath of late been so dim-sighted.

3. As Midnight is a time of greatest Hardship and visible Danger. The Air is then Raw and Cold, which tender Virgins cannot bear without the hazard of their Health; and therefore such have pleaded, they needs must Die if sent to Prison, not knowing that such a moist Cellar is Christ's House of Wine, *Cant.* 2. 4. Yea, Lions then are wont to Roar, *Psal.* 104. 2. 21. which nothing but a Louder *Cry* will make poor feeble Virgins not to fear. Thieves also are then abroad, therefore Men judge it not their Duty (but their sin) to walk at Midnight, without a more than Ordinary Call, *viz.* a *Cry*: Though all are set (by Christ) upon their Watch at such a time, *Mark* 13. 35. 37. which

one would think is Call sufficient. But we are apt to fit our Duty for the Meridian of our Interest, and not to venture out if self-concernments lye at Stake, unless a greater Cry be made within, as sometimes was in *Egypt*, which made them all to rise at Midnight, *Exod.* 10. 29, 30. though Robbed by it, *v.* 36.

Quest. 6. What's meant by those words, *Go ye out to meet him?*

Answ. 1. These Virgins were Now Asleep; and Going is an Act of one awakened: which therefore intimateth the Rouzing up of drouzy Habits into awakened Exercises. That Rising Sun will have the Sap of Radical Dispositions drawn up into the Branches of Respective Actions. There is no visible Difference between the Wise and Foolish (the Dead and Living) while asleep; whom Christ will now Distinguish, by putting them upon Motion. He is content to eat his Spouses Honey-comb, together with her Honey, *Cant.* 5. 1. but Roots alone will not content him, when also Fruits are not laid up for him, as is expected from a Spouse, *Cant.* 7. 13. He therefore hath called them out of Darkness into Light, that they might shew forth his Vertues, 1 *Pet.* 2. 9. and not onely have them Dormant in their Habits. This is their Duty alway; therefore he takes no Notice of their present slumbring, but puts them on immediate Action, or Going out to meet him, as they would have him Own them.

2. These Virgins had gone out Before, who yet are bid to go out Now; which therefore intimates The Repetition of their former Practice with fresh Amendments. He doth not check them for what they had done, nor is he yet fully satisfied with it, who else would not have *Vain* (or *Needless*) Repetitions, *Mat.* 6. 7. Their First going out was Warrantable, but not faultless; else should no place have been sought for the Second, as in Relation to that first Covenant, *Heb.* 8. 7. That first was from *John Baptist*'s Cry; the Influence whereof must first Decrease, before the Bridegroom's Voice is heard. Yea, that at first was (mostly) upon the first *Adam*'s Motion, whose weakness must first appear; then comes the Son himself, as in Relation to the Law and Gospel, *Rom.* 8. 3. Indeed that first going out was very Mercenary; therefore he putteth upon this Second, to try the Nobleness of their Principle. However, Christ is for a Second Edition, which usually is Corrected; and his best Wine is kept by him untill the last, *John* 2. 10.

3. The Virgins (at their first going out) did verily Expect the Bridegroom's Coming then, as their Design to Meet him signified, who Now are bid go out again, together with an Additional Notification of his Coming: which therefore intimateth, The Re-assuming of their former Expectation,

The Parable of the Ten Virgins Opened. 113

Expectation, upon a fresh and surer Ground. They took *John Baptist* to be the Bridegroom; wherein he checks their over-hastiness, by telling them, that his Own Coming was not till now to be Expected. Their former Hope was meerly grounded upon Providence; he therefore now more plainly expounds the Scriptures, unto the Revival of their Dying Expectations, as *Luke* 24. 27. He taketh pleasure in his Peoples Hope, *Psal.* 147. 11. whose very Expectation shall not Perish, *Psal.* 9. 18. therefore he catcheth at sinking *Peter*, though his first Confidence was not a grounded Faith, *Mat.* 14. 28, 29, 30, 31. They were now Tossing to and fro (or Nodding) by Reason of the Bridegroom's Tarrying; therefore he giveth them at last this stedfast Anchor.

4. One's going out to Meet another, is both a Token of Respect, *Gen.* 9. 1. and a sign of Longing to behold him with the first, *Numb.* 23. 15. which therefore intimateth his present Expectations of that Nature from them, with reference unto himself. He then expecteth to be Worshipped by all the gods, both Men and Angels, *Psal.* 97. 7. and Saints will Honour him at such a time, *Rev.* 19 7. which Time is therefore hinted by this *Cry*. But chiefly is this desired by him, as going out to Meet him is a signal of their Longing to behold him with the first; and therefore he that Heareth, is bid say, *Come*, *Rev.* 22. 17. and to evince it by this Going. Which cannot but be readily performed by the Saints, with reference unto their Lord and Friend, their Brother, Husband, and Blessed Saviour. Nor may it irk them to go forth a little, since he is pleased to come the greater part of the way, by far, onely requiring their meeting him in the Air, who comes to them from Heaven, out of Respect and Love.

5. These words import their going out of something, in Order to their Meeting of the Bridegroom. Which things then to be gone out of, are as followeth.

1. They are to go Out of all their sinful Defilements of a Common Nature, which hath been their Duty alway, 2 *Cor.* 7. 1. but Now is so by way of Eminency. And if the Name of Christ obligeth hereunto, 2 *Tim.* 2. 17. much more the Notice of his Coming as a Bridegroom, and as a Judge. His Day will be upon the Lofty, *Isa.* 2. 12. therefore Go Out of Pride. The Meek will then most probably be hidden, *Zeph.* 2. 3. therefore Go Out of Passion. The Time will Now be very short, *Rev.* 10. 16. therefore Go Out of Earthly-mindedness, 1 *Cor.* 7. 29. 30, 31. The Face of the Covering will be Destroyed, *Isa.* 29. 7. therefore Go Out of Formality. The Lord alone will be Exalted, *Isa.* 2. 17. therefore Go Out of Slavish Fear and Fleshly Confidence,

Q   *v.* 22.

v. 22. A sin of meer Omission will send some then to Hell, *Mat.* 25. 41, 42. therefore Go Out of Negative Christianity. Preachers and others will then be termed Workers of Iniquity, *Mat.* 7.22,23. therefore Go Out of bare Material Duty, into its Life, and Power, and Spirituality.

2. They are to Go Out of *Babylon*, as far as may be from the Beast, especially from the Whore, or Antichrist in his more Spiritual appearances. This Latter was a Duty alway, the neglect whereof was never so severely punished as Now it will be. Now, Temporal Judgments will be entailed upon Spiritual Sins, and it is then High Time to Go Out thence, *Rev.* 18. 4. Yea, every one that is then found in *Babylon* shall be thrust through, *Isa.* 13. 15. therefore let none stand still, but let *Jerusalem* come into their Remembrance, *Jer.* 51. 50. And though the Beast's Name (as that of Priests) may falsly be continued unto some; yea, though some still retain the Number of his Name, yet may both these escape that Brand of visible Reprobates, which then will be the Portion of his Worshippers, and such as do receive his Mark; or more down-right and Manifest Compliers with that Interest, *Rev.* 14. 9, 10, 11. Were these things rightly understood as to their Sence and Time, enquiries of that Nature would not be thought unuseful.

3. They are to Go Out of Privacy into an Open Testimony, as they had done before, at their first going forth. This also was an Ancient Duty, the Neglecters whereof (in times of utmost Danger) are threatned by Christ himself to be Denyed by him, as being the Deniers of him, *Mat.* 10. 27, 28. 33. Upon the first Rise of the Man of Sin, the Woman then fled into the Wilderness, *Rev.* 12. 14. as that denoted her want of former Outward Glory, but not from fear of Bloody Cruelty, (as *Brightman* well Observes upon the place) onely to shew, that such Apostates did falsly call themselves Christ's visible Churches. Which also followeth upon the Privacy of Church-worship, which is a Worshipping of the Beast, unto the Clouding of Professors Saint-ship, and the destroying of a proper Accident, *viz.* Visibility, which is inseparable from a Churches Essence: And though Repentance may recover Saint-ship, yet such a failing layeth Churches wast, till New Erected, and which may prove to their Advantage.

4. They are to Go Out of those Old Heavens, which then must Pass away (at least, be changed) together with the Earth of Civil Constitutions. This Going out of Churches is Warrantable in the fore-named case, yea, and a Duty; but at this time there will be no visible Churches to continue in, although Church-state may still remain. Thus was it

with

The Parable of the Ten Virgins Opened.

with the Jewish Church, at Christ's first Coming: Thus will it be with Temple-state, at his next Personal Coming, *Rev.* 21. 22. Yea, thus it was with present Constitutions, a little before his Coming in *Constatine's* Time, *Rev.* 6: 13, 14. and as the sixth Seal concluded, so will the sixth Trumpet. We Now are in the Expectation of those New Heavens, *Isa.* 65. 17. and then the former shall not be Remembred. Upon the Reviving of Temple-work, the Temple is said to be then Founded, *Hag.* 2. 18. therefore we then must have New modelling. Therefore we Read of no Beasts (or Pastors) just when the Seventh Trumpet soundeth, *Rev.* 11. 15, 16. as having lately Disappeared since, *Rev.* 14. 3. untill *Rev.* 15. 7. Now, Officers and Churches are wont to go together. Wh ch is more plainly hinted by Christ's Resolving to spew those *Laodiceans* out, *Rev.* 3. 16. who were the Last of those Typical *Asian* Churches under the Dragon's or Satan's Dispensation, *Rev.* 2. 10. 13. who must be laid aside a little before the setting up of Christ's own Throne, *Rev.* 3. 21.

5. They are to Go Out of Lower Good attainments into an Higher state of Evangelical Perfection. Their Childish things must now be put away, as 1 *Cor.* 13. 11. their Wheat must out-grow its Blade and empty Ear, *Mark* 4. 28. they should endeavour to be more than Babes in Christ, else will they want that Wedding Garment of an Healthful Appetite for Christ's strong Meat, *Heb.* 5. 14. when he shall make his Marriage-Supper, *Mat.* 22. 4. 12. They must be Accurate as to the Matter of Duty; all which must diligently be added unto Faith, 2 *Pet.* 1. 5. Yea, both Obedience and Believing must be compleated, by having Respect unto the Scripture as their Rule, God's Glory as their Highest Aim, and the Second *Adam*'s Spirit as their Root and Principle. And thus as Natural Beauty consists of Integrality, Symmetry, and Complexion; so is a Gospel-Saint made up of Body, Soul, and Spirit; or Nature, Animality, and Spirituality: as *Salem*, *Sion*, and *Millo* were all United into one *Jerusalem* in *David*'s Time, 2 *Sam.* 5. 6, 7. 9. which therefore was called a City Compact, *Psal.* 122. 3. and the Perfection of Beauty, *Psal.* 50. 2. as *Sion* was a Type of Gospel-Saints, especially in *David*'s Time, and when he Ruleth over all *Israel*, which fully Answereth unto the Seventh Trumpet's founding, *Rev.* 11. 15.

6. In Order unto all which before mentioned, They are to Go Out of Themselves at such a time, and every of their self-concernments into a Self-denying frame of Spirit, else will they neither follow Christ, *Mat.* 16. 24. nor yet Prepare to Meet him. *Amos* 4. 12. They must go out of sinful self, else will they not say to their Defilements, *Get you hence*, *Isa.* 30. 22. They must go out of Worldly self, else will they

The Parable of the Ten Virgins Opened.

not leave their *Babylonish* Accommodations, or felf-fecuring Privacy in times of Danger. Yea, they muſt go out of Spiritual felf in fome Refpects, elfe will it irk them to leave their Old Heavens, and to count all things lofs for that which is more Excellent, *Phil.* 3. 8. Such muſt not then talk of Ceiled Houfes, *Hag.* 1. 4. nor yet receive Honour o e of another, *John* 5. 44. nor value Man's Judgment, 1 *Cor.* 4. 3. nor Judge of Things or Perſons, according to Appearance, *John* 7. 24. nor yet call ought a Priviledge, fave as it is of Chriſt's Appointment, and no way interfering with our Duty.

Queſt. 7. Why will Chriſt have the Virgins thus to Meet him, by Going Out?

Anſw. 1. That fo they might be Throughly thus Awakened, which is one Branch of Going Out, and by their Going is Effected: Since, if the Sleeper's Rifing and ſtanding up doth tend to his Awakening, *Eph.* 5. 14. *Iſa.* 51. 17. much more his Going alfo, in this Moral fence, as in the Letter, *Mat.* 26. 45, 46. By which awakening here, is meant the Actuating of that Light and Grace which formerly had been afleep; and which their Walking doth Accomplifh. The Powerful Repetition of former Duties muſt needs awaken more and more, efpecially when there are freſh Additions of a Rouzing Nature, fuch as this Second Going Out affordeth. He that Walks out at Midnight, will rub his Eyes, efpecially when going in untrodden paths, and lying open unto utmoſt Danger. He alfo muſt needs be Throughly wakened, whofe way is up-hill, and full of ſtumbling ſtones; fuch as that eminently is (if rightly Walked in,) which leadeth out of thefe Old Heavens, and Lower Good attainments.

2. That fo his Coming Now might herein (as in other things) Refemble his Perfonal Coming at the laſt; when thofe Alive fhall be caught up into the Air to Meet him, 1 *Theſ.* 4. 17. and in the Clouds, together with thofe Newly Raifed from the fleep of Death, *v.* 16. being ſtrangely Changed, 1 *Cor.* 15. 52. There, muſt be a Meeting Now, as will be Then: which Meeting is Now at Midnight, as it will Then be in Clouds and Darknefs: Sleepers will Then awake, fo will they Now; fome unto fhame, and fome to Everlaſting Life, *Dan.* 12. 2. Chriſt will Then Come in Perfon, and with the Laſt Trump of All, 1 *Cor.* 15. 52. as Now in his Returning Witneffes, and with the Laſt Trump of Seven, *Rev.* 11. 15. There muſt be Now a Going Out of Lower things, as will be Then a being caught up into the Air, out of what is Defigned to the Flames, and into an Higher, Clearer, Purer State, and more immediate Communion with the Lord, till thefe Old Heavens and Earth be done away.

3. That

word) did Re-aſſume that Work which had been laid aſide through former Diſappointments, *Luke* 5. 5. Yea, bare Going out to Meet another, doth Evidence Reſpect and Longing to behold him; both which are Signs of Honour. Eſpecially when ſuch Go out, not onely from Satan and the Man of Sin, but alſo from deareſt ſelf-concernments, both Natural and Spiritual; or when that is Accounted Loſs for Chriſt, which formerly hath been Accounted Gain, *Phil.* 3. 7. ſuch as our Outward Intereſt is, much more ſome Higher Priviledges.

4. That ſo his Harbinger might not out-ſhine himſelf, in that Regard. The People went Out of Old *Jeruſalem* into the Wildeinneſs to Meet *John Baptiſt*, *Mat.* 3. 3. 5. So did theſe Virgins at their firſt going out, ſuppoſing *John* to have been Chriſt himſelf, *John* 1. 25. Yea, *Iſrael* went out of ſome Accommodations, when they went out of *Egypt*, *Numb.* 11. 5. who yet fell ſhort of *Canaan*, *Numb.* 14. 29, 30. Now, ſhall the Servant be above his Lord? Or ſhall the Morning-ſtar ſeem brighter than the Sun? Shall we Go Out to ſee a ſhaken Reed, *Mat.* 11. 7. and not much more to Meet this Rock of Ages, who never failed, *Iſa.* 42. 4? Shall we go out of *Egypt* to Moun, *Sinai*, and not from thence to *Sion*, the City of the Living God, that Heavenly *Jeruſalem*, *Heb.* 12. 22? Thus we are apt to prefer Inferiour Governours before this King, *Mal.* 1. 8. 14. but he now ſtandeth upon his terms, and will count thoſe unworthy of him, who Love ought More than him, *Mat.* 10. 37. who leave not All when he Calls for their going out to Meet him.

5. To ſave them from that Harm which thoſe lie open unto who keep within at ſuch a time, in Competition with this Going out. Sleep in a Moral ſence is alway Dangerous, and much more Now; *Mark* 13. 36. therefore he would awaken them by Going Out. And their firſt going out, would onely Aggravate their Preſent ſitting ſtill, *Gal.* 5. 7. therefore he puts them upon this Neceſſary Repetition. The Death of Hope betrayeth into ſlumbring; therefore he would Revive their former Expectation of Meeting with him, upon their going out this Second time. They who Deſpiſe him, will lightly be eſteemed, 1 *Sam.* 2. 30. therefore he Calls for their Reſpect, by Going out to Meet him.

him. He that is Wicked at that time may juftly then be given up, *Dan.* 12. 10. and as it was ever Dangerous to keep in *Babylon's* fins, fo (at fome fuch a time) in Old *Jerufalem's* ftate, *Jer.* 21. 9. Yea, Babes may then not be Admitted into the Temple Opened, much lefs felf-loving Privateers. Therefore Chrift Calls for Going out to meet him in every of thofe regards.

6. That fo he might confult for their being Crowned at his Coming, (and in a way of feeming Righteoufnefs) becaufe of their being then found Working, who formerly had been afleep. Satan Rocks men afleep; Chrift bids them Watch: and he that fets on Work will Pay the Workman's Wages, as fuch are Actually employed, juft at the time of Payment. The Bridegroom's Favours will be very Rich; but none fhall Wear them, becaufe of former Service, fave as they Now go out afrefh, and thereby evidence their Love of his Appearing, whom then the Righteous Judge will Crown therewith, 2 *Tim.* 14. 8. Therefore this *Ifaac* Calls for Going out, *Gen.* 27. 3. and not fo much from Love of what is brought, as that his Soul might Blefs the Bringer, *v.* 4. And *Jacob's* timely Kid, *v.* 9. will be more Acceptable and Effectual, *v.* 27. than *Efau's* Venifon Afterwards, *v.* 30. 33. though fauced with Tears, *v.* 34. This will clear up the Righteoufnefs of his Rewarding Wifer Virgins, and Waving others, who do not then go out as heretofore.

7. To Intereft Obedient Virgins in the Benefit of their very Going out to Meet him, whofe Labour and want of fleep will be fufficiently Requited by their very Walking. How chearful is an Active Spirit when rouzed up, whom fleep or fitting ftill makes dull and fad! And if one fingle Act of Duty doth Refrefh, much more will Repetitions of that Nature Chear a Gracious Heart. It alfo cafeth a Spoufes Heart, if her being fick of Love may any way be evidenced, or made known to her Beloved, *Cant.* 5. 8. which Going out to Meet him doth evince. Yea, One's very going out to Meet him as he Cometh, is to be caught up from Earth into the Air, or part of One's way to Heaven. There can be no Peace in fin; nor Singing, till out of *Babylon,* nor grounded Satisfaction in finful Privacy; nor in Chrift's Temple, if he be Abfent; nor in a Childifh Spiritual ftate, Compared with the fulnefs of that Joy which doth Accompany one's being Called out from thence into a nearer Union and Communion with the Bridegroom, by going out to meet him.

8. To Work them for that Thing, 2 *Cor.* 5. 5. or make them Meet to be Partakers of that Inheritance, *Col.* 1. 12. which he hath then to give. Then every Eye fhall fee him, *Rev.* 1. 7. therefore they muft

be

be wakened. Their Priviledges will be then Restored; therefore their Duty also must be Repeated, and Hope Revived. That Heavenly Kingdom will not be Inherited by Flesh and Blood, 1 *Cor*. 15.50. therefore they must be Changed, *v*. 52. by Going out. They will be then Cloathed with Change of Raiment, but therefore their filthy Garments will first be taken away, *Zech*. 3.4. Then *Babylon* will be no more, *Rev*. 18.21. to their Rejoycing, *v*. 20. who are come Out from thence, *v*.4. They will be then Confessed by him, *Mat*. 10.32. therefore they must not be Deniers of him by sinful Privacy. They must be emptied of other things to make room for what is more Excellent. And if they were not got above what is combustible, they would not so Glorifie God in the Fires as they shall then do, and Sing because of his dreadful Majesty, *Isa*. 24.15.

9. Because he Longs to see them (and their Graces) with the first: therefore he comes to meet with them, and puts them upon Going out to meet with him. He doth long bear in mind the Kindness of on's Youth, *Jer*. 2.2. because such are the first Ripe in the Fig-tree, at her first time, *Hos*. 9.10. especially when little Children (in their Bravery) go out at Midnight to Meet their Father, who hath been long Absent from them. He fain would hear his Spouses Voice, and see her Comely Countenance, *Cant*. 2.14. therefore he bids her Rise and come away, *v*. 10. affectionately protesting unto *Joshua*, *Zech*. 3.6. when lately come out of *Babylon*, *v*. 2. and Gloriously Attired, *v*. 4. what he will then do for him, if Persevering in those ways, *v*.7. Now, their Going out to Meet the Bridegroom, doth give him both to see them sooner, and in the Glory of that Beautifying self-denyal, which otherwise had not been seen if they had kept Within.

10. That so he might thus Try the Measure of their Strength, and Nature of their Oyl, in Order unto a plain Distinguishing between the Wise and Foolish Virgins, who hitherto were in Appearance all alike. They all went out at first, with Lamps and Vessels, wherein the Special Oyl was yet an hidden thing. And while the Bridegroom tarried they did all of them sleep and slumber; so that no visible Difference yet appeared. Yea, when the Cry is made, they All Arose and Trimmed their Lamps; nor do they seem to Differ, untill their Going out this Second time, and then they Part. This Second Transplantation will throughly Try the Nature of that Root, whose Leaves (yea, and some kind of Fruit) were formerly as fair as any other. This Casting of the Corn will fully sever it from Lighter Seed as well as Chaff; and, therefore Christ takes this Course to make that Precious, wherewith he then will sow the Earth afresh.

Use 1. At·

Use 1. Although the Bridegroom tarrieth beyond the Virgins Expectation, yet at the laſt it will be truly ſaid by ſome, *Behold, he Cometh*. The Truth of a Promiſe may not be therefore called in Queſtion ſimply becauſe it is Prolonged, and Mis-timed by the Generality of Profeſſors. Chriſt hath thus wiſely Ordered it, to ſtumble ſome, to Humble the moſt Knowing Men; and to Try all, whether their Faith be grounded on his Word, or on their own and others Apprehenſions. But yet the Viſion will not Lie, which doth Oblige our waiting for it, becauſe it will come ſurely and not tarry, *Hab*. 2. 3. Nor may a former Expectation have been a meer Deluſion, ſave as *John Baptiſt* hath been thought (by his Diſciples) to be the Bridegroom, who onely was the Bridegroom's Friend or Harbinger, *John* 3. 26. 28, 29. However, let God be True, though every Man ſhould prove a Lyar, at leaſt in part miſtaken, as being the Fruit of Darkneſs and Over-haſtineſs.

2. That Diſpenſation of the Bridegroom's Coming is very Notable, or much to be Obſerved, as doth appear from Chriſt's prefixing that Word [*Behold*] unto his Signification of its Near approach. And if that Night was much to be Obſerved, in which God brought his People out of *Egypt*, *Exod*. 12. 42. much more this Day, in which the Lord our Righteouſneſs will lead the Seed of *Iſrael* out of the North to their own Land, *Jer*. 23. 6, 7, 8. That was their firſt Redemption; this will be the ſame a Second Time, *Iſa*. 11. 11. Now, as Relapſes are moſt Dangerous, ſo Reſtaurations are moſt Remarkable. That was attended with following Checks and ſore Temptations in the Wilderneſs, but this will put the Gentile-Saints in full poſſeſſion of their own Land, untill the Jews Converſion. That onely was Afflicting to *Egyptian* Dragons, and not to any of the *Iſraelites*; but this will ſadly fall upon the Goats, or ſlothful Servants, and Fooliſh Virgins; which therefore is much more to be Obſerved by all ſorts of Perſons.

3. When all the Virgins have done looking for the Bridegroom, then is the ſureſt ground for our concluding his Near Approach, for then doth Chriſt himſelf affirm it, which formerly had onely been preſumed. Therefore he tarrieth untill ſome kind of falſe Alarm hath made the Generality to be Secure; and then, Behold, he comes indeed. What cauſe have all to ſtand continually upon their Watch, unleſs they mean to be ſurprized by him, whoſe very Coming is not known, ſave that it will be at the moſt unlikely time. How weak are they who therefore think the Time is not ſo nigh at hand, becauſe the preſent Expectation of it is not ſo General as heretofore it may have been. This doth beſpeak our Hearkning to that Cry, which giveth Notice of the Bridegroom's

The Parable of the Ten Virgins Opened.

groom's Coming when all the Virgins are fast asleep, at least wise not to count it therefore of no weight, since at some such a time the truest signification that yet ever was, will then be made.

4. Christ here doth give some further Notice of his present Coming besides that of his Harbinger, which seemeth to be more than was at his first Coming in the Flesh, and which is worth our taking Notice of. He came not then to Judge the World, *John* 12. 47. as now he doth, *Rev.* 11. 18. And shall a Judge shew more of Gentleness (as this Redundant warning hinteth) than did a Saviour? But though he now will Execute the Judges Office, yet doth he enter on it with a Saviours Heart: And therefore he doubly warneth Now, because his present Work will be more Dreadful. How loth is Christ that any at this day should Perish, 2 *Pet.* 3. 9.! How are we more engaged to him than were the *Pharisees,* who onely had *John Baptist*'s Cry: And if the Despisers of that single Invitation were then shut out for ever, *Luke* 14. 24. how can those Foolish Virgins hope to enter, who have out-stood a Second Notice. Therefore this Cry had need be heeded, which else will doubly call for Wrath and Vengeance upon its Disobeyers.

5. This Cry is made at Midnight, or when the Virgins are asleep: which further shews the Riches of his Grace, who waiteth for the fittest Time wherein to make its freeness Evident, especially since they had been Aakened once before, or when they first went out of *Babylon,* as is evinced from their Dreaming then, *Psal.* 126. 1. Indeed Christ bad Relapsing Slumberers to sleep on now, and take their Rest, to shew what they Deserved: But yet (to evidence the Riches of his Love) he also bad them to Arise, *Mat.* 26. 43. 45, 46. as here he dealeth with these Virgins Lest Men should boast of Congruous worth, with reference unto the Grace of God in Christ, it therefore is bestowed on them, when in the height of Incongruity or unworthiness to receive it. Thus did Christ Personate a *Macedonian,* entreating *Paul* to come and help them, *Acts* 16. 9, 10. Yea, thus unloveliness is his Time of Love, *Ezek.* 16. 6. 8. who then is moved to Heal, when nothing but Discouragements are to be seen, *Isa.* 57. 17, 17. The Voice of that Cry had need be hearkned unto, which otherwise doth so abound with sin-accenting and sorrow-heightning Grace.

6. How sadly are they Mistaken who think a going Once out will serve the turn, which is that great Soul-ruining Mis-apprehension among the Virgins or Professors. The World lyes still in Wickedness, 1 *John* 5. 19. and doth not stir at all: But Virgins are such as have gone out at first, and then they Rest, who Generally perish in that state. When *Israel* first went out of *Egypt* they went out All together, *Exod.*

The Parable of the Ten Virgins Opened.

12. 41. whose Carkasses yet Generally fell in the Wildernefs, *Numb.* 14. 29. becaufe they were not also free to go out Thence into Land of *Canaan,* when called thereunto by thofe of another Spirit, *v.* 24. 3❀ Thus alfo All the Jews went out of Nature into *Mofes,* 1 *Cor.* 10. 2. but not from Thence into the Righteoufnefs of God in Chrift, *Rom.* 10. 3, 4. (which is Revealed from Faith in *Mofes* to Faith in Chri t, *R.m.* 1. 17.) and therefore they were not faved, *Rom.* 10. 1. And thus one may have (virtually) forgotten that he was purged from his Old fins, 2 *Pet.* 1. 9. who having efcaped groffer Lufts, is not a Partaker alfo of that Divine Nature, *v.* 4. whofe firft appearance is Gofpel-Faith, *v.* 5. All are partakers of the Earthy *Adam*'s Image, but they muft bear the Image of the Heavenly alfo, 1 *Cor.* 15. 49. or not Inherit his Heavenly Kingdom, *v.* 50. nor yet be faved, *Eph.* 2. 8. fave as they are God's Workman-fhip Created in Chrift Jefus, *v.* 10. Let us therefore (at the firft) Go out of Ignorance into Knowledge; and then (a Second time) Out of the Form of Knowledge into Practice, *Rom.* 2. 20, 21. Let us (at firft) Go out of Difobedience into Duty; and then (a Second time) out of Material Legal Duty, or the Letter, into the Newnefs of its Spirituality, *Rom.* 7. 6. Let us (at firft) Go out of Superftition into Godlinefs or Right Worfhip; and then (a Second time) out of the Accidental Form of this Right Worfhip, or Notional Profeffion of it into its Life and Power, 2 *Tim.* 3. 5. Thus in the General.

And as to fuch a Particular Duty and Time, peculiarly referred unto in this Parable; thofe are much miftaken, who think a former-going out will ferve Chrift's turn at Prefent. He fpeaketh Now, with reference unto the Virgins Prefent ftate, which intimates his Expectation of their Progrefs beyond or out of thofe attainments, which in their Time and Place were not to be Defpifed. He is for Adding unto his Peoples Priviledges, *John* 10. 10. who therefore may expect the like from them in point of Duty, 2 *Pet.* 1. 5. Nor do fuch properly walk in any of his ways (as all the Saints are faid to do, *Pfal.* 119. 3.) who onely take one ftep therein, and fo defift. However, fuch as do onely Go from the *Pharifees* unto *John* the *Baptift,* and not from *John* to Chrift, will be Inferiour unto the leaft in the Kingdom of Heaven, *Mat.* 11. 11. if not in danger of Reverting unto the *Pharifees* again. Therefore if we have formerly gone out of *Babylon* or Old *Jerufalem* which Then was, we Now muft Write that Copy over a Second time, with reference unto what is Now in Being, above what formerly hath been departed from.

And that we may thus fully follow God, in Anfwer to this *Cry,* thefe following Motives will be of Ufe. *Mot.* 1.

Mot. 1. The Call is clear to each of those fore-named steps at such a Time. The most of which were Duties from the first; but Now, by way of Eminency. Sin was Defiling alway, but Now *Jerusalem* will be search'd with Candles, *Zeph.* 1. 12. Woe therefore to the Filthy and Polluted then, *Zeph.* 3. 1. It ever was unlawful to Comply with Spiritual *Babylon*, *Dan.* 1. 8. and 3. 12. but now some further self-delivery is enjoyned, *Zech.* 2. 7. which formerly was not a Duty, *Jer.* 29. 4, 5, 6, 7. Christ never warranted the Privacy of Solemn Worship; but now the Re-assuming of surceased Temple-work is urged from the Lord himself, and by his Messenger in his Message to the People, to shew the clearness of their Call unto it, *Hag.* 1. 12, 13. At such a time the Ancient Priests must be New Consecrated, and the Old Altar purged before God will Accept their Offerings upon that Altar, *Ezek.* 43. 26, 27. And Spiritual Growth is Eminently Now expected, the want whereof will sadly signifie, since as the House of *David* will Then be as an Angel, so will the Feeble be as *David* in that day, *Zech.* 12. 8.

2. The Way is safe, and more especially at such a Time. He Walketh Surely who walketh Uprightly, *Prov.* 10. 9. Since Angels are charged with him in all such ways, *Psal.* 91. 11. and a clear Call to Duty, turns Night, (yea, Midnight) into Day, or seeming Danger into Security, *Isa.* 11. 8, 9, 10. However, the greatest Suffering is that of Sin, *Hos.* 4. 14. All outward Tribulations are nothing to inward Peace, *John* 16. 33. God's Loving Kindness is better than Life it self, *Psal.* 63. 3. The Soul is of more worth than all the World, *Mat.* 16. 26. and present light Afflictions (in the way of Duty) are most at Work, as to the Crown of Glory, 2 *Cor.* 4. 17. Yea, at This Time the Holiest ones are likeliest to be hid from outward Dangers, *Zeph.* 2. 3. God will be for a Sanctuary unto self-hazarding Non-confederates, *Isa.* 8. 12. 14. The Timely returners to Temple-work shall have no cause to fear, *Hag.* 2. 5. And he that goeth out of Old *Jerusalem* (both City and Temple) at such a time, may thereby save his Life, *Jer.* 21. 9.

3. The Walk is Recreating. Sin makes the Soul to Cry, *Who shall Deliver me*, *Rom.* 7. 24. and to thank God, through Jesus Christ, so far as it is Obtained, *v.* 25 And who would not be glad to lose his filthy Rags for Change of Raiment? What merry singing is there in the ways of God, *Psal.* 138. 5. as his Redeemed come to *Sion,* *Isa.* 51. 11. from out of Melancholick *Babylon*, *Psal.* 137. 1, 2, 4. The Open Field is far more sweet and chearing than to be self-shut up in sinful Privacy; yea, suffering in such a way doth yield the Matter of Rejoycing, *Acts* 5. 41, 42. Christ Spouses also are sometimes more Delighted in the

The Parable of the Ten Virgins Opened.

Fields and Villages than in *Jerusalem*, or any of its Gardens; especially when likely (there) to have more sweet Communion with their Beloved, *Cant.* 7. 11, 12. And what a Recreating toil it is to mount with Singing to the Height of *Sion*'s Hill, *Jer.* 31. 12. from whence a Breathed Traveller may see the more of Heaven, and all these Earthly Lower things beneath him.

4. Thus shall we sooner see the Bridegroom by Going out to Meet him, than if we stay behind. *Follow Holiness, without which no Man shall see God*, Heb. 12. 14. as shall the Pure in Heart; *Mat.* 5. 8. for unto such Christ Promiseth the Manifestation of himself, *John* 14. 21. Nor is he to be seen in *Babylon*, save by some Extraordinary way of Revelation, *Dan.* 10. 1. but they shall see Eye to Eye, whom God shall bring again from thence to *Sion*, *Isa.* 52. 8. Then also was the Spirit poured out, *Acts* 2. 4. when those were all with one accord met in One place, *v.* 1. where all might come, *v.* 6. and therefore the Doors were not then shut for Fear, as formerly they were at Evening, *John* 20. 19. or when at Supper, *Mark* 16. 14. And at this time a Spouse may seek Christ long enough, in Bed, or in his Ancient Temple, and yet not find him, *Cant.* 3. 1. nor in the City or Old *Jerusalem*, *v.* 2. nor till she hath passed from the Watch-men, *v.* 3, 4. And since Christ comes from Heaven, 1 *Thes.* 4. 16. the Higher that we go, the sooner we shall see him, *v.* 17.

5. Such onely will go with Christ unto the Marriage, who thus Go out to meet him, because none else will then be ready, before the Door is shut, *Mat.* 25. 10. He who then hath not his Clean or Wedding-Garment on, will onely have that silencing check, *How camest thou hither*, Mat. 22. 12 ? therefore go out of sinful Defilements. This Marriage-feast and *Babylon*'s Funerals will contemporize, *Rev.* 19. 2. 9. 17, 18. therefore Go out of *Babylon*, for fear of being not then alive. Christ then will be ashamed of Them, *Mat.* 10. 33. who formerly have been ashamed of him, or have denyed him, by letting fall their Open Testimony, *v.* 27, 38. therefore go out of sinful Privacy. This same New Earth and Heavens will be laid upon the Old ones Ruines, *Isa.* 65. 17. therefore go out from hence, for fear of perishing in that Rubbish. And if we look for those, what manner of Persons should we be, 2 *Pet.* 3. 14. in point of growth, *v.* 18. therefore go out of Lower good Attainments. In Order whereunto, these following Helps may be of Use so far as there is yet room for such a Practice.

Help 1. Let not your Oyl be then to Buy, which *is* the undoing of Foolish Virgins at such a time: Endeavour to be satisfied (with all preventing speed) as unto what the Cry requireth; and please not your selves

Some may Cry up the Light and Strength of Nature as they pleafe, but nothing fhort of Gofpel Grace will make Men Run and not be Weary, or not to faint with Walking, *Ifa.* 40. 31. when Youths will fail, *v.* 30.

2. Let us be Searching what manner of Time the Spirit of Chrift here fignifieth; as did the Ancient Prophets, with reference to his firft Coming, 1 *Pet.* 1. 11. unlefs we think the Time is come, we fhall have no more mind to Walk (at fuch a Midnight) than had thofe Jews to Build, *Hag.* 1. 2. Some may fuppofe the Virgins firft going out was in the Days of *Conftantine,* and that the Bridegroom's Coming here will not be till the Jews Converfion, at Chrift's Perfonal Coming, or *John's* New *Jerufalem.* But they who firft went out, and after fell afleep, are they who are bid Now go out again: therefore the Firft and Second going out cannot be fo many hundred Years afunder, as from the Time of *Conftantine* untill Chrift's Second Coming. The Jews muft alfo be Converted before Chrift's Perfonal Coming, or elfe that fudden Change then, 1 *Cor.* 15. 51, 52. would leave no room for Mourning, *Zech.* 12. 10. or Building Houfes, *Ifa.* 65. 21. which Jews will alfo not be Converted, untill the fixth Vial be poured out, *Rev.* 16. 12. before which time the Temporal Kingdom will be Reftored, *Rev.* 11. 15. therefore the Bridegroom will firft come unto the Gentiles, who will prepare the others way by drying up *Euphrates, Rev.* 16. 12. or cafting out the four Monarchs, *Zech.* 1. 21.

3. Labour to be Awakened Throughly, which is the firft ftep in going out, and maketh way for all the reft. Chrift doth defign their being thus Awakened, by Calling for their Going out; and he would have them to Awake, in Order to their going on, as being both the firft Beginner, and Means of Perfecting that Work begun. One May fit ftill who is Awake, but Muft fit ftill, if faft afleep: who, till awakened Throughly, will go but fomewhat Odly and Unfteadily. And as Men would awake, fo they muft unfold their Hands, *Prov.* 16. 10. and Open their Eyes, *Prov.* 20. 13. and draw the Curtain, or give way unto the Light, *Eph.* 5. 14. Such alfo may not be Offended with a Friendly Touch, *Mat.* 17. 7. nor with fome Louder Noife, or gentle

Nip,

Nip, if need requireth, *Mat.* 26. 40. Such also muſt Ariſe, as do theſe Virgins, and not lye ſtill in ſuch a Tempting Poſture. Yea, they muſt Rub their Eyes, and ſhake themſelves, *Judg.* 16. 20. or Offer ſome Holy Violence unto their ſluggiſh Frame : Nay, they muſt alſo be at Work, or fall upon the Trimming of their Lamps, and entring on their going out, elſe will they ſleep again, *Mat.* 26. 46.

4. Gird up your Loins (or Go with a good Courage, *Jer.* 1. 17.) and let your Lamps be Burning, *Luke* 12. 35.. or your Affections flaming; ſo will you Open to Chriſt's Knock, *v.* 36. or Anſwer to his Cry. He that abhors not Evil, will be deviſing Miſchief on his Bed, and never ſet himſelf in a way, ſave that which is not good, *Pſal.* 36.4. Go out of the midſt of *Babylon,* Delivering every Man his Soul from God's fierce Anger, in this day of her Deſtruction, *Jer.* 51. 45. And though a Lion may be abroad, yet (to prevent our ſinful Privacy) let us Remember, the far worſe Biting Serpent is within at ſuch a Day, *Amos* 5. 18, 19. Plead with your *Mother,* Plead; who Now is not the Wife of Chriſt, as formerly ſhe may have been, *Hoſ.* 2. 2. And ſtand not Mincing of the Matter, as you would not deprive your ſelves of Mercy, *v.* 4. And he that doth not Grow or Multiply his preſent Talent, will have it taken from him at Chriſt's Coming, *Mat.* 25. 28.

5. Expect to loſe your Company, at leaſt, one Half, or All the Fooliſh Virgins at this Second Going out. *Noah* was very ſingular in point of Righteouſneſs, *Gen.* 7. 1. or Going out of ſinful Defilements, wherein the Generality Periſhed. At *Babylon* ſhall fall the ſlain of all the Earth, *Jer.* 51.49. excepting ſome few, who then will Go away, *v.* 50. *Haggai* and *Zechariah* were the onely Two remaining Witneſſes for Temple-work in their Day, *Ezra* 5. 1. And *Jeremiah* was much alone in ſtirring up others to Go out of Old *Jeruſalem* into *Babylon* or Confuſion. And when the Harveſt (or time of Cutting down) is come, the Corn is Generally Dead at the Root, or hath done Growing, ſave here and there a ſingle Ear. Few Trees can bear a Tranſplantation, few ſeek the things of Jeſus Chriſt, few will endure to Walk in this Narrow way, few perſevere unto the End; and who ſhall Live when God doth this? Therefore he now that ſtays for Company, will be ſhut out with his Companions.

MAT.

MATTHEW XXV. 7.

Then all those Virgins Arose and Trimmed their Lamps.

IN this Verse we have an Account of that which followed upon the fore-named *Cry, viz.* All the Virgins Arising thereupon, and Trimming their Respective Lamps. By which word [All] we are not Necessarily to Understand each Individual Virgin before mentioned; several of which might Now be Dead, both in a Natural and Mystical sence: but onely All, who Now Remained, and had not lost their Appellation by some more gross and late Pollution since their first Going out.

From whence the Observation is as followeth.

Observ. Upon the fore-named *Cry,* All the Remaining Virgins (both Wise and Foolish) are made to Rise and Trim their Lamps.

Quest. 1. What is the Meaning of that word, *Arose ?*

Answ. 1. Their Rising (upon this Account) doth intimate Their being made to Hear that *Cry,* in Answer unto which they do Arise. This signifies the *Cry* to have been very Loud, else would it not have been Heard by so many Persons fast asleep. Now, have they not heard ? Yes verily, *Rom.* 10. 18. although they have not all Obeyed, *v.* 16. for who hath so Believed our Report ? That Everlasting Gospel, *Rev.* 14. 6, 7. doth seem to have been Preached before these Virgins fell asleep, as also, that Double Notification of *Babylon's* fall, *v.* 8. the first whereof was then Accomplished: Between which First and Second Fall there is a Warning given, *v.* 9. which seemeth to be the *Cry* here made, and also to have been made already. All sorts of Compliers with the Beast, and with his Mark (in Fore-heads or in Hands, that is to say, with reference to more Apert Commands or Covert Prohibitions) have been fore-warned, and they have Heard it.

2. Arising intimateth their being Now in a Capacity of Speaking, Hearing, Seeing, Weighing, and Going out, if they had pleased, more than before, while fast asleep. And have they not already been in that Capacity ? Could they not have Discoursed what was Offered, and heard Replyes, and see what he that Runs might Read, *Hab.* 2. 2 ? Could they not have Considered what formerly they had rot heard, *Isa.* 52. 15. before it was Condemned, *John* 7. 51 ? Yes, could they not

have

have walked out, as unto any visible Rub, save what was of their own Creating? 'Tis true indeed, Man can do nothing of himself, *Acts* 17. 28. at least-wife not in Spiritual Cases, 2 *Cor.* 3. 5. but Men forbear not upon that Account; and Common Influences might suffice as to the Matter (or more External Part) of such a work. And in that Case Affected Ignorance is not Invincible, nor will Pretended inability Excuse, *Luke* 14. 18, 19, 20. when Blind and Maimed ones shall be brought in, *v.* 21.

3. Arising (hereupon) doth intimate their Understanding and Approving (in part at least) what is Declared and Required by the *Cry*. One may be throughly wakened by that which vexeth, who then endeavours to sleep again: But being told, the Bridegroom Cometh, and being bid Go out to meet him, he will not Rise, who doth not competently understand the Notice, and like the Motion. And hath not this also been to be seen of late among the Virgins? Have not their Swooning Expectations been Revived, as *Tabitha*, so as to sit up a little, *Acts* 9. 40? Have not some Heard, that Christ (in his Witnesses) is both Alive and Risen, *Luke* 24. 23? Yea, have not some of Themselves been Plausibly convinced, because his Dead Body was not to be seen, although they saw him not Alive, *v.* 24? Yea, have they not Approved in their Hearts and Consciences, at least, some part of what the *Cry* requireth? Which further proves its having been already made; though with submission.

4. Arising intimateth the Sleepers Moving out of his former Place and Posture. Some Men can slumber as they stand, but yet not sleep, till either Laid, or sitting in some convenient place; both which are inconsistent with Arising. And hath not such a variation been Apparent? I mean, some kind of Rising up (with Arms unfolded) from easier Seats and self-indulging Postures? Some have been strengthened, as *Jacob* was, to Rise and Sit, though onely upon the same Bed still, upon the Hearing of *Joseph's* Coming, *Gen.* 48. 1, 2. and his not being able to leave his Bed, was from his present Weakness, and Near approaching Death, *Gen.* 49. 33. Others have also Risen out of their Seat, as *Eglon* did, upon his Hearing of a Message from the Lord, *Judg.* 3. 20. who yet then Perished, *v.* 21. because of his former evil Practices. But some have also left their Bed and Walked, as did that Damsel, upon Christ's speaking to her, *Mark* 5. 41, 42. who formerly had been asleep, *v.* 39.

5. Arising upon the *Cry*, doth intimate their getting in a readiness for some further Action, as *Josh.* 8. 3. *Mat.* 8. 15. and as is evident from the joyning of their Rising, with the Trimming of their Lamps: Which leadeth to the next Enquiry. *Quest.* 2. What

The Parable of the Ten Virgins Opened.

Quest. 2. What seemeth to be meant by the Trimming of their Lamps?

Ansv. 1. -Trimming of Lamps doth intimate (by Necessary consequence) the taking Notice of their present state, in point of Oyl or Light, which could not but be then perceived, and as the Issue evidenced. While Men are fast asleep, (yea, till they Rise and are at work) they know not clearly what they Have or Want, which shou'd encourage us to be upon our constant Watch, as we would know our Happiness or Misery. Sleep doth Benight the Understanding, and onely fil's the Head with Solacing or Frighting Dreams, for which there is no Real cause, as upon wakening doth appear. And have not the slumbring Virgins been thus undeceived upon the fresh stirring of their Affections, Typified by these Lamps? Some have been on.ly Frighted into the Exercise of their Remaining strength, as *Sampson* was, upon his first Awakening, by a Cry, *Judg.* 16. 9. But others have found, that shaking of themselves could do no good, no more than it did him at last, *Judg.* 16. 20, 21.

2. Trimming of Lamps doth intimate their being Cleansed from that Soil, which formerly hath been Contracted by length of Time, or falling snuffs, or burning too near the bottom. Lamps will contract Pollution meerly through discontinuance of constant Dressing: And so will good Affections, when not constantly looked after, 1 *Chron.* 29. 3. 9. 18. Much more will unremoved snuffs defile; or that more Gross and Earthy part, which doth Attend our best Affections; Especially when Lamps are suffered to burn too Low, or when our very Light is Carnal, which doth discolour our Affections, and threatens the Extinguishing of our Light or Judgment, *Rom.* 1. 21. And have not the Virgins Lamps been All thus Trimmed? Whilst they were slumbring, their former good Affections were much Eclipsed from want of Daily Rubbing, from their being onely Snuffed or Reproved by their own Back-slidings, and from the Degenerating of their Wisdom into Carnal Policy, which since hath been Amended.

3. Trimming the Lamps doth intimate their being also newly Tipt, or Beautified with some fresh Adorning; the former being now decayed with Age and filth, and partly by a present securing. And have not the Virgins Lamps or good Affections been lately thus Adorned? Some could not be at Rest untill they had put on again that Coat of Zeal for Christ, which formerly they had put off; till they had turned unto him, from whom they with the Generality had Revo'ted, in Answer to that Call, *Isa.* 31. 6. Yea, others also have endeavoured to set a fair Gloss or Face upon their fading Lamps, or Dying good Affections,

by

by wishing that it had been otherwise, and witnessing unto the betterness of others Practices. Thus have these sought to Paint their Faces, whereas the former have Recovered their Native Lustre; though both are in Appearance very Trim to what they sometimes were, themselves and others being Judges.

4. Trimming the Lamps doth intimate their making shew, of getting fit to March, or to Go out and Meet the Bridegroom; which partly their Arising promised, much more this Super-added Preparation. And hath not such a shew been made? Yea, have not some begun to March? Whom others also have Accompanied, so far as Oyl or Light hath lasted. Some have Reformed many Moral Evils of a Common Nature. Some have Repented of more gross Compliances with Spiritual *Babylon*. Some are more Open (yet) in their Religious Worship, but are not free to Promise it for the Future, nor yet to Confess a former failing. But most are stumbled at Going out of this Old Earth and Heavens, or Lower good Attainments, desiring first to Bury their Aged Parents, *Mat.* 8. 21. or Friendly to Part with them, at least, *Luke* 9. 61. and to fetch something out of their Old House, at least their Cloaths, *Mat.* 24. 17, 18. not being able to go out of Lower things.

Quest. 3. How comes this *Cry* to be so Generally Rouzing?

Answ. 1. Because it is so very Loud; in which Case *Baal* must needs have heard if he had onely been asleep, 1 *Kings* 18. 27, 28. as God did *Rabshakeh*, *Isa.* 37. 23. The Lord hath lately Cryed aloud, both by his Providences, and by some Publick Testimonies. How did the late Plague Alarm all our Virgins, among whom it Raged most Remarkably? Yea, how were Harlots Frighted with the Fire, and much more others? The Meaning whereof hath been made out unto some Men of Wisdom, *Mic.* 6. 9. and partly, unto some Foolish Virgins also. And doth it not conclude them Dead, who are not yet at all awakened? Nor will continuing Sleepers be Excused, by their pretending Not to have Heard; since all Men shall be Judged by that Law which hath been once Proclaimed, though not particularly sent to every one who should have Enquired after it, which yet hath been so loud, as Generally to Raise the slumbring Virgins.

2. Because it is undoubtedly Divine, the Hearing whereof made wicked *Eglon* to arise, *Judg.* 3. 20. and those to be Obedient, who had surceased Temple-work through Slavish Fear, when once they understood the Lord's own Voice and Message by the Prophet, whom God himself had sent as his own Messenger, *Hag.* 1. 12, 13. The Voice of God can break the Cedars, or stout-hearted ones, *Psal.* 29. 5. Yea, it

it can make the Hinds to Calve, *v.* 9. or Fearful Creatures (such as Hinds are, *Cant.* 2. 7.) to bring forth, although with much Pain, as doth that Creature, *Job* 39. 3. The word of Man may be (and in some Cases should be) Dis-regarded, *Gal.* 1. 8. but if it be received as the Word of God, it works Effectually in them who do Believe it, 1 *Thes.* 2. 13. Now, all the Virgins do believe this *Cry* is Christ's; and it is self-evincing, because 'tis Scriptural; and then they must be one day Judged by it, who therefore Now cannot but be awakened.

3. Because this Cry Without is Seconded by Conscience from Within, which maketh room for its Reception. Conscience is in the Soul of Man, as is the Drum within his Ear, which doth receive an Outward sound, and so transmits it to the Brain, or Understanding, unless that Drum be spoyled, and then no Cry Without is Understood. Science alone is ineffectual, but Conscience is knowing Together with, or Co-attesting unto the Truth and Weight of what is Offered by another. Now, that which is here Notified by the *Cry*, is readily Ecchoed unto by awakened Consciences, which do Remember, Christ May be Coming, and then it is a Duty to Go out and Meet him. And when a *Cry* without is Answered by a *Cry* within, the deepest sleeper must needs awaken, and do something, untill the Ear be Deafned, and Conscience some way satisfied, so as to cease its Bawling Noise.

4. Because the Persons cryed unto are Virgins or Professors, and so more easie to be awakened than others are. These were not Dead, but onely fast asleep, who therefore were more likely to Rouzed up, at least-wise by some Louder Call. Professors are Described also by their Nearness unto Christ, *Eph.* 2. 17. which is a great advantage, in point of Hearing, above what others have. The *Cry* is also more Particularly Directed to the Virgins here, which promiseth a suitable Entertainment, *Prov.* 22. 19, 20, 21. and in which Case, a *Jehu* will arise, 2 *Kings* 9. 5, 6. And though Proud *Pharaoh* Knew not God, upon his Hearing of a Message from him, *Exod.* 5. 1, 2. Yet none of these Virgins are so Atheistical, as to Reject what seems to be Divine. And though some former Professors may have made away their Conscience, 1 *Tim.* 1. 19. Yet Virgins (whilst Remaining such) have something of a Tender Spirit in them, which doth Oblige their Hearkening thereunto.

5. The Wiser Virgins might be concluded light of Hearing, and of an Obedient Disposition, with whom the Foolish Yet were in Communion; and if but one of a Company be awakened, he may awaken all the rest. Spouses are never so fast asleep, but they both Hear and Know the Voice of their Beloved, *Cant.* 5. 2. Christ's Sheep are to

could be afforded by the Wiser Virgins, yet might the Foolish be thus awakened, who otherwise, perhaps, had not been much Affected with the *Cry,* save as some of their own Companions did enliven it by their Example, which are more Prevalent with some than Precepts.

Quest. 4. Why do the Foolish Virgins (also) Rise and Trim their Lamps, who had no Oyl to lead them further, as had the Wise?

Ansiv. 1. These being at the present wakened, must needs do something, who scarcely could do less than Rise and Trim their Lamps. They were awakened by the *Cry,* whether they would or no; and to lye still with Open Eyes, or to Rise up and to be altogether Idle, would onely make their Consciences Rage the more, till it be made to sleep again. Thus are some Hurried in that, which as they never Thought to have Begun, so neither do they mean to Prosecute it, save till some fair Occasion be afforded of Quarrelling therewith, and of Returning into their Former state. This is the Fruit of Injudicious good Affections or Rash Engagements, whereof Men soon Repent, *Mat.* 21. 30. and which are easi'y desisted from, without much inward real conflict, *Ruth* 4. 4, 5, 6. Trust not unto the Force of Natural Conscience, no more than to the hasty springing up of Seed in Stony Ground, which hath no Root, *Mat.* 13. 5, 6.

2. They possibly might not Yet perceive their want of Oyl, untill their Lamps were Trimmed, Labouring still under that Mistake, which made them at the first to venture out, through sleightiness and self-conceit. They who seek not to un-deceive themselves in Time, may justly be given up to strong Delusions, that they shall verily believe a Lye; and they who sleep with Empty Vessels, will scarcely Dream of ought but Fulness; nor yet awake (in Spiritual Cases) with any other (Timely) apprehensions. When Souls fall once in Love with Naked good Affections, they seldom prize a Spiritually enlightned Judgment, untill it be too late to Rectifie that Fundamental and Soul-damning Error. It is with Spiritual Pride, as with a Tympany, which (being Chronical) is hardly Cured, especially in Case of a Relapse, or when a Soul hath formerly been warned of it, as all the Virgins or Professors were, when first enlightned.

3. They fain would go as far as might be with the Wiser Virgins, with

than otherwise they would have done, because they scorn to come behind their Fellows. Communion also begetteth Love; and Love confirmed Ruth (who yet had not a better Principle) to keep her Mother Company, *Ruth* 1. 15, 16. Yea, Natural Conscience will Regret, to Part with Ancient Precious Friends, when barely put upon Repeating their Joint former Practice, untill some more than Ordinary Let doth intervene, and till a plausible pretence or colour shall be Offered for such a Parting.

4. They might do This without any Prejudice to Themselves; and in that Case, some easier work will not be stuck at by a Foolish Virgin. 'Tis nothing (in Comparison) for one Awakened to Arise: Nor can the Trimming of One's Lamp (or stirring of some good Affections) much Disquiet any Man whose Principal Interest, or Corruption is yet untouch'd. Thus Satan is content to Gratifie the sinner's bawling or awakened Conscience, by giving him a Dispensation to Hear, and Read; and Pray sometimes, untill that Crying fit be over. Nor is a Worldly Interest endangered by what this Trimming of the Lamps importeth, no more than *Nicodemus* his Coming unto Christ (by Night) did him; since he was yet within the Compass of that Law, *John* 9. 22. And though an Harlot will not do thus much, yet is the most Foolish Virgin Wiser than to distast a Bosom Friend, by Grudging that which may be safely granted.

5. They might think (being Foolish) this was All; untill the *Cry* is, as it were, Expounded by the Wiser Virgins Going further: So prone are Hypocrites to Magnifie their own Performances. Or they might think this would suffice at least; either to carry them out, as at the first, or to Excuse them, in Case they did not Go, having thus shewn their good Affection by Trimming of their Lamps.

First, they might think their Trimmed Lamps would be sufficient to carry them out this Second time, as well as at the First; when they did onely take their Lamps, but no Oyl with them; not minding the Difference that Now was, both as to the Work it self, and also the strength of their Affections. The Work it self was Then more Easie, and their Affections were more Lively, than at the Present: But when

poo-

poor *Sampson*'s Hair was cut, he still was apt to Fancy that shaking of himself would serve the turn, as heretofore at other times, *Judg.* 16. 19, 20. This trusting unto fore-Experiences is many times the Ruine of unsound Professors, who Argue from a former Practice, unto their Future perseverance, and so betray themselves into the Tempter's hand through their Presumptuous Confidence. *David* indeed might safely Argue his following Succefs from what he formerly had met with, 1 *Sam.* 17. 37. because he went in the Name (or Strength) of God, *v.* 45. which Hypocrites do not pretend unto; and therefore, since their Good is not in their Own Hand, *Job* 21. 16. it is no wonder if their Lamp or Candle be put out, *v.* 17.

Secondly, they might (at least) suppose, This would Excuse them, in Case they went no further; having thus shewn their Willing Mind, or good Affections, by Trimming of their Lamps. Thus some poor Creatures are apt to Fansy, that good Desires will serve the turn, who therefore plead a Love for Christ, such as those Virgins had, *Cant.* 1. 3. who yet were not Espoused to him. These Good Affections are the Bane of Hypocrites, who think to Borrow upon Practice, by their Presenting Christ with good Desires; but he will not be Mocked. Onely themselves are fully satisfied, if they have but a liking of Christ's ways, a Love for Walkers in them; especially if they are Up and Doing, to the Height of their pretended Light. Indeed Christ sometimes doth Accept a Willing Mind, but that Relateth onely to Invincible Inability, and not to Foolish Virgins, but the Wise, 2 *Cor.* 8. 11, 12. both which are sadly mis-applyed by them to themselves.

6. This Work is of a self-paying Nature, as well as safe: and *Ephraim* (that silly Creature, *Hof.* 7. 11.) is willing to Tread out the Corn, *Hof.* 10. 11. or Work and Eat together, *Deut.* 25. 4. so is a Foolish Virgin. The first Going out was attended with present Pay, wherein the Foolish Virgins therefore Joyned; so is their Second Rising and Trimming of their Lamps, though not their Second Going forth: And Carnal Jews will follow Christ whilst they are filled with his Loaves, *John* 6. 26. who Walked no more with him, *v.* 66. when nothing but Spiritual (or invisible) Bread and Flesh is promised to them, *v.* 51. But Rising doth Refresh the Conscience much, so doth the finifying of Affections: Since it is Natural unto Maids or Virgins to think more on their Ornaments than on their Rest. *Jer.* 2. 32. Yea, they would not else be accounted Virgins; the Preservation of which Name or Title doth Plentifully Recompense the Foolish Virgins present Labour, who therefore are thus at Work.

Use 1. As none were to be counted Virgins Heretofore, save they

they who at the first went forth to meet the Bridegroom; so when the *Cry* is made, none are to be Accounted Virgins Then, save they who thereupon Arose and Trimmed their Lamps; since All the Virgins (at such a time) are said to do so. And so long onely doth the Warrant of Communion last with such, and of their being Owned as Professors; who Differed from the Wise at first, as to Reality; but from This time they cease to have the Name of Virgins given to them, and as that Name is Common to the Foolish with the Wise, in point of Visibility. This shews the sadness of their visible State, who are not moved with the *Cry*, since they have thereby forfeited the Name of Virgins, in Christ's Account, as having slept the sleep of Death. Yea, they who are not Parted Now from such as These, will not themselves be counted Virgins.

Use 2. Here we may see one sad Effect of sleep or slumber, *viz.* the marring of our Lamps at least, as their being Trimmed (by awakened ones) evinceth. Now, Virgins usually are very Neat; therefore this consideration might suffice to keep such ever waking, as they would not spoyl their Trimming. How Glorious was their first Love, when shining with a Lively Exercise thereof, and Burning with an Holy Zeal for Christ at their first Going out, together wherewith their Glory also hath been lost. Man's Eye is eminently the Seat of Beauty, which therefore needs must be Eclipsed, together with the Closing of his Eye with sleep, which is Death's Image. In point of visibility, Darkness it self is staining, *Job* 3. 5. and sleep will Ruffle the finest Ornaments in Reality; therefore none would be seen in their Night-Habits, nor will they lye down to slumber, till they have either put off their Bravery, or ceased to be studious about its Preservation.

Use 3. Hence we may Learn, how far the Wiser and Foolish Virgins may go together. They All went out at first, they All were overtaken with a slumbring Spirit; and now they All Awaken, Rise, and Trim their Lamps together. It is a Mercy to be Awakened, but many are so, to their shame, who either sleep again, or onely Muse and Talk a little, and to less purpose, if that be all. It is some further Mercy to be Raised up, which yet an Hypocrite may be Interested in, who may not onely Hear Christ's Voice, *Luke* 13. 26. and be in a Capacity of doing more, but also may Approve what is more Excellent, *Rom.* 2. 18. Yea, Foolish *Galatians* may Begin to Run, *Gal.* 3. 3. and 5. 7. Nay, such may also Trim their Lamps, as do these Foolish Virgins; an Empty House may be both Swept and Garnished, *Mat.* 12. 44. Such may do many things, *Mark* 6. 20. and Promise more, *Mat.* 21. 30. No Judgment can rightly pass upon Professors, till we

shall

shall see who have Gone out, by their Admission to the Bridegroom's Marriage.

MATTHEW XXV. 8.

And the Foolish said unto the Wise, Give us of your Oyl, for our Lamps are Gone, or (as the Margin hath it) are Going out.

IN this Verse we have the first visible Difference between these Virgins; and by the Foolish Virgins own Confession. From whence the Observation is this.

Observ. Upon the Virgins being (All of them) Raised by the *Cry* at Midnight, the Foolish do acknowledge their want of Oyl or Light, who therefore Call upon the Wise to give them of their Oyl.

Where'n we have presented to us their seeming sence of wanting Oyl; their own Confession of it, and Desire of Supply, together with the Cause of both, *viz.* the failing of their Lamps. All which do fairly offer these following Questions to be considered of.

Quest. 1. What is that sence of wanting Oyl, which doth here seem to be in Foolish Virgins, with reference unto themselves?

Answ. 1. It is a sence at Last, but not in Time, *viz.* not in Due Time. They should have lookt to this at first, but were too Hasty then, having enough to serve their present turn, and not desiring to have more; till meer Necessity doth enforce it. And thus, when Flesh and Body are consumed, a Foolish Man may mourn at Last, and be convinced of his wanting Wisdom, *Prov.* 5, 11, 12. Thus did the light of Hell's Fire (at Last) make *Dives* see his want of Care, which he himself Despaired to Redeem, onely would have his Brethren to be warned by him, *Luke* 16. 27, 28. Yea, thus poor Living *Esau* did perceive at Last, how Foolishly his Birth-right had been Sold by him, when it was now too late to gain the Blessing, *Heb.* 12. 16, 17. 'Tis not the depth of Sence, save as it also is in Time, which can Advantage late enlightned ones, or make it out, that such Impressions are any other, but what a Natural Man may have and perish with. Untimely self-sowing and appearing Corn is Ploughed up, because it is not seasonable.

2. There

The Parable of the Ten Virgins Opened.

2. There may be (in such) a sense of want, but not of any Proper or self-worth, Relating to this Special Oyl. A Natural Man may be in Love with Grace's Portion, but doth not see the Native Beauty of her Person, abstracted from the other. These Foolish Virgins saw they could not Go without the Wiser Virgins Oyl, else would they not have Mourned in its Absence, till Interest did shew it to be Necessary. Whereas a Gracious Soul would have All Grace at Present, and consequently some whereof there is no present Need; such as is Suffering Grace in times of Peace; and such a Degree of any Grace which is not Absolutely Necessary to Salvation. This sense of worth appeared in these Wiser Virgins, who took Oyl with them at the first, although that present Expedition might have been made without it.

3. It is a Passive sense, or from a Forreign Evidence, rather than from an Active self-enquiry. They did not search their Vessels, as they should have done, untill their Lamps were Going out, which did Necessitate the Present taking Notice of their wanting Oyl, else had they still been Ignorant. Thus one may Accidentally be Made to see, what otherwise he would not have Enquired after, no more than *Ahab* did *Elijah* or *Micajah*, if he could fairly have avoided them. Spiritual Convictions are cross to Flesh and Blood, which *Felix* had no time to hear, *Acts* 24. 25. which *Pilate* ran away from, *John* 18. 38. and *Balaam* would have shunned if he could: Yea, some Professors stand in need of being urged unto self-examination, 2 *Cor.* 13. 5. which yet a Gracious Heart is Active in, *Lam.* 3. 40. but very few others. And though an Hypocrite may Go exceeding far, yet Generally he is no Voluntier in such a Service, save as that Young Man's self-conceit made him ask Christ, *What lack I yet*, *Mat.* 19. 20?

4. It is a sense of Consequents, but not of a Procuring Cause. They saw into the Emptiness of their Vessels, but not their wretched Negligence, who else might have Prevented this before. 'Tis rare to find a Cordial self-condemning Hypocrite, with reference to self-contractions of a Moral Nature, who yet are deeply sensible of wanting Care in other Cases. *Cain* was sensible of his Punishment, *Gen.* 4. 13. and *Pharaoh* (in that Respect) of sin, *Exod.* 10. 16. and others also of their wanting Grace, but not of being Accessary thereunto, through wretched slightiness. Such either lay that Cause at Satan's Door, *Gen.* 3. 13. or falsly charge it upon God, *James* 1. 13. or else Translate it unto others, 1 *Sam.* 15. 24. but sin is a Brat disowned by its Natural Mother, save where Grace also is. Whereas an Holy Heart is chiefly sensible of his being Active unto (or an Occasion of) that want of Oyl,

The Parable of the Ten Virgins Opened.

which otherwise could be more easily endured by him, if it were onely in a way of Suffering, and not of sin.

5. It is a Natural sence, but no way Spiritual. Grace is not Spiritually to be discerned in its Total Absence, as it now was with These, who took No Oyl with them, and so could not be Spiritually Affected towards it; else might one Exercise Grace before he hath it. The Spirit of a Man may know what is in him, yet with respect unto the things of God, that knowledge is nothing which is not from his Spirit: And so the deepest Natural sence is Spiritual Non-sence, 1 *Cor.* 2. 11. Whereas a Gracious Soul sees what he hath or wanteth, by vertue of an Heavenly Beam, Comparing Spiritual things with Spiritual, 1 *Cor.* 2. 13. So that (in such) a sence of Absence is both more clear and less Afflicting, because it Argueth some kind of Presence. Convictions issuing from Natural Conscience, are either Flashy or Enraging: But Heavenly and Spiritual Light is to be known, as by the plainness of its Demonstration, *John* 16. 8. So by the Dueness of that Composure which doth Accompany the deepest sensibleness Occasioned by it, *Acts* 9. 3. 6. Compared with *Judas* his Conviction, *Mat.* 27. 3. 5.

6. It is a sence of wanting Oyl in Lamps, but not in Vessels; the Latter whereof is of far greater Consequence, as is a sound Mind (or Honest Heart) Compared with the best Affections. Thus were the *Pharisees* Apprehensive of some Lesser failings, but not more Weighty Matters, *Mat.* 23. 23. as some are sensible of Actual sins, but not Original; or of their wanting such Particular Fruits, but not the Root of a Renewed Principle. Whereas good *David* did bewail his being shapen in Iniquity, *Psal.* 51. 5. and begged the Renewing of his Heart and Spirit, *v.* 10. as *Paul* did most Lament his Body of Death, *Rom.* 7. 24. and took more Notice of his Mind than of his Members, *v.* 23. 25. But if an Hypocrite may have some Present stirring of Affections in him, his Conscience is so weak, as to be satisfied without a Change of Mind, or Spirit of Grace, which is the onely Conservator and Ennobler of good Affections. This is the utmost of that sence, (Relating to the want of Oyl) which may be in a Foolish Virgin, or unsound Professor.

Quest. 2. What is the Nature of that Confession which is here made by Foolish Virgins, as to the Failing of their Oyl or Light?

Answ. 1. It must be onely in a way of Counterfeit, or of Pretending the want of Present Light, because they had no mind to Walk, as was exhorted unto by the *Cry.* Thus one of those Invited Ghests made shew, as if he Could not Come, *Luke* 14. 20. whose want of Will was all the Cause, else might his Wife have come with him, and both

of

of them should have been Welcome. Indeed good *David* once did feign himself bereft of Reason, 1 *Sam.* 23. 13. and *Peter* made as if he knew not Jesus, *Mat.* 26. 27. but neither of them did persist herein, as do these Foolish Virgins. And thus, as some are willingly Ignorant, 2 *Pet.* 3. 5. so others scorn to be Accounted Blind, *John* 9. 40. who yet will seem as if they did not see that which is Manifest in their Conscience, 2 *Cor.* 5. 11. and want not Light, but onely Grace to use that Talent, the Hiding whereof will not excuse from being cast into that outer Darkness, where they shall weep in vain, *Mat.* 25. 30.

2. They here Confess a Weighty Failure without Affection suitable thereunto. The want of Oyl (at such a time) is of the saddest consequence, yet do not we read of their Lamenting, but onely saying *Our Lamps are Gone, or Going out.* Man is endued with Affections, which (since the Fall) are Dislocated or Mis-placed, as to their Proper Objects. An Hypocrite is never Moderate save with Respect to Spiritual Losses, which he can signifie without Complaining. Thus some confess their want of Light, whose Gummed Eyes are not so much as washt with Natural Tears. Affections are both the Outward Evidence, and stirrers up of Inward Sense; which they who Bridle now, when need requireth such a vent, will Weep the more hereafter, unto the multiplying of their fruitless sorrow. Unsound Professors may be Affectionate, 1 *Sam.* 24. 16. but unaffectionate Confessions (in Momentous Cases) have small appearance of their being found, but like the Foolish Virgins.

3. Much Partiality may be Observed in their Confession.

1. They confess their Want, or Suffering onely, but not their sin, or want of Care to be supplyed at the first. Most Bodily Sicknesses are from Intemperance, yet few Complains of the one, are truly sensible of the other; much less will they Confess it, save in a Case of Gross Exorbitancy. The bare acknowledgment of one's Suffering transfers the Cause upon another; but the confessing of it's in bred Root doth add Disgrace unto the Plaintiff's sorrow. Thus some bewail their want of Spiritual strength, as being an heavy Portion from the Lord; but take no notice of their sluggishness, as being Accessary to their own enfeebling. And it is easier to be Convinced of a sin, than to Confess it, as *David* found, *Psal.* 32. 3. and much more *Sau'*, till he was forced thereunto, 1 *Sam.* 15. 30. Indeed 'tis Folly to complain of Punishment, and not of Sin, which is the Cause, *Lam.* 3. 39. but yet 'tis very Natural, and more especially to Foolish Virgins.

2. They do Confess the Present Failing of their Oyl, but not their taking No Oyl with them at the first, as Christ had truly said concerning

-ing them, *Mat.* 25. 3. They would be thought to have had that, which now they do confefs was Gone, or Going. How weak are they, who ground the Fallible Nature of Holy Oyl, upon thefe Foolifh Virgins falfe Pretenfion; as if They were to be believed more than Chrift. But thus an Hypocrite would fave the Reputation of his former ftate, when forced from his prefent Claim. What Paint do fuch beftow upon Profeffed Tombs, by feeking to Embalm that which they do acknowledge to be Dead. But thus, a wrong Foundation is not owned, together with the failing of a Superftructure; and though fome lefs mifcarriage may be confeffed, yet is felf-honour (in an Higher cafe) confulted for, in fuch Profeffors deepeft felf-condemnations, as was apparent in *Saul's* Example, 1 *Sam.* 15. 30.

3. They onely do Confefs the Failing of their Lamps, and meerly with Refpect unto this prefent Expedition: But not fo *Plainly*, their want of Oyl; at leaft-wife, not their having (Now) No Grace at all. All have their Failings, faith an Hypocrite, and I have mine: making no Difference (in point of kind) between himfelf and others, but onely in Degree. *Agur* confeffeth himfelf to be Beneath a Man, *Prov.* 30. 2. and *David* himfelf, to be *Behemoth*, or a Beaft of the Plural Number, *Pfal.* 73. 22. whilft Hypocrites will call themfelves of the Holy City, *Ifa.* 48. 2. the Seed of *Abraham*, *John* 8. 33. the Temple of the Lord, *Jer.* 7. 4. Thus fome confefs their want of Light into a Duty urged unto; but Judge that Ignorance to be confiftent with the Main, and are offended with the Queftioning of their Spiritual ftate, meerly becaufe that Oyl is wanting. It would be well if All were thus Ingenuous: But *Ananias* and *Sapphira* would rather Dye, than make a full and free Confeffion; and of this Nature is that Acknowledgment which is here made by Foolifh Virgins.

4. They do not Deny this Going out to be the Wifer Virgins Duty; yet will they not confefs their own fitting ftill to be their fin; but Judge their want of Oyl or Light, fufficiently to Vindicate them from that Charge. A Gracious Heart is fenfible of unknown Errors, and doth defire to be cleanfed from fecret faults, *Pfal.* 19. 12. not counting himfelf to be therefore Juftified, fimply, becaufe he knoweth Nothing by himfelf, 1 *Cor.* 4. 4. but Foolifh Virgins are not Careful (at leaft, not felf-condemning) in fuch a cafe. It fatisfieth fuch, if they can fay, We have no Light into fome kind of Practice; the total Neglect whereof is therefore not Accounted fin, till they fhall come to be Convinced. Particular Actings of this Nature may fometimes be in Wifer Virgins; but yet this is the Principle of Foolifh ones, which therefore fhould be

Cautelously

Anſw. 1. We may not Diſpute the point with God, as to his Soveraignty and Dominion, *Job* 25. 2. by vertue whereof the Stars are ſaid to be Not Pure in his ſight, *v.* 5. nor yet the Heavens clean, *Job* 15. 15. Yea, who may therefore charge his ſinleſs Angels with ſome kind of Folly, *Job* 4. 18. becauſe of their Ignorance compared with his Infinite Omniſciency. And if Man juſtly may impute the Father's ſin unto his Innocent Child, much more may God impute the firſt Man's Diſobedience u to others, *Rom.* 5. 19. whoſe Ignorance (in that Reſpect) was Abſolutely Invincible. And into which Reaſon, (*viz.* the Soveraignty of his Will,) the Righteouſneſs of *Adam*'s Fall is Ultimately to be reſolved, together with the Hiding of his Mind from others. *Mat.* 11. 25. becauſe it ſeemeth good to him, *v.* 26. This is enough to ſilence the Subtileſt Diſputant, who elſe might be too hard for his Opponent, as to the Equity of God's finding fault, at leaſt-wiſe in ſome Caſes, or with Reſpect unto Man's being Hardened by the Lord, *Rom.* 9. 18, 19, 20.

2. Pretended, or Willing Ignorance is ſo far from Excuſing any one, as that it ſadly Aggravateth a Neglect of Duty. If ſome were truly Blind, they would Comparatively have no ſin, *John* 9. 41. but either Themſelves diſdain to be ſo called, *v.* 40. or elſe it is Apparent otherways, that either they do falſly Pretend unto the want of Knowledge, *John* 7. 27, 28. or that (at leaſt) they Might Know if they Would; 2 *Pet.* 3. 5. This kind of Ignorance is of a Lying Nature, *Lev.* 6. 3. which is not Expiated, but by a deeper Humiliation, or Greater Offering, *v.* 6, 7. for any Soul or Perſon, *v.* 2. than if his Ignorance were Real, *Numb.* 15. 27. This ſeemeth to be the Caſe of all theſe Fooliſh Virgins, or ſome of them, at leaſt, who would think ſcorn to be accounted ſhallow; yea, who preſumptuouſly Neglect thoſe Means of Light which are afforded to them, and thereby are in danger of being cut off, *Numb.* 15. 30, 31. and Now by God himſelf, who hath the Preſent Execution of ſuch Laws, *Heb.* 10. 28. 31.

3. Invincible Ignorance may be ſufficient to Excuſe from Actual ſin ; but not when Means of Light are Miniſtred, though not Convincingly underſtood. Original ſin (as all confeſs) is chargeable upon Infants, whoſe Ignorance is yet invincible: But Actual ſin is not imputed, ſave with Reſpect unto a Law Proclaimed, which alſo may be underſtood. Thus Heathens who are Ignorant Invincibly of Goſpel-Laws, ſhall not

Equally (for kind) Obliged to take Notice of its Laws; which also Might be understood, were they but careful in the use of Means.

4. One may be at the present Guilty of a sin, *Lev.* 4. 13. who yet is not Obliged to Confess it, (or offer a Particular Sacrifice for it) untill he is Convinced of it, *v.* 14. *Lev.* 5. 4, 5, 6. save onely in a General way, or from an easie suppofition of its being Possible, *Ezek.* 45. 20. One may confess a Real sin, who yet may therein Lye against himself, unless he also is Convinced of it; therefore Conviction must go before Confession. Yet is that Person Guilty before the Lord, and consequently bound from Peremptory self-acquitting, though not engaged to make a Positive Acknowledgment. Such therefore ought to Grant that in the Notion, which they are not yet bound to charge upon themselves, as to a known Particular Application. Yea, such ought also to be self suspitious, and to confess the Possibility of their failing, though none should urge them to any more than barely General self-condemnation, unless such seem to dally with their Light.

5. One may Transgress at Present, in his Not Doing such a thing, who yet is not immediately engaged Now unto the Practice of it, till he shall be enlightned thereinto. Though an Erroneous Conscience doth not Affirmatively bind me unto sin, *Acts* 26. 9. 15. yet doth it Negatively bind from Duty, untill that Duty is cleared up, and yet my present Non-performance of it may be sinful. God will be first Served with the Head (or Knowledge) in every Sacrifice, *Lev.* 1. 8. and would have every Man to be Persuaded in his own Mind, *Rom.* 14. 5. else Real Duty may Rationally (or unto such a Man) be sin, *v.* 23. Yet his Not Doing of it (from Erroneous Doubting) is also sinful; because that Ignorance is self-contracted, where Means afforded are not convincing. Self-blinding Men are not first bound to see, but to anoint their Eyes, *Rev.* 3. 18. Yet their Not Acting from want of Sight, is to be charged on them as sin whilst they are Blind.

6. One's Self Contracted (Real) Ignorance, may somewhat lessen both Guilt and Suffering, but doth not Take them quite away. He that doth not his Master's Will through lack of Knowledge, shall be yet Beaten, although with fewer stripes, *Luke* 12. 48. which Argueth his being somewhat Guilty, because fore-warned, *v.* 46. though he had
now

The Parable of the Ten Virgins Opened. 14?

now forgotten it. And though there is little Difference between the Guilt of Ignorance in Rulers, *Lev.* 4. 22, 23. and Inferiour Persons, *v.* 27, 28. yet is a sin of Ignorance in Priests (or Eminent Professors) *v.* 3, 4. Equivalent to that of All the Congregation, *v.* 13, 14. Yea, with Respect unto the same sort of Persons, some sins of Ignorance (according to the Worth of Duty) are of a Deeper die, *Numb.* 15. 24. than are some other, *Lev.* 4. 13, 14. And so far is a Multitude from lessning the Guilt of Ignorance, as that it is the greatest Guilt of all; appearing from the Sacrifice required in that Case, *viz.* A Young Bullock and a Goat, *Numb.* 15. 24. which Goat (in such a case) was more than was required from any other sort of Persons (save the Multitude) for any sin of Ignorance whatsoever.

Quest. 4. What kind of Desire is that (Relating unto Oyl or Light) which is here signified by the Foolish Virgins to the Wise?

Ansvv. 1. It is a Partial (but not Compleat) Desire, and therein suitable to their fore-mentioned Confession. They do not say, Help us to such a Measure of this Oyl, as you seem to be furnished with; much less do they Desire to have their Vessels filled with it; but onely, *Give us* [*Of*] *your Oyl*; as if some Lesser quantity would serve their turn. An Hypocrite may crave some Part of Grace, or just so much as Conscience and Occasion doth require, who yet is loath to bear the whole, for fear of being too much burthened. Thus some would have Restraining Grace, *Numb.* 22. 34. and Saving Grace at last, *Numb.* 23. 10. Others are for the Highest Notions of Spiritual Knowledge, *Prov.* 18. 1. A third is for that Good by which Eternal Life may be Obtained, *Mat.* 19. 16. together with the saving of his Earthly Interest, but not otherwise, *v.* 21, 22. This Argueth that Water is not Elementary, save unto Fishes; since other Creatures when most athirst, are yet afraid of being Drown'd in its Abundance.

2. It is not a Desire of Oyl (at all) in Vessels, but onely to supply their Fading Lamps, as the subjoyned Reason of their Desiring it doth Evidence. An Hypocrite is most sollicitous about his Lamps or good Affections, which if he can but competently keep from Going out, the Deadness or Extinction of his Principle and Judgment is not the Matter of his Lamentation. Such mostly are Delighted in that kind of Preaching which worketh most upon Affections, however dark the Mind is left; yea, possibly Mis-guided, by Reason of a Zeal for God, but not according unto Knowledge, *Rom.* 10. 2. This is too Natural unto the Best, so far as Folly is remaining in them; but is Predominant in Foolish Virgins, who altogether are deprived of Heavenly Wisdom. But yet these wiser Virgins took Oyl in their Vessels; nor are such satisfied with others

Oyl

The Parable of the Ten Virgins Opened.

Oyl in that Respect, as these poor Foolish Virgins would have been; but are for being taught by their Anoynting, and not by any Man whatever, 1 *John* 2. 27.

3. It is a Desire of Oyl from Man, (or from the Wiser Virgins) but not from Jesus Christ. Means are not to be Dis-regarded; but yet, if any Man lack Oyl or Wisdom, he is first bid to Ask of God, *James* 1. 5. as *Solomon* did, 2 *Chron.* 1. 10. but so did not these Foolish Virgins. An Hypocrite will not Delight himself in God, *Job* 27. 10. A Common Jew will first spend all upon Physitians, *Luke* 8. 43. and Carnal Hearts content themselves with Applications made to Instruments. How few add Prayer unto their Hearing, save in a Formal way of doing both; and thence it is they are no more Advantaged by either. Whereas a Gracious Heart doth know Christ onely hath the Key of *David*, *Rev.* 3. 7. both as to the Speakers Utterance, *Col.* 4. 3. and Hearers Entrance, *Acts* 16. 14. therefore such chiefly sue to him. And if a Man may Hypocritically Desire Light of God, *Numb.* 22. 19. much more of Man, who is less Dreaded, and who cannot detect his close Dissimulation.

4. It is not Properly a Desire, but rather a Demand, made up of much appearing Pride and Discontent; as those words [*Give us*] do import. *Abraham's* Servant could Humbly say unto a Virgin, *Give me* [*I pray thee*] *a little Water*, Gen. 24. 43. But *Israel* (in a way of Chiding) said to *Moses*, *Give us Water, that we may Drink*, Exod. 17. 2. So do these Foolish Virgins speak unto the Wise, as *Jacob* bad *Laban* to Give him his Wife; not in a way of Supplication, but Demand, *Gen.* 29. 21. *Give me thy Son*, said he unto that Woman, in a way of Courtesie, not to himself, but her, 1 *Kings* 17. 19. So say these to the Wife, else they must Part, as if Continuance with them were a kindness to the Wife. Yea, these bid, *Give us of your Oyl*, as *Israel* (Atheistically) said to *Moses*, *Give us Flesh*, Numb. 11. 13. which was not in his Power to do; no More than Man can give Light to another. Thus is an Hypocrite's Desire made up of Pride and Passion, instead of Vertue, Grace, or Common Reason.

5. It is a Lazy Desire this of having Light freely Given, without any store of Cost or Pains. We may not Sell the Truth, but yet are bid to Buy it, *Prov.* 23. 23. And as with our Laborious Searching for it, *Prov.* 2. 4. so by our Chearful Suffering the Loss of all for that Excelling Knowledge, *Phil.* 3. 8. But Man (as Man) knows not the Price of Oyl or Spiritual Wisdom, *Job.* 28. 13. Nor will an Hypocrite Give ought for Truth, at least not hazard the Loss of All, as doth an Heavenly Merchant for this Pearl, *Mat.* 13. 45, 46. An Hypocrite

is

The Parable of the Ten Virgins Opened.

is free to Hear what may be underſtood by one that's half aſleep, and could do ſomething, if he might not Suffer; but otherwiſe he pleadeth Poverty and Weakneſs of Capacity in this Caſe, though not in other Matters of Equal Difficulty and Expence. If Light be darted in upon them, or if they might but ſave their Money, ſome would accept of *Given* Oyl, who elſe will neither Buy nor Walk till forced to it; and not then neither, ſave onely in a way of outward ſhew.

6. It is a cold Deſire this, not uttered with any ſign of Earneſtneſs, as *Acts* 2. 37. nor Seconded with Importunity, as *Mat.* 15. 2:. although the other did not plainly ſay, *Not ſo,* (which words are added by our Tranſlators;) nor do they Abſolutely gain-ſay the Motion made, but onely bid them [rather] go to them that Sell, *Mat.* 25. 9. *Paul* Thrice beſought the Lord for Grace untill he had it, 2 *Cor.* 12. 8, 9. and *Jacob* ſaid unto the Angel, *I will not let thee Go, except thou Bleſs me,* Gen. 32. 26. Nor is the Cordialneſs, much leſs the Grace or Spirit of Supplication evidenced but by an Holy Violence and Perſeverance, *Eph.* 6. 18. One might have thought, in ſuch a Weighty Caſe, the Fooliſh Virgins would have Repeated their Deſire, and then have Proſecuted it with cogent Arguments, at leaſt, have bitterly lamented their Repulſe, inſtead of ſilent Acquieſcing in a firſt Denyal. But Hypocrites do either Counterfeit a good Deſire, or at the beſt are onely preſſed thereunto by that which is too Weak to bear them out untill it be obtained.

Queſt. 5. How came the Fooliſh Virgins Lamps (or good Affections) to go out, before their Work was done?

Anſw. 1. Becauſe they were not fed with Oyl out of their Veſſels, or from a well-informed Judgment. 'Tis ſaid, they took No Oyl at firſt; and then, Not in their Veſſels, to be ſure: Therefore their Lamps could not be Laſting. Life in Affections onely is but like unto Sap reſiding in a Branch, which being ſevered from its Root, may ſprout a little (eſpecially if thruſt into ſome Moiſter Ground) but in a ſhort time will come to nothing. Indeed there is a Gradual Difference (in point of Laſtingneſs) between ſome Natural Mens Affections, compared with others, as is between their Bodily Conſtitutions; but though ſome may Live longer, yet all are Mortal, ſave as they are Preſerved and Animated by an Immortal Soul or Judgment; and Violence of Exerciſe doth onely ſhorten their continuance. As we would therefore have our Lamps not to go out, ſo let us take heed of Empty Veſſels.

2. Becauſe the very Lamps of Fooliſh Virgins (or their Affections, as in Themſelves conſidered) are much Inferiour to the other's in point

of Laſtingneſs. Saints are compared to Green Firr-Trees, *Hoſ.* 14. 8. whoſe very Boughs (which anſwer unto Spiritual Affection,) retain their Greenneſs Long: But Hypocrites Affections at the beſt are onely Carnal; and if a Carnal Mind be Death, *Rom.* 8. 6. much more are ſuch Affections Mortal. They alſo that are Chriſt's, have Crucified that Inordinacy of Affection, which others ſtill Labour under, *Gal.* 5. 24. and Violent Paſſions are of no long continuance. Yea, Hypocrites Affections are like thoſe Lamps or Candles, which have ſome ſwailing Thief in them, or ſome Particular Object fixt upon, which (as a Sucker) makes the Branch to wither: whereas a Good Man guideth his Affections with Diſcretion, *Pſal.* 112. 5. which therefore laſt the longer. Thus we may Learn, both why the Fooliſh Virgins Lamps go out, and how we may ſecure our own, *viz.* by getting our Affections Sanctified.

3. Becauſe the very Oyl wherewith the Fooliſh Virgins Lamps are fed, is alſo differing from the others in point of Fatneſs, Purity and ſelf-multiplying; all which are Influential to its Laſtingneſs. The Fooliſh Virgins Oyl was onely Common at the beſt; and Nature's Oyl (compared with that of Grace) doth quickly ſpend it ſelf, and upon thoſe fore-mentioned Accounts, as may be thus made out.

1. Spiritual things are alſo Fat, and conſequently not ſo apt to waſt. Such is the Moiſture of the Olive-Tree, *Judg.* 9. 9. eſpecially of Chriſt, *Rom.* 11. 17. and of thoſe Bleſſings obtained through Faith on him, *Iſa.* 55. 2. and through Communion with him, *Pſal.* 36. 8. and 63. 5. *Jer.* 31. 14. Therefore Affections fed with ſuch like Conſiderations are of a more laſting Nature; and thence it is that True Believers are not ſo ſubject to Back-ſlide, becauſe their Motives to continue ſtill are of a more Lively and Eternal make, *John* 6. 67, 68. But choiſeſt Earthly Delicates, in point of Moral Nouriſhing, are very Lean, *Pſal.* 106. 15. which leave the Eater's ſtomach alway Craving, *Pſal.* 78. 29, 30. therefore Affections fed therewith, are apt to faint upon their being diſcontinued; and he that onely Drinketh of ſuch Water will Thirſt again, *John* 4. 13. Yea, Lower things are no way ſatisfying, *Iſa.* 55. 2. while they continue, *Eccl.* 1. 8. and Increaſe, *Eccl.* 5. 10. Therefore Souls Acting upon that Account (in ways of Duty) are at the beſt uncertain, compared with others, *Prov.* 19. 23. and 14. 14.

2. That which is Spiritual, is alſo Pure, 1 *Tim.* 4. 12. and Pureſt Oyl (at leaſt-wiſes in a Myſtical ſenſe) will burn the longeſt time; therefore that Sacred Lamp which was to be alway burning, was Ordered to be fed with pure Oyl-Olive beaten, *Exod.* 27. 20. Now, a Divine Command is Pure, *Pſal* 19. 8. ſo is that Wiſdom from above,

James

The Parable of the Ten Virgins Opened.

James 3. 17. yea, so is a Believers Hope of Future Glory, 1 *John* 3. 2. therefore Affections fed with such like Arguments, are of a long continuance. Since God's Command endures for ever, so doth his Duty whose Outward Peace gives place to Purity, and whose very Hope is of a Soul-purifying Nature. But Earthly Lower Motives are Compounded, as is the Matter whereof some Lights are made, which therefore quickly spend themselves with spitting, and leave a Noisome Snuff behind them. Therefore the Foolish Virgins Lamps go out, with an Offensive smell unto the Wise, who thenceforth cannot bear to have Communion with them any longer, but wish them also to be Gone, *Mat.* 25. 9.

3. That which is Spiritual, is of a self-multiplying Nature also, wherein the Wiser Virgins Oyl is like that of the Widows, 2 *Kings* 4. 3, 4. and that which Multiplyeth in its pouring out, must needs be Lasting. Inherent Grace is (partly) therefore Everlasting, because it is alway Growing, *Psal.* 92. 12. 14. so is a Suffering Saints future Glory, 2 *Cor.* 4. 17. and Present Consolations, 2 *Cor.* 1. 5. yea, his Faith also, 2 *Thes.* 1. 3, 4. therefore Affections fed with such a kind of Oyl, are as a well watered Tree, whose Fruit and Leaf continue in a Time of Heat and Drought, *Jer.* 17. 7, 8. But Lower things are of a Passing Nature, 1 *John.* 2. 16, 17. uncertain at the best, 1 *Tim.* 6. 17. and at the last will come to Nothing, *v.* 7. yea, Perish with the Using, *Col.* 2. 22. therefore Affections fed therewith must needs be of a fading Nature; especially since Lower Motives are apt in time to Deaden Men's Affections unto Spiritual Objects: whereas that which is Spiritual, is also the Preserver and Embalmer of that Affection, which is thereby maintained.

The Truth of all which may yet more fully be made out, by taking a Particular Notice of those Motives (or that Oyl) wherewith the Lamps or good Affections of unsound Professors unto Duty, are maintained. All which are Fading. As,

1. When Duty is Affected for its Novelty, which may not be so easily perceived at the first, as afterwards. *Athenians* spent their time in nothing else but telling and hearing some New thing, *Acts* 17. 21. who therefore had some Affection for *Paul*'s New Doctrine, *v.* 19. which afterwards was Mocked by them, *v.* 32. Thus did the Jews Affect *John Baptist*'s Light, though onely for a Season, *John* 5. 35. or during its Prime and Flower, as ὥρα signifieth, from whence ὡραῖος is derived, signifying Beautiful, *Rom.* 10. 15. because a thing in Season is so, *Eccl.* 3. 11. And upon this Account the Foolish Virgins might Go out at first; but therefore were their Lamps or good Affections soon Extinguished.

148   *The Parable of the Ten Virgins Opened.*

guished. Whereas a Gracious Heart Affects the Nature of his Duty, who therefore stores up All, both New and Old, *Mat.* 13.52. and Loves it to the End, as Christ doth him, *John* 13.1. But he that Marrieth a Woman for her Beauty, is oft a Widdower before his Wive's Decease; and upon that Account poor Foolish Virgins are soon Divorced from that Duty, which was Espoused onely for its Beauty.

2. When Duty is undertaken from a Passionate Pang, or strong Impulse upon their Spirits thereunto, which doth betray some into Error, and maketh all to faint in ways of Truth. Impulses are uncertain things, which therefore never can beget a fixed Frame; as in those Ancient Prophets, whose strange and sudden Variations from themselves did thence arise. Impulses are suspitious things, especially since the Perfecting of a surer Rule: And when a Call is not Exceeding Clear, Danger will represent it as a meer Temptation, unto the Failing of ones Real Duty. Impulses also are oft-times Contradicting; and Interest in that Case, will have a Casting Voice, as being alway Next to Conscience, and in its silence evermore supreme. Whereas a Gospel-Saint is Taught to Heed that Written Word, 2 *Pet.* 1.19. which is both certain, safe, and self-agreeing: Therefore his Duty (Built upon that Rock) will stand, when other Bottoms fall together with their Buildings.

3. When such a Path is Walked in, not for the way it self, but for the sake of One's Companions, in point of Quality, Respect, or Number; it being Natural to have Men's Persons in Admiration, *Jude* 16. And thus a Ruler's Faith, or Practice of the *Pharisees*, is by some Men Accounted the strongest Argument, *John* 7.48. Others will Serve that God who is the God of their Respected Friend, *Ruth* 1.16. Others will be concluded by the Generality of Professors, right or wrong, 2 *Sam.* 16.18. But as few Men of Rank are Called, 1 *Cor.* 1.26. So fewer of them will continue Faithful in a Trying hour, *Jer.* 5.5. and Love unto One's self will hazard a Parting with Dearest Friends in times of Danger, *Mark* 14.50. and as the Generality are never Right, *Mat.* 7.14. so few are free to Die for Company, or Persevere in Duty upon that Account, whatever they Profess, *Mat.* 26.35. Whereas the Righteous holdeth on his way, *Job* 17.9. as doth a Traveller upon some earnest Business, though all forsake him, 2 *Tim.* 4.16.

4. When Duty is Affected (Mainly) for it's suitableness to Common Reason. Reason is good, as is the Law, if used Lawfully, 1 *Tim.* 1.8. else Duty needs must be imperfect in point of Lastingness, as well as Form and Matter. Right Reason (at the first) did shew the Equity of Man's Obedience to the whole of his Creator's Will, as it

was

The Parable of the Ten Virgins Opened. 149

was Then signified, or might be afterwards; but Reason is much Impaired by the Fall, as is the Law, *Rom.* 8. 3. save as fallen Man is under it to Christ, 1 *Cor.* 9. 21. Faith is the proper Form of Gospel-Duty, which therefore (as in the *Greek*) is called the Obedience of Faith, *Rom.* 1. 5. and therefore Duty bottomed upon Reason, must needs be apt to Putrifie, as is Man's Body when severed from his Soul, or its Substantial Form. Natural Reason doth Oppose some part of that Material Duty which is required, *Mat.* 16. 21, 22, 23. therefore that Rational or Legal Man, *Mat.* 19. 20. could not go on unto Perfection, *v.* 21, 22. Whereas a Gospel-Saint sees that by Faith alone, which might have been known by Reason, *Heb.* 11. 3. who therefore seeth also that which Reason never would have Evidenced, *viz.* the Duty of his Losing all, in ways of Proper Gospel-Duty, *Luke* 14.26. *Acts* 21. 12, 13. *Heb.* 11. 24, 25, 26.

5. When Duty is performed in the strength of Resolutions, or meer Natural Courage, which are a Means and Mercy not to be Despised, but yet not to be Trusted in, as *Peter's* instance sadly sheweth, *Mat.* 26. 35. 74. Courage may carry through a Natural Undertaking, 2 *Sam.* 10. 12, 13. and Vows of Old were of Religious Force, *Judg.* 11. 39. but other Armour is prescribed in Gospel-times, *Eph.* 6. 10, 11. Christ having chosen what is Weak, that so no Flesh should Glory in his Presence, 1 *Cor.* 1. 27. 29. Courage is under the Command of Reason, and when the Captain Runs, (as Reason will, in Spiritual Cases) the stoutest of his Souldiers cannot stand, for lack of Conduct: And Resolutions are depending upon Courage, which therefore needs must Run together with it. Whereas a Gracious Heart is not so much for saying what he will do, as Labouring to set Duty home upon his Heart, *Psal.* 44. 20, 21. and waiting upon God for Light and Strength, *Psal.* 25. 4. 5. Opposing Faith to Natural Fear, *Psal.* 56. 3. who therefore is not Moved, *Psal.* 16. 8. and 62. 2.

6. When Duty is affected in a time of Safety, and upon that Account. Birds hatched in a Summers Season are Generally Gone (at least-wise will not sing) in Winter: Whereas those Primitive Christians were most Faithful, who were Converted in a Time of Persecution. Men walking in the Fields for Recreation, are driven back by an appearing storm: but therefore such will neither Sow nor Reap, *Eccl.* 11. 4. Peace is a Mercy, *Acts* 9. 31. to be Prayed for, 1 *Tim.* 2. 2. but he that is not an hardy Souldier, will never be a Faithful Christian, 2 *Tim.* 2. 3. Therefore a Gracious Heart is not for Lingring till the storm be over, because he longeth to be Master of that great Temptation. Yea, therefore God inureth His unto some kind of daily

Tryals,

7. When Pride is the Main Impulsive unto Duty, as to its being either first undertaken upon that Account, or therefore (chiefly) Persevered in. Thus Honour did excite the *Pharisees* to be Obedient; and others (having once Begun) will not Desist, for fear of being Mocked: Both which are of Inferiour Use, but not fit to be trusted with the Chief Command in a Religious Service. The Lust of the Flesh, (or Worldly Pleasures) and the Lust of the Eyes (or Worldly Riches) do seem both of them (Generally) to be preferr'd before the Pride of Life, or Worldly Honour, 1 *John* 2. 16. to shew the Weakness of this Latter Motive, compared with the other Two, though All of them are Worldly, and consequently of a Passing Nature, *v.* 17. Few will Begin to Run in Wisdom's Paths, if Honour be the Onely Prize; much less will they Persist herein, if Pleasures and Profits be thereby Hazarded, through Fear of Persecution; since in that Case, it is accounted One's greatest Honour to consult for such a Principal self-preservation, though by Disgraceful self-contradicting Practices.

8. When Duty and Affections are Contracted, meerly because of Present wages expected thereupon. Those never will be Faithful Souldiers unto Christ, who are not satisfied with the publick Faith of Heaven in that respect, and present Necessaries, 2 *Cor.* 4. 18. 1 *Tim.* 6. 8. These Foolish Virgins (at their first going out) had store of such Encouragements, together wherewith their Lamps (or good Affections) are Now Extinguished. An Heart that is Taken with the World, doth ever incline, as doth a Needle, to that Load-stone wherewith it hath been Touched; and Gospel-Duty is yet directly Opposite thereunto; as is the South unto the North. Therefore Christ doth Prepare his Voluntiers with such like Proclamations at the first, *Mat.* 8. 19, 20. shewing the inconsistency that is between Love of the World and of the Father, 1 *John* 2. 15. at least-wise in Respect of Lastingness, *Mat.* 5. 24. There is some Fatness in Earth'y Blessings, which yet will Fade, if not bedewed da ly, *Gen.* 27. 39. so will those Lamps (or good Affections) which Mainly are maintained with that kind of hungry Oyl.

9. When Duty is under the Sole or Principal Command of Natural Conscience, and slavish fear of Condemnation entailed upon Disobedience.

The Parable of the Ten Virgins Opened.

dience. T'... lso is a Serviceable Under-Officer, Commissionated by Christ himself, *Mark* 16.16. and therefore all Fear of Suffering is not Diabolical, save when it is Supream, *James* 2.19. But Natural Conscience is subject to be feared in some, 1 *Tim.* 4.2. and in all Unbelievers, to be Defiled, *Titus* 1.15. yea, to be weak:ned in the Best, 1 *Cor.* 8.7. therefore not fit to be confided in, save as it is Accompanied or back'd with Faith unfeigned, and without which it is not good, 1 *Tim.* 1.15. And as Christ's Future Promises are nothing (with a *Demas*) to this present world, 2 *Tim.* 4.10. so present Suffering (in the way of Duty) will easily be too many for an Hypocrite's future fears of such a Nature. Therefore Christ doth not trust Conscience with his People's Guidance, but doth Himself dwell in them by his Spirit, and is ch in-dwelling Spirit doth enable them to keep what is Committed to them; 2 *Tim.* 1.14.

10. VVhen our Affections unto Duty are meerly bottomed upon the sense of high: t proper Priviledges from the Lord himself, which are believed to be had in such a way. 'Tis true indeed the Love of Christ (for what he hath already done) is of a Soul-constraining Nature, 2 *Cor.* 5.14. next unto which is Hope of Future Glory, 2 *Cor.* 4.17. but as the Saints Duty is not proper, so neither can it be ensured, save as it issueth chiefly from a Nobler and more Lasting Principle. A Child of Light may walk in Darkness, *Isa.* 50.10. whose Duty (in that Case) would fail, if he were onely animated by a sense of Priviledges. Therefore so many stumble in the ways of Christ, because they meet not with those In-comes from him which were too peremptorily Expected, and too much Leaned on. Christ was Delighted in God's will, as such, *Heb.* 10.7. therefore he Fainted not, though seemingly forsaken by his Father, *Mat.* 27.46. and nothing short of that same Oyl (wherewith he was Anointed) *viz.* the Love of Naked Duty, will keep our Lamps from Going out.

Use 1. God alway can, and in due time he will constrain the Foolish Virgins to confess their being Inferiour to the Wise, in point of Oyl, or some more choice Accomplishments. Thus *Pharaoh* was enforced to confess, that *Moses* was more prevailing than Himself with God in Prayer, *Exod.* 8.8. and *Balaam* also, that his Present state was not so Happy as that of *Israel*, *Numb.* 23.10. Yea, *Saul* at last was made to signifie that *David* was more Righteous than himself, 1 *Sam.* 24.17. As God can punish the stoutest Heart, *Isa.* 10.12. and cause the Arrogancy of such to cease, *Isa.* 13.11. So he can make the proudest *Pharisee* to call himself the chiefest sinner, 1 *Tim.* 1.15. who sometimes thought he had wherein to Trust, *Phil.* 3.4,5. *Ahab's* false Prophet

The Parable of the Ten Virgins Opened.

Prophet scorned to be thought Inferiour to *Micajah*, 1 *Kings* 22. 24. untill he went into an inner Chamber to Hide himself, unto the shame of his Profession, and then he saw it, *v.* 25. Compliance with an *Ahab*'s will, and base unworthy self-withdrawing ear, evince the Absence of God's Spirit in Men, and will at last convince such of their false pretending thereunto in Times of Peace.

2. Those are not Worthy to be called Virgins, who are Condemned by these Foolish Virgins Carriage to the Wife, in such a Case and Time. These do not call the other Desperate, Schismatical, or self-conceited, for Offering to go out without their Company: *Eliab* therefore was an Invidious Fellow, who neither would Engage (Himself) with that *Goliath*, nor yet let *David* go without a Censure, 1 *Sam.* 17. 28. These do not call their Darkness Light, nor boast of their new Trimmed Lamps, but do Confess their going out: *Saul* therefore was exceeding Impudent, who did assert his having been Obedient, against both Sense and Conscience, 1 *Sam.* 15. 13, 14. These do not scorn to be Instructed, nor Totally Neglect the use of Means, but freely come unto the Wise, to be partakers of their Oyl: Therefore proud *Amaziah* was near his End, who scorned to be Taught by his Inferiour, 2 *Chron.* 25. 15, 16. So were *Eliab*'s Sons, who causelesly Railed upon *Moses*, but scorned to come up unto him, to have the Case Decided in a Friendly way, *Numb.* 16. 12, 13, 14. 32.

3. The Foolish Virgins Lamps are alway apt to fade, and will at last Go out, especially at such a Time, or when the Cry is made. They are (at best) but as a Morning Cloud, *Hos.* 6. 4. unrooted Seed, *Mat.* 13. 5. Houses upon the Sand, *Mat.* 7. 26. Professors, *Deut.* 5. 28. without an Heart, *v.* 29. and of an Earthy make, 1 *Cor.* 15. 45. or without strength, *Rom.* 5. 6. all which evince their being apt to fail. Yea, such will (at the last) come down indeed, since Hypocrites will not alway Pray, *Job* 27. 10. nor yet Believe but for a while, *Luke* 8. 13. but will be choaked with the World, *Mat.* 13. 22. being onely Zealous for Men's Traditions, *Mat.* 15. 2. or meerly Counterfeiting Good Affections, *Mark* 7. 6. And more especially at such a time, when God will lead Back-sliders forth with workers of Iniquity, *Psal.* 125. 5. Discovering Foundations unto the Neck, *Hab.* 3. 13. when two third Parts shall be cut off, *Zech.* 13. 8. and Chaff shall be burnt up, *Mat.* 3. 12. in Order to the Purging out of Rebels from among his People, *Ezek.* 20. 38.

This is a Failure of High Concernment, which I shall therefore a little shew the Symptoms of. And so the Symptoms of Decaying good Affections (or Fading Lamps) are briefly these.

Sympt. 1. When

Sympt. 1. When onely in an hour of Temptation there seems to be a want of Light into that Truth or Duty, which formerly (and in cool Blood) was never Doubted of. If *Peter* knows not Christ, *Mat.* 26.72. nor *Nabal*, who Famous *David* is, 1 *Sam.* 25. 10. nor *Israel*, what's become of *Moses*, *Exod.* 32. 1. It is not so much from Ignorance, as want of Love. That Lamp (and not its Oyl) is to be blamed, whose Light is alway clear, untill some Nip or Gust of Wind doth put it out: and in that Case Men wrongfully complain of Darkness. 'Tis true, Back-sliders never were Judicious; and yet their not Continuing in the Truth, is nextly caused by the failing of their Affections, and is a sign thereof. A Real Friend doth Love (a Thing or Person) alway, *Prov.* 17. 17. therefore Adversity will make no Alteration, so long as Friendship doth continue, however injudicious that Affection is. And let no Man deceive himself, his Turning aside from Christ cannot be from a Better Light, but want of Love.

2. When every small Occasion is improved by Professors, whereon to fall, or be Offended. Love covereth a Real Sin, *Prov.* 10. 12. and Charity believeth all things, 1 *Cor.* 13. 7. especially when there is Ground for Confidence (as in this Case there is) that such a Thing or Person is not Culpable, when most suspected. But when the Foolish Virgins Motion (for Oyl or Light) is soon Denied, especially when *Haman*'s suing for his Life is most unreasonably misconstrued, *Esth.* 7. 8. Yea, when a Man is therefore called an Enemy, for telling that which cannot be denyed to be a Truth, *Gal.* 4. 16. Such Mens Affections certainly are Altered. Well might they be Concluded to be Envious or Dis-affected, *Mat.* 27. 18. who could not say, what Evil Christ had done, and yet Cryed out to have him Crucified, *v.* 23. Whereas he that doth Love his Master, will not Accept of Freedom Offered, *Exod.* 21. 5. Nor will *Ruth* leave her dearly Beloved Mother, although she hath a fair Occasion Ministred, *Ruth* 1. 15, 16. nor will ought separate a True Believer from his Love of Christ, *Rom.* 8. 35.

3. When Means afforded for Satisfaction (as to the Truth of such a Duty) are very sleightly attended unto, if at all. He daily Meditateth in the Law of God, who dearly Loveth it, *Psal.* 119. 97. and he that Cordially desireth Heavenly Wisdom will separate himself (from other Business) to seek it, *Prov.* 18. 1. Nor is a Love-sick Spouse Discouraged (by what she meeteth with) from the Pursuance of her Beloved, *Cant.* 5. 6, 7, 8. But Dilatory Hearers, who feignedly are for a more Convenient Season, *Acts* 24. 25. and such as put a Question, but stay not for its Answer, *John* 18. 38. especially they who will not so much as come unto the Light, *John* 3. 20. Yea, they who

who Perfunctorily converse about Enquiries of this Nature, or do not Hear in Hearing, *Mat.* 13.13. do plainly evidence their want of Love unto the Truth, 2 *Thef.* 2. 10. Thus some are easily convicted of Decaying good Affections, because the strenuousness of their Endeavour doth no way suit the shew of their Desire.

4. When Ordinary Light is not sufficient, without some more than Necessary Demonstration; which yet in other like Cases is by such Persons thought to be unreasonably expected by another. God made Man upright, or Plain-hearted, but he hath found out many bad Inventions or Evasions, *Eccl.* 7. 29. and out of his own Mouth shall he be Judged, *Luke* 19. 22. Some things of Old were Darkly hinted, much more in Gospel-times, *Psal.* 49. 4. *Mat.* 13. 34. to Try Men's Ingenuity, *Mat.* 15. 15, 16. or who are of that Chosen Number, that will Obey as soon as they shall Hear, *Psal.* 18. 44. Love made the Spouse (when half asleep) to Hear the Voice of her Beloved, *Cant.* 5. 2. And *David*'s Delighting in the Will of God, did make him light of Hearing, *Psal.* 40. 6. 8. And if *Elisha* had not been very Candid, he wou'd not so readily have known the Meaning of *Elijah*'s Mantle cast upon him, 1 *Kings* 19. 19, 20. 'Tis true, Man's Reason may not Dictate Gospel-Duties, yet is there room for Candour in such Cases; and Persons Dull of Hearing, *Mat.* 13. 15. have not the Love of God in them, *John* 5. 42.

5. When clear Convictions are not Accompanied with speedy Actions: it being an undoubted sign of Weakness in that Child, which stayeth long in the place of breaking forth, *Hof.* 3. 13. A strong Affection is rather apt to be too forward, as *Moses* was, to have his Sister healed, *Numb.* 12. 13. as *David* was to Build a Temple, 2 *Sam.* 7. 2. 5. and as the People were to make Christ King, *John* 6. 15. however such are in Pain, till they have Vent, and then are most Refreshed, *Job* 32. 19, 20. Faith is not Hasty, *Isa.* 28. 16. and Hope can wait, *Rom.* 8. 25. but Love is all upon the Spur, and if there be nothing from Without to hinder, one Day is then Accounted a Thousand Years, 2 *Pet.* 3. 8. Therefore such are for making Haste, *Psal.* 119. 60. and not conferring with Flesh and Blood, *Gal.* 1. 16. but do immediately endeavour to comply with signified Duty, *Acts* 16. 10. Whereas *Lot*'s Lingring still in *Sodom*, *Gen.* 19. 16. after a double *Item* given, *v.* 12. 15. did plainly evidence he had no great Affection to be gone.

6. When Souls are glad of being Hindred, and who are therefore Catching at, or readily at least improve the first Advantage fairly Offered for such a Purpose. As Hatred watcheth for anothers Halting, *Jer.* 20. 10 and Envy seeketh for Occasions, 2 *Cor.* 11, 12. or false

Witnesses, *Mat.* 26. 59. so Love Deviseth Liberal things, *Isa.* 52. 8. and waiteth to be Gracious, *Isa.* 30. 18. *David* was Glad when others did invite him unto Duty, *Psal.* 122. 1. whose Soul did break with Longing for it, *Psal.* 119. 20. and 41. 1, 2. Nor would *Paul* be disswaded with Heart-breaking Importunities, *Acts* 12. 13, 14. but did what in him lay, to shun Obstructions, *Gal.* 1. 17. and sadly Bewailed, *Rom.* 7. 24. his being sometimes Captivated, *v.* 23. or Hindred from that good which he fain would have done, *v.* 19. Whereas they have but small Affection for their Duty, who wait but for a Wind to carry them off, *John* 6. 65, 66. or willingly Obey Man's countermand, *Hos.* 5. 11. yea, they who do not cast about to be Delivered from a forcible Captivity, *Jer.* 41. 13, 14.

7. When any thing is loved More than Christ or Duty, *Mat.* 10. 37. A Child may truly Love his Parents both alike, and Christ did duly Love All his Disciples, *John* 13. 1. though *John* was Eminently his Beloved, *v.* 23. but Christ is not Beloved Duly, if Life it self (as well as our Relations) be not Hated by us in Competition with our Duty unto him, *Luke* 14. 26. *David* Desired Nothing upon Earth, Compared with God, *Psal.* 73. 25. Nor was *Paul* moved with the fear of Losing All, if what he had to do for Christ might be but finished, *Acts* 20. 23, 24. and nothing short of this, will clearly Evidence a True Disciple's Love, *John* 21. 17, 18. And though a Temporary failing of this Fruit in *Peter*, *Mat.* 26. 34. might be consistent with its Never failing Root, *Luke* 22. 32. yet they who fall with him, and do not also Rise again, will not be Credited, as to the Truth of their Professed good Affection. An Hypocrite may Suffer much, but yet their Lamps are quite Gone out, who do Habitually Affect ought more than Christ, and do thus Evidence it.

8. When that Reproach which some Men cast upon the ways of God, is Lightly born by those who do Profess to walk therein. How would the Wiser Virgins have been Moved, in case the Foolish had Reviled them, because of Going forth. Love is made up of Sympathy, and as in Christ, *Acts* 9. 4. so in his People, *Psal.* 69. 9. And though *Paul* would have some Opposers to be Taught with Meekness, 2 *Tim.* 2. 25. yet could not he bear Blaspheming Jews, *Acts* 13. 45, 46. Yea, *David's* Love to God made him Hate the Haters of him, and to be Grieved with them, *Psal.* 139. 21. as with his greatest Enemies, *v.* 22. Two contrary Masters cannot be served with the same Affection, *Mat.* 6. 24. and next unto a Saint's being Angry with himself, 2 *Cor.* 7. 11. he cannot but Declare against the sins of others, *Mic.* 3. 8. Passion is to be watched over, *Eph.* 4. 26. and Personal Cases call for Moderation,

Numb. 12. 2, 3. but let us have a care of smothering Zeal by our Discretion, so as to make our Love for Christ a Matter Disputable.

9. When Souls are Satisfied with Ignoble and Dull Performances of that Duty which God requireth, Love scorns to be affrighted into Duty, 1 *John* 4. 18. or basely to be Hired thereunto, *Dan.* 5. 17. yet will it Act unto its utmost, as that which *David* did with good Affection, 1 *Chron.* 29. 3. he also did with all his Might, *v.* 2. Some Pray and Hear, as they shou'd Buy and Marry, 1 *Cor.* 7. 29, 30. and as the manner of their Acting is, such is the Measure of their Affection, and suitable thereunto (at last) will be the Nature of their Pay, 1 *Sam.* 2. 30. The weakest Creature hath an Heart, and Soul, and Mind, and Strength, wherewith God (in the first place) should be Loved, *Mark* 12. 30. and may not Christ justly say to thee, as *Delilah* did to *Sampson*, *Judg.* 16. 15. *How canst thou say, I Love thee, when thine Heart* (in a Duty) *is not with me, but hast oft Mocked me, and not yet told me wherein thy great strength lyeth?* A Customary Yawning, Drouzy, Wandring, Sleighty VVorshipper of God, is one whose Lamp (or good Affection unto Duty) is either Gone, or Going out.

10. VVhen Souls are not Affected duly with anothers Duty, wherein Themselves are not so properly concerned. Indeed some will Commend that Duty unto others, wherein Themselves would be Excused, *Mat.* 23. 4. This is a self-condemning Approbation, *Rom.* 2. 18. 21. But others onely Cry that Duty up wherein Themselves are Eminently Engaged: But this is self-Love, and not a Proper Love of Duty. Love is commensurated by its Object, therefore Christ doth not call that Love or Friendship which is not both Indefinite, *John* 14. 15. and Universal, *John* 15. 14. forbidding his Disciples to fault that Good which others did who walked not with them, *Mark* 9. 38. 39. *Moses* Desired, that all the Lords People were as he, *Numb.* 11. 29. and others stedfastness was that by which *Paul* was Preserved alive, 1 *Thes.* 3. 8. Yea, *John* Rejoyced in Christ's out-shining him, *John* 3. 26. 29 The Spirit in a Saint may Lust to Envy, *James* 4. 5. but Men of an Habitual Invidious Spirit (approving nought but what is in themselves) are void of Love to Christ or Duty.

These are the Symptoms of Decaying Lamps, or good Affections; in Order unto the keeping whereof Alive, (for Christ and Duty,) these Motives may be of Use.

Mot. 1. Affections in Man are Noble Faculties, and Spiritual Objects are the Highest, which God hath therefore aptly joyned, *Col.* 3. 1. and such no Man should put asunder, *Mat.* 19. 6. *Adam* in Paradise had

The Parable of the Ten Virgins Opened. 157

had all the Creatures in their Prime, yet could he not find an Help meet for himself among them all, *Gen.* 2. 20. that shews the Nobleness of Man's Affections, whose Nature is still the same, but that Man's Foolish Heart is Darkened, *Rom.* 1. 21. *Eph* 4. 18. VVill any wise Man stitch Rags together with Silver Threds? Or spill Rosewater upon the Ground? Or cast away his Love and Person upon a Foolish VVoman? S ch are these Lower things, Beggarly, *Gal.* 4. 9. Earthly, *Phil.* 3. 19. and Foolish, 1 *Tim.* 6. 9. VVhat Pity it is, that Princes Daughters, *Cant.* 7. 1. should Marry so much beneath themselves, when Courted or Desired by him, *v.* 10. who is the King of Kings, *Rev.* 19. 16. the Treasury of wisdom, *Col.* 2. 3. the greatest Heir imaginable, *Heb.* 1. 2. and chiefest of Ten Thousand in point of Beauty, *Cant.* 5. 10.

2. Affections in Man are Lasting, especially his Love or Charity, which will Abide when Faith and Hope shall fail, 1 *Cor.* 13. 13. and Spiritual Objects are the most Incorruptible, *Rom.* 1. 23. whilst Earthly things are of a Fading Nature, *Isa.* 24. 4 why should our Eyes then be set thereupon, *Prov.* 23. 5? VVill any wise Young Man lay out his whole Estate upon a falling House, when he might have a better? How sweet are Christ's Embraces, *Cant.* 2. 6. whose Arms are Everlasting, *Deut.* 33. 27. compared with other Lovers, whom we must be Divorced from by Death, 1 *Tim.* 6. 7. if not before? Affections will continue with us unto all Eternity, but not their worldly Objects; and how will Sinners grieve in Hell, who (through meer Foolishness) will then have Nothing to fix their Love upon. VVhereas they whose Affections Now are wholly given up unto the Lord, will be so far from wanting what to Love Hereafter, as that Love (in its Happiest Exercise) will be the Chief (if not the Sole) Survivor of their Affections.

3. Love is of God, 1 *John* 4. 7. who therefore is called the God of Love, 2 *Cor.* 13. 11. and in a Natural sence as well as Spiritual, since he is the Father of our Souls or Spirits, *Heb.* 12. 9. and consequently (also) of our Affections. Now, shall not he that Plants a Vine, *Mat.* 21. 33. Receive its Fruit, *v.* 34? Shall he that Feeds a Flock, not eat the Milk thereof, 1 *Cor.* 9. 7? Shall not a Father be first Served with his Child's Activity? Houses are firstly at their Builder's Service; Rivers return unto the Sea, from whence they came, *Eccl.* 1. 7. Trees shed their Leaves upon the Ground that bears them: And then shall *Israel* onely bring forth Fruit unto Himself, *Hos.* 10. 1. Is it a small thing with us to take God's Jewels, Broidered Garments, Oyl and Honey; yea, his very Sons and Daughters, and give them (from himself)

to others, *Ezek.* 16. 17, 18, 19, 20? To Love ought more than him without whom nothing could be Loved, is most unworthy, and the just matter of greatest self-abhorring.

4. Affections seem to be the clearest Evidence of God in Man, as to his Infiniteness; in which regard, Low finite Objects are no way Adequate thereunto. There may be a Desire in Man of More than is attained by him, or clearly understood, or can be had, or should be Aimed at, yea, more than he is able to Receive, so Boundless are his Affections, and therefore Meet for none but Christ. Some things may be desired, which are forbidden, *Gen.* 3. 6. and sinful Objects should not be Loved, *Rom.* 12. 9. but let him be *Anathema Maranatha*, who Loves not Christ, 1 *Cor.* 16. 22. Some Die of Love unto the Creature, because they cannot have it: but none are more than Sick of Love for Christ, *Cant.* 5. 8. who at the last, will be self-manifesting unto such as Love him, *John* 14. 21. No Earthly thing should be Affected overmuch, but Love to Christ will never turn into a Lust, *Deut.* 6. 5. Yea, Spiritual Objects will make room for their Reception and Comprehension, *Eph.* 3. 17, 18. and as the Lord is satisfying, *Psal.* 73. 25. so he that Loveth him, Loves other things in their due manner, *Mark* 12. 30, 31. All which bespeak our Love for him.

5. Affections are the Gloss of Actions, and without which the greatest Doer, and utmost Sufferer is as nothing in God's Account, 1 *Cor.* 13. 3. Love is the fulfilling of the Law, *Rom.* 13. 10. the first Fruit of the Spirit, *Gal.* 5. 22. whose Sallet is better than a stalled Ox, *Prov.* 15. 17. and a Man's Kindness is his Desire, *Prov.* 19 22. Yea, all the Substance of his House (compared with Love) is utterly to be contemned, *Cant.* 8. 7. Christ's Love is better than Wine, *Cant.* 1. 2. and his Loving kindness, than Life it self, *Psal.* 63. 3. nor doth the Cedar Wood, or Silver Pillars, or Golden Bottom, or Purple Covering, so much set out his stately Chariot, as that its Midst is Paved with Love, *Cant.* 3. 9, 10.. Yea, Christ doth also count his People's Love much better than Wine, *Cant.* 4. 10. remembring *Israel's* Kindness, *Jer.* 2. 2. whom he oft proved to know their Love, *Deut.* 13. 3. his Valuation whereof appeareth by what he hath prepared for such as Love him, 1 *Cor.* 2. 9. and therefore *David* Desired no greater Mercy than what he had for such, *Psal.* 119. 132.

6. Affections are the Bringers forth of Actions; and as no Work is done at all, in Case Affections be wholly wanting; so where these are not strong and Lively, nothing is done with Joy, or without Difficulty. Judgment is as the Head, and our Affections as the Feet: Therefore he cutteth off the Feet, who sendeth by a Fool, that wanteth both, *Prov.* 26.

The Parable of the Ten Virgins Opened.

26. 6. At least-wise, our Affections are as the Wheels unto a Chariot, which Driveth Heavily when those are taken off, *Exod.* 14. 25. Love is the sleight of Acting, which doth not call its Duty Grievous, 1 *John* 5. 3. nor is it Quenched with many Waters, *Cant.* 8. 7. but doth constrain, 2 *Cor.* 5. 14. in spight of all Discouragements, 2 *Cor.* 12. 15. Whereas Men void of Love to Christ complain of Weariness, *Mal.* 1. 13. wishing the Work were over, *Amos* 8. 5. and waiting for an Opportunity of being Discharged from it, which he who Loves his Matter will not Accept of, *Exod.* 21. 5. Let us therefore keep up Affections, unless we have a mind to cast off Duty.

7. Affections have a re-acting Influence upon the Judgment, as they are Weak or Lively, which should provoke our Care in that regard. Lamps in the Letter, do onely spend their Oyl or Light, which (in the Mystery) is Multiplyed by a flaming good Affection, and Drieth up together with its Going out. Nay, though Oyl may be in the Vessel, yet is there no Proper Light, save as that Oyl is fire in the Lamp or good Affection. Therefore Men never want sufficient Light for that which they Affect, but Generally do complain of Darkness, together with the setting of their Love. Those Jews had not the Love of God in them, *John* 5. 42. who therefore said; they Knew not Christ, *John* 7. 27. although they Knew him well enough, *v.* 28. Nor is it to be wondred at, since Things or Persons not Affected are not much Heeded; yea, most Men's Judgments are Commanded by Affections since the Fall: Therefore if once our Lamps go out, we shall no longer see our Way into a Dis-affected Duty.

8. Affections also are very Tickle, and therein like to Lamps, which (if they be not Guarded) will soon Blow out. A Garment may have lost its Gloss, whose Substance is not yet Consumed; a Razor may have lost its Edge, which is not yet Gap't or Broken; a Flower may have shed its Leaves, whose Root and Stalk do still continue: Such is the Fading Nature of Men's Affections. The Spouses Heart (or Judgment) was Awake when her Affections were asleep, *Cant.* 5. 2. and there may be Love in the Root for Christ, as was in *Peter*, whose Fruit or Exercise was wholly gone when he Denied him. Yea, one may Act for God, and yet without Affection; Witness not onely *Zipporah*'s Angry Duty, *Exod.* 4. 25. and others snuffing at it, *Mal.* 1. 13. but also the Consistency that is between One's giving Alms, *Mat.* 6. 2. and yet omitting Mercy, *Mat.* 23. 23. yea, all a Man's Goods unto the Poor, yet without Charity, 1 *Cor.* 13. 3. Affections are like Crystal Glasses quickly crackt, but not by Man to be Amended.

9. If our Affections be not fixed upon Christ, they will then fasten

otherwhere unto our Dif-advantage. One may have Power over his own Will, in point of Marriage, 1 *Cor*. 7. 37. who yet mu t needs Affect fomething or other; and if not Chrift then either Sin or Creature-comforts will have all. *Incline my Heart unto thy Law*, (faith *David*) *and not to Covetoufnefs*, Pfal. 119. 36. *q. d.* if Thou doft not fecure me for thy felf, then *Mammon* will be fure to have me. Affections cannot keep their Virgin-ftate, but will Efpoufe fome Early Object: And when Souls are not alway Ravifh'd with Chrift's Love, the Serpent will creep in upon them. Yea, if ought elfe be Mafter of our Affections, God will be Hated by us, *Mat.* 6. 24. there being no Middle kind of Abnegation (on either part) between him and the Creature, as is between one Creature and another. Therefore let us Affect Chrift and our Duty, elfe will it not be long before we Hate them both.

10. God's Love unto his People doth provoke their fuitable Return, elfe will they be Inferiour unto Publicans, *Mat*. 5. 46. and Sinners, *Luke* 6. 32. He Loved them firft, which doth prevent Upbraiding, but calls for after-love, 1 *John* 4. 19. His Love to them furpaffeth Knowledge, *Eph*. 3. 19. and fhall their Love to him not be made known at all, or very little? He Loves them with an Everlafting Love, *Jer*. 31. 3. And did a ftream yet ever fail (without a wonder) whofe Spring continued? No Man hath Greater Love from any, than have the Saints from Chrift, *John* 15. 13. and are they not then unworthy of him, in cafe they Love ought More than him, *Mat*. 10. 37? He loved them, when in their Blood, *Ezek*. 16. 8. whilft they were Sinners, *Rom.* 5. 8. and fhall not they love this altogether lovely one, *Cant*. 5. 16. whofe fharpeft Rebukes are big with Love, *Rev*. 3. 19? efpecially fuch who have had much forgiven, *Luke* 7. 42. Nothing can feparate them from the Love of God in Chrift, *Rom*. 8. 39. who then fhall feperate Chrift from their Love of him, *v.* 35, 37, 38?

11. Love is the greateft Factor, and many times with very little Charge, which fhould Encourage us to keep it up (for Chrift) with utmoft care. A good Man fets his Love upon the Lord, therefore God Promifeth to Deliver him, becaufe he thereby feems to know his Name, *Pfal*. 91. 14. whereas bare want of Love (to Chrift) incurrs the faddeft Excommunication, 1 *Cor.* 16. 22. Yea, *David's* Love was amply Recompenfed, when it was onely in his Heart to Build an Houfe for God, 2 *Sam.* 7. 11. 1 *Chron*. 28. 3. therefore the Pooreft Saint fhall be Rewarded for their Benevolence, which fome could never Evidence, fave by their good Affection, *Mat*. 25. 34, 35. And if Saints fhall be dealt with by the Lord, according to their Love, their Portion then muft needs be Endlefs, for fuch hath been their good Affection, however

fhort

The Parable of the Ten Virgins Opened. 161

short their Actions be. Yea, therefore both Their Happiness and others Misery will be Eternal, or Answerable to their Endless Love.

12. Saints do Profess much Love for Christ, Soul-love, *Cant.* 1. 7. and their being Sick thereof, *Cant.* 2. 5. yea, their being alway ready to break with an Indefinite Longing after his Judgments or their Duty, *Psal.* 119. 20. If *Peter's* Question were put by Christ to any here, *John.* 21. 15. their Answer would be like his, as to the Truth (if not t e Measure) of their Affection; and would be Grieved (as he was, v. 17.) if their Profession of that Nature be not Credited; yea, all the People would say Amen unto that Curse, 1 *Cor.* 16. 22. as *Israel* did of Old unto those Comminations, *Deut.* 27. 26. Therefore these Foolish Virgins would be thought to have so much Affection still, as to Desire more; or rather they onely meant the want of Light, (and not of Love,) by this Confession of Lamps going out. *O therefore Love the Lord, all ye his Saints,* Psal, 31. 23. and do not onely make a shew thereof, *Ezek.* 33. 31. but let it be without Dissimulation, *Rom.* 12. 9. and not in Word, 1 *John* 3. 18. since Grace is onely like to be their Portion who Love Christ in sincerity, *Eph.* 6. 24.

13. There can be no true inward Peace or Satisfaction so long as there is a Restraint upon Affection towards Christ and Duty. As Anguish shut up is strangling, *Job.* 7. 11. so is a Gracious Heart in Pain while its Affections are unduly stopt, in point of Godly sorrow, *Psal.* 32. 3. Strong Desire, *Job* 32. 19, 20. and Holy Zeal, *Psal.* 39. 2. *Jer.* 20. 9. *Psal.* 119. 20. *It therefore is good to be Zealously Affected alway in a good thing,* Gal. 4. 18. Yea, a good Conscience (if Awakened) is not at quiet, nor doth enjoy it self with Comfort so long as its Affections for Christ are Dead; and therefore *David* Prays for being Quickned in God's way, *Psal.* 119. 37. according to his Word, *v.* 25. and for his Names sake, *Psal.* 143. 11. so would he call upon him, *Psal.* 80. 18. And with what Faith can they (who Love not Christ) expect the Manifestation of his Love to them, which is so promised onely, *John* 14. 21? Yea, with what Face can they Desire it otherwise, as if it were not all the Reason in the World, that a Wive's and Husband's Love should be Reciprocal, *Hos.* 3. 3.

14. The Going out of Lamps (or Failing of our Affections) is one sad Sign of Foolish Virgins, and more especially at such a time, or in these latter Days. Poor un-espoused Virgins may have a Love for Christ, *Cant.* 1. 3. what shall we then think of such who Love him not, since all the Upright are there said to Love him, *v.* 4? The best Material Actions are not so Characteristical (of visible Saint-ship) as Affections; and Filial Duty is thus Distinguished from that of Servants,

Y *Phil.*

Phil. 2. 20. 22. therefore the shedding of this Flower exceeds the Falling of that Fruit, in point of Spiritual Discrimination. The Cooling of Professors Love is said to be the Predominant Distemper of such a Time, *Mat.* 24. 12. and Time-Temptations are dreadful Symptoms. Thus are the Wife and Foolish Virgins (here) Distinguished: And Typical *Ephesus* is Threatned with un-churching (and consequently, with being visibly un-Sainted) for leaving her first Love, *Rev.* 2. 4, 5.

15. Extinguished Lamps (in such a Day as this) will hardly be ever Lighted more untill the Door be shut. The Nearer that any Union is (as that of Brethren) the Greater is its Division upon a Breach, and so much the more Hard is its being re-united, *Prov.* 18. 19. And as Affections are Enobled by their Objects, so love for Christ Degenerating into sleightiness, doth therefore enter into the Depth of Putrefaction, as Best things do, when fallen into Decay, which consequently are most irrecoverable. Thence is it, that so few Adulterers (or Backsliders) do Return, *Prov.* 2. 19. so Boisterous is that Affection which is not kept within the bounds of its allowed Object. And Time-Temptation, (such as this is at present) are more especially Malignant or Incurable, because they are a Spiritual Plague or Token of God's Displeasure, by which his Own are separated from the World, *Psal.* 12. 7. Therefore let our Affections be well Guarded Now, unless we mean to have those Lamps put out for ever.

16. Let us duly weigh that dreadful Sentence passed upon such as love not Christ, 1 *Cor.* 16. 22. There was of O'd, and there still is a Two-fold Ordinary Spiritual Censure upon Offenders; the one of which was, to be shut out of the Camp for so long time, *Deut.* 23. 10. which was a Type of that With-drawing, 2 *Thes.* 3. 6. 14, 15. The Other was, to be cut off, *Exod.* 12. 15. which Answereth unto Gospel-Excommunication, *Gal.* 5. 12. Yet might a Person (so dealt with) be Taken in again, 2 *Cor.* 2. 8. But some were not to be so much as Prayed for, 1 *John* 5. 16. as being never to be forgiven, *Mat.* 12. 32. but to be called *Anathema*, or set aside, untill the Lord shall come, which *Maranatha* signifieth; the former of which is a *Greek* word, the other *Syriack*, which latter was the common Language of the Jews at that day: To intimate, that he who loves not Christ, was to be Cursed by *Jews* and *Greeks* (or *Gentiles*, 1 Cor. 1. 24) till Christ shall come and say, *Depart ye Cursed*, *Mat.* 25. 41. Not but that every sin deserveth Death, *Rom.* 6. 23. nor but that sinners (of this kind) may be Recovered; onely to Represent the Danger of not loving Christ, next unto that of sinning against the Holy Ghost.

And

The Parable of the Ten Virgins Opened.

And as we would keep our Affections up for Christ and Duty, these following Helps may be of Use.

1. Let us stand Gazing upon these Objects, as those Apostles did, when Christ Ascended, *Acts* 1. 10. nor shall we need to fear our being therefore checked, as they were then, *v.* 11. because their stedfast looking Terminated upon his Flesh, unto our Admonition. As is the Sight, so is Impression; Beholding Changeth, 2 *Cor.* 3. 18. and Vision doth Assimilate, 1 *John* 3. 2. Yea, *Job* concluded the working of his Friends Affections towards him, in case they would but look upon him, *Job* 6. 28. as looking upon Christ doth make his Piercers mourn, *Zech.* 12. 10. with Supplication. Therefore *Job* made a Covenant with his Eyes, *Job* 31. 1. and Drunkards are bid to take heed of looking upon the Wine, *Prov.* 23. 31. Yea, when Christ would not be Overcome, he bids the Spouse to Turn away from him, *Cant.* 6. 5. So Powerful is Sight upon Affection. And if Ten Thousand Objects were in View, Christ would appear to be the chiefest of them all, *Cant.* 5. 10.

2. Let us endeavour also to Trim such Objects, since our Affections unto Things and Persons are much Inflamed by the Bravery of their Adorning, as Harlots too well know, *Jer.* 2. 33. Nor doth Christ need to be set out by us, save as an Eye of Faith can Dress him with his Own, or rather see him as he is, or as he (at the least) will at the last appear in Glory. Men therefore Hide their Faces from him, *Isa.* 53. 3. because his Visage is first marred by them, *Isa.* 52. 14. either by stripping him of his stately Robes, or by discolouring them with their Evil Eye. Could we but look at Jesus, as he is Now set upon his Father's Throne, *Heb.* 12. 2. how should we Run with Patience the Race that is set before us, *v.* 1. Since Duty hath the same Debentures, and which as surely will be discharged. 2 *Tim.* 2. 12. Yea, how would Duty at the Present Ravish, could we but Eye its Native Beauty, our being therein most like to Christ, together with that Peace which doth attend it.

3. If any One Duty would be alway loved by us, so let our Love be Universal, and let us not Despise the least; at least-wise not the Greater Branches of it, such as Time-Duties are by way of Eminency. He that Despiseth any of his ways, shall Die, *Prov.* 19. 16. his Love thereunto will Decay; it being with Obedience, as with a Faggot, the smallest of whose sticks (when plucked out) doth loosen all the rest. A Killing Cold is oft-times got (in tender Bodies) by leaving off a Thinner Garment; yea, by not having it closely Girt about us.. Much more if Weightier Matters are Disesteemed; it being with our Affections,

fections, as with a Civil State, which soon will come to Nought, when Babes and Children are in Chief Command, *Isa*. 3. 4. Time-Truths are as the Bond of Duty, which being once flackned, doth hazard the Dissolution of our Love in General, as both Experience and the Scriptures Witness; and without Love to which no True or Lasting Love to any other can safely be concluded otherways.

4. Let our Affections unto Christ be Genuine, or Kindly, and not Enforced. One may be Over-awed to Love another, but Souldiers Prest into a Service are not to be Confided in; therefore Christ onely is for Voluntiers. How hard a Matter it is to keep Affection up (in a Religious Duty) unless the Spirit be kindly raised! Whereas Enlarged Hearts can Run, *Psal*. 119. 32. and spend themselves, 2 *Cor*.6.11. without being Wearied, 2 *Cor*. 12. 15. Spontaneous Earthly Fruits are most Abiding, so is that Love which is most Natural: God's Love is therefore Everlasting, *Jer*. 31. 3. because he Loveth Freely, *Hos*. 14. 4. Therefore God and his People are called each others Portion or Inheritance, *Jer*. 10. 16. because the Naturalness of their Affection (each unto other) is like an Estate in Land, which is not Subject unto Casualties, as Money is. An Arrow forced out of a Bow will fall within a while; whereas Beams Darted from the Sun, continue in their Strength and unconstrained Vigour.

5. Let not our Love be over-violent, I mean, not so, as to be Supream, in Competition with our Judgement. A Sober Traveller will soonest come unto his Journeys end; whilst he that's all upon the Spur will quickly Tire, both Horse and Man, *Gal*. 5. 7. They who receive Man as an Angel, *Gal*. 4. 14. are apt (ere long) to count him as an Enemy, *v*. 16. therefore, unless such could be Zealously Affected alway, *v*. 18. 'tis better to be Moderate, 1 *Cor*. 4. 6. Some (in our Days) have been too fierce to hold. *So Run, as that we may Obtain*, 1 *Cor*. 9. 24.' and he that striveth for the Mastery, is Temperate, *v*. 25. which seemeth to be meant by Lawful striving, 2 *Tim*. 2. 5. We should Love God with all our Heart and Soul, and Mind, and so with all our Strength, *Mark* 12. 30.' else as an injudicious love is alway Carnal, (though fixt upon a Spiritual Object,) so it will never last; and violent Exercise doth onely Post a Mortal Body so much the faster into its Grave.

6. Let our Affections unto Duty be kept up in their constant Exercise, as we would have them to continue. That Lamp which is not always Burning, will go out. If (in this case) we cease to Love, Affection will soon Die, as doth Man's Body without continual Breathing; Loves Breath and Life is in the Nostrils of its Exercises. He that would row

against

The Parable of the Ten Virgins Opened. 165

against the Stream, (as every of Christ's Lovers doth) must have a Care of Missing any one stroak, for fear of being Turned quite away. This some have found to be the Issue of Religious Intermissions, under pretence of waiting for the Spirit, till Love unto that Duty hath been quite Extinguished. And as indulged sluggishness is one Symptom of our Dying Love, so is it a Cause thereof; as stirring up this Heavenly fire (by a Lively Exercise) is likeliest to prevent its Going out. When we have once Raised the Bell of Duty, a steady pull may keep it up with ease, which else will Fall, and may not Rise again.

7. Let us not Hanker after other things. Sin Killeth our Affections quite, and if the Creature hath too much, Christ will have none at all, 1 *John* 2. 15. A right up burning Lamp will last the longest; but when its Light doth waste on either side, it swaileth much, and hazards an Extinction. Christ sitteth light, *Mat.* 11. 30. but *Mammon* (got up behind him) Tireth us, in ways of Duty. Could we but lay aside these heavy Weights, how should we Run with Patience the Race that is set before us, *Heb.* 12. 1? How can some wonder at the Cooling of their scattered Love! It being therewith as with Sun-beams, which are not burning, save as they are United, *Psal.* 86. 11. We cannot Approve our selves to God, unless we study, 2 *Tim.* 2. 15. and studying is inconsistent with Diversions, untill our Eyes are turned from beholding Vanity, *Psal.* 119. 37. This savouring so much what is of Man, (though onely in a way of Longing for them) destroys our Taste of better things, *Mat.* 16. 23. and our Desires thereof.

8. Let our Affections (unto Christ and Duty) be of the Noblest Kind, both as to their Rise and Maintenance. Christ may be Embraced by Carnal Arms, and in that case, the Ivy (about an Oak) may wither soon, because its Root is of a Weak Decaying Nature. Professors (Generally) are onely careful to fix upon a Spiritual Object; Whereas the Suitableness of their Affections is as Essentially required of them, else are they neither Holy, nor will be Lasting. And though there is an Holy Driving Terror, 2 *Cor.* 5. 11. and other Drawing Considerations, *Hos.* 11. 4. yet will our Motion never be Perpetual, save as our being Wisdom's Children, *Mat.* 11. 19. is evinced by the Naturalness of our Affection to its Naked Wayes. And to that end, let us not too much eye Encouragements in such a way, lest by that means our Love should be Debased: But let those Chambers (or Accommodations) be so joyned to the Temple of our Duty, as that their Beams may not be fastned into its Wall, according to God's own Order, 1 *Kings* 6. 6. else will it Threaten both the Weakning and Defacing of that House, in case those Chambers be taken down, which otherwise is no way Dis-advantaged.

9. Let

9. Let us be careful with whom we Ordinarily (at least-wife Intimately) do Converse, since though Communion with the Wise cannot secure the Foolish Virgins Lamps from Going out; yet are Companions apt to Influence, *Prov.* 13.20. *Saul* (if among the Prophets) will also Prophesy, 1 *Sam.* 19.24. And *Joash* his good Affection was Preserved, so long as good *Jehoiada* Lived, 2 *Chron.* 24. 2. but otherwise Love will cool, *Mat.* 24.12. Affection for Duty (since the Fall) is very crazy; and Persons (Aguishly Disposed) upon the sight of others so Affected, are apt to shake. Thus many Hopeful Virgins (of later Years) have Buried their Ancient Love (for Duty) in the Bosom of a Dis-affected Yoak-fellow; which is a fair Warning unto Others to Marry in the Lord, 1 *Cor.* 7.39. Come out of *Babylon*, for fear of being Touched with her Sins, *Rev.* 18.4. Since any one Root of Bitterness is apt to Trouble and Defile, *Heb.* 12.15. though it be but a little Leaven, 1 *Cor.* 5.6. Consult Experiences, and let us Act accordingly.

10. Let us endeavour to ashame our selves, both by our Own and Others Practices, provoking hereunto. Oh how Affectionate are sinners in their way, Doting upon their Lovers, *Ezek.* 23.10. and seeking to out-vye each other in their Inordinacy, *v.* 11. Yea, falling in Love with Pourtraitures upon the Wall, *v.* 14.16. and being inflamed with the Remembrance of former Lewdness, *v.* 19.21. And is it not a shame that Christ should have less Love than Satan? Nay, Saints themselves have heretofore been Zealous in an Evil way, as *Paul* had been, who therefore (when he was Converted) followed after Holiness in himself, as he had sometimes Persecuted it in others, *Phil.* 3.6.12. Yea, all these Virgins had been full of seeming Love for Christ, as those for *Paul*, *Gal.* 4.15. And is it not a shame that *Israel* should come short of Heathens, in point of Lasting, *Jer.* 2.10? Nor can it be denyed, but that Saints have Affections still, who can give no good Reason for their Abatement toward Christ, *Jer.* 2.5.31. and in that case, as Christ will not Accept the Creatures Leavings, *Mal.* 1.8. so doth he sadly Curse such a Deceitful Sacrificer, *v.* 14. and such a puff upon a Candle new blown out, may be of use to blow it in again; yea, with the Help of Christ's Breath therein, and of his Hand behind it, this may regain the deadest Lamp.

11. Let us be deeply Humbled in the sence of our Decaying Love for Christ, as we would ever get it up again, and keep it Lively. Cold peccant Humours lye exceeding Low, as Melancholy in the Stomach, which maketh Heart-sick before it will come up; as she Experienc'd, *Cant.* 5.8. upon the Cooling of her Love, *v.* 2, 3. And *Peter* eminently

The Parable of the Ten Virgins Opened. 167

nently, till he had Wept moſt Bitterly, *Mat.* 26. 74, 75. and then he Loved Chriſt (ever after) to the Death, *John* 21. 17, 18. Chriſt would be glad to hear Back-ſliding *Ephraim* to bemoan himſelf, *Jer.* 31. 18, 19, 20. Such Breakings forth upon our Lips would comfort .o.y Evidence ſomes hopes of a Recovery, *v.* 20, 21. Theſe Fooliſh Virgins do confeſs their Fading Lamps with un-affected Hearts, who Go to Buy more Oyl, *Mat.* 25. 10. but not with Weeping, as *Jer.* 50. 4. nor do they Return with ſelf-condemning, *Mat.* 25. 11. that ſhews their Hopeleſneſs, *v.* 12. Remember whence we are fallen, and Repent, as we would Riſe again, *Rev.* 2. 5.

12. Let us be much in Prayer, that God wou'd Direct our Hearts in the Love of him, 2 *Theſ.* 3. 5. and that he would incline them to his Law, *Pſal.* 119. 36. and not to any Evil thing, *Pſal.* 141. 3. As he is the Father of Lights, *James* 1. 17. ſo his Almighty Hand muſt Guard our Lamps, as doth a Lanthorn, elſe every Guſt of Wind will blow them out. He turneth the Heart to Hate, *Pſal.* 105. 25. and *Eſau's* Hatred into Love, *Gen.* 33. 4. who alſo can prepare the Heart unto himſelf, by keeping that Affection up (for ever) which elſe is Subject to Decay, 1 *Chron.* 29. 18. This Fire firſt cometh from Above; and though fore-named Helps may lay the ſticks together, yet Prayer muſt Blow it up, elſe will it ſoon go out. Had theſe Poor Fooliſh Virgins gone to Chriſt, (who onely went to their Companions,) they might have gained from himſelf, what neither was in their own Power to keep Alive, (*viz.* their Lamps,) nor in the Others to Reſtore.

MATTHEW XXV. 9.

But the Wiſe Anſwered, ſaying, Not ſo, leſt there be not enough for us and you; but Go ye rather to them that Sell, and Buy for your ſelves.

IN theſe words we have the Wiſe Virgins Anſwer unto the Others fore-going Motion. Wherein we may Obſerve, Firſt, a Gentle Denying of them, rather Implyed in that word [*but*] than plainly ſignified; thoſe word [*Not ſo*] not being in the *Greek.* Secondly, a Satisfactory Reaſon rendred; *Leſt there be not enough for us and you.* Thirdly, a Giving them (yet) what Help they can, by way of

Ex-the Others great Miscarriage, whose Lamps were now Gone out, through want of Care to take Oyl with them at the first?

Answ. 1. These Foolish Virgins here do not Provoke the Wise unto their Faces by any unhandsome word or carriage: and in that Case, few will Begin to Quarrel upon Christ's Account, till Passion is stirred up by Personal Provocations. There is a great Fault among Professors in that regard, who count Plain dealing Passion, and so Desist therefrom, untill themselves are throughly vexed, or Passionate indeed; and then such will speak out. We ought to follow Peace with all Men, *Heb.* 12. 14. but not to Purchase it by Theft and Murder, such as Mans sinful silence is, to Christ and to his Brother, *Jer.* 23. 30. *Ezek.* 33. 8. Thus doth self-love dispense with Duty, under a Pretence of studying Peace, till Interest hath made such Furious, instead of being truly Faithful, which seldom is of any use, *James* 1. 20. save onely to Discover those Passionate Reprovers Dissimulation.

2. The Wiser Virgins might Perceive the others inability to bear plain down-right dealing at the present; and this might cause their being silent. Rebukes are Pearls too good for Swine, *Mat.* 7. 6. Nor may a Scorner be Reproved, *Prov.* 9. 7, 8. And when that Prophet was bid forbear, he Warrantably did so, as a Token of the others Ruine, 2 *Chron.* 25. 16. As Men would not be cast out, so let them take heed of Mocking, *Gen.* 21. 9, 10. and as they would not be let alone, so let them take heed of being Joyned to their evil ways, *Hos.* 4. 17. Yea, let them Encourage others as they would Healingly be Reproved by them, *Psal.* 141. 5. Saints have not so many smiles from Christ (as yet) because they cannot bear them; nor others (upon that Account) some fructifying showers from his Clouded brows. And though (at such a time) Gentiles may be compelled to come in, *Luke* 14. 23. yet Old Professing Jews will soon Discourage their Inviters, *v.* 24.

3. These very Wise Virgins were lately wakened out of their sleeping with the other, which might Occasion their want of Zeal. Distempered sleep (such as this was) doth Naturally tend to make the Spirits dull; and much more in a Moral sence. Conscience in *David* was fast asleep when he could be so fierce against that in Another, whereof himself was then so Guilty, 2 *Sam.* 12. 5, 6, 7. 'Tis meet for Slumberers

The Parable of the Ten Virgins Opened.

to Rub their Eyes, before they can Discern (at least Reprove) another's sluggishness. Christ's Teaching was Authoritative, in Competition with that of Hypocrites, *Mat.* 7. 29. whose guilty Conscience (when Appealed unto) made them Desist from prosecuting their Impeachment of another, *John* 8. 7. 9. And as those Typical Snuffers were made of purest Gold, *Exod.* 37. 23. so Persons Newly Raised from a Fall, have seldom so much Confidence, as to Rebuke their fellows, till throughly purified from Enfeebling guilt.

4. They might be Tender in Judging upon the present case; how far a failing of this Nature was their sin; or how far such a sin might be consistent with the Main; or whether their Lamps were not Recoverable: And therefore onely might Exhort instead of sharp Rebuking. Christ did more deeply Censure the Foolish Virgins of his Time, than his Disciples could well bear, *Mat.* 15. 12. and some Wise Virgins (at this Day) like not such kind of Tartness. Few are Convinced, that Ignorance doth not Excuse from sin, or that Time-Duties are of such Importance, as to have Saint-ship gathered up thereinto: who therefore dare not Judge Men upon that Account. And since the Scripture so much calls for Gentleness, it is a thing so grateful of it self, as that few Men can bear it's Contrary in any case, though every whit as plainly Warranted, especially among Back-sliders. But those Tormenting Witnesses were onely Two, *Rev.* 11. 10. the Generality are Moderate.

5. Wise Virgins alway are Inferiour to the Foolish, in point of Interest; which is a sore Temptation, not to Irritate, and which but few can overcome. Soundest Professors generally are Poor, compared with others, 1 *Cor.* 4. 8. and Poor Men use Intreaties, leaving rough Answers to the Rich, *Prov.* 18. 23. who seldom themselves are so dealt with, save by a more than Ordinary Prophet, as of Old. Soundest Professors also are but few: And where is that *Micajah*, who dareth to Rebuke four hundred Lying Flatterers? Yea, Foolish Virgins are of the first Magnitude, unto the dwellers upon Earth, as is the Moon, because of its being nearer unto sense: And as Proud *Pharisees* deride Plain dealing, *Luke* 16. 14. presuming upon their high Esteem, *v.* 15 so none but Christ and *John* durst roughly handle them, until the Spirit was poured down, *Acts* 2. 17. 23. and when that Dispensation comes again, *Isa.* 32. 15. then stammerers will speak plainly, *ver.* 4.

6. The Lord himself might have a Righteous Over-ruling Hand, in their being silent unto such, at such a Time. He hath the Key of Utterance, *Col.* 4. 3. and when he Shutteth, no Man can Open, *Rev.*

The Parable of the Ten Virgins Opened.

3. 7. A Moral (or Preceptive) Bar is alway laid upon his People's Reprehensions, in some Cases, or when clear Duties are Disputed; *Hos.* 4. 4. and sometimes an Effectual (or Physical ;) Bar doth force them to be dumb. Thus *Naaman*'s halving it with God, (after so full a Conviction and Obliging Mercy,) was justly Punished with *Elisha*'s silence and seeming Approbation, 2 *Kings* 5. 17, 18, 19. The Time is Now haitning, for God himself to Answer such Hypocritical Enquirers of him, *Ezek.* 14. 4. who therefore will not let his Servants speak, *v.* 3. And thus some are not Plainly spoken unto, *Mat.* 13. 13. least they should See and Hear, and Understand, and be Converted, unto their being Healed, *v.* 15.

Quest. 2. What is the Meaning of that Denial which is here made (by these Wise Virgins) unto the Foolish Virgins Motion for Oyl or Light?

Answ. To which I Answer.

First, Negatively.

1. It is not to be understood, as if the Wise Virgins were (in the least) unwilling to have lent what Help they could, in case the Other had been truly serious. This would not have consisted with their Wisdom, but would have signified their being also Foolish; since the Lips of the Wise Disperse Knowledge, but the Heart of the Foolish doth not so, *Prov.* 15. 7. A Gracious Heart Longeth to Impart that Spiritual Gift, whereof he doth partake, *Rom.* 1. 11. doing therein to Others, as he would be dealt with by them, *v.* 12. Oyl is Diffusive, especially where Gifts and Graces are in Conjunction: therefore it sadly signifieth, when utmost Spiritual Help is not Afforded, from Envy, Sluggishness, or Spiritual Pride : Satan may Hinder, once and again, 1 *Thes.* 2. 18. so may Diversions otherways, *Rom.* 15. 22. Yea, sometimes *Paul* was Hindred by the Holy Ghost, *Acts* 16. 6, 7. who else did count himself a Debtor unto All, *Rom.* 1. 14.

2. Nor is it meant, as if the Wise Virgins (absolutely) were unable to have given Oyl unto the Foolish. 'Tis true, all Man's sufficiency (for such a work) is of the Lord, 2 *Cor.* 3. 5. as well as Efficacy, 1 *Cor.* 3. 7. yet are Men workers together with him, 2 *Cor.* 6. 1. who therefore have this Oyl or Treasure in their Earthen Vessels, 2 *Cor.* 4. 7. *Paul* could Beget, in Bonds, *Philem.* 10. and he that is not Able to be a Spiritual Father, was Typically of Old debarred from that Priest-hood, *Lev.* 21. 20. which was a Type of Gospel Saint-ship, 1 *Pet.* 2. 9. nor might such enter into the Congregation, or be Accounted *Israelites*, *Deut.* 23. 1. Nor will the Saints Oyl (in this Respect) forbear to Multiply, so long as there are any chosen Vessels

left.

left for it to over-flow into, as 2 *Kings* 4.6. or not untill Election hath gone bearing Children; and then this Oyl will stay, as did that Widdows, serving to pay its Owners Debts, and for Subsistance, 2 *Kings* 4. 7.

3. Nor is that Cautionary Reason [*Lest there be not enough for us and you*] to be Interpreted, as if this Spiritual Contribution would Exhaust the Wiser Virgins store, as at the first blush it seemeth to import. There was no Lessening of Christ's Vertue, by what went from him, *Luke* 8.46. nor is the Sun darkened by its shining: Nor is a Saint the Poorer for his Spiritual Liberality. Yea, Grace is thus kept Bright with Use, which otherwise might gather Rust, and so Corrupt, as Gold it self is apt to Canker, *James* 5.3. unto its Owner's Disadvantage. And as unmeet with holding tendeth unto Poverty, so he Increaseth, who duly scattereth, *Prov.* 11.24. and watereth himself by watering others, *v.* 25 as Talent-Occupiers do Experience, *Mat.* 25.20. Lamps, in the Letter and Mystery, herein Agree, that neither of them are Diminished by Lighting Others: Mystical Lamps herein are singular, because their Oyl is Multiplyed by Distribution. Thus much as to the Negative. But then,

II. Affirmatively. They might thus speak unto the Foolish Virgins.

1. To prove the Cordialness of their Desire, if not to check their sleightiness and Carnality therein. When that *Samaritan* Woman sleightily and Carnally desired Christ's Ever-living water, *John* 4. 15. he onely Answered her with a Diversion, *v.* 16. *q. d.* I will be otherwise sought unto before a Motion of that Nature shall be satisfied. However Cordialness is thus Expreimented. Thus *Joshua* tryed the Truth of *Israel's* Professing to Serve the Lord, *Josh.* 24.16. by his Rejecting of it, *v.* 19. till they had Doubted it, *v.* 21. and then he let it pass, *v.* 22. Thus *Naomi* refused *Ruth's* first Resolution to Accompany her, *Ruth* 1. 10. 15. meerly to prove her stedfastness, *v.* 16, 17, 18. as did *Elijah* to *Elisha*, 2 Kings 2.2. and Christ himself unto those two Disciples, *Luke* 24. 28, 29. Had not the Foolish Virgins been indifferent, so Modest a Denial would have wrought another way; therefore this Tryal was not unwisely made.

2. To Check the Foolish Virgins coming Onely unto them for Oyl, without any further Pains or Cost, who therefore bid them (*rather*) *Go to them that Sell, and Buy.* Thus *Naaman* was bid to Go and Wash in *Jordan*, 2 Kings 5. 10. and those Ten Lepers to Go and shew themselves unto the Priest, *Luke* 17. 14. and *Israel*, to Buy of *Esau*, Meat and Water, *Deut.* 2. 6. not from unwillingness to Gratifie

wish, when either God is likely to be Robbed, or some more sad Distemper to be Indulged.

3. To shew the Wise Virgins sense of having Oyl little enough, and none to spare, as (in Propriety of Speech) the Other's Motion did import: Therefore these Answer, *Lest there be not enough for us and you.* As he that Loveth Silver, is not satisfied, *Eccl.* 5. 10. So he that Loveth Oyl (or Grace, and Spiritual Light,) is as the Sea, which is not Full, though all the Rivers run into it, *Eccl.* 1. 7. Thus is a truly Gracious Heart Distinguished from Hypocrites, by his being alway fearful, lest he should not have Oyl enough, which others are afraid of having too much of. And more especially Wise Virgins are sollicitous, with reference unto Time-Truths and Duties; which are Expensive, and therefore need the greater Stock: Yea, which are also very Curious, and therefore need the clearest Light. 'Tis true, their Lighting others is no way self-diminishing; but their Denial here may onely intimate unto the other, how Low they were in their own Eyes, and what an High esteem they had of Oyl, as to its Worth and Use.

4. To signifie (perhaps) how Difficult it was for them to make this Present Duty out, unto another, above Most other Duties. 'Tis true, Time-Truths are very Plain, as Excellent things are, to him that Understandeth, *Prov.* 8. 6. 9. yet are they hardly to be understood by Others, 2 *Pet.* 3. 16. and to be uttered by the Best, *Heb.* 5. 11. Few at this Day perceive that More is in this Second going forth, than at the First: Nor can it be yet made out, but with a stammering Lip, as was fore-told, *Isa.* 28. 11. or with a strange Tongue, as *Paul* explaineth it, 1 *Cor.* 14. 21. Truths are but rarely seen, at their first coming up, till God (in Time) shall make some clearer Revelation, *Phil.* 3. 5. or till the Customary Practice of Sober Christians, shall silence them who seem to be Contentious, 1 *Cor.* 11. 14. 16. Let not the Foolish Virgins wonder, in case the Wise (at first) have no more Light into untrodden Paths, than will just serve their turn; as is here hinted.

5. These bid the Other go, and Buy Oyl for Themselves; because they would have them see with their Own Eyes, and not with Others, in Matters of this Nature. Unsound Professors (like some bad Husbands)

The Parable of the Ten Virgins Opened.

bands) Live most upon Borrowing: But Gospel-Saints are for the Proving of their Own work, *Gal.* 6. 4. and working with their Own Hand, 1 *Thes.* 4. 11. and being perswaded in their own Heart, *Rom.* 14. 5. Thus shall Men have Rejoycing in their own selves, *Gal.* 6. 4. Thus shall they have Reward, according to their own Labour, 1 *Cor.* 3. 8. thus Trees are to be known by their own Fruit, *Luke* 6. 46. nor will the Best Seed abide with him, which hath not Root in Himself, *Mat.* 13. 21. Therefore Wise Men are onely for the Use and Distribution of what is their own, *Prov.* 5. 15, 16, 17. and they who make the Truth their own, have right to call Heaven their own also, though Earthly *Mammon* be Another's, *Luke* 16. 11, 12. and this is Buying for ones self.

6. They might thus speak to get rid of the Others Company, whom they now had no Pleasure in, so much as to Discourse any longer with them.

1. Partly, Because of their Back-sliding from a former Practice and Profession. They had gone out Before; but now their Lamps were Gone, or Going out, and with a Noisom smell unto these Wiser Virgins, which might Occasion this Quick (though Fair) Dismission. God hath no Pleasure in him that draweth back, *Heb.* 10. 38. because Apostates are as Smoak unto his Nose, *Isa.* 65. 5. therefore Christ will not Parley with these late Returners, *Mat.* 25. 12. no more than do these other now. Nor is it to be wondred at, since Mystical Lamps are apt to go out for Company, *Mat.* 24. 12. yea, their very Snuffs are most Offensive, like Dead Mens Carkasses, which do Occasion those Alive to stop their Noses, *Ezek.* 39. 11. and so their Speech must needs be Hindred. As Men would have Discourse (with Christ, or with his People) to be Convinced; so let them take heed of wearying others with such bad Savours, or Dead Affections.

2. Because the Wise Virgins might perceive their being unlikely to Convince the other, by any thing Offered for such a purpose. These Foolish Virgins (Doubtlesly) had already heard, what could be said, and wherefore should they hear the same again, who had no mind to be the Truth's Disciples, *John* 9. 27? The Cry had cleared up the Nature of this Duty: Nor do they Complain of wanting ought, but Lamps, or good Affections thereunto; and when the Judgment is not Supream, 'tis but in vain to Reason with Mens Affections. It was an Argument of *Abigail*'s Wisdom, to be silent, till *Nabal*'s Reason was Restored, 1 *Sam.* 25. 26. 27. nor will Men Plough upon the Rock, *Amos* 6. 12. yea, Saints are bid with-draw from strifes of Words, and from Perverse Disputings, 1 *Tim.* 6. 4, 5. If Men will not Believe, Christ will

say

Anſw. It muſt be meant of Chriſt, or of his S
no other whom theſe wiſe Virgins would ḷi.d the (

Now, as to Saints, the Generality of Profeſſ
theſe Virgins; therefore They cannot be the Se
of them do bid the other half, to Go and Buy elſe

'Tis true indeed, there have been Two Anoin
Oyl) by way of Eminency, *Zech.* 4. 14. wh
Chriſt) are termed Olive-Branches, *v.* 12. but
reference unto others, *v.* 11. and theſe are ſaid t
Oyl out of Themſelves, through their Two Go
Sanctifi.d Mediums, *viz.* the VVord and Praye
this is (in Effect) to Sell; ſo that ſuch Eminentl
the Maintainers of others Lamps with Oyl, *Zech*
ſhare (with Chriſt himſelf) in ſuch a Title, abo
Profeſſors. Onely it thence will follow, that ſlur
gins are no Proper VVitneſſes; ſince (when Awa
Challenge to themſelves the Name of Oyl-Emp
it unto Others,) which yet is given by Chriſt unto
11. 4.

But yet I rather chuſe to give this Title (here)
is the Heir of all things, *Heb.* 1. 2. and conſeq
prietor, or Proper Seller of this Commodity.
Perſon be Repreſented here, by that word [*the*
cauſe he hath his under-Servants, but alſo thoſe Se
Rev. 3. 1. by whom he Selleth theſe Commoditi
with his Approbation, *John* 16. 13. And ſo we r
wherewith Chriſt's Shop is Furniſhed, and under
being put to Sale. In which regard, I ſtand here
ſome Apprentice) inviting Paſſengers to come an

1. Do you lack any Meat or Drink, poor Hung
Come Buy and Eat, *Iſa.* 55. 1. here's Meat and
6. 55. This water will prevent your future Thirſt
that Eateth of this Bread, ſhall never Dye, *John*
will be Cheated otherwhere, *Iſa.* 55. 2.

2. Do you lack any VVine, poor Drooping He
yea, come Buy VVine, *Iſa.* 55. 1. this VVine is well
Iſa. 25. 6. Old VVine, which is the Beſt, L

The Parable of the Ten Virgins Opened. 175

which is better than any Wine whatever, *Cant.* 1.2. nor is it measured out by Cups, but Flaggons, *Cant.* 2.5. whereof one may with safety (as well as freedom) Drink abundantly, *Cant.* 5.1.

3. Do you lack any Milk, poor little Children? Come hither, yea, come, Buy Wine and Milk, *Isa.* 55.1. both which may safely be Drunk together, *Cant.* 5.1. and this Milk is sincere, which therefore is to be Desired, 1 *Pet.* 2.2. that New-born Babes may Grow thereby: It is the Milk of that Red Heifer, *Numb.* 19.2. and of that Goat, *Lev.* 16.20. both which are very Nourishing: This Milk is under the Spouses Tongue, *Cant.* 4.11. because she lyeth sucking at Christ's Breast.

4. Do you lack any Cloaths or Money, poor Naked Beggars? *I Counsel thee* (saith Christ) *to Buy of me Gold Tryed in the Fire, and White Raiment, that thou maiſt be Cloathed*, Rev. 3.18. His Gold will never Rust, nor will his Garments Moth-eat: his Robes will cover all your Nakedness, so will his Money pay your Debts: His Cloaths will add Inherent Beauty, his Money answereth all things, however poor its all Possessor seemeth, 2 *Cor.* 6.10.

5. Once more; Do you lack your Sight, poor Foolish Virgins? Christ also hath Eye-salve to Sell, which he doth Counsel you to Buy of him, *Rev.* 3.18. That is the Oyl here spoken of, (or the Commodity now in my Hand) with reference unto which, Christ is here called a Seller. The Nature of which Oyl hath formerly been cleared up: It onely now remains to shew, why Christ is called the Seller of it, or wherein he is like a Tradesman? which thus appeareth.

1. Tradesmen have store of what they put to Sale, and so hath Christ. Here is enough for him and others; therein he differeth from these Wise Virgins. He hath the Treasury of Wisdom, *Col.* 2.3. in whom all fulness dwelleth, *Col.* 1.19. and such a Fulness as is to be Received from, *John* 1.16. As none have cause to wave his Offer, from their pretending to have enough, *Gen.* 33.9. so none hath cause to fear his being Prejudiced by it, since he hath all, as *Jacob* said, *v.* 11. and as the *Hebrew* word there signifieth. He promiseth to fill the widest Mouth, *Psal.* 81.10. and hath enough for all the VVorld; yea, satisfieth ever Customer, and yet he is the same for ever. His uncreated Oyl can Make (with one word speaking) whatever Oyl the Creature needeth; therefore his stock must needs continue.

2. A Tradesman hath Authority to Sell, and so hath Christ. He is the Proprietor of what he hath, by Vertue of the Father's Gift, *Mat.* 28.18. and his own Purchase, *Phil.* 2.8, 9. and is it not Lawful for him then, to do what he will with his own, *Mat.* 20.18? He can produce

176   *The Parable of the Ten Virgins Opened.*

duce his Letters Patents 3. therefore fear not to Trade with him, for him hath God the Father Sealed, *John* 6. 27. Buy what you pleafe of him, it never shall be Taken from you, if Good and Needful, *Luke* 10. 42. Yea, though his Servant (*Isaac*) did mistake the Person, yet *Jacob* had the Blessing still, because the Master did so Order it, *Gen.* 27. 33. Robbers, *John* 10. 1. may Sell what they have stollen, *Jer.* 23. 30. but shall not therefore Profit others, because not sent, v. 32.

3. Tradesmen are Free to deal with any, and so is Christ. *Ho, every one that Thirsteth*, Isa. 55. 1. *and whosoever will*, Rev. 22. 17. Rich or Poor, Old or Young, Good or Bad, one or other, let him come. His Voice is to the Sons of Man, *Prov.* 8. 4. and unto Thee, yea, even to Thee, *Prov.* 22. 19. *And he that cometh to him, shal in no wife be Cast out by him*, John 6. 37. He onely findeth fault with Men's unwillingness, *John* 5. 40. nor doth he Turn away from any, till they have Judged themselves unworthy of his Gracious Offer, *Acts* 13. 46. Yea, former Provocations are no Let to Persons pricked in their Hearts; for unto such the Promise is, by way of Tender, as well as others, *Acts* 2. 37, 38, 39.

4. That which a Tradesman Selleth, is the Buyers own, between them two; so is it between a Soul and Christ. Therefore his Gifts are said to be without Repentance, *Rom.* 11. 29. because they are Sold, as to Assurance, though freely Given, *Rom.* 8. 32. as to any Proper Price, *Isa.* 55. 1. A Gift bestowed upon Servants, is onely theirs till such a Time, *Ezek.* 46. 17. before which Time, it may be Taken away, if mis-improved, *Hos.* 2. 8, 9. but Spiritual Riches are a True Believers own, *Luke* 15. 11, 12. who is a Son, *John* 1. 12. therefore his Gift is a Possession by Inheritance, *Ezek.* 46. 16. 'Tis firmly Promised, 1 *John* 2. 25. and with an Oath, *Heb.* 6. 17. before sufficient Witness, 1 *John* 5. 7. an Earnest whereof is also given, *Eph.* 1. 14.

5. Tradesmen Invite their Customers, but do not offer to Enforce them, save onely in a way of Moral suasion; and so doth Christ. He onely hinteth the Happiness of being Interested in his Offers together with the Danger of Refusing them, *Mark* 16. 16. and that's the whole of his Compelling to come in, *Luke* 14. 23. He may be Heard to say, *How long will ye Love Simplicity*, Prov. 1. 22? *When will ye be wife*, Psal. 94. 8? *Why will ye Die*, Ezek. 18. 31? but else, be at your Choice, whom you will Serve, *Josh.* 24. 15. The Man of Sin is for Coercion, *Rev.* 13. 16. but herein partly doth the easiness of Christ's Yoke appear, because it is not Put upon a Person's Neck, till he is willing to Take it up, *Mat.* 11. 29, 30.

6. Tradesmen

The Parable of the Ten Virgins Opened.

6. Tradesmen are wont to Part with no Commodities, but upon such proposed terms; no more doth Christ. Onely Christ herein differeth much from other Tradesmen, because Himself is not Advantaged, nor is the Soul at all Impoverished by any of those terms insisted on. Which are as followeth:

1. You must Come unto him. His Chapmen are oftner bid to Come, than Buy, *Isa.* 55, 1. to intimate, that if they mean to Buy, they must be sure to Come. He May be found of such as do not seek him, *Isa.* 65. 1. but Ordinarily he will be first Enquired of, *Ezek.* 36. 37. *Joseph* had Corn enough, yet must his own Brethren Come and Buy, *Gen.* 42. 2. yea, they must come again, or starve, *Gen.* 43. 2. And then he hath his Price, although they had their Money still, *v.* 22, 23. Yea, they must Come to Him, *Mat.* 11. 28. and not unto their Fellows onely, as did these Foolish Virgins. The Father hath Committed all to him, *John* 5. 22. as *Pharaoh* did to *Joseph*, *Gen.* 41. 55. such also must Come, as Coming doth import Believing, *John* 6. 35. not Absolutely with Respect to full Assurance, in point of Present or Future Interest; but yet with reference to his Ability and Will, upon such terms as are propounded by him, *James* 1. 6. *Heb.* 11. 6. and by a Special Faith, *Eph.* 3. 8.

2. You must come Mourning over all your former sleightiness and Provocations. Acknowledge your Offence, till when he Goeth from you, *Hos.* 5. 15. but humble your selves, then will he Hear, 2 *Chron.* 7. 14. take with you Words, *Hos.* 14. 2. as did that Prodigal, *Luke* 15. 18, 19. so will this Father Run and Meet you, *v.* 20. Thus must Transgressors come, Going and Weeping, *Jer.* 50. 4. which doth evince their being led by him, in a straight way, and their being welcome to him as a Father, *Jer.* 31. 9. *Pour out thine Heart like Water before his Face,* Lam. 2. 19. which is a Secondary kind of washing, *Isa.* 1. 16. *Then Come* (faith he) *and let us Reason,* v. 18 and Self-bemoaners are Affectionately remembred by him, *Jer.* 31. 18. 20. Money in water, is (in Appearance) double; onely this water must be clear, 2 *Cor.* 7. 10. and you must put no value thereupon, however Christ accounteth of it.

3. You must reduce indefinite desires into Particulars. When Chapmen come into a Shop to Buy, they are first asked, What would you have? Blind *Bartimeus* cryed unto Christ, (Indefinitely at first) *Thou Son of David, have Mercy on me.* Mark 10. 47. but when he came to Jesus, *v.* 50. Christ asked him, *What (in Particular) he wou'd have done unto him,* v. 51. Christ onely Echoeth unto the Creatures Voice; which (if Particular) is suitably replyed unto, *Mark* 10. 51, 52.

A a till

The Parable of the Ten Virgins Opened.

till when, his Call is as Indefinite, *v.* 49. as is the others Cry, *v.* 48. And therein have a Care to pitch upon what is of greatest Worth and Need; so will Inferiour things be added, *Mat.* 6. 33. without asking, 1 *Kings* 3. 11. 13. You would have Oyl, (faith Christ,) what kind of Oyl? The very Best (say you) the Purest Oyl: So may you have both it, and what is Common also.

4. His Offer must be duly Prized. It may be Tendred unto All, but is not Sold, save unto such who thereto Eminently are Invited, *Isa.* 55. 1. *Mat.* 11. 28. There must be so much sense, both of its Worth, and of our Need thereof, as to Provoke the Will, *Rev.* 22. 17. else shall we never Buy it of him. 'Tis true, there is a Passive Union first, (or pre-communication of Christ's Commodity) which doth Beget Desire; but till there be an Active cloze, (proceeding from that Desire Exercised,) there is no Full or Proper Interest. It is a Marriage-contract this, wherein the Man first takes the Woman, but she must also take the Man; till when, the Marriage is not Compleated: Nor can ought else be Sold or Bought.

5. You must receive this Oyl into your Vessels, else will Christ never Sell it, meerly to feed your Lamps, or flashy Present good Affections. It was not desired by these Foolish Virgins, save onely with respect unto their Lamps; and therefore (Possibly) the Wise Denyed them; so will Christ certainly. In case you would have Oyl (faith Christ) where is your Vessel? *Give me thine Heart*, Prov. 23. 26. *and I will fill it*, Psal. 81. 10. If there be no Vessel, his Oyl will stay, 2 *Kings* 4. 6. and 'tis Absurd to think, that Oyl (or Wisdom) can be Subjected, save in the Judgment. Some onely would have Oyl applyed to their Itching Ears; others, unto their Tongue, to make it Nimble; others, unto some VVound, till it be Healed: But Grace or VVisdom is not Thine, unless it entreth into thine Heart, *Prov.* 2. 10. no more than sinful Temptations are, untill the Heart be therewith filled.

6. Your Vessels also must be Emptied; else can you not Receive his Oyl, which is not Sold by him, untill it be immediately Delivered. Some other Liquors will Incorporate; but Darkness will as soon Agree with Light, as Sin with Grace. Some fain would keep their Puddle-water still; and so Christ's Oyl should spill upon the Ground, which he will not endure. And what a Fool is he, who doth refuse Christ's stately Robes; because he may not have them put upon his Filthy Garments? Let go your Airy self-conceit; else that alone may be sufficient to Obstruct the best Replenishment: As in a Stomach filled with wind. Yea, Christ will not be won, save with the Loss of Common Oyl, and all

The Parable of the *Ten Virgins Opened.* 179

all thofe things which heretofore have been Accounted Gain, *Phil.* 3. 7, 8.

7. You muſt receive the whole of his Commodity. Chriſt is an whole-Sale Merchant onely. He is a Vine, whoſe Fruit is Cluſtered. He doth not Sell his Oyl by Drops or Spoonfu's; you muſt have All or None. His Water is not to be had, but by a Quill united to his Conduit-Pipe. Some are ſo Moderate, ſo Partial in their Defires, as that Chriſt hath no mind to Parley with them. Yea, his whole Shop and Perſon too muſt go together, to every of his Speeding Chapmen; *Ruth* and her Land might not be ſeparated, *Ruth* 4. 5. And what a Mercy is it unto Saints, that Chriſt and all his Spiritual Bleſſings are thus United, *Eph.* 1. 3. unto their being made Compleat in him, *Col.* 2. 10! How readily is this Accepted of, in other Cafes, ſave with Reſpect to Chriſt's Commodit es!

8. You muſt be content to take it as it Cometh; which (at the firſt) may not be ſo Delightful, as afterwards. If any part of Chriſt's Commodities may be called worſe than other, the Beſt are Laſt; but you muſt take them as they Riſe, that being the Cuſtom of his Shop. There is a Teaching and a Crowning Oyl; an Oyl for Light, and Oyl of Gladneſs; Oyl for a Sacrifice, and Oyl for Food : But *Leah* muſt firſt be had, *Gen.* 29. 26. and Supper is not until the Work be over, *Luke* 17. 7, 8. nor may we receive the Promiſe, till we have done the Will of God, *Heb.* 10. 36. Thoſe never will go Through with Chriſt, who will not Buy, ſave what is clear (unto an Eye of ſenſe) at its firſt running; who will not learn the Chriſtian's Primmer, becauſe his Croſs is the firſt Letter in that Row, *Mat.* 16. 24. who would have the Bottom of Chriſt's Oyl firſt poured out, which cannot be expected.

9. You muſt be willing to lay all down, both in a Myſtical and Literal ſence, giving him leave to Take it if he pleaſeth, and without grudging. He onely deals with Generous Chapmen, who value him above their All, in any Reſpect whatever. Thoſe are not worthy of him, who Love ought More than him, *Mat.* 10. 37. nor ſhall thoſe Comers ſpeed with him, who Hate not what is Deareſt to them, in caſe he calleth for it, *Luke* 14. 26. His Terms are theſe; thy Gold and Silver, and Wife and Children, (the Goodlieſt of them all) are Mine, as *Benhadad* ſaid to *Ahab*: 2 *Kings* 20. 3. nor will he be ſatisfied with thy bare Aſſenting hereunto, *v.* 4. unleſs they be Delivered up, when called for, *v.* 5, 6. Indeed he either will not take this Money, as *Gen.* 42. 25. or will reſtore an hundred-Fold, *Mark* 10. 30. but yet it muſt be all laid down, as *Gen.* 43. 21, 22. yea, Spiritual Priviledges alſo.

10. You muſt be alſo very Thankful, with reference unto (at leaſt-wife,

wife, notwithstanding) the hardest terms which have been signified. This will Evince its being Given, in your esteem, as it so is, in his account; whose being called a Seller here, yea, whose fore-named Price insisted on, doth no way Interfere with the Freeness of his Gift. His great Design is to set forth the Glory of his Grace, *Eph.* 1. 6. which is Eclipsed by Men's unthankfulness, or by a Cloud upon their Brow. This hath been the Practice of all his speeding Chapmen; this you must do, or he and you will not Agree: And though a Cheapner may think much, yet is Dis-satisfaction inconsistent with its being Sold. Therefore say not, 'Tis Naught, 'Tis Naught, as many Buyers use to do; since, when thou hast it, I dare be bold to say, thou wilt Boast of it, *Prov.* 20. 14,

11. You must be sure to hold your Purses. That's one of this Seller's Terms; *Come buy, yea, come,* but without Money, *Isa.* 55. 1. Plead not for more, because of what you have; plead not for any, because of your Deserving it, or being Worthy to receive it. Count not your Duty Payment, stay not till you have got a Price, or Present in your Hand: But come as Poor and Vile in your own Eyes as may be; Christ onely deals with Spiritual Beggars. Some hope to speed, because they are full handed; *thy Money Perish with thee*: Some dare not come, they are so Poor; but if thine Heart be willing to Accept him, as aforesaid, come and Welcome. I do not say, that Christ is thine, but thou maist freely come and Buy; yea, none but Nothings are Traded with.

12. You must Engage to keep this Oyl; which as he will not Take away, *Luke* 10. 42. so neither must you Let it Go, *Prov.* 4. 13. He Selleth by Indentures, putting his Fear into the Heart (his Oyl into the Vessel) upon those Terms, *Jer.* 32. 40. *Jer.* 50. 5. 2 *Tim.* 1. 14. That which is subject (wholly) to be Lost, is neither any special Oyl, nor was it ever Sold by him: Yet shall a careless Loser (of Common things) pay more for what is Lent, than doth the Buyer, *Exod.* 22. 7. 9. But he that bids you Buy the Truth, doth also charge you not to Sell it, *Prov.* 22. 23. And since his Commodity is your Life, *Prov.* 4. 13. you would be a Loser by its Sale, though all the World should be Exchanged for it, *Mat.* 16. 26. *Esau* had not the Blessing, because he was Free to sell his Birth-right, *Heb.* 12. 16, 17. which *Jacob* would never part with more, and thereby evidenced his having Bought it.

13. You must Improve this Oyl for him, and not Receive his Grace in vain, 2 *Cor.* 6. 1. or turn it into Lasciviousness, *Jude* 4. 'Tis not else sold; nor is that Holy-Oyl, which is thus apt to be Abused. There is some kind of Oyl which may be set before an Idol, *Hos.* 2. 8. but that

is

The Parable of the Ten Virgins Opened. 181

is Common, and likely to be taken away, *v.* 9. which doth evince its being not sold, but Lent. Let your Design be good, in your Desiring Oyl or Light, and you shall have it: Oh what an easie Price is this! And as a Demonstration of its being thus improved, he doth expect to be first served by you, in a way of self-denyal, or first Fruits; leaving the Residue for you to gather. Nor will a Wise Servant grudge to Occupy that Talent for his Master's Use, which doth redound at last unto his own Advantage.

14. As you would Buy, or Lastingly partake of the Root and Fruit of this good Olive-Tree, *Rom.* 11. 17. take heed of Boasting, *v.* 18. with reference unto the Root or Branches, or with respect unto the Thing it self. Boast not, as to the Thing it self, which is not Theirs who are not Humble, 1 *Pet.* 5. 5. it being the Nature of this Oyl to keep all other things below it self. Boast not against the Branches, or such who Now may want this Oyl; but carry your selves, in that respect, as these Wise Virgins do unto the Foolish; which did more fully evidence their having Bought it, than did the others Motion for some part thereof. Boast not (especially) against the Root or Christ, as if he did not Bear thee: As if he were Beholden to thee for thy Fruit; as if it were not His, while it is Thine, which that wise Servant did confess, *Luke* 19. 16. and by that means he had the whole, with some Addition, *v.* 24.

15. You must not Trifle, but see unto this work betimes. There is a Time of Finding, *Psal.* 32. 6. *And those that seek me Early shall find me,* saith Essential Wisdom, *Prov.* 8. 17. When once the Master of this Shop or House hath shut the Door, some Men will seek to enter in, but not be able, *Luke* 13. 24, 25. Oh seek him therefore, while he may be found, *Isa.* 55. 6. while he is Calling, while you are waking; while sin is Modest, while you are somewhat Tender; while Satan is Restrained, and Christ at work, whether by his Spirit, Word, or Providences. I would Discourage none, by telling them my Present Fears, as to the Foolish Virgins Case; but it is high time to Run and Cry, Lord, Oyl for me, before the Door be shut.

16. You must be willing to Communicate this Oyl (or Light) to others also, as you are able, and as Occasion is afforded; unless the Scripture gives a Dispensation: The wise Virgins (here) do seem unable; and scorners are not to be Instructed, *Prov.* 9. 8. but otherwise you are Receivers, that you might Give, *Mat.* 10. 8. Your Light must shine before the World, *Mat.* 5. 14, 15, 16. and not be Covered, or in a secret place, if you would have your Candle Lighted (or sold) by Christ, *Luke* 11. 33. When thou art Converted, strengthen others, *Luke* 22. 32.

whose

Sale, wherein thine All is called for, *Mat.* 10. 27, 28. Without submitting to which Term, this Oyl is never Sold to any, *Mat.* 13. 46.

Quest. 4. Why doth Christ chuse to Sell his Oyl?

Answ. 1. That so it might be Represented sure; as being fairly Bought and Sold. Gifts are depending upon the Givers good Affections, *Hos.* 13. 11. but *Jacob* kept the Birth-right still, which he had Bought, (and consequently, the Blessing also) though *Esau* Hated him, *Gen.* 27. 41. And though God's special Gifts are said to be without Repentance, *Rom.* 11. 29. yet is a Doubting Conscience better satisfied with Christ's being said (as here) to Sell it, according unto Common Rules of Judging. Therefore God Buys his People with a Price, that so they might be His, without Dispute, 1 *Cor.* 6. 20. Yea, therefore he sometimes Sold them unto others, *Judg.* 2. 14. to make those Buyers think, they had a Lawful Title to them, *Isa.* 49. 24. Now, God is willing to shew abundantly his own Immutability unto the Heirs of Promise, *Heb.* 6. 17. who therefore calls his Gift their Purchase.

2. To hint the Worth of his Commodities. Gifts usually are lesser things; as Thread and Paper: But things of Worth are Evidenced by a Price demanded. Indeed Christ is Invaluable, *Prov.* 8. 11. therefore he must be Given, or not be had: But yet the Soul must Buy him with his All, *Mat.* 13. 44. to shew his Worth as much as may be. Men will not Run and Cry for Apprehended Trifles; therefore there doing onely so for Christ, doth intimate his being Valued by them. Especially when *Paul* did freely suffer the Loss of All things for his sake, Accounting his former attainments Dung, Compared with him, *Phil.* 3. 8. And though a sinners sin is nothing, because it wants the good of Being; yea, worse than Nothing, because that Soul had better not have Been, *Mat.* 26. 24. Yet is it his right Eye, *Mat.* 5. 29. the Loss whereof doth Argue Highest Valuation, *Gal.* 4. 15.

3. That so his Chapmen's Honour (as well as Satisfaction) might be consulted for, by him, (and by this means) together with his own. He hath made all things (Firstly) for Himself, *Prov.* 16. 4. because there is no Higher End; which therefore doth accordingly Oblige his Creatures in all their Actings, 1 *Cor.* 10. 31. who also are

En-

The Parable of the Ten Virgins Opened.

Encouraged to Honour him, by his confulting for their Honour, in a Second place, 1 *Sam.* 2. 30. He doth put Honour upon Himfelf, by ftanding upon fome kind of Price: His People alfo do much Honour him, by their Accepting him upon his own Propofals: And he will therefore alfo have them Buy, that fo their Generoufnefs might be thus Evidenced (as was by *David*, 2 *Sam.* 24. 23, 24.) And feeming Riches, who can thus Purchafe their very Purchafer, by that precious Faith, 2 *Pet.* 1. 1. which is fo All-commanding, *Mat.* 15. 18.

4. To fignifie its being not to be Challenged, as a Debt; nor upon Terms, fave with its Owner's Leave. That which is fairly Sold, may be Demanded, in way of Righteoufnefs; therefore if Saints confefs, *The Lord is Juft and Faithful to Forgive*, 1 John 1. 9. becaufe (in Chrift) they have laid down his Price; till when, both Parties are at Liberty. A Tenant's Rent may be Required; but not a Tradefman's unbought Ware: Nor can fuch be Conftrained to Sell, no more than Chapmen are to Buy. No Flefh muft Glory in His prefence, 1 *Cor.* 1. 29. which as the Freenefs of his Gift confulteth for, *Eph.* 2. 9. fo doth his Sale: That fo, his being Dif-obliged might Appear, both as a Benefactor, and as a Tradefman; which doth Exclude all kind of Boafting.

5. That fo his Commodity might be the more Endeared, as Bought things are. Propriety. (though meerly from a Gift) doth much Endear, 1 *Kings* 21. 3. efpecially when it is purchafed; as that Ew-Lamb was as his Daughter who had bought it, 2 *Sam.* 12. 3. Thus *Jacob* would be Buried in that Field which *Abraham* Bought, *Gen.* 49. 29, 30. He that had Bought a piece of Ground, muft needs go fee it, though at a Coftly Rate, *Luke* 14. 18. And *Sion's* prime Argument with God, to be remembred, was, her having been his Ancient purchafe, *Pfal.* 74. 2. Mothers (ufually) are moft Affectionate, becaufe their Children coft Them Deareft, *Prov.* 4. 3. and 31. 2. and God is very careful of thofe whom he hath purchafed with his own Blood, *Acts* 20. 28. So was Chrift unto *Paul*, whom he had won (or Bought) with Lofing all his former Gains, *Phil.* 3. 8.

6. That Foolifh Virgins might be Difcovered, who fain would have Oyl Freely Given, and keep their Money ftill, from finful fleightinefs, and bafe felf-love, if not from Envy, and for a wicked End. The pooreft Chapman hath fome Money, *Ifa.* 55. 2. which he might keep, if it wou'd either profit him, or not be vainly fpent elfe-where: And in that Cafe, he doth but fhew his own unworthinefs, who Grudgeth Chrift the having of it. Thofe Men deferve to be uncafed by him, who will not give (for his Commodity) what doth not profit them to keep;

and

and from a Design thereby to Act unto his Dis-advantage. Thus also will their Mouth be stopt, with reference unto their being Denied, and others Speeding, since his Commodity is at the Buyers Service.

Quest. How is that Freely Given, *Rom.* 5. 15. which yet is Sold? Either by God or Christ.

Answ. 1. The Father Selleth, because the Son laid down his price, unto the full, in point of Matter, for his Elect; both as to God's vindictive Justice, and Distributive. Vindictive Justice had her Full payment from him, for the sins of his Elect; because he was made sin for them, 2 *Cor.* 5. 21. and was not Spared or Remitted, *Rom.* 8. 32. Distributive Justice had her Full, because he did whatever the Law required, *Heb.* 7. 26. whose Universal Righteousness (without Restraining it unto his Death) is that by which his people Reign in Life, *Rom.* 5. 17. Yet is it also There called a Gift, because the Benefit of his Obedience is made over unto Others, which Rigorous Justice doth not Admit; and therefore it is onely pleaded at the Throne of Grace, *Heb.* 4. 16. Thus Selling and Free Giving are consistent, with Respect unto the Father.

2. The Son doth also Freely Give, though he is here said to Sell.

1. Because the price (insisted on) is Nothing, Compared with the Worth of his Commodity. This Oyl (or Wisdom) is Invaluable; man knoweth not the price thereof, *Job* 28. 13. it cannot be got for Gold or precious Stones, *v.* 15, 16. yea, all the things to be Desired are not to be Compared with it, *Prov.* 8. 11. How then can those forenamed terms be called a price? Which either Relate to filthy Rags, or Matters of no Real worth at all, save in a person's Estimation. Now, if a Pepper-corn be paid, it hath the Name of Price, in Law; but if an Earldom should be Sold for one brass Farthing, would it be therefore said, Not to be Given? Therefore Christ's proper Name must needs be *Giver*; however, Commonly, he may be called a Seller: His Name is Wonderful, *Isa.* 9. 6. or a Free-Giving Tradesman.

2. Because Himself is not Advantaged by any of that fore-said Money, or as the Buyer is, by his Commodity; which therefore (as to Him) is Freely Given. What gets He by thy Coming to him? He Bottleth up his people's Tears, not for Their Worth, but as his *Memorandum*, *Psal.* 56. 8, 9. The Emptyings of thy Vessel are no Gain to Him, as thy partaking of his Fulness is to Thee. And as thy Praises add no Real greatness to him; so what Receiveth he of thy hand, if thou be Righteous, *Job* 35. 7. *Nehem.* 9. 5? Yet will no Man be at this Cost and pains, who doth not Value this Commodity above those Terms. From whence it followeth, that as the Creature is a Buyer, so Christ is properly a Giver, though called a Seller: 3. Because

3. Becaufe the Chapman is not Damaged, but much Enriched by his very parting with this Money, as well as by what is Exchanged for it. Thy very Coming unto Chrift, is both a Labour and Recreation, *Mat.* 11. 28, 29. Thy Godly forrow is not to be Repented of, 2 *Cor.* 7. 10. no more than fweating in a Fever. Thy Thirfting after him, doth make his Tafte the more Delightful, *Prov.* 27 7. It is a Mercy to have thy Veffel Emptied of what is in it; and yet a greater Mercy to have it called for, in Order to its being filled with Grace, *Pfal.* 81. 10. Yea, it is not for thine Advantage, to have his Oyl run fomewhat Thick at firft, and Clearer afterwards, *Luke* 16. 25? Its being Improved for Him, will prove thy Gain at laft, *Luke* 19. 16, 17. fo will thy greateft Loffes for its fake, *Mat.* 5. 10. the Expectation whereof doth onely make continued Enjoyments fo much the more fafe and fweet, *Heb.* 11. 17. 19.

4. Becaufe he is the Sole Proprietor, as of his own Commodity, fo of the Buyer's Money alfo: And in that cafe, felf-payers are Free-Givers. Thou canft not check him with thy Coming to him, becaufe thou Liveft and Moveft in him, *Acts* 17. 28. Thy forrow is an Affection in thee, of his Creating; the Exercife whereof thy fin hath alfo made to be a Moral Debt. What haft thou (as to Outward Bleffings,) which thou haft not Received from him, *Ezek.* 16. 10, 11, 12? And may he not then Require their being All laid down, without a Commutation? Thine whole Activity is from himfelf; thy Praifes and Improvements are his Due: Yea, he it is who worketh in thee, to Will and Do, according to the Terms propofed, *Phil.* 2. 13. therefore if *Abraham* were Juftified by works, he hath whereof to Glory, but not before the Lord, *Rom.* 4. 2. for who hath firft given to him, and it fhall be Recompenfed, *Rom.* 11. 35. elfe paying him with his own, doth onely evidence the Freenefs of his Gift.

Ufe 1. Wife Virgins have very Low and Jealous thoughts of their own Spiritual ftock, as is here fignified; and more efpecially, when Newly wakened out of their finful flumbring, for which there is fufficient Reafon. Sleep is Expenfive, as Sicknefs is, whereof this is one kind; and therefore Love it not, for fear of coming unto Poverty, *Prov.* 20. 13. However fuch are apt to be fufpitious, beyond their Ground; Departure from the Lord, being both the Fruit of unbelief, *Heb.* 3. 12. and caufe of fuch-like Doubting. Yea, a Returning Prodigal is to be known by Holy humble Apprehenfions of his worth, *Luke* 15. 19. and Oyl or Wifdom, *Eccl.* 7. 23. Indeed, the truly wife are ever Lowly, *Prov.* 19. 2. whilft others think they have Enough, not onely for Themfelves and Others help, but alfo to fpare fome part for

Satan,

Satan, who therefore are bold to dally with his Temptations; but such Men's Folly shews their Real want of Oyl, or wisdom.

3. Wise Virgins are (in the first place) for Themselves, with reference unto their Spiritual Interest. It is not onely warrantable, but (in this case) it is their Duty and their Wisdom. In Outward things Man ought to Love his Neighbour as Himself, in Opposition unto Malice, *Lev.* 19. 18. and in Respect of Truth, though not Degree, save in some more than Ordinary Cases, 1 *John* 3. 16. but not in Spirituals. And though *Paul* wisht himself accurst from Christ (for others) in point of Spiritual Priviledges, *Rom.* 9. 3. wherein he also might have a Special warrant; yet did he not wish his being a Transgressor for their sake, save as Christ was by way of Imputation. God's Glory should be preferred by us, before our own Salvation; but let us not do Evil, though Good may come, *Rom.* 3. 8. in that Respect, *v.* 7. Therefore, with reference unto Duty, it was the Spouse's Grief, that she had kept others Vineyards, and not our own, *Cant.* 1. 6.

3. Wise Virgins are very loath to say, *Not so*, unto a Motion made for Spiritual help, in any case whatever. Those words [*Not so*] are not in the *Greek*, but added by our Translators, as being grounded upon the wise Virgins silence. Nor do they Absolutely bid the other Go elsewhere, but onely rather; and with Respect unto the Foolish Virgins greater benefit, who by that means might have Oyl without borrowing. Some do with-hold anothers Due, when it is in the power of their hand to do it, *Prov.* 3. 27. but Saints are forward to be Charitable, *Psal.* 112. 5. save as meer Duty doth forbid them: Christ had Compassion upon others, and as with reference unto their Bodies, *Mat.* 15. 32. so much more with Respect unto their Souls, *Mark* 6. 34. And Christians have their Name from him; nor are Men worthy to be so called, in case they be of *Nabal*'s Churlish Disposition, 1 *Sam.* 25. 11.

4. Wise Virgins are for giving satisfaction unto others, with reference unto their very Negatives. Some will not hear the strongest Reason Offered against themselves, *Zech.* 7. 11. these Men are Beasts, 1 *Cor.* 15. 32. Others will give no Reason for their Practice, but their Will, *Exod.* 15. 9. these are not Prudent Men, *Prov.* 26. 16. Others expect that every Light Excuse should serve the turn, *Luke* 14. 18. but those were Carnal Jews, or Foolish Virgins. How shamefully have some endeavoured to silence those with Childish Answers, who have been serious in desiring Oyl, or Spiritual help. But Grace is not for Dallying, especially not in Momentous cases, but alway is provided of a Rational Answer with Holy fear, 1 *Pet.* 3. 15. expecting that
Christ

The Parable of the Ten Virgins Opened. 187

Christ will one day call for an Account (or Reason) of Idle words, *Mat.* 12. 36. Nor can they be supposed to have Faith, who are unreasonable or Absurd, 2 *Thes.* 3. 2.

5. Poor Foolish Virgins are not likely (in these latter days) to gain Oyl from the Wise by their Communion with them, or addresses to them. Together with the Rising of God's Light and Glory upon *Sion*, Professors of an Earthy Spirit will be covered with Gross Darkness, *Isa.* 60. 1, 2. None of the wicked at such a time shall understand, *Dan.* 12. 10. the Matters of their Peace will then be hidden from their Eyes, *Luke* 19. 42. and as the unlearned (then) so will the Learned be, in point of Ignorance, *Isa.* 29. 11, 12. Christians Communion (heretofore) may have been both Preventive and Recovering; but henceforth no more of that Vine, untill its Fruit shall be renewed, *Mat.* 26. 29. Newly Awakened ones love not to stir; Helps ready to be laid aside are very weak, and when the payment is, the work is over: Therefore this Dispensation must needs be fixing. I would not Discourage from the use of Means, but Doubt their Efficacy at this Day, with Respect unto Foolish Virgins.

6. It may not be wondred at, if Wise and Foolish Virgins be Observed (in these latter days) to have but little Intercourse, as is here signified. There is not any thing considerable doth befall us, but is Revealed, *Amos* 3. 7. if Men did but consult the Scriptures, *Luke* 24. 27. Thus, as to this particular, between the time of Christ's Ascending, (which Answereth unto that of of his VVitnesses, *Rev.* 11. 12.) and the Descending of the Holy Ghost, (which Answereth unto the Seventh Trumpets sounding,) Christ's Party were alone, *Acts* 1. 13, 14. choosing some other instead of *Judas*, v. 15. and did not meddle with the Jews till afterwards, *Acts* 2. 1. which Answereth unto the Viols Dispensation. And thus, untill the Spirit (in these latter days) is poured from on High, the Fruitful Field (or Old Professors) is counted for a Forest, *Isa.* 32. 15. not sown with Exhortations, nor Ploughed with Reproofs. This Interval is rather a time of Prayer and silence, *Rev.* 8. 1. alluding unto that, *Luke* 1. 9, 10.

7. VVise Virgins (at such a time) are freely willing to let the other Go from them, for mutual good. VVhat shall we then judge of them, or by what Name must they be called, who cannot bear a separation from their Old Companions by any means? Some count it strange, that others do forbear their wonted Intercourse: But can a wise Man delight to Reason with unprofitable Talk, *Job* 15. 2, 3? Such are Exhorted to save Themselves from that untoward Generation, *Acts* 2. 40. who are Offended with plain down-right dealing, and Non-compliance with a

sinful

finful Prohibition, *Acts* 5. 28. Nor can the Foolish Virgins Go and Buy Oyl for themselves, unless Communion with the wise be discontinued, as is here hinted. The onely way to Benefit Apostates, is to let them Go; who otherwise are apt to Bless themselves with being so far owned, therefore with-draw, 2 *Thes.* 3. 14.

8. Wise Virgins lend what help they can, by way of Exhortation and Direction unto those whom they may not be able to Instruct. This is the Last Remedy to be used; a bidding Ordinary means farewell; like that last digging about a Barren Fig-Tree, *Luke* 13.8,9. or bringing the Matter unto *Moses*, *Exod.*18.26.Thus is the Spirits willingness Evinced, together with its weakness; thus is a Departing Saint's breath sweet unto the last: thus is Christ Evidenced by them to be above them, and this is Grace's Valediction unto far-spent sinners. Indeed Man's utmost help is onely Ministerial; and Christ reserveth some peculiar work unto himself, *Mar.* 9. 18. whom therefore these wise Virgins send the other unto. When Instruments are out of Breath, and Ordinary Means have tryed their utmost; yet is there hope in him, who can recover from the Grave: And thus far Grace is willing to Accompany a Dying Creature, which is the Last Office to be performed.

9. Christ will be (now) Gone unto, by such as want his Oyl or Light, and will not come to them, as heretofore his manner was, *Eph.* 2. 17. He will be Enquired of at such a time, *Ezek.* 36. 37. and will be sought for, *Hos.* 3. 5. till when he Goeth and returneth to his place, *Hos.* 5. 15. or Heaven, 1 *Kings* 8. 30. The Temple sometime was his dwelling place, *Psal.* 76. 2. but now his Glory is removed thence, *Ezek.* 11. 23. untill it shall Return, *Ezek.* 43. 4. Therefore he must be followed by such as mean to find him, *Cant.* 3. 1,2. This is the Fruit of sinful Dallying, *viz.* the Hiding of his Face, *Deut.* 32. 20. or self-with-drawing, *Cant.* 5. 6. and in that case, self-stirring up is Necessary, *Isa.* 64. 7. 'tis well if that will serve. Time-sinners must not onely seek, but also strive, *Luke* 13. 24. and such do but deceive themselves, if they conclude their having of this Oyl (which formerly hath been Neglected) without some more than Ordinary Cost and Pains, as is here signified.

10. Oyl [*for our selves*] was alway both our Duty and our wisdom to be Labouring after, which in these latter days will eminently be urged unto and insisted on by all wise Virgins. Foundations (now) will be Discovered, *Hab.* 3. 13. there will be no room for Borrowing; nor will Professors be Advantaged, save by what is their own. Their Motion here doth evidence Christ's Design, which is, to have Men
Principled

Principled for their Duty, and not to satisfie themselves (as these poor Foolish Virgins would have done) with bare Revived Lamps or good Affections, wherewith Christ is not satisfied, nor his People. Wise Virgins may be known by this, their putting others upon self-enquiries; who therefore will not lend a Form of Knowledge, lest that should satisfie without its Power. Such may be thought to be reserved; but as Christ hath a Righteous Hand therein, so they may have an Holy Aim, *viz.* the others greater Benefit.

11. There are Oyl-Sellers still, whom Men are bid to Buy it of, as they would have it for Themselves. Christ onely can Estate a Soul in Light, and by that means secure it; which else is apt to be Removed; nor will he Recompense a Man, save with Respect unto what is his own, 1 *Cor.* 3. 8. But you must Buy it, and its Price hath been already set; nor will one Farthing be abated: Therefore let none presume his Interest therein, who hath not (doth not) come up unto those fore-named Terms. And 'tis a Mercy that it may be had; which these Wise Virgins do suppose, else would they not have bid the other Go and Buy: Nor is the Door said to have been shut till afterward, *Mat.* 25. 10. The near Approaching of which Day doth call for Mutual Exhortation, *Heb.* 10. 25. while it is called, *To Day,* ·*Heb.* 3. 13. before it be too late. And as a Bargain of this Nature would be struck up, these following Directions may be of Use.

1. You must be content to Go, or (in some sence) to Part with those Wise Virgins, whom (heretofore) a Right of walking with (in point of State-Communion) hath been Challenged. Keep with them still, as Precious Friends; but cease from any Higher Claim, or from pretending unto the sameness of your Spiritual Case and State with theirs. There is that Maketh himself Rich, who yet hath Nothing, *Prov.* 13. 7. and as that Man is not Relieved by another, so neither will he work himself, till eased of that foolish Fansie. The *Pharisees* were not Baptized of *John, Lu.* 7 30. because unwilling to confess their sins, *Mat.* 3. 6, 7, 8. Nor would those Jews come unto Christ, *John* 5. 40. who boldly called God their Father, *John* 8. 41. no more than Persons unconvinced of their Blindness, will Buy Eye-salve, *Rev.* 3. 17, 18. Oh let us rather Buy Oyl twice than be without it, from Groundless self conceit.

2. Set out his Oyl with highest Commendations, as to its Virtues, Worth, and Need. Think not to have its Price abated by your sleighty undervaluings, as in your dealing with other Tradesmen. Others bid See for Love, and Buy for Money; but here, your Money is your Love: Therefore he biddeth most for Oyl, who doth most

Prize.

Prize it. Wife Virgins Hide their Love from Men, left they should else be sleighted by them: But Christ's Admirers have learnt the Art of Gaining upon his Affections. Children will Cry for what they would have, and so must you for Spiritual Knowledge, *Prov.* 2. 3. *Oh that thou wert my Brother*, faith the to Christ, *Cant.* 8. 1. And say you unto Wisdom, *Thou art my Sister*, Prov. 7.4. *Get Understanding with all thy Getting*, Prov. 4. 7. Exalt her, *v.* 8. who Loveth him that Loveth her, *Prov.* 8. 17. Our Estimations, Sighs, and Tears, are Currant Gold with Christ, though nothing Valued by other Tradesmen.

3. Take heed by any means of Dallying with him. Make not Two words, for Fear of a Denyal. He came no more unto those *Gadarens*, who did but once desire him to be gone, *Luke* 8. 37. nor would he ever after deal with those who had Rejected his first Offer, *Luke* 14. 24. Were it not to Befriend you, (to Pleasure You more than Himself) he would not Sell it: And Love Despised is the most Provoking. Yea, he who fell not in with *Paul's* first Offer, never desired more the sight of that Commodity, *Acts* 24.25. However this Tradesman's Lowest Price is at the first, as Late Repentants do Experience, who formerly have Dallied with his Offers: How Cheap did *Lydia* Buy, *Acts* 16. 14. Compared with those Second Comers, *Acts* 2. 37. You cannot be without his Oyl, nor doth your Conscience think it is too Dear; therefore Accept it with Thanksgiving: And when you have it, your having been so long without it will be your onely Grief.

4. Have Patience though, and do not hastily fling away: Christ deals with none (as an Eventual Seller) but Sober Chapmen. Inordinacy of Desire is a Lust which he will not indulge in any: Men either do not Ask, or Ask amiss; who therefore have not their Desire, *James* 4. 2, 3. Your Time is alway ready, so is not his, *John* 7. 6. who will not Serve his Mother, till such an Hour, *John* 2. 4. And *Moses* was made to tarry one week longer, whom nothing else would serve but Now, *Numb.* 12. 13, 14. Thus many poor Creatures want their Oyl, because they cannot wait, 2 *Kings* 6. 33. but fling out of Christs Shop (with *Saul*) into the Devil's, 1 *Sam.* 28. 6, 7. and there are Cheated, *v.* 14. You are but Beggars, in the Form of Buyers; therefore demean your selves accordingly. And do not Passionately retort or turn away, though his first Answer should be rough; but give good words, *Psal.* 22. 2, 3. and wait his Leisure, *Psal.* 123.2. whose Oyl cannot be had else where, and is thus given, *Psal.* 27. 14.

5. Be sure you do Design it for your selves, (next unto him,) and
for

The Parable of the Ten Virgins Opened. 191

for your own beſt good, as theſe Wiſe Virgins Exhortation hinteth. Expect the firſt Queſtion put(next to What do you lack)will be, Whom is it for? Would you have Oyl, meerly to Boaſt thereof, or to Inſtruct another; or onely to Accommodate a Worldly Intereſt? There's other Oyl good enough for ſuch a purpoſe. This Holy Oyl muſt not be put unto a Common Uſe, *Exod.* 30. 31. 33. Some would have Healing Oyl, to ſin more freely; and Fragrant Oyl, to gain the Virgins good Affections; and Lightſome Oyl, to make a ſhew: But Holy Oyl is not put into ſuch polluted Veſſels. *Abraham* had more than Ordinary Light, and he was careful to Improve it, *Gen.* 18. 17. 19. And *Paul*, together with his filled Veſſel, had ſomething given to ſecure it, 2 *Cor.* 12. 7. And though Grace makes the Change, yet the Indulging of Lower Aims is inconſiſtent with a Grounded Hope of ever Buying it.

6. Conſult not with Fleſh and Blood; our own, or others. The Fleſh at beſt (or in a Natural Reſpect) is Weak, *Mat.* 26. 41. much more in a Moral ſence, *Gal.* 5. 17. and therefore Fleſh and Blood cannot Inherit, 1 *Cor.* 15. 50. for theſe will never Buy. Dull Fleſh hath no great mind to Go, *Prov.* 6. 10. Proud Fleſh thinks ſcorn to have the eaſieſt Terms Impoſed, 2 *Kings* 5. 11. 13. Self-loving Fleſh would part with Nothing, much leſs with All, *Mat.* 19. 21, 22. therefore this ſelf (or Fleſh) muſt be Denied, before Chriſt will be followed, *Mat.* 16. 24. Conſult not herewith in others neither, as *Abſalom* did with *Huſhai*, and *Rehoboam* with his Companions, unto the Ruine of them both. The Serpent will tell thee, Chriſt is too Dear, and may abate, *Gen.* 3. 4, 5. Relations will bid thee (firſt) to provide for Them: And Carnal Friends will break thine Heart with their Diſſwaſives, *Acts* 21. 13. *Peter* took Chriſt to do, for being too forward, *Mat.* 16. 22. whom therefore *Paul* would not conſult with at the firſt, *Gal.* 1. 16, 17, 18. Nor will a Bargain of this Nature be concluded, till ſuch are ſilenced by us, as *Peter* was by Chriſt, *Mat.* 16. 23.

7. Mind his Commodity before you do Refuſe it; and under this ſingle denomination (here) of its being called Oyl; yea, meerly with Reſpect to that Particular uſe of Oyl intended here, *viz.* its being Serviceable in point of Light; which may induce your Buying of it.

1. The Light is ſweet, *Eccl.* 11. 7. and doth Rejoyce the Heart, *Prov.* 15. 30. therefore the Light is put for Joy and Gladneſs, *Eſth.* 8. 16. *Pſal.* 97. 11. by which the Heart-chearing influence of a Godly Ruler is deſcribed, 2 *Sam.* 23. 3, 4. Yea, God's own Love (which is the choiſeſt Cordial) is called the Light of his Face or Countenance,

Pſal.

Psal. 4. 6. Now, would you not be glad of Joy? Come then, yea, come and Buy this Lightsome (and this Gladsome) Oyl. When *Sampson* had lost his Eyes (or Light) how did he Grind in the Prison-House, *Judg.* 16. 21. it may be his Teeth together, in way of Indignation and Vexation, chusing to be Avenged upon others for his Two Eyes, by Losing his very Life, *v.* 28. 30. which Now was not Desirable. Yea, therefore Hell it self is Represented by a place of Darkness, where Grinders are, *Mat.* 8. 12. as Heaven is a place of Light, *Col.* 1. 12. and Joy, *Psal.* 16. 11. to shew the Pleasantness of Light (as in it self considered,) and Dolefulness of being in the Dark.

2. Light giveth Life and Being unto visible Objects, which otherwise are as if they were Not, as to our being Solaced with their sight: Yea, we had better Not to hear of Beauty, than to want Eyes or Light, by which to see it. Man seeth not (at least not chiefly) by Extramission, as Owls and such like Creatures do; therefore His very Eyes are useless, if in the Dark; who onely Heareth, what others See. Death and Destruction have heard of Wisdom, *Job* 28. 22. but sinners know not that Eminent Gift, *John* 4. 10. because there is no Light in them, *Isa.* 8. 20. How marvellously would it Affect, could Men but see the Amiableness of God's Tabernacles, *Psal.* 84. 1. the many Flowers in *Sion's* Land, *Cant.* 2. 12. much more the Glory of God himself, as it appeareth in his Sanctuary, *Psal.* 63. 2. *John* did behold Christ's Glory, in his Lowest state, *John* 1. 14. but others saw no Beauty in him, who therefore did Despise him, *Isa.* 53. 2.

3. Else will you not have the Comfort of what you do Enjoy. Souls in a state of Darkness may Really be Interested in Electing Love; but till Christ gives them Light, *Eph.* 5. 14. such cannot know it: without his Holy Enlightning Spirit, there is no Joy of his Salvation, *Psal.* 51. 11, 12. Thou hast the Scriptures, but till thine Eyes are Opened, thou canst not understand them, 2 *Cor.* 4. 4. because they are Spiritually to be Discerned, 1 *Cor.* 2. 14. Thou hast the Tender of that Marvellous Light, 1 *Pet.* 2. 9. the Sun of Righteousness doth shine upon thee, but yet thy Darkness cannot Comprehend it, *John* 1. 5. God is not far from every of you, *Acts* 17. 27. yet can you not see or know him, untill the Son Revealeth him, *Mat.* 11. 27. therefore such Groundedly cannot Joy, save in the Creature. Nor can you see the Creature Neither, so as to Rejoyce therein aright, save as this Sun doth make that Moon conspicuous, *Psal.* 16. 5, 6. or as God's Light doth shew the goodliness of that Inheritance.

4. You will not else be apt to Blush or be Ashamed, whatever cause there may be of it. It is a shame to speak of those things which are
done

The Parable of the Ten Virgins Opened.

done by some in secret, *Eph.* 5.12. because all Manifestation is by the Light, *v.* 13. How did Enlightned *Ezra* Blush, to mention the sins of others, *Ezra* 9. 6. much more to stain his own Profession with the least unseemly Motion, *Ezra.* 8. 22! Light is Subjected in the Eye, *Mat.* 6. 22. which Eye is therefore apt to water with every Mote, and will not suffer spots to rest upon the Garment: Thence is it, that Enlightned ones are alway Neat. But sinners are in Darkness, *Mat.* 4. 16. who therefore cannot be Ashamed, *Jer.* 6. 15. Sin being Virtually upon their Back, where vilest Spots may be (and be Continued) with utmost Confidence, till they shall be Ashamed and Confounded both together.

5. You will not else have any Spiritual Heat or Warmth; which alway is Accompanied with Spiritual Light. The Natural Sun may warm him who is Blind, as to his Bodily sight; but so doth not the Sun of Righteousness, save whom he also doth Enlighten. There may be true Spiritual Light or Grace without any Apprehended Warmth or Comfort, *Isa.* 50. 10. but there can be no Grounded Peace, where Grace is wholly wanting, *Isa.* 57. 21. This is that Oyl of Joy, *Isa.* 61.3. and without which there is no Laughter, save what is Mad, *Eccl.* 2. 2. Darkness and Sorrow are Co-incident, and both of them are Consistent with the Light of Earthly Sparks, *Isa.* 50. 11. All Wisdoms Paths are Paths of Peace, *Prov.* 3. 17. which is a way that others know not, because their Paths are crooked,*Isa.*59.8.and therefore their Case must needs be sad.

6. You will not else be Spiritually helpful unto others; at least,there is no Promise for it upon other Terms, *Jer.* 23. 22. Christ was Anointed first, and with this Special Oyl; and then his Preaching was Effectual, *Isa.* 61. 1. but, *What hast thou to do* (saith God unto the Wicked) *to Declare my Statutes,* Psal. 50. 16? whom others are bid to let alone, and with Respect unto their Blindness, *Mat.* 15. 14. Lips may Salute the Ear; whereas Heart Answereth unto Heart, *Prov.* 27. 19. nor can it be Expected (in an Ordinary way) that Nature should work Grace; or that a sinner should Beget, save in his own Likeness, as *Gen.* 5. 3. Christ's Image (in a true Believer's Conversation) is a Preaching Picture, 1 *Pet.* 3. 1. while Graceless Gifts are but a silent kind of Speaking, *John* 6.63. nor can the Flesh Reveal that which is Spiritual, *Mat.* 16. 17. no more than Nature can Receive it, 1 *Cor.* 2. 14. Since Darkness Comprehendeth not this Light, *John* 1. 5.

7. You will not else be able to prevent your doing Mischief unto others and your selves. *Paul* was Injurious, and yet Ignorant, 1 *Tim.* 1. 13. untill he was enlightned from Above, *Acts* 9. 3, 4, 5. Nor can

C c   Men

Men (in the Dark) Difcern, although the Prince of Life be Killed by them, *Acts* 3. 15. 17. How will Chrift's Piercers Mourn when they fhall fee him, *Zech.* 12. 10. perceiving how they have broken his Commands, by Rufhing on them; and how they have trod him under Foot? Yea, as to ones felf, Wife Men (or Virgins ftored with Oyl) fore-fee the Evil, and Hide themfelves,*Prov.* 22. 3. while others Pafs on, as *Balaam* did, upon the Swords point, untill his Eyes were Opened, *Numb.* 22. 31. Thence is it, that fuch are apt, either to be fnared, *Ifa.* 8. 15. or elfe to kick againft the Pricks, *Acts* 9. 5. and run upon the Boffes of God's Buckler, *Job* 15. 26. if not to ftumble and fall upon that Breaking Rock, *Ifa.* 8. 15. becaufe there is no Light in them, *v.* 20.

8. You will not elfe find the way, wherein you ought to Walk; and fo be fubject either to fit ftill for want of Light, or to go wrong, if not Turn back; or at the leaft, to walk uncomfortably, and unacceptably, though poffibly in a Right Path. Darknefs difpofeth more for fleep than any kind of Action, *Pfal.* 104. 23. which will be fad for him whofe Neceffary work requireth utmoft fpeed, *Heb.* 3. 7. And in the dark, Men (if they walk) are apt to Wander, *John* 12. 35. fave in a broad and Beaten Road, which Chrift's is not, *Mat.* 7. 14. Yea, fuch are prone to wheel about into their bad Old way again, and fo (being Giddy with frequent Turning) to Fall and Rife no more. Nay, though by chance fuch may hit Right, yet are they fubject to be drawn afide, *Prov.* 9 15. and though they fhould go on, yet as it is uncomfortable, fo they were Superftitious ftill, who Worfhipped the True, but unknown God, *Acts* 17. 22, 23.

9. You will not elfe Go forth to Meet the Bridegroom, no more than do thefe Foolifh Virgins for lack of Oyl or Light: and fo you will not enter with him to the Marriage. Chrift's Coming is unto *Sion*, *Ifa.* 59. 20. and *Sion*'s way is Narroweft at the laft: Therefore Men (in the Dark) will There be moft fubject to Miftake. This Going forth is a Time-Truth and Duty; and but Two Hundred (of *Ifrael*'s Thoufands) have Underftanding of the Times, 1 *Chron.* 12. 22. therefore without peculiar Light Men are not like to hit this way. The greateft Robberies (as in the Letter) are Near this City, efpecially when Travellers are Benighted: Therefore (in fuch a Cafe) none will ftir out. And if you Go not forth to Meet him, you will not come with him unto the Marriage, which will be very fad, as may be made out afterwards.

10. You will not elfe be fit to hold Communion with the Wife; as being Convicted to be Foolifh Virgins, by wanting Oyl or Light at

such a Time. I wonder how any can imagine that Light and Darkness should Agree, 2 *Cor.* 6. 14. or why they are Offended with Dividing upon that Account, which is as Old as since the first Creation, *Gen.* 1. 4. True *Israelites* have Light, and in their Dwellings, by which they are Distinguished from Dark *Egyptians*, *Exod.* 10. 23. and not to be enlightned is a sign of Death, *Job* 33. 30. Nor was the first Creation Perfected, (much less the Second) so long as Darkness was upon it, *Gen.* 1. 2. So that both State-Communion with the Wise, yea, and Communion with their State, depend upon your having of their Oyl or Light: Nor will you else Partake of their Inheritance in Light, *Col.* 1. 12. or Light of Life, *John* 8. 12.

MATTHEW XXV. 10.

And while they went to Buy, the Bridegroom came; and they that were Ready went in with him to the Marriage; and the Door was shut.

THis Verse referreth to the Time of Christ's own Coming as a Bridegroom, with reference unto the Perfecting of that Redemption, which Gentile Saints must first be Interested in, as hath been cleared up before. Whose Coming then, is Amplified here; 1. By the Nick of Time, or while the Foolish Virgins went to Buy. 2. By the Qualification of those who are Admitted to the Marriage, [*They that were Ready.* 3. By the Exclusion of all others, against whom *the Door was shut.*

The summe of all which may briefly be comprized in this General Observation following.

Observ. While Foolish Virgins Go to Buy their Oyl or Light, the Bridegroom Cometh; together with whom they who are Ready go in to the Marriage: and thereupon the Door is shut.

Quest. 1. How do these Foolish Virgins Go to Buy?

Answ. 1. Negatively; Not in a Right or Serious manner, which never is in vain, *Isa.* 45. 19. as is their seeming Labour here, because they were not Ready in due time. Those went to see *John Baptist*'s Light, *Mat.* 11. 9. with seeming Joy, *John* 5. 35. who had no mind to Buy it, (at least some of them, *Luke* 7. 30.) upon his Terms,

The Parable of the Ten Virgins Opened.

Mat. 3. 8. *Ezekiel's* Hearers came to Cheapen his Commodity, (and with a shew of Love,) but had more mind to Buy a Worldly Interest, *Ezek.* 33. 30, 31. which was enough to silence them, *v.*33. when their Desolation came upon them, *v.* 29. Poor *Zedekiah* was content to Hear what *Jeremiah* would say unto him, *Jer.* 38. 14. but was afraid of being seen (by others) in that Shop, *v.* 24. nor did he Buy. Thus might these Foolish Virgins Pray for Light, but with Dissimulation, as *Jer.* 42. 20. or stumbling-blocks set before their Faces, as *Ezek.* 14. 3.

2. Affirmatively: Their going to Buy doth rather seem to intimate their staying otherwhere, (under a false Disguise) till such a Time.

1. Till that Practice, of Going out (to Meet the Bridegroom) is grown more General among Professors. I am perswaded this is the Case of many, who have no mind to see the Light of a Command, till they shall have the Light of Company. When divers Torches are abroad, some Men Delight to walk at such a Time, and spare the Cost of Buying for themselves: But single Lights are not sufficient to guide Dim-sighted Hypocrites in Narrow ways. When Christ himself was left alone, then *Peter* did not seem to know him, *Mat.* 26. 74. untill the Mist before his Eyes was (by a Beaming Look from Christ) dissolved into a shower, *Luke* 22. 61, 62. but if Sobriety be the Fashion, a flanting Courtier will be Sober, (though meerly indeed for Fashions-sake;) and if Christ's Way be once a Common Road, then Foolish Virgins have Bought their Oyl, or want no Light.

2. Till it be safer walking in such a way. Darkness is sometimes put for outward Danger, and Light for Safety, *Job* 29. 3. Nor hath a Foolish Virgin Light in the way of Duty untill its Danger is Removed. A Godly Man is sometimes Tempted to sit still, at such a Time, *Psal.* 39. 1. but yet (Habitually) he is a God-like Man, to whom the Night shineth as the Day, *Psal.* 139. 12. nor doth he stumble in his way of Duty, although it may Expose him unto Danger, *John* 11. 8, 9. But Sufferings are the sinners Onely (Apprehended) Darkness; who therefore cannot see their way untill that Cloud be Taken up, which giveth Light to all True *Israelites*, *Exod.* 14. 20. So long as those were in a strait or Visible Danger, they Hid themselves in Caves and Thickets, 1 *Sam.* 13. 6. in Mount *Ephraim*, untill the Enemy began to Run, and then they also had Light enough to follow hard after, 1 *Sam.* 14. 21.

3. Till Goers out to Meet the Bridegroom are seen (by them) to be Rewarded; or to Go in with him unto the Marriage. Great is the Light of Earthly Recompences; the Expectation whereof made purblind

The Parable of the Ten Virgins Opened. 197

blind *Judas* hit the way to Chrift, untill he miffed of them, and then he Loft his way again, *John* 12. 6. *Mat.* 26. 14. How ftrongly did *Balaam*'s Wages make him fee that way, the Dangeroufnefs whereof was Obvious unto an Affe's Eye, *Numb.* 22. 23. and therefore a finners way feems Right unto himfelf, although its End is Death, *Prov.* 14.12. This Recompence of Reward enlightned *Mofes* into the way of Suffering Duty, *Heb.* 11. 25, 26. and when the Bridegroom's Favours are beftowed upon his Followers, *Mat.* 19. 28. that Glory will Difcover others having Gone afide; who will not then want Light, (had they but Leave and Time) for their Returning; till when, they do Complain of Darknefs.

4. Untill fome Greater (Apprehended) Danger doth Accompany their fitting ftill, than was in going forth to Meet the Bridegroom. The Old Heavens fhall pafs away with a great Noife, 2 *Pet.* 3. 10. which may Awaken thefe Foolifh Virgins out of their Loytering flumber, and fo may give them Light. The Clapping of Chrift's Door (when it is fhut by him in Anger) may ftartle all that are without, and make them Run, to be Admitted in, who formerly Pretended Ignorance, as to their Going out When Houfes are on Fire, then Blindeft Sluggards will have Light fufficient into that way, wherein a Lion (formerly) was faid to be, *Prov.* 22. 13. VVhen Life will be Endangered by finful feeking to Preferve it, *Mat.* 16. 25. while God will be a Sanctuary to his Faithful Non-compliers, *Ifa.* 8. 13, 14. then will the Foolifh Virgins feem to have got Oyl or Light.

Queft. 2. VVhy will Chrift Come at fuch a Time?

Anfw. 1. In Anfwer to his People's Prayer, *Luke* 18. 7. which is Effectual, *Jam.* 5. 16. fometimes to alter his feeming Purpofe, *Exod.* 32. 14. *Ifa.* 38. 1, 2. 5. and then much more to Haften his Promifed Coming, 2 *Pet.* 3. 12, 13. Prayer will not let him Reft, till he doth Come, *Ifa.* 62. 6, 7. and in that Cafe, it is Commiffionated to Command him, *Ifa.* 45. 11. Yea, fingle Importunity (diftinct from Friendfhip) is Reprefented by him, as moft Prevailing, *Luke* 11. 8. *Sion* may fay (at fuch a time) *God hath forgotten her,* I fa. 49.14. *But can a Woman forget her Sucking Child,* v. 15.? Can fhe endure long to Hear it Crying? Therefore he doth forbid his People's Praying when he is purpofed not to Hear, *Jer.* 7. 16. fince elfe he could not be in quiet. Now at this time a Spirit of Supplication will be poured out. *Zech.* 12. 10. which (like Reverfed Thunder) will fhake the Earth and Heavens; fo will Chrift Come, *Hag.* 2. 7.

2. To fatisfie the Expectation of his Poor; which fhall not Perifh for ever, or alway be forgotten, *Pfal.* 9. 18. Thefe Virgins had Expected
him

People's Hope, *Psal.* 147. 11. and Christ doth know what sore Temptations Disappointments are, *Mark* 11. 12, 13, 14. therefore if it were otherwise, he would have told them, *John* 14. 2. to Difference his People's Hope, *Rom.* 5. 5. from that of Hypocrites, *Job* 8. 13. else would the Saints Perswasion (in Matters of Duty also) be Despised by the World.

3. To make good his own Promise, signified by the Cry, as in Relation to his First Coming, *Luke* 1. 72. who therefore bad it to be Written, because these things are True and Faithful, *Rev.* 21. 5. yea, plainly written upon Tables, because the Vision will surely come, and will not Lye, *Hab.* 2. 2, 3. There is a Promise of his Personal Coming at last, *Acts* 1. 11. before which Time there is a Promise also of his Coming to the Gentile Saints, as hath been cleared up; and he is ever Mindful of his Covenant, *Psal.* 111. 5. He therefore brought his People out of *Egypt*, for he Remembred his Holy Promise, *Psal.* 105. 42, 43. he therefore laid aside the Jewish Covenant, that so his Promise might be sure, *Rom.* 4. 16. which also (therefore) is Confirmed with an Oath, *Heb.* 6. 17. nor will an *Abraham* therefore stagger at it, *Rom.* 4. 20. or *Sarah*, because he is adjudged Faithful, *Heb.* 11. 11.

4. To make the shadows flee away, as at his first Appearing, *Col.* 2. 17. which also will be Resembled by his After-Comings. Shadows of Old were of God's own Appointing, *Heb.* 8. 5. and were continued, untill they grew unreasonably long, compared with the Substance, and then Christ came to Take them quite away, *Heb.* 10. 9. So in these Gospel-times, some kind of Shadow (Form, or Type) is Now required, *Rom.* 6. 17. and suffered to continue (in such an Individual Appearance of it) till Power and Form are shamefully Disproportionable; then such Appearances are to be turned from, 2 *Tim.* 3. 5. Yea, Christ himself will Come, *Isa.* 25. 9. to swallow up such Covering Vails, *v.* 7. and once more will Discover the true Substantial Forms of Gospel-worship, *Ezek.* 43. 11. He therefore will Come at such a Time, that so the Ark of his Testimony may be seen within his Second Temple Opened, *Rev.* 15. 19.

5. To take unto Himself his own great Power, and Right of Reigning, *Rev.* 11. 17. Indeed his Throne was Stablished of Old, *Psal.*

The Parable of the Ten Virgins Opened. 199

93. 2. who was the King or Law-giver unto *Israel*, *Acts* 7. 38. and as his own (Spiritual) House was first Erected at his first Coming, *Heb.* 3. 6. so was his Temporal Kingdom also, in the Days of *Constantine*, *Rev.* 12. 5. both which (*viz.* the Temple and the City) will be Restored (as of Old) together with the Full Return of *Babylon*'s Captivity, *Zech.* 6. 13. Then she that Halted shall be made a Remnant, *Mic.* 4. 7. and *David*'s Tabernacle shall be Raised up, *Amos* 9. 11. and then it shall be said, *Thy God, O Sion. Reigneth,* Isa. 52. 7. He will be King, *Hos.* 13. 10. sought for by all True *Israelites*, *Hos.* 3. 5. it shall be Given him, whose Right it is, *Ezek.* 21. 27. And he will then Come to take possession of it, first in his Saints, the High ones, *Dan.* 7. 27. or such as *Joshua* was, *Zech.* 6. 11.

6. To Judge the Dead, *Rev.* 11. 18. which may be Construed divers ways. Possibly with reference unto All sorts of Persons; who will be then virtually Dead, and after that comes Judgment, *Heb.* 9. 27. Or thus; To Judge the Dead, that is, the Wicked; who will be then (Mystically) Awakened unto their Everlasting shame, *Dan.* 12. 2. Or rather thus; To Judge the Dead, that is, to Judge Things over again, which have been long since Dead and Buryed, in Order unto the passing of a Righteous Sentence thereupon. Then will some principles be Generally Embraced, which have been thought to be Seditious : Then will some Truths be fully Vindicated, which have been called Errours, if not Heresies : Then will some Practices Appear to be Traditional, which have been said to be Christ's own Apointments. Men's turning things up-side down, shall be esteemed as the Potters Clay, *Isa.* 29. 16. for God will then Alter them, *v.* 17.

7. To give Reward unto his Servants, both Great and Small; *viz.* his Prophets, Saints, and such as Fear his Name, *Rev.* 11. 18. or Fathers, Young Men, and Little Children, 1 *John* 2. 13. Typified by the Ancient High-Priests, and Priests and Levites. Then will be the Time of Paying off his Hired Labourers, *Mat.* 20. 8. of giving double unto Sufferers, for their shame, *Isa.* 61. 7. and of Convincing others (by this means) that verily there is a God, who Judgeth in the Earth, *Psal.* 58. 11: Then will the Pelican, *Psal.* 102. 6. be turned into a Flock of Doves, *Isa.* 60. 8. or Solitary ones be set in Families, *Psal.* 68. 6. Then will the Sons of *Zadock* have their Right of Priest-hood, *Ezek.* 44. 15. or Faithful ones, the Chiefest Name among Professors: Then will the Saints (the High ones) have the Kingdom, *Dan.* 7. 27. and the Chief Priest (or Eminent Saint among them) shall be their Prince, *Ezek.* 44. 3. Compared with *Lev.* 8. 31. *Rev.* 3. 11.

8. To Punish Transgressors, and to Destroy them that Destroy the Earth,

Earth, *Rev.* 11.18. Then Wife and Foolish Virgins will be fevered, in a Providential way, *Mat.* 25.12. Then will Back-fliding Priests (or Eminent Old Profeffors) be at leaft Degraded, *Ezek.* 44.10.13. and thofe will have the Loweft place of all, who have unfruitfully enjoyed Greateft Means of Light, as *Capernaum* (in Chrift's Day) is threatned, *Mat.* 11.23. which was the Metropolis of *Napthali*; and therefore *Napthali* his place is Laft (or Loweft) in *Ezekiel*'s City, *Ezek.* 48.34. which Anfwereth unto This Coming of the Bridegroom. But as to Perfons more Grofly Vicious, Chrift will then Come to Cut them off, for all their Cheating and Falfe Swearing, *Zech.* 5.3. for all their Revellings, *Amos* 6.7. Whoredoms and Oppreffions, *Mal.* 3.5. and more Efpecially for their Perfecutions, *Pfal.* 79.10. who then fhall be drunk with their own Blood, *Ifa.* 49.26.

9. To Ceafe Difquietments, and fettle Peace, with Truth and Righteoufnefs among the Profeffors upon Earth. Chrift will then Come as King of *Salem*, *Heb.* 7.1. and Prince of Peace, *Ifa.* 9.6. being his peoples Peace, when the *Affyrian* cometh, *Mich.* 5.5. and give them Peace in his Second Temple, *Hag.* 2.9. in way of Covenant, *Ezek.* 34.25. Yea, he will fpeak Peace to the Heathen alfo, *Zech.* 9.10. nor fhall they Learn War any more, *Mic.* 4.3. This King of *Salem* (alfo) is *Melchifedec*, *Heb.* 7.1. and he will Reign in Righteoufnefs, *Ifa.* 32.1. which fhall look down from Heaven, *Pfal.* 85.11. then will Oppreffors be confumed, *Ifa.* 16.4. and following Exactors will be Righteous, *Ifa.* 60.17. Yea, he will then Difplay the Banner, becaufe of Truth, *Pfal.* 60.4. Determining Matters Controverfal, in his Valley of Decifion, *Joel* 3.14. and turning a pure Language to the People, *Zeph.* 3.9. that he may be One Lord, and his Name One, *Zech.* 14.9.

10. To Eafe the Creature of its prefent Bondage, perfectly at his Laft Coming, *Rom.* 8.21. a Tafte whereof will Now be given. The Creature groaneth yet, becaufe of its unfruitfulnefs, and cruel Ufage, and finful Mis-improvement; all which fhall then be much Rebuked. The Rivers of *Judah* (then) will flow with Waters, and Hills with Milk, and Mountains with New Wine, *Joel* 3.18. God will Then hear the Heavens, and they the Earth, and it the Fruits thereof, for *Jezreel*'s fake, *Hof.* 2.21,22. The Righteous will (then) be Merciful to his Beaft: the Creatures may not Prey fo one upon another, *Ifa.* 10.6. nor will they be Deftroyed fuperfluoufly, as Now they are. Men fhall not Drink Wine with a Song, *Ifa.* 24.9. or finfully abufe the Creature; but fear the Lord and his Goodnefs, *Hof.* 3.5. therefore the Heavens,

The Parable of the Ten Virgins Opened.

Earth, and Sea, are bid then to Rejoyce, because of Christ's Coming to Judge the World, *Psal.* 96. 11, 12, 13.

Quest. 3. Why doth not Christ stay untill the Foolish Virgins do Return?

Answ. 1. Because his own set time was fully come, beyond which 'tis not fit that he should Tarry for any sort of Persons whatsoever. Himself is Ready, so is the Bride; yea, all the Wise Virgins also: And can it be Expected then, that he should Tarry for some few Foolish Loyterers? He lately had Engaged for his Speedy coming, *Mat.* 25. 6. and Mercy must give way to Truth; yea, All his Name (or Attributes) unto his Word, *Psal.* 138. 2. The five Wise Virgins are for his Present Coming; and though the other five would have him stay, yet shall not he Then have a Casting Voice, upon his own Account? If Time and Tide will stay for none; much less will their Creator: Especially since his Present Coming is with State; and Earthly Kings will scorn to Tarry till sluggish Servants get them ready.

2. Because he else might Tarry long enough, or rather, Not come at all, if not untill these Virgins have bought Oyl: Therefore that can be no Let unto him. As Oyl is put for Special Grace, so Foolish Virgins (in that Day) will never Buy it, (as their Exclusion Evidenceth;) nor as 'tis put for Spiritual Light into this Duty, of Going out to meet the Bridegroom. Nor will they have Light into the Matter of that work before his Coming; because their Light is wholly Borrowed from that which followeth upon his being Come. Now, if he must come before they will have Oyl, then if he means to come at all, he must not stay for them. They will have him come first, with reference to their Enlightning Motives; therefore he will not Tarry for them, although by that means they are shut out for ever.

3. Because the time of shewing Mercy (unto such, and in some sence) is Now Expired. The Attribute of Mercy is inseparable from God's Essence, *Exod.* 34. 6. yet is its Exercise Commanded by his Will, *Rom.* 9. 18. And though he Delighteth in that Exercise, *Jer.* 9. 24. yet hath he Bounded it by such a time, beyond which time he will no more have Mercy, *Hos.* 1. 6. Now, when the Seventh Trumpet begins to Sound, *Rev.* 10. 7. then Time shall be no longer, *v.* 6. and partly in this Respect, for that contemporizes with the shutting of this Door. These Virgins are Dead before that Time; and though Christ is so Civil, as to wait a while; yet when their being Dead is out of Doubt, (as now it is) he then will stay no longer. His Patient Spirit will not alway strive with sinful Man, *Gen.* 6. 3. but hath its Limits set by him, who can make way for Anger, *Psal.* 78. 50.

Dd   4. Because

The Parable of the Ten Virgins Opened.

4. Because they have had Warning, Means, and Time enough. What could they Reasonably desire more? They had the Scriptures from the first, which shew the worth and Need of Oyl: And 'tis but the Fansie of some in Hell, that other Applications would be more Effectual, *Luke* 16. 31. They had the Benefit of Conversing with the wise, by whom Christ worketh Now, as if Himself were present, *John* 14. 12. At their first Going forth they should have taken Oyl with them: And Errors in the first Concoction are not wont to be Corrected in the Second. They had been wakened by the Cry; and Repetitions seldom profit them who are not benefited by the Preacher's Voice, *John* 9. 27. They did confess their want of Oyl, and made a shew of going to procure it, but did not Act accordingly; and so had nothing to Object against the Justness of Christ's being wearied with such kind of Dallyers.

5. Because they are not worth the waiting for. They onely stood in need of beeing Buryed, for which Christ will not stay at all, since he would not have others do so, upon that Account, *Mat.* 8. 22. They seem to be Mad, or Fools in Grain; and if an *Achish* had no need of such, 1 *Sam.* 21. 15. much less hath Christ, so as to Tarry for them, they had sufficiently Despised him, by disregarding all his counsel, who therefore are not worthy to be so much Honoured by him, 1 *Sam.* 2. 30. They did but cheat the other Virgins all this while with flattering words; And therefore neither Christ nor They would be Abused by them any longer. Nor would they ever have been good for ought, in case they should have come by being tarried for; therefore Christ might design their being turned off by Coming, while they were Parted from the Wise.

6. Because he else would miss of his Main Purpose; which is, to Cast some out for ever, *Mat.* 8. 12. by coming on them unawares, *Luke* 21. 34, 35. An Absolute Decree of some Men's sad Exclusion, is easily consistent with a present (visible) Possibility of their Admission; both which are hinted in those words, *The Children of the Kingdom shall be cast out,* Mat. 8. 12. And though Christ hath enough for All, *Mat.* 22. 4. yet but a Remnant onely shall be saved, *Rom.* 9. 27. Since Tophet also is Ordained for some, *Isa.* 30. 33. and Everlasting fire, *Mat.* 25. 41. as is the Kingdom for some others, *v.* 34. And therefore (chiefly) Christ is Resolved thus to come, while such (who are Ordained to this Condemnation, *Jude* 4.) are either Revelling, *Mat.* 24. 49. or minding Earthly things, *v.* 37. or fast Asleep, *v.* 43. or (at the least) out of the way, as these poor Foolish Virgins will then be.

Quest. 4. VVhat

The Parable of the Ten Virgins Opened. 203

Quest. What is the Import of that word, *Ready?* They that were Ready.

Answ. 1. The same *Greek* word doth elsewhere signifie, Fore-Ordained; and is Translated (in that sence) Prepared, *Mat.* 25.34. 1 *Cor.* 2. 9. *Heb.* 11. 16. and thus it is here partly meant, with reference unto the Persons Interested in this Priviledge, of Going to the Marriage. Such as were Ordained to Eternal Life, ('tis said) Believed, *Acts* 13. 48. and none (hereafter) will be Glorified, save they who (through fore-knowledge) were of Old Predestinated, *Rom.* 8. 29. All are Invited, but none will come, save whom the Father draweth, *John* 6. 44. or who are Given by him to the Son, *John* 17. 2. Those must Expect to be put by, whose Names cannot be found upon Record, when Ancient Registers will be enquired into, *Ezra* 2. 62. Let us therefore make our Calling and Election sure; Election by our Calling, 2 *Pet.* 1. 10. and This, by adding unto Faith all other Vertues, *v.* 5. and in Abundance, *v.* 8.

2. The same word also else-where signifies a Thing, or Persons being Purely Ordered (or Prepared) by the Lord himself; and in a way of singular Discrimination. Thus sitting at Christ's Right Hand and his Left, is said to be Prepared (or made *Ready*) by the Father, for some Persons above others, though of the same kind with them, *Mat.* 20. 23. And thus [*They that were Ready*] may Import, those whom the Father hath peculiarly Designed hereunto, Above-their Fellows, who (in their Day) may possibly have drank as Deeply of Christ's Bitter Cup as these. This lays the Dust of self-conceit in any, who are Admitted to the Marriage; and will Occasion their Crying, Grace, Grace, at such a time, *Zech.* 4. 7. This is of Use to Moderate our over-earnest Expectations and Desires of sharing in that special Priviledge: And this doth Eminently Declare, that Foolish Virgins shall never Enter; since many Wise ones will not be suffered to see that day, as *Mat.* 13. 17.

3. The word (here used) doth most commonly Import One's being Prepared for such a work, 2 *Tim.* 2. 21. or in a present Readiness to set about it, 2 *Cor.* 10. 6. And in a Three-fold sence.

1. With Respect unto a Person's Will. Thus *Peter* was Ready to go with Christ to Prison, in point of present (Apprehended) Willingness, *Luke* 22. 23. And *Paul* was Ready, not onely to be Bound, but also to Die for the Name of Jesus, *Acts* 21. 13. And thus, None but the Wise Virgins were (at present) willing to go with Christ unto the Marriage; since whosoever will, may freely Drink those Living Waters, *Rev.* 22. 17. The Foolish Virgins were Habitually

D d 2   willing,

willing, as is evinced by their Coming afterwards: But yet not Actually; for then they would have made more Haste. They had a sluggish will, but not Industrious, *Prov.* 13. 4. untill the Summers Heat was over, which is the onely Time for Harvest-work. They had a will unto the Place, but not unto the way that led thereunto: And such are said to have no will for Life, *John* 5. 40. which yet All do Desire.

2. VVith reference unto a Person's Freedom otherways, or having Nothing else to Do. Thus were the Jews Ready to have killed *Paul*, and waited onely for an Opportunity, *Acts* 23. 21. Thus also are the wife Virgins Ready, at such a Time, as having laid aside all other busness, (or being at a Moments warning,) and onely waiting for their Lord's Appearing, *Luke* 12. 36. But Foolish Virgins are not yet at Leisure. How long will it be, before a Sluggard thinks it time to Rife, *Prov.* 6. 9, 10? And when the Drunkard doth Awake, he yet will at the same work again, *Prov.* 23. 35. *To Morrow shall be as this Day* (saith he) *and more Abundant*, Isa. 56. 1. Such think there's time enough; therefore they will take the other Cup, *Luke* 12. 45. and make part civilly with their Old Relations, *Luke* 9. 61. at leat-wife fetch their stuff out of an House on Fire, *Luke* 17. 31. and so are not yet Ready to follow Christ.

3. VVith reference unto a Persons Fitness (every way) for such an Undertaking. Thus Saints are bid to be alway Ready to give an Answer to every Man, 1 *Pet.* 3. 15. that is, to be Prepared for it. And in this sense it is here Chiefly meant.

VVhich kind of Readiness (for the Bridegroom's coming) consisteth (as the Scriptures signifie) in these Particulars.

1. Sobriety is Required, with reference unto the Near approaching End, 1 *Pet.* 4. 7. such as this Dispensation is. Thus are we to be Sober in our Speech, not being vain or over-talkative: In our Behaviour, not being Light or Indiscreet: In using the Creature, not Exceeding our Estate or Comeliness: In worldly Employments, not being Covetous or Carking: In Judging others in a Doubtful case: In minding others Judgments of us. since the great Judge is at the Door: In Relation to others Prosperity and our Affliction; not to Repine or Envy: In Matters of Revenge, not to prevent the speedy Recompenser: In Disputable self-justifyings, not to be Peremptory: And in Relation to the Bridegroom's Coming, not to be over-hasty in our Expectations or sad Conclusions. Thus are we to be very Sober, both as to our Inward Frame, and Outward shew.

2. Such must not have their Oyl to Buy; as Oyl importeth Special
Grace,

be the Portion of the *Gentiles*, *Mal.* 1. 11. or another sort of Persons. And Light into the Present work (of Going out to meet the Bridegroom) is here Particularly meant by Oyl; as that which is Expresly Requisite, and without which, the Having of Grace will hardly be made out. Were this Believed, how would it startle some, who make light of their being (yet) in the Dark.

3. Such must have gone forth a Second time to Meet him. Therefore the Bridegroom Tarried, because the Wise Virgins were not Ready (then) in that Respect. They had (indeed) Gone out Before; but Chri t Now comes in Kingly State: And King *Ahasuerus* had his Virgins Doubly Pur fied, six Moneths with Oyl of Myrrh, and other six Moneths with Odours, *Esth.* 2. 12. Those never will be Ready to go in with Chri t, who are contented with a Separation from more Gross Pollutions. Men use to pass through several Rooms before they come into the Presence Chamber: Nor can it be Expected, that a Child's First Coat should ever suit a Manly Growing Dispensation. If we believe that all these things shall be Dissolved, *What manner of Persons should we be*, 2 Pet. 3. 11? Or with what Face can we suppose, that Nothing more should be required Now, than what hath formerly been done by us?

4. Such must have Mourned over all their former failings; and not content themselves with bare Reforming. Christ cometh with the Clouds, *Rev.* 1. 7. and we must Go with Rain, or Weeping, *Jer.* 31. 9. as for an onely Son, *Zech.* 12. 10. Covering our selves with shame, for we have sinned, *Jer.* 3. 25. and sad Bemoaning for our Evil ways, *Jer.* 31. 18, 19. Yea, and this Mourning must be Apart, *Zech.* 12. 12, 13. with reference unto Secret faults, and Freedom for an Holy Roaring, and as an Evidence of our being upright. And as a Proof hereof, our former Idols must be cast away with Detestation, *Isa.* 30. 22. Yea, we must Bear God's Indignation, *Mic.* 7. 9. Acknowledging it as the Punishment of our Iniquity, *Lev.* 26. 40, 41. and not confess the sins of others onely. There are yet few Reformers, but fewer Mourners between the Porch and Altar, *Joel* 2. 17. and yet till then, we are not Ready for Christ's wiping at his Wedding, *Rev.* 21. 2. 4.

5. Such must be Holily Resolved (in the strength of God) to be
more

The Parable of the Ten Virgins Opened.

m..e Faithful to him for the time to come. Though other Lords may have been owned by us, *Isa.* 26. 13. though other ne'r have been confided in, *Jer.* 3. 23. yet shall it be so no more, *Hos.* 1... Some are more Open for Christ, than heretofore; who yet will promise nothing, if a fresh Temptation cometh: These are not Ready, they want the Girdle of an Holy Resolution; nor will they confess a former sin. But we must joyn our selves unto the Lord in a Perpetual Covenant, *Jer.* 50. 5. or be One Spirit with Christ, which joyning to him doth Import, 1 *Cor.* 6. 17. Bound in the Spirit, as *Paul* was, whatever might befall him, *Acts* 20. 22. Thus he that Loseth his Life, shall save it, *Mat.* 16. 25. and none will Reign with Christ on Earth, save they who are thus (virtually at least) beheaded for him, *Rev.* 20. 4. or are full Followers of him, *Numb.* 14. 24.

6. Such must be made up of Earnest Wrestling, and patient Waiting; which is a Rare Conjunction, at such a time. Some may be content to wait, but from the want of Holy Earnestness, or from a sinful Indifferency and slightness of Spirit, Relating unto such a Mercy; as is evinced by their Negligent Use of Sanctified Means. Others are Earnest enough, but yet unable to Wait, 2 *Kings* 6. 33. Ready to Give up all, if not Relieved by such a time, as 1 *Sam.* 11. 3. But where shall we find a silent Cryer, *Exod.* 14. 15? A Submissive pleader, *Jer.* 12. 1? Or Lawful Striver, 2 *Tim.* 2. 5? Yet are we not fit to Drink till very Thirsty, and yet duly Cool: till furnish'd with a Spirit of Supplication, *Zech.* 12. 10. and yet willing to wait, *Isa.* 8. 17. *Micah* 7. 7.

7. Such must be able to Bear the Manner of Christ's Appearing, which will be very strange; and therefore Blessed will they be, who are not then Offended in him, *Mat.* 11. 6. He will Come in the Night, *Rev.* 16. 15. and some will therefore think he means to Steal, or take by Violence; wherewith weak ones will be Offended: as in a Spiritual case, the suddenness of a Convincing word makes some poor Creatures the more Averse. His Coming will be Terrible; and therewith Children will be Offended; as some poor Childish Creatures are with Threatning Calls unto Repentance. His first Appearance will be small, and therewith some will be Offended, *Zech.* 4. 10. as *Judas* was, and others are, because Christ's Present Pay is mostly Spiritual. And therefore Blessed is the people who know his Joyful sound, *Psal.* 89. 15.

8. Such (now) must be upon their constant Watch; who formerly, perhaps, had been Asleep. Christ here concludeth with that Exhortation, *Mat.* 25. 13. to shew wherein this Readiness doth consist; and that the unready Virgins were now fallen into a Second slumber, under a

pretence

viledge, *Luke* 21. 28. Death's picture (as sleep is) must not then be upon a Living Man; but Gracious Habits must be Actuated: The Flowers must appear, *Cant.* 2..12. and Spiritual Beauty must want Nothing but that Light to make it Manifest.

9. Such must have on their VVedding Garment; else will they not continue there, however (possibly) they may come in, *Mat.* 22.12, 13. which VVedding Garment plainly hinteth some kind of Spiritual Bravery, in the General, (whatever its particular import may be;) or something of a more than Ordinary Nature. Then *Joshua* must be clad with Change of Raiment, as well as have his filthy Garments taken from him, *Zech.* 3. 4. Yea, a fair Mitre also must be set upon his Head, *v.* 5. which (in a croud) will evidence his being a High-Priest, or a Professor of the Highest Rank. Then will the Defence be upon all the Glory, *Isa.* 4. 5. or outward Priviledges and Eminent Graces will go together. Then will there be a Glympse of Heaven upon Earth, (that Dispensation being called the Kingdom of Heaven;) and therefore Flesh and Blood, (or what is short of being Spiritual) will not Inherit that Heavenly Kingdom, as at the last, 1 *Cor.* 15. 50.

10. Such also are bid to have their Lights (then) Burning, *Luke* 12. 35. or all their Graces in the Highest Exercise. Saints must not onely (then) be truly Spiritual, but Zealous also, *Rev.* 3. 19. or serving the Lord with spiritual Fervour, *Rom.* 12. 11. Flame is the Form of Fire, and therefore Flaming Lamps (or Burning Lights) doth Evidence, not onely the Having of Oyl (or Truth of Grace;) and Oyl both in the Lamp and Vessel; But Holy Judicious Affections (also) Exercised in their Height and Glory. Luke-warm Professors (then) will be cast out; and nothing but this Sacred Flame will then secure from being (in some Measure) Burned. Affections (then) must be called off from all combustible (or Lower) Objects; and (being Fired) must be fixed upon Christ; who will then come in Flaming Fire, (as at the last, 2 *Thes.* 1. 8.) and therefore will be met with burning Lights by all his Bride-Maids.

11. Such must be Doubly Cloathed then, with both an Under and an Upper Garment; or something on them (*viz.* Imputed Righteousness) as well as in them, *viz.* Inherent Grace, *Psal.* 45. 13. Christ Graces

[*In*]

The Parable of the Ten Virgins Opened.

[In] a Soul, are fine and white, or shining, but yet not Clean or Pure, *Isa.* 64. 6. *Prov.* 20. 9. and therefore Clean (or Pure) fine Linnen must needs import, what is Imputed through Believing: And both these sorts of Righteousnesses are required unto One's being Ready for the Marriage, *Rev.* 19. 7, 8. 'Tis true, these alway go together in Reality, 1 *Cor.* 6. 11. but yet they may be (and are) severed in Men's Fancies, though sinfully, since God hath joyned them, *Mat.* 19. 6. Absurdly, since Duty is the Fruit of Faith. And self undoingly, since none will be Admitted, with Christ's Approbation, *Rev.* 7. 15. save they whose Robes are washed in his Blood, *v.* 14. Woe then to them, who call Imputed Righteousness an Airy Notion,

12. Such also are then bid to let their Loins be Girt, *Luke* 12. 35. as being one undoubted Branch of Readiness for any Service, 2 *Kings* 4. 29. Which Girting (in a Spiritual sence) must be with Truth, or Uprightness, *Eph.* 6. 14. a very Rare Girdle at such a time, *Mic.* 7. 4, 5. Formality (then) will be Predominant, 2 *Tim.* 3. 5. but Christ will utterly abolish Idols (or Appearances) in that Day, *Isa.* 2. 18. Though *Jezebel's* Face was Painted, 2 *Kings* 9. 30. yet *Jehu* bad *Throw her down*, *v.* 33. much more will Jesus (at his Coming) cast such *Jezebels* into a Bed of Sickness, *Rev.* 2. 20. 22. Wood is Combustible, *1 Cor.* 3. 12, 13. though never so fairly Gilded: and therefore Hypocrites (then) will be surprised with Fear, because they cannot dwell (as can the Upright) with Everlasting Burnings, *Isa.* 33. 14, 15. Be therefore sincere, *Phil.* 1. 10. or such as will abide the Judgment of the Sun.

Quest. 5. What are we to Understand by this word, *Marriage*?

Answ. Thereby is planly meant Christ's Union with his Kingly Dispensation upon Earth; which will Resemble that of Marriage, in all these following Respects.

1. Marriage is not Convenient in a time of Persecution or Distress, 1 *Cor.* 7. 26. though it is Lawful then, *v.* 28. The Absolute prohibiting whereof is that first Act, by which the Man of sin is to be known, 1 *Tim.* 4 3. since it is Honourable in All, *Heb.* 13. 4. And thus, Christ alway had a Power of Marrying in this sence, (as *Paul* and *Barnabas* had in the Letter, 1 *Cor.* 9. 5.) although he Taketh not that Power to himself till such a Time, *Rev.* 11. 17. He had All Power given him, at his first Coming in the Flesh, *Mat.* 28. 18. the Absolute Denying whereof is therefore a Denial of his being Come, by which the Antichrist is to be known, 1. *John* 4. 3. Onely he would not then improve his Power in that Respect, lest he should give Offence at such a time, *Mat.* 17. 25, 26, 27. 2. The

2. The Ancient High-Prieſt might not Marry with an Harlot, or one Divorced, or Prophane, *Lev.* 21. 14. Nor might an *Iſraelite* Marry with an Heathen, *Deut.* 7. 3, 4. Nor may Saints Marry in Goſpel-times, ſave in the Lord, 1 *Cor.* 7. 39. or in an Holy, Meet, and Honourable way. And thus is Chriſt's Diſpenſation Ordered. He will not Marry with one Divorced, therefore the Jews Old Miniſtration will not be Reſtored for ever, *Ezek.* 16. 61. eſpecially, ſince he is (Now) Divorced from that Wife a Second time, which is the utmoſt of his Indulgence, and more than uſual, *Jer.* 3. 1. He will not Marry with an Harlot; and therefore Antichriſt's Diſpenſation is Blaſphemouſly called Chriſt's, *Rev.* 17. 3. 5. He will not Marry with one that is Prophane, or Heatheniſh; therefore his Kingdom is not of this wicked World, *John* 18. 36. The Kingdom of Heaven (ſtrictly taken) is Reſerved for his Father, 1 *Cor.* 15. 28. therefore Chriſt's Bride is upon Earth, *Rev.* 21. 2. when fit for Marriage.

3. Marriage conſiſteth in the Husbands Taking, *Deut.* 25. 5. and in the Womans being Given by her (Living Father) *Deut.* 22. 16. So is Chriſt Married to his Kingdom, which he Received of his Father, *Luke* 19. 12. and doth not Take it, *Rev.* 11. 17. till it is Given him, *Ezek.* 21. 27. As in Relation to Particular Souls, he Marrieth none, ſave whom the Father Giveth, *John* 17. 2. So it is with Reſpect unto his Kingly Power. He Cometh as a Thief, unto the World, *Rev.* 16. 15. but by the Door, as to his Father's Approbation, *John* 10. 1, 2. He will not Marry without his Father's Full Conſent, wherein he is a Pattern to his Children. Nor do the Saints (the High ones) Take the Kingdom, *Dan.* 7. 18. till it be given them, *v.* 27. though others may exalt themſelves, (pretending thereby) to Eſtabliſh the Viſion, but they ſhall Fall, as heretofore ſuch did, *Dan.* 11. 14.

4. Eſpouſals were wont to be before a Marriage, *Mat.* 1. 18. *Deut.* 20. 7. which is of great Uſe, if not a Duty ſtill. And thus, Chriſt was Contracted, or made ſure unto his Throne of Old, *Pſal.* 33. 2. in which regard, that Diſpenſation is his Wife in Law, *Deut.* 22. 24. and therefore woe be unto him that Forceth her, *v.* 25. as worldly Powers have done, (eſpecially ever ſince *John Baptiſt*'s Coming in the Myſtery,) whom therefore Chriſt will put to Death, though nothing ſhall be done unto the Humb'ed Crying (although Betrothed) Damſel, *v.* 26. *John Baptiſt*'s Coming was to Prepare the Bridegroom's way, *Mat.* 3. 3. and whoſe Eſpouſing Teſtimony therefore was of Uſe, *John* 5. 33. which Cuſtome alſo is Obſerved, in a particular Soul's Uniting unto Chriſt, *Hoſ.* 2. 19. onely there muſt be ſome further Progreſs made;

there-

The Parable of the Ten Virgins Opened.

therefore they hinder the Lamb's Marriage, who could be satisfied with *John Baptist*'s work.

5. Princes are wont to Marry (first) by Proxies; or by some other Persons Representing them, and so doth Christ. He was an Husband unto *Israel*, Jer. 31. 32. yet were they Married (first) to *Moses*, being Baptized into him, 1 Cor. 10. 2. Thus are Saints Married (or Espoused) Now by others unto Christ, 2 Cor. 11. 2. Thus also *Sion* is (first) Married by her Sons; although Christ is the Bridegroom, with Respect unto that Dispensation, *Isa.* 62. 5. Christ hath a Throne (or Kingdom) of his own, *Rev.* 3. 21. which Dispensation (at the last) is called his Bride, *Rev.* 21. 2. with reference unto his Personal Marrying of it: But yet this King will Honour some of his Saints, by letting Them Marry that Ministration first, *Psal.* 149. 9. that he might first Sup with Them, *Rev.* 3. 20. thence all Dominions ('tis said) shall Serve and Obey Him, when yet his People (chiefly) do Possess the Kingdom, *Dan.* 7. 27.

6. Marriage Creates the Nearest Union, and fullest Communication, or most sweet Communion. So is it here, since Christ will then Rest in his Love, *Zeph.* 3. 17. or Center in a sweet Deportment towards All, but more especially his Chosen ones, whom he will then Evidence his Conjugal Affection unto, his Everlasting kindness, *Isa.* 54. 8. Affected with their former Sufferings from others, *Zech.* 1. 15. and from Himself, *Isa.* 40. 2. Jer. 31. 20. Accepting what they Offer, *Mal.* 3. 4. and satisfying their Desires, *Zech.* 13. 9. as *Esth.* 5. 6. Paying their Debts, *Mat.* 25. 34, 35. 40. and deeply Revenging all their Injuries, *Zech.* 2. 8.

7. A Marriage cannot be, unless the Bride and Bridegroom be there Present, at least-wise in their Representatives. Thus Christ was Present when he first Married *Israel*, *Acts* 7. 38. thus it is also from the Presence of his Spirit (in an Instrument) if any Soul be Married to him, or Discipled, *Mat.* 28. 20. and when his Kingly state shall be set up, its Name will be, *The Lord is there*, Ezek. 48. 35. His Personal presence is reserved till the Last; but yet the Bridegroom will Now come, else could there not be a Marriage. Prepare for his Appearing then, so as that Saints shall say, *Loe, This is He*, Isa. 25. 9. Yea, others then will Look upon him, either with weeping Eyes, *Zech.* 12. 10. or with self-hiding from his Face, as *Rev.* 6. 16. His spiritual Presence hath been suspended; but he will come again, in that Respect, to fill the second Temple with his Glory, and Constitute a proper Marriage.

8. Increase is wont to follow upon Marriage, in way of Blessing from

from the Lord, *Gen.* 1.28. fo doth it upon Chrift's. Thus *Ifrael* Multiplyed more than others after her being Married unto Chrift, *Ezek.* 5.7. unto the Aggravating of her Adultery. Thus alfo, Gofpel-Saints are therefore Married unto Chrift, that fo they might be Fruitful unto God, *Rom.* 7.4. and it was fore-told, that Gentile-Saints fhould Multiply more (in point of Number) than did the Ancient Jewifh Wife, *Ifa.* 54.1. And when Chrift fhall be further Married to his Kingly Difpenfation, *Ifrael* and *Judah* will be fown with the Seed of Man, *Jer.* 31.27. they fhall be Increafed like a Flock, *Ezek.* 36. 37. unto their own Admiration *Ifa.*49.21. and Place fhall not be found for them, *Zech.* 10.10. The Children that *Sion* will then have, fhall call for Place wherein to Dwell, *Ifa.* 49.20.

9. Marriage is during Life, fince God hates Putting away, *Mal.* 2.16. fave in the cafe of Adultery, *Mat.* 5.32. therefore to have been the Wife or Husband of more than one, (by Reafon of unmeet Divorce) is fuch a fcandal, as incapacitateth for a Gofpel Church-Office, 1 *Tim.* 3.2.12. and for the Place of a Widow, 1 *Tim.* 5.9. Thus Chrift's Betrothing is for ever, *Hof.* 2.19. whofe Marriage-Covenant with Particular Souls doth undertake for their being Loyal to him, who therefore Never will be Divorced, *Jer.* 32.40. And though Chrift Now Difowns the Jews (his Ancient Wife) *Hof.* 2.2. yet did fhe firft play the Harlot, *Jer.* 31.32. as the Bill of her Divorce will Evidence, *Ifa.* 50.1. Nor will he put away his Wife, as to the Gentile-ftate, till they prove Falfe to him, *Rom.* 11.22. nor ever alter his Married Difpenfation (with them, or with the Converted Jews) but upon their Departing from him firft.

10. Marriage doth not Neceffitate the Husband's Conftant Prefence though; but is confiftent with his (fometime) Difcontinuance, unto the Bride-Chamber-Children's Mourning, *Mat.* 9.15. though Harlots are Glad thereof, *Prov.* 7.18,19. Particular Souls Experience this, unto their forrow; though as the Fruit of their Apoftacy, as in Relation to the prefent Jews, *Cant.* 8.1. or Senfuality, as in the days of *Conftantine*, *Cant.* 5.2. or fad Formality, as after the Return of *Babylon's* Old Captivity, *Cant.* 3.1. according unto *Brightman's* Cafting of thofe feveral Times. And with Refpect unto Chrift's Marrying with his Difpenfation; fome think his Second Perfonal Coming will be Difcontinued: Though I am not of that Opinion, fince Saints will then be ever with the Lord, 1 *Thef.* 4.17. But yet, his Glorious prefence, with Reftored Gentile-Saints (if not the Jews) will be (I think) but for a Time; to make Room for his After-coming, to wit, in Perfon.

11. Mar-

The Parable of the Ten Virgins Opened.

11. Marriages of Old were Solemnized in such a way; wherein Christ's Union with his Dispensation doth Resemble Marriage. As thus,

1. It was most Honourable, that a Marriage should be known; and so is Christ's Coming (as a Bridegroom) Notified here before hand, for all the World to speak, if they have ought against it. He never used to steal a Marriage, by Creeping into Houses, as Suspitious Person, do, 2 *Tim.* 3. 6. but published his Purpose unto *Pharaoh*, *Exod.* 5. 1. and the King of *Babylon*, *Jer.* 51.61. Thus was his Personal Coming Published, *Mat.* 2. 2. and 3. 3. thus is his Spiritual Kingdom to be managed, *Mat.* 10. 27. thus was his Temporal Kingdom first set up, *Rev.* 12. 4, 5. and thus (I am perswaded) it will be Restored, as in the Type, 2 *Sam.* 2. 7.

2. Marriage is a time of more than Ordinary Joy to all there present, as well as to the Bride and Bridegroom; which is of Use still among the Jews, as saith *Buxtorfius*, *Synag. Juda.* Therefore the Rising Sun is Represented by a Bridegroom's Coming out of his Tent or Chamber, with others Joyful Acclamations, *Psal.* 19. 5. And thus *John Baptist* (who was the Bridegroom's Friend) Rejoyced greatly, because of the Bridegroom's Voice, *John* 3. 29. And as there is Joy in Heaven, upon a Souls Marrying unto Christ, *Luke* 15. 10. so doth it make those Glad on Earth who are that Bridegroom's Friends, *Acts* 11. 23. And thus Christ's Coming here, will be Received with many shoutings, *Zech.* 4. 7. and all kind of Musick, *Rev.* 15.2,3. and holy Dancing, *Jer.* 31. 13. And as the Bride hath cause to Joy (especially considering what a Match this is) so Christ will then Rejoyce as doth a Bridegroom, *Isa.* 62. 5, whose Heart is then most Glad, *Cant.* 3. 11.

3. Marriage also is a Time of Feasting; especially when Kings are Married, as when *Ahasuerus* Married *Esther*, *Esth.* 2. :8. for which some Poor (no doubt) might fare the better. Thus *Israel's* first Marriage was called a Feast, *Exod.* 5. 1. in which regard, their Flocks and Herds must all go with them, *Exod.* 10. 9. And therefore God's making a Feast for Christ (in Gospel-times) is called a Marriage, *Mat.* 22. 2. And as that Publican made a Feast, upon his being Married un-

The Parable of the Ten Virgins Opened. 213

4. Much Company is wont to be at all Marriages; so will there be at such a time. When Souls are Married unto Christ, the Angels flock to see Repenting Sinners, *Luke* 15. 10: So when the Church in *Corinth* was Espoused, 2 *Cor.* 11. 2, the Angels came to their Solemnities, 1 *Cor.* 11. 10. How great a mixed Multitude there was, *Exod.* 12. 38, when *Israel* was Espoused in the Wilderness, *Jer.* 2. 2: and when Christ wedded his Dispensation in Gospel-times, his Chariots were twenty thousand, even Thousands of Angels, *Psal.* 68. 17. Thus in the days of *Constantine*, we read of an innumerable Multitude, *Rev.* 7. 9; and a great Voice of *much* People afterwards, *Rev.* 19. 1, together with the Fall of *Babylon*, *vers.* 2. Then All will gather themselves to *Sion*, *Isa.* 60. 4; as all the City did to *Naomi*, at her Return, *Ruth* 1. 19: and whose Thundering Voices will evince the Second Temple's being opened, *Rev.* 11. 19.

5. All sorts of persons *(Then)* are in their greatest Bravery; so is it at Christ's Marriage. Then *Solomon* is crowned with a stately Crown, *Cant.* 3. 11. The Bride is brought, in Cloathing of wrought Gold and Needle-work, *Psal.* 45. 13, 14. yea God will Then appear in Glorious Greatness, *Tit.* 2. 13. as Earthly Parents are most fine upon their Childrens Wedding-day. Bridegrooms are wont to Deck themselves with Ornaments, and Brides with Jewels, *Isa.* 61. 10. so will Christ come with Power and great Glory, *Mat.* 24. 30; and part of that Bride's Ornament will be, her Numerous Train, *Isa.* 49. 18; but chiefly, the Garment of Salvation and Robe of Righteousness, *Isa.* 61. 10. Then also will the House be Garnished, *Isa.* 4. 2; and Meanest Servants will be finified with Outward Blessings and Moral Vertues, as *Rev.* 22. 2; but more especially, the Brides Companions (or all wise Virgins) will then be Honourable, *Psal.* 45. 9, 14.

6. Marriage-Solemnities (of Old) were in the Night; which Christ doth here allude unto; And so are all his Marriages. He married *Israel* (at least-wise call'd them to be married) in the Night, *Exod.* 12. 42: and Married (or Betrothed) Souls are called out of Darkness, 1 *Pet.* 2. 9. and in the Night he will come as a Bridegroom, in this Parable. He was Betrayed in the Night, 1 *Cor.* 11. 23; and in the Night will he Return. The Natural Day began at Evening, *Gen.* 1. 5; so will this Day of the Son of Man, *Zech.* 14. 7. as ancient Visions were wont to be in the Night, *Job* 4. 13. Christs Kingdom cometh not with Observation; therefore Not in the Day; but as the Lightning, which shineth out of Darkness, *Luke* 17. 20. 24. This sheweth His Affection to that Dispensation; and will trie who love sleep above it. It will be a Night of Rioting unto the Wicked, 1 *Thess.* 5. 7. and Sorrow to the Saints,

Psal.

Pfal 30. 5. and Drowzinefs unto all, save them who fet themfelves to watch.

7. Bridegrooms are wont to be Met (of Old) and fo to be conducted to the Marriage; which alfo Chrift requireth here. Thus *Ifrael* Met him in the Wildernefs, *Jer.* 2. 2. for There he found her, *Hof.* 9. 10. Thus a Betrothed (or Believing) Soul, muft Come unto him, *John* 6. 35. and thus his People muft prepare to *meet* him in the latter days, *Am.* 4. 12. When *Abraham* had overcome thofe four great Kings, then did the King of *Sodom* goe out to Meet him, *Gen.* 14. 17: and when Chrift fully hath fubdued the four Monarchs, then *Abraham*'s Seed muft goe and *meet* with him. Thus when he cometh to his People (in the latter dayes) he will be found of them without, who mu't then Lead him into their Mothers Houfe, *Cant.* 8. 1, 2. Who muft be then Ready alfo with Oyl prepared, and Strength to bear his terrible Appearing, 1 *Joh.* 2. 28. fo as to *meet* him with Thankfgivings, *Revel.* 11. 16, 17.

Queft. 6. *How can Chrifts Union with his Difpenfation (in thefe Latter Dayes) be called a Marriage, fince it is granted, to have been Once fet up Before?*

Anf. 1. Becaufe this Reftauration followeth a former Juft Divorce. Chrift married the *Gentiles* (at his firft Coming) as he had done the *Jews* before, *Rom.* 11. 22. Now as Gods Ancient *Ifrael* comm'tted Whoredom before their going into *Babylon*, fo did the Gentile-Churches before the Man of Sin arofe, 2 *Theff.* 2. 3. And as thofe *Ifraelites* were put away for their Adultery, when they were firft carried Captive, *Jer.* 3.-8. fo muft the Gentile-Churches (and Profeffors generally) be Divorced (by a parity of Reafon) at their firft going into *Babylon.* Thence is it, that as the Temple was then fhut up, fo was the City (or Temporal Dominion) alfo, Trodden under foot, *Rev.* 11. 1, 2; as in the Letter, of Old. And therefore the Return of that Captivity (with reference unto them both) may well be called a Marriage, (as it is, *Hof.* 2. 19, 20. *Jer.* 3. 14. *Ifa.* 62. 4, 5.) becaufe it followeth a Divorce, with reference to that [Numerical] Difpenfation, although Once more Reftored in Kind. And this Return is not compleat (with reference unto us Gentiles) untill the Bridegrooms coming, in this Parable, whatever fhew thereof (like that of Betrothing or Efpoufals) may go Before. Now if Chrifts Union with his Kingly Difpenfation in thefe Latter dayes, doth follow a Juft Divorce from what had been Before; fuch doe but then plead an Harlots Caufe, who Argue for his Ecclefiaftical or Temporal Kingdom, from what hath been Before (or fince) the Rifing of the Man of Sin; fave onely in a late Preparatory way to this

enfuing

The Parable of the Ten Virgins Opened. 215

enfuing Marriage, from what of Later years hath come to pass, in order thereunto.

2. Becaufe the Glory of this Latter Houfe (or Difpenfation) will be Greater than of the Former, *Hag.* 2. 9. Now when the New Heavens and Earth shall be created, the former shall not be remembred, *Ifa.* 65. 17. Chrift Married (at the firft) when He was Young, (as fome Great Perfons ufe to doe.) Who, (in relation to his Spiritual Kingdom, when it was firft fet up,) was Therefore call'd a Child, *Act.* 4. 27. and a Man-child, with reference unto the firft Erecting of his Temporal Kingdom, *Rev.* 12. 5. both which muft needs be Myftically underftood. Now Infant-Marriage is not taken notice of, when one is married Afterwards at his full Age, as Chrift is at this time; from whence the Name of Marriage therefore (ever after) doth Commence. This fecond (alfo) will Eclipfe the former, becaufe the Glory of Chrifts Spiritual and Temporal Kingdom (Now) will be united, which Heretofore were fevered. Now as Chrifts ancient Marriage with the *Jews*, was to be quite forgot in Gofpel-times, *Jer.* 3. 16; fo will his Second Marriage with the Gentiles, quite Deftroy the former, by reafon of that Glory which Excelleth, as 2 *Cor.* 3. 10: therefore this Latter onely hath that Name.

Queft. 7. How may we Reconcile Chrift's coming (here) To the *Marriage*, with that Returning [*From*] the *Marriage*, *Luke* 12. 36 ?

Anf. 1. By varying the Circumftances of Time and Place, with reference unto the fame Wedding in point of Subftance. Chrift went to Receive his Kingdom, when he Afcended, and after the Receiving of it to Return, *Luke* 19. 12 : and yet, at his Return (together with the feventh Trumpet's founding,) he is then faid to Take it, as if he had not Taken it before, *Rev.* 11. 17. which plainly fheweth, a Double Taking of His Temporal Kingdom; the one, in Heaven; and the other upon Earth; yet doth he not Take it, in the fecond fence, till his Returning from having taken it in the former. And in like manner, he may be faid to have been *Married* [*Firft*,] in Heaven, when he Afcended, (fince *Marrying* and Receiving are the fame;) and yet he doth not Take (or *Marry* that Difpenfation upon Earth, till his Returning from that former Wedding. And fo, his Knocking (*Luke* 12. 36.) muft onely intimate his fudden Coming, confiftent with a going out to meet him.

2. By altering the Tranflation of that *Greek* word ['Ἐκ] which is there rendred *From, Lu.* 12.36; but yet it may be read [*by reafon of*] and fo that Place and this will nothing differ, although fore-named Circum-

ftances

stances be not varied. And thus, the same *Greek* word is rendred [*of*] *Rom.* 9. 11. 30 ; with reference unto Works and Faith and Him that Calleth ; that is, [*because*] or [*by reason of*] as easily may be collected. And in that sence Christs coming [*To*] the *Marriage* here, and his Returning (in *Luke*) by reason of the Wedding, may well agree ; since his Return, (*viz.* from Heaven,) will be [*because of*] his Wedding upon Earth. Nor need we stick at the word *Return*, if we referre it unto Heaven, which He is now Gone into, who sometime was on Earth ; especially since his *Marrying* is so Desireable, as that Earth therefore may be call'd his Home ; and so his Coming (for such a purpose) may well be call'd *Returning*, in the strictest sence ; yet doth the *Greek* word onely note *Removing*.

3. By varying the Case, in *Luke* and *Matthew*. The Latter of which (or this in my Text) doth plainly relate unto Christs *Marrying* with his Dispensation. But that in *Luke* may possibly referre unto another Parable, by which the Virgins are exhorted to be Watchfull, as Servants are, for their Lord's Coming, when he shall Return from Feasting at some Persons Wedding. In which last sence, Christ doth compare himself (in *Luke*) unto an Housholder, who taketh liberty (Himself) to Feast abroad, or to be at another's Wedding in the Night ; yet doth he expect, his Servants should be well employ'd at home, and ready to Open at his first Knock. Christ is Now Feasting upon his Fathers Throne, *Rev.* 3. 21 ; yet will he have his Servants (upon Earth,) to *watch*, that when he shall Return from thence, (which in regard of Feasting is call'd a Wedding,) unto his proper Marriage here, they might immediately receive him. Thus *Luke* and *Matthew* are Reconciled.

Quest. 8. Wherein consists the Priviledge (hinted here) of Going with Christ unto the *Marriage*, at such a Time ?

Ans. 1. Such will enjoy more Intimate and Near Communion with the Bridegroom; which is a precious Priviledge. Christ then will onely have the Bride, as *Joh.* 3. 29 ; but all his Friends will have his Presence: So as to see his Face, *Rev.* 22. 4 ; and hear his Voice, *Joh.* 3. 29 ; and have their fill of his Embraces, *Cant.* 8. 3. Their Eyes shall then behold him in his Beauty, *Isa.* 33. 17. and if the Bride be worth one's Coming to have seen, *Rev.* 21. 9 ; much more the Crowned Bridegroom, in that Day of his Espousals, *Cant.* 3. 11. The Saints future Happiness consisteth in their being with him, 1 *Thess.* 4. 17 ; which therefore *Paul* so much Desired, *Phil.* 1. 23. the Fulness of Joy being in his Presence, *Psal.* 16. 11. which therefore doth forbid his Peoples Mourning, *Mat.* 9. 5. How did good *Davids* Soul and Flesh *thirst* to behold his Glory

in

in the Sanctuary, *Pſal.* 63. 1, 2; which will be then so fully Opened, as that his Hidden Ark will then be seen, *Rev.* 11. 19.

2. Such will then Clearly see the Bride in all her Glory; which is a great Priviledge, *Rev.* 21. 9, 10. She will be then Visible unto All, as was Christ's spiritual Glory at his first Appearing; which yet was Actually seen but by a Few, *Joh.* 1. 14. Others may see her at a Distance; as will the saved Nations, the New *Jeruſalem*, *Rev.* 21. 24. but these shall see Eye to Eye, when the Lord shall bring again *Sion*, *Iſa.* 52. 8. And if the Promiſes were Embraced (or Joyfully beheld) when they were yet far off, *Heb.* 11. 13; much more when *Sion* shall be Reared up, will it be worthy to be Looked on, *Iſa.* 33. 20. Much less will such Mistake the Bride, as others will, who therefore will Despise that Dispenſation, as some men do those Books whose Authour is not known. Nor can the Saints know what they Ought to do, save as they have knowledge of the Times, 1 *Chron.* 12. 32. or of their proper Diſpenſation; which therefore is a Priviledge.

3. Such will be Witneſſes of that Solemnity; or of the mutual Taking and Giving, that will then be between the Bride and Bridegroom; which will be both their Honour and Advantage. What running is there, to see Two (Earthly) Princes meet? much more, when both the Bridegroom and the Bride come down from Heaven, *Rev.* 21. 2, 3; or when this Moon and Sun shall meet, without Eclipsing each others Light: then will the Morning Stars sing, and all the Sons of God will shout for Joy, as at the first Creation, *Job* 38. 4. 6, 7, and they Alone. Much of Gods Majesty will appear, *Iſa.* 24. 14. which yet will not occasion Singing, (or comfortable Satisfaction) save to this little Remnant, *v.* 13. Strange things will then be done, the Righteousneſs whereof will onely be resolved into Sovereignty, *Pſal.* 75. 7. or into Chriſt's Taking, by vertue of the Father's Giving, and Bleſſed is the Non-offended Person in Christ's Day, *Mat.* 11. 6. or such as know the Joyfull Sound, *Pſal.* 89. 15.

4. Such then will be the Brides Companions, or Maids of Honour, *Pſal* 45. 14. and which Kings Daughters will then be Ambitious of; *v* 9. That Bride will deal well with all her Servants; but these will be her Fellowes, rejoycing with her, *Iſa.* 66. 10. and being Dandled upon her Knees, *v.* 12. and Eminently Delighted with the Brightneſs of her Glory, *v.* 11. These will have liberty of coming with the Bride unto the King, *Pſal.* 45. 14. these Friends shall Eat and Drink together with them both, *Cant.* 5. 1. and it will be their Joy, that Chriſt himſelf ſhall have the Bride, *Joh.* 3. 29. whileſt others are unsatisfied with their Portion, *v.* 26. Theſe will be the greateſt Favourites, as *Joſeph* was

next to *Pharaoh*, *Gen.* 41. 40. yea, These will be both *Sion*'s Children and her Husband, in Christ's stead, *Isa.* 62. 5. and thus *Eliakim* (having the Key of *David*'s House) shall be a Father to the Inhabitants of *Jerusalem*, *Isa.* 22. 21, 22. and be the Ruler of Christ's Houshold, *Lu.* 12. 42.

5. Such then will have the Comfort of their Garments of Salvation, *Isa.* 61. 10. or of those Ornaments, which Maids cannot forget, *Jer.* 2. 32. It is their present Duty to be getting Ready, in that regard; but yet their Change will not be till that very Moment of the Bridegroom's Coming, as 1 *Cor.* 15. 51, 52. Then will God sprinkle clean water on them, and cleanse them from all their filthiness, and put a New Spirit in them, *Ezek.* 36. 25, 26. which will Refresh, as well as Beautifie, *Isa.* 61. 10. when *Israel* shall be brought again from *Egypt*, *Psal.* 68. 22. where they have lien among the Pots, then will they be as Doves with silver wings, and Feathers of Yellow Gold, *v.* 13. The Remnant of *Israel* shall not do Iniquity, *Zeph.* 3. 13. no other Lord (but Christ) will then be mentioned, *Isa.* 26. 13. nor will their Garments then be stained with Reproaches, as hitherto they have been; but Others (or they with whom they do converse) shall call them in a serious way, the Holy People, *Isa.* 62. 12.

6. Such then will be uncloathed of their filthy Garments, *Zech.* 3. 4. Corruption must not Inherit Incorruption, 1 *Cor.* 15. 50. Their stony Heart will then be Taken away, *Ezek.* 11. 19. and wickedness will be carried (in a covered Ephah) to be Established in the Land of *Shinar*, upon her own Proper Base, *Zech.* 5. 8. 11. Nor will they onely have got Victory over the Beast, but over the very Number of his Name at such a Time, *Rev.* 15. 2. viz. Compliances of the most Refined Nature. This will Occasion them to sing the Song of *Moses* and the Lamb, *Rev.* 15. 3. viz. more fully and Distinctly (as this Particularized Duplicate importeth) than when the Virgins first went out, *Rev.* 14. 3. The Best (till Then) will have Iniquity (in Principles or Practices) Reproachfully abiding in them; which Eminently (then) will Pass away, *Zech.* 3. 4. unto their Honour and Refreshing. Such then will be Enlightned (as the Margin hath it) when their Light is come, *Isa.* 60. 1. Abandoning what formerly they did Esteem, *Isa.* 30. 22. Yea, shaking off their Dust, and Loosing themselves from all the Binds of their Captivity, *Isa.* 52. 2.

7. Such then will Eat and Drink, *Isa.* 65. 13. or Feast it with the Bride and Bridegroom, at Wines and Fat things full of Marrow, *Isa.* 25. 6. yea, he will then come forth and Serve them, *Luke* 12. 37. who therefore cannot Fast or Mourn, *Mal.* 9. 15. That Chamber (or Accommodation) whose Prospect is toward the North (which was the

most

The Parable of the Ten Virgins Opened. 219

most Honourable side of Old, 1 *Kings* 7. 39.) will be for the Sons of Faithful *Zadok*, *Ezek.* 40. 46. God will then make it known, the Silver and Gold are His, *Hag.* 2. 8, 9. when they from *Sheba* shall bring Gold, *Isa.* 60. 6. and Iron shall be turned into Silver, *v.* 17. for in the Gentiles Glory will the Saints then boast themselves, *Isa.* 61. 6. But yet the Prime Dishes (at this Feast) will be the Full Discovery of their Duty, *Ezek.* 43. 11. and Grace to Practise what formerly hath been Neglected, as in the Type, *Nehem.* 8. 17. together with their Hearty Welcome to that whole Provision, *Jer.* 32. 41. and their Being satisfied with the Consolations of that Bride, *Isa.* 66. 11. yea, Flourishing like an Herb, *v.* 14. or Thriving by them, increasing Holy fear together with Enlargement, *Isa.* 60. 5.

8. Such will (thence-forward) be secure from Grosser Persecutions or Oppressions. Destructions (then) will come to a Perpetual End, *Psal.* 9. 6. when Christ shall have prepared his Throne for Judgment, *v.* 7. which at this time will be, *Rev.* 11. 18. As such shall walk with Christ in white, *Rev.* 3. 5. and eat of the Hidden Manna, *Rev.* 2. 17. so will they not be hurt by any such kind of Second Death, *Rev.* 2. 11. for they shall eat of the Tree of Life, *v.* 7. Then will the four Horns be frayed away, *Zech.* 1. 21. and the *Assyrian* also smitten with a Rod, *Isa.* 30. 31. there shall be no more a pricking Bryar to the House of *Israel*, *Ezek.* 28. 24. such Enemies being either wasted, *Isa.* 60. 12. or brought (at least) into a Full subjection, *v.* 14. The Saints Heart (then) shall Meditate Terror, with reference unto their Old Oppressing Officers at Home, and Forreign Adversaries, *Isa.* 33. 18. but Violence shall not be heard, for all such Officers, will be made Peace, *Isa.* 60. 18 nor shall they see a fierce (Besieging people any more, *Isa.* 33. 19. but will (in that regard) have Liberty to walk Abroad (which formerly they could not do, *v.* 8.) or to behold the Land that is afar off, *v.* 17. *viz.* the uttermost of their Borders, in peace and safety, *v.* 20.

9. Such then will be Discharged from any kind of Future Toyling whatever. Their Oyl, or their Anointing (then) will have Destroyed the *Assyrian* Yoke, *Isa.* 10. 27. and then Christ's Yoke (when severed from the other) will be easie. Their Garment of praise, *Isa.* 61. 3. will then Excuse them from servile work, *v.* 5. save what is suitable unto their Royal Priest-hood, *v.* 6. the meaner part of which Employment (also) will then be put upon the Better sort of Late Back-sliders, *Ezek.* 44. 11, 12, 13, 14, 15, 16. Nor will they be so weary (then) with Running in the way of Duty, nor faint with walking; but shall renew their strength, yea, seem to Mount up with wings

as Eagles, *Ifa.* 40. 31. Such will Abound with Service then, *Ifa.* 66. 23. but yet without Complaining; the Labour of a Duty being then removed, when they shall get shut of Clogging Humours, and have a New Heart beftowed on them. Thence is that ftate Defcribed, by their conftant finging, and fitting at a Feaft, *Ifa.* 65. 13, 14. and yet by ferving God (in his Temple) Day and Night, *Rev.* 7. 15. becaufe that Service (then) will be their Meat and Drink, or Matter of Delight; not faying (as thofe of Old) *When will the New Moon be Gone,* Amos 8. 5 ? But, *Let us Go fpeedily to Pray before the Lord,* *Zech.* 8. 21.

10. Such will have the Comfort of each others Company. Then all the Precious ones will be together, *Zech.* 14. 5. like fo many Jewels made up into a Bracelet, *Mal.* 3. 17. which as an Ornament that Bride fhall wear, *Ifa.* 49. 18. for wherefoever the Body is, thither will the Eagles be gathered together, *Luke* 17. 37. Then will thofe Saints be alfo of One Heart and Way, *Jer.* 32. 39. as were the Primitive Chriftians, *Acts* 4. 32. not Envying or Vexing one another, *Ifa.* 11. 13. but Serving the Lord with one confent, and joyntly calling upon his Name with a Pure Language, *Zeph.* 3. 9. whofe Name will then be One, *Zech.* 14. 9. Yea, thefe Wife Virgins then will be Divided from the Foolifh, as Sheep from Goats, *Mat.* 25. 32. no ftranger uncircumcifed in Heart fhall enter (with *Ifrael*) into the Sanctuary, *Ezek.* 44. 9. but *Jerufalem* fhall be Holy, *Joel* 3. 17.

11. Such then will there continue, none being Caft out, *Mat.* 22. 13. but he that wants his Wedding Garment, *v.* 12. which fhews the Poffibility of fome Hypocrites creeping then in, as heretofore, *Gal.* 2. 4. But Sons will abide in that Houfe for Ever, *John* 8. 35. and Faithful Overcomers will be as Pillars in God's Temple, who fhall no more Go out, *Rev.* 3. 12. Indeed God's People (in the General) will from that time be no more termed forfaken, *Ifa.* 62. 4. nor will they have any more to do with Grofs Idolatry, *Hof.* 14. 3. which yet may be confiftent with their Gradual declining in the General, till Chrift himfelf fhall come in Perfon, 1 *Thef.* 3. 13. But yet particular Saints (who come at firft with Chrift unto this Marriage) will be an Earneft of that more Univerfal fixing afterwards. Yea, fuch will Grow, *Hof.* 14. 5. paffing with Chrift from one Room to another; and reaping the Benefit of that Increafing Difpenfation, all their Time.

12. All this will then be Accented unto the Saints, by their Peculiar fharing in it; or by the quite contrary Portion of the Generality at fuch a Time. Darknefs fhall cover the Earth, when *Sion's* Light will Rife upon the Saints, *Ifa.* 60. 1, 2. when Chrift fhall bid [*Thefe*] Come, in Order unto intimate Communion with himfelf, *Mat.* 25. 34. He

The Parable of the Ten Virgins Opened. 221

then will say to Others, *Depart from me*, v. 41. The Nations will be Angry then, *Rev.* 11. 18. whilst These are giving Thanks, v. 17. who see the Justness of Christ's ways, *Rev.* 15. 3. or who will be Witnesses of that Solemnity. When Saints will be the Bride's Companions, *Psal.* 45. 14. then others shall entreate her Favour, v. 12. as *Haman* did *Esther's*. The Best of Hypocrites will want their Wedding Garment, *Mat.* 22. 11. when these Wise Virgings will be Ready. Yea, when these shall be white; Those will do wickedly, or be filthy still, *Dan.* 12. 10. When Saints shall Eat, then Others will be Hungry, *Isa.* 65. 13. and Howl, while Saints are Singing, v. 14. The Seventh Trumpet soundeth Peace to These, and Woes to Others, *Rev.* 11. 14, 15. And when the Saints are gathered together, *Zech.* 14. 5. then will the Mount of Olives (or their Adversaries) be Divided, v. 4. And as Sons will continue in this House; so others will be heard to Knock in vain.

Quest. 9. What doth this shutting of the Door Import?

Answ. 1. The securing of those within; partly, from Going out Again, as 2 *Kings* 6. 32. but chiefly from harm without. Thus did the Disciples shut the Doors, although from sinful Fear, as *Calvin* noteth, *John* 20. 19. Thus was *Nehemiah* Tempted to Meet some others in the Temple, with its Doors shut upon them, but would not yield thereunto, *Nehem.* 6. 10, 11. thus did those Angels (Lawfully) pull *Lot* in, and shut the Door against those wicked and Mischievous *Sodomites*, *Gen.* 19. 10. And so it may be here. Admitted Virgins shall not Depart, for Christ hath shut them In: Nor shall any Enter, to do them Hurt, for he hath shut them Out. Thus *Sion* shall no more be made to Drink the Cup of Trembling, *Isa.* 51. 22. her uncircumcised Enemies shall no more come in to her, *Isa.* 52. 1. Christ will be no more wroth with her, *Isa.* 54. 9. and in her Land there will be no more Violence heard, *Isa.* 60. 18. Yea, Satan will then be in some Measure Bound, or signally Rebuked, *Zech.* 3. 2. till such a Time; as at Christ's Personal Coming.

2. The shutting of this Door importeth chiefly, the Keeping of Others out, from sharing in the Priviledge of those within, which will be sad.

1. Since this Door is shut against Professors, who have been wont to be within. Dogs are shut out, and no Man heeds their Howling: But when some kind of Children are cast out, what weeping and gnashing of Teeth must needs then be, *Mat.* 8. 12. VVhat means this Noise, said poor Presumptuous *Joab*, 1 *Kings* 1. 4? So will the Foolish Virgins say, when they shall hear the Clapping of this Door against them,

them. The Top-stone of *Ishmael's* Misery was, that he (a Son) should be cast out, *Gen.* 21. 10. to Die in a Barren VVildernefs, without a Miracle. Such will then Cry, as sometime *Sion* did, *Jer.* 8. 15. *We Looked for Peace, but no Good came; and for a time of Health, and behold Trouble.* This Virgin-troop will then be more Confounded, becaufe they Hoped and were Afhamed, like the Troops of *Tema, Job* 6. 19, 20. which will rejoyce Hell from beneath (or Men more Grofly wicked) that Virgins are Excluded as well as Harlots, *Ifa.* 14. 9, 10.

2. Since they are fhut out from the Marriage; which Feaft their Teeth will water at, who had no ftomach to their work of Going forth to Meet the Bridegroom. If thefe were onely Excommunicated from the Service there, they would no more value it, than many do (Now) the Prelates Cenfures; in cafe that Lightning went alone. But they muft neither Eat nor Drink, *Ifa.* 65. 13. nor Tafte of Chrift's Marriage Supper, *Luke* 14. 24. nor be the Bride's Companions, as was Defired and Expected by them. And though Hell may fee into Heaven, (as through a Cranny of that Bolted Door) yet will the fight of water there, but onely Aggravate thofe Seers Torment, *Luke* 16. 24. and fo the Hearing of that Heavenly Mufick, will but increafe the others Howling, *Ifa.* 65. 14. An Hypocrite (chiefly) is in Love with Priviledges, (as Harlots are with Gifts;) the want whereof will therefore lay the Top-ftone of their Mifery, when that Door fhall be fhut upon them.

3. Since it is fhut by Him, who fhuts, and no Man Openeth, *Rev.* 3. 7. Indeed his Opening is firft mentioned there, *Rev.* 3. 7. becaufe his Prime Defign (at his firft coming) was not to Condemn or fhut, but Save or Open, *John* 3. 17. but he Now comes to fhut that Door which had been Opened by him heretofore. And well may he make bold to fhut the Door, becaufe he is the Mafter of that Houfe, *Luke* 13. 25. which therefore none may Open without his Order. Nor is it like, that any other would have fhut it of their own Accord; Saints being rather over-tender: But when 'tis fhut by Him, they Dare not (will not) Open it without his Leave. Nay, when he fhutteth, no Man Can Open; as when He Openeth, no Man Can Shut, *Rev.* 3. 8. This Door is not upon the Latch; therefore uncivil Perfons cannot enter: And none but *Eliakim* hath the Key, *Ifa.* 22. 22. therefore 'tis but in vain to hope from others: This Door is alfo Everlafting, *Pfal.* 24. 7. therefore not to be Broken through.

4. Since fhutting out, and being Caft into uttter Darknefs, go together, *Mat.* 8. 12. The Punifhment of ⌈ *Lofs* ⌉ would be the lefs, if

The Parable of the Ten Virgins Opened. 223

this of [*Senfe*] did not accompany it: nor is it fo bad to Die of Faft-ing, (much lefs to want a Feaft,) as to be Fed upon (Alive) with gnawing Never-dying Worms, *Mar.* 9.48. Nor is the want of Greater Light fo much afflicting, as to be caft out into the Outer Darknefs, a Place of darknefs as Darknefs it felf, and where the Light is as Darknefs, *Job* 10.22. How great muft needs that Darknefs be, *Mat.* 6. 23. compared wherewith, the Inner Darknefs is fome kind of Light. This needs muft be a Place of Weeping, to which is added, Gnafhing of Teeth, *Mat.* 8. 12. not in a way of Deriding Saints, as heretofore in their Afflicted State, *Pfal.* 35. 16. or of Infulting over them, as *Lam.* 2. 16. much lefs of being Ready to Devour them, as *Job* 16. 9. but in a way of being Vexed, as *Pfal.* 112. 10. and grievoufly Tormented, as *Mark* 9. 18.

5. Since others will be then Within. The Mifery of Man, (arifing from fome kind of VVant) is meerly grounded upon his Fancy: if None had ftately Houfes or rich Fare, then every one would be Content without them: but Envy flayeth filly Ones, *Job* 5. 1. Nor would the bare want of Neceffaries fo Afflict, in Cafe that VVant were Univerfal: but it muft needs Increafe poor ftarving *Lazarus* his Pain, to Know, that *Dives* fared Delicioufly, *Luke* 16. 19. 21. whofe Scale was therefore Juftly turned afterwards, *v.* 25. but very Heavily, as *Dives* thought *v.* 24. This will be the Foolifh Virgins Cafe; whofe being caft out, will make them VVeep; but Others being In, will caufe the Gnafhing of their Teeth, *Mat.* 8. 12. and meerly for want of being Ready, which they had Timely Notice of, but loft the Blefling as did *Efau*.

Ufe 1. The Virgins will part with mutual Freedom, before the Bridegroom's Coming. Indeed, the Wife (firft) Bid the other goe; but yet the Foolifh (Readily) Accept the others Motion. Which [*Bidding*] is, for fpiritual Gain; but this [*Accepting*] is for a Carnal Intereft, as hath been opened. Now they will part, at leaft-wife in Affection: not fo Delighting each in other, as heretofore: Since Differences in Opinion (efpecially with reference unto Time, Truths and Duties,) are apt to Alienate if not Provoke, *Numb.* 14.6.10. Yea, fuch will part in point of Practice alfo; the One fort going out to Meet the Bridegroom, the other going to Buy Oyl: As *Ruth* and *Orpah* did, with reference unto their Mother *Naomi*, *Ruth* 1. 14, 15. Nay they will Part in point of wonted ordinary Communion alfo: as *Paul* and *Barnabas* did, becaufe of *Mark*, who had Deferted his bounden Duty, *Act.* 15. 38, 39. This Parting (probably) will be Gradual: but let it Certainly be Expected, and not be Wondred at.

2. The

2. The Foolish Virgins onely (and not the Wise) are said to Goe, or Leave the Others Company: which is Observable. The Name of *Separation* hath been alway Infamous, although the Scripture clearly Owns it, 2 *Cor.* 6. 14. but at this Day the Foolish Virgins are the Separatists, however Apt to charge it upon others. There hath been formerly, a Lawful (Proper) Separation made by Saints, from Others: as when the *Jewish* Way was separated from, by those *Act.* 19. 8. who sometime were Obliged to walk therein. But yet, Backsliders (Returning to their Ancient Duty) cannot so Properly be said to separate from their bad Companions, since there was never any Lawfull Union, and so no need of a Divorce. However, the present case is Plain: the Foolish Virgins separate from the Wise, as to their former Joynt Practice, of Going out to meet the Bridegroom. Let no man therefore Check wise Virgins by that Name, which is not Theirs, nor (Absolutely) Infamous.

3. It is here said, *They went to Buy,* who (as it hath been Proved) went to *Sleep:* from whence is hinted, that sinfull Actions are Covered over with fair Pretences; and more Especially in these Latter dayes. Herein consisteth much of that Deceitfulness which lurketh in the Heart, *Jer.* 17. 9. and Sin, *Heb.* 3. 13. Thus bold Complyers are termed Wise in Christ, 1 *Cor.* 4. 10: and Wantonness is called Love, *Prov.* 7. 18. yea, Persecution is counted Wisdom, *Exod.* 1. 10, Zeal, *Phil.* 1. 6. and Duty, *Act.* 26. 9. Some men Declare their Sin, as did *Lots* eldest Daughter, (having learnt that in *Sodom, Isa.* 3. 9.) in calling her incestuous Infant, *Moab,* which signifieth, *Of her Father,* Gen. 19, 37: but Others are more subtile, such are the Foolish Virgins. Conscience (in such) will not permit a full Profession: and as That would have crackt their Credit quite, so would it have stopt their mouths from ever Claiming a Right of Entring afterwards.

4. Their false Hypocrisie is not Detected, (by any Word Discovering it,) but as they did Pretend [*to goe and Buy*] so is it here Delivered. They did profess ('tis like) this was their End: and Eminent Professors are not Hastily charged with Lying. However, Christ may (yet) let it pass for Currant: to Harden them in their (undiscovered) Sin: to learn us Moderation in a Disputable Case: and to Reserve their Manifestation till his Coming, unto the Heightning of their Confusion, by shutting them out, who (till that time) were not Convicted: or, by their being Apprehended, Tryed and Executed all at Once. Methinks I see the Reason here, of some mens Confident self-justifying; of others unaccustomed forbearing them in way of Censures, and of God's Ordering it to be so: Others will be more fully satisfied, when they

The Parable of the Ten Virgins Opened.

they shall see that following sudden Revelation of God's righteous Judgement at the Bridegrooms Coming.

5. Deceitfull Shews will not Advantage in this Day of Christ; since he will Come, while Foolish Virgins are gone to Buy, (as they Dissemblingly pretend) unto their being shut out for Ever. Some may seek Deep to hide their Counsel from the Lord, *Isa.* 29. 15. but this shall be esteemed as the Potters Clay: for shall not their Creator know, *v.* 16? He searcheth the Heart, to give to every Man his Due, *Jer.* 17. 10. Therefore Ought got unjustly, will not Prosper, *v.* 11: and this the Churches (or Professors) shall be made to Know, *Rev.* 2. 23. Yea, when it is thus, in point of Turning things upside down, *Isa.* 29. 16. within a very little while, the Lord will turn such seeming fruitfull Fields (or Glorious Hypocrites) into a Forrest, *v.* 17. Those do but Hasten his Appearing to their shame, who seek to cover evil Actions with fair Disguises, *Isa.* 66. 5. as Christ Then cometh here, upon the Foolish Virgins, for our Warning.

6. Peculiar Service (done for Christ) will suitably be Rewarded (by him) upon Earth, since all the Wise Virgins will be Admitted to the Marriage. Then Christ will gird himself, *Luke* 12. 37. and serve them: his Feast of Wines, *Isa.* 25. 6. will make them to forget their former Misery, as *Prov.* 31. 7. Yea he will then swallow up Death in Victory, *Isa.* 25. 8. and take away their Rebuke from off the Earth. When apt to faint (by reason of some Wildernefs-temptations) in fleeing out of *Babylon*, let this *Jerusalem* come into our Mind, *Jer.* 51. 50. or what God hath Prepared for him that waiteth for him, *Isa.* 64. 4. Then will their Foolishness appear, who have desired to be Excused from this Supper, *Luke* 14. 18. when they shall see, *Luke* 13. 28. how Blessed a thing it is to have been Called thereunto, *Rev.* 19. 9. the Truth whereof is signified there, by its being ordered to be Writ, and by a superadded Testimony.

7. This Feast may not be Tasted though, untill the Bridegroom's Coming; since these wise Virgins are here said to goe [*with Him*] unto the Marriage. We therefore have need of Patience, *Heb.* 10. 36: yea therefore Christ may put his Knife unto our Throat (or Exercise us with Delays) because we are so given to Appetite, *Prov.* 23. 2. And since Himself Expecteth, *Heb.* 10. 13: shall not we watch with him, *M. t.* 26. 40? those have no Faith, nor yet good Manners, who cannot Feed upon a Promise, nor be content to fare as doth their Master, *Job.* 13. 16. 'Tis for Our Interest to have Him with us; whose Presence (at the Table) make's our Spikenard smell, *Cant.* 1. 12; and in whose Absence, the very Bride-chamber Children Fast, *Mat.* 9. 15. Let us not

therefore be too Hasty: especially since they who Now are Full, will then be Hungry, *Luke* 6. 25. as having had their Portion.

8. There is a Readiness required for this Feast; 'and without which, none are Admitted to the Marriage. Some kind of Duty is Immediately incumbent on us, while in the Gall of Bitterness, *Act.* 8. 22, 23; but yet All (proper) Priviledges have their Fitness pre-required. We must be wrought for Glory, 2 *Cor.* 5. 5: nor will the Blind and Lame, (or Men defective mainly in their Light and Walking) ever Enter into *David*'s House, 2 *Sam.* 5. 8. Though Duty is required, apart from Priviledge; yet Priviledges may not be Expected without suitable Duty. Indeed, this Marriage will be as Burdensome to Unready Persons, as such themselves will be to Christ and his Companions; as Heaven it self would be an Hell to Sinners. And uppermost Seats will be Reserved for the greatest Gallants in that Day; or she shall stand at Christ's Right-hand, whose Clothing is the Gold of *Ophir*, *Psalm.* 45. 9.

9. The Marriage-Feast (at such a Time) will be in some Place which hath (as it were) a Door; as its being [*shut*] importeth. All may be Invited thither, but none will *share* therein (as Guests) save they who are Admitted with Approbation. This will be a peculiar Priviledge; which they shall know, whose Carelesness (in point of fore-required Duty) will Exclude them. The *New Jerusalems* Gates shall not be shut at all, *Rev.* 21. 25; to shew the Absoluteness of its Security: yet will there be Angels standing at them, *v.* 12, to keep those Out who have no Right to Enter, *v.* 27. so will it be Now. And as there shall be faithfull Keepers of the Sanctuary then, *Ezek.* 44. 16; so Carefull *Eliakim* will have the Key of *David*'s House, *Isa.* 22. 22; by Means whereof, Communion-Acts (relating unto Priviledge as well as Duty) will be secured.

10. The Door of Mercy will (in some sence, and unto some) be shut on Earth; or in this lesser Day of Judgement. It is (Insensibly) so at Present, unto particular Souls, as to Christ's striving with them by his Spirit of Grace: but it will Then be so more Evidently, in point of Priviledges; yea, though some (at that time) will seek to Enter, *Luke* 13. 24. Nor will it be to be Wondred at, since all the (Intended) Guests will be then Come, and set at Supper; and in that case, the Gates (in Great Houses) are alway shut. And as there will be no scaling of that high Wall, *Rev.* 21. 12; nor strength to force a passage through this Door: so neither will late-got Oyl or Tears be able to shoot its Lock for Ever. Those are mistaken sadly, who do conclude

the

the standing Open of Christ's Door till Death; and more especially in these Latter Days, as Foolish Virgins will Experience.

11. It therefore highly doth concern the Virgins or Professors of our Days to get themselves Ready as fast as may be. And in the Pressing whereof, I shall content my self with urging hereunto, as that word [*Ready*] appertaineth unto Virgins in the Letter; and as the same *Greek* word is used, *Rev.* 19. 7. with reference unto the Bride at such a time. In Order unto the setting home of which Exhortation, these following Motives may be of Use.

Mot. 1. This getting Ready is that Great work of Time incumbent on us, which therefore had need be chiefly minded by us alway, and much more Now. What is required of the Bride, but to be Ready, *Rev.* 19. 7? What of each Guest? but to have on his Wedding-Garment, *Mat.* 22. 12? Yea, what doth God require, from first to last, but to Put off Old former Cloaths, *Eph.* 4. 22. and that we Put on New, *v.* 24? The onely thing required of Spouses (by their Husband at this Feast) will be, to make themselves as Fine as may be; as once a Person told his Lady, upon a like Occasion. Nor came we (indeed) into this World to Eat and Drink, or Buy and Sell; but to get Ready for our Change. Earth is a Trimming place for Heaven, and Time should be Employed for Eternity. He that is Ready in this Spiritual sence, hath done the work belonging to his Day. Therefore we cannot be too Early up at such a work.

2. It is the Property of Virgins to be self-adorning; *Can Maids forget their Ornaments,* Jer. 2. 32? Such kind of forgetfulness seemeth to be inconsistent with thir state; next to their being termed Harlots, such cannot bear to be Reproached with their want of Neatness; whom if we Differ from (in this Respect) as to their Nature, how can we take it ill, not to be called by their Name? Harlots of Old were to be known by some particular kind of Vail, *Gen.* 38. 14. and Spiritual Sluttishness is such a Vail or Covering which sheweth Persons to be no Virgins. All sorts of Professors therefore have disowned their Companions, as they have seen them to be careless in their Habit, Compared with their Fellows. So that Remisness in our Holy self-adorning will very much Darken the visibility of our being Virgins or Professors, and Hazard the Total Loss of our Repute.

3. *Unready* Virgins (to be sure) are not wise, or truly Gracious, at least not in Appearance; since all the wise Virgins are Described here, by their being Ready; as if those terms were Convertible. There is much wisdom required unto this work of Dressing One's self aright: And Heavenly wisdom is much evinced, by One's being daily Conver-

The Parable of the Ten Virgins Opened.

fant thereabout. Fools Pride themselves in some one single part of man's Attire; but wife Men are ashamed to be seen till they have All, *Psal.* 119. 6. Fools are not Careful, as to the manner of their being drest: But Holy wisdom maketh to be Curious; not onely in having All one's Garments on, but every thing also in its Place; and so Preserved from being Loose or stained. Children and Fools are chiefly for their Food and Play, but spiritual Neatness is both the wise Man's VVork and Recreation, his Meat and Drink; who therefore alway is at his Brush and Looking Glass.

4. Professing Spouses are Princes Daughters, *Cant.* 7. 1. which doth Oblige Possessors (Eminently) to be sollicitous in this regard, as such are in the Letter. Ordinary Garments may Become a Beggar, (as Moral Vertues do a Carnal Man,) but not the Children of a King; who are forbidden strange Apparel, *Zeph.* 1. 8. but not Compleat, at least, not in a Spiritual sence. Did such consider the Nobleness of their Descent, *John* 1. 13. the Nature of their High Calling, *Phil.* 3. 14. The Glory of Kings Daughters Cloathing, *Psal.* 45. 13. it would ashame them into an Evidencing of their Heavenly Breeding, by laying out their time in getting Ready. If Earthly Gallants will not have one Hair amiss, much more should Heavenly Courtiers Hate a spotted Garment, *Jude* 23. and be continually Adding to what they have; since spiritual Fashions (also) Alter; and *Joshua* (Now) must have his Change of Raiment, *Zech.* 3. 4.

5. Thus shall we have more Love and Honour from Christ and others. How very plain are some in their Night Habit; yea, how did *Michal* Despise her Husband *David*, when he was stripped of his stately Robes, 2 *Sam.* 6. 20. Nor was the self-undressing Spouse's Fairness witnessed unto by her Companions, *Cant.* 5. 9. till she had first put on her Coat again, *v.* 3. 5. But when a Child is Neatly Drest, how is it Dandled by its Father; so will the King Desire his Spouse's Beauty, *Psal.* 45. 11. when Clad in Gold, with her Retinue, *v.* 9. Thus shall we also be more Amiable in the Eyes of others; both Saints and Sinners. VVhen *Ephraim* and *Judah* shall be Neat, or Clean from their Defilements, *Ezek.* 27. 23. then will they Unite in Love, *v.* 19. and be no more Divided, *v.* 22. Yea, Carnal Creatures will then Respect us, if not Love us; such being apt to honour others, meerly because of their Apparel, whom otherwise they do not much Regard.

6. God will be Glorified in us by this means, which is a self-sufficient Motive to get Ready, Saints Dress themselves and Christ at once; as their unhandsomness disgraceth him, whom they call Husband. Their Change of Raiment shews the fulness of his Wardrobe; their washed Robes,

Flesh, 1 *Tim.* 3. 16. becaufe the Father's Glory was to be feen in him, *John* 1. 14. as His in Us, when we are Ready.

7. Thus fhall we be more ufeful (at the Prefent) unto others, with whom we do converfe ; which is a Motive (ftrong enough) to make us Haften. All are more apt to mind Examples, than a Rule: Although God's Law was ftill the fame, yet when there was no King (or Judge) in *Ifrael*, to put that Law in Practice, then every one did what feemed good unto him, *Judg.* 17. 6. So is it in the want of Exemplary Saints. Children will gather Wood, when Fathers make the Fire, and Mothers knead the Dough for an Idolatrous Ufe, *Jer.* 7. 18. Some are Adventurous to be Offenfive in their Habits, *&c.* becaufe they fee Profeffors fo altered. How ready were the People to withftand the Prohibition, when they had Leaders to go before them, *Hag.* 1. 12. Now, *Paul* was willing to be from Chrift (a while) for others good, *Phil.* 1. 23. 34. much more fhould we get Ready therefore; which is indeed the way to be with him, at leaft-wife fooner than can be elfe expected.

8. Elfe fhall we ill Requite his Love, in Tarrying all this while, for fuch a purpofe. Chrift is Affectionate, unto the Height: who did Exceedingly Defire to eat his Laft (or Death-importing) Paffeover, *Luke* 23. 15. much more to fee th's Wedding day, as ever did a Youthful Bridegroom, *Ifa.* 62. 5. whofe waiting therefore, is like that of a Dropfie Man for Drink, which Exercifeth Patience to the utmoft. Now, as he partly tarrieth, untill the Vintage (*viz.* the wicked) be fully Ripe. *Rev.* 14. 18. So more efpecially, untill the Wheat (or Harveft) be fo, *Mat.* 13. 30. or till the Bride be Ready, *Rev.* 19. 7. whofe Readinefs confifteth (Mainly) in the Readinefs of her Companions. And if for our Expediency, he Tarrieth Now, as he did fometime (therefore) Go away, *John* 16. 7. fhall we then Trifle ? VVould not that be, as to His Grief, fo to Our fhame, if not the Aggravating and Occafioning of our Exclufion.

9. Thus fha'l we haften (what in us lieth) the Coming of this day of God, which is a Duty, 2 *Pet.* 3. 12. and that which All (in words) Defire, *Mal.* 3. 1. And as we are to Haften it by our Prayer, *Ifa.* 62.

The Parable of the Ten Virgins Opened.

7. So (more especially) by our getting Ready, 1 *Pet.* 1. 13. else that we not Comp'eatly Haflen it. As Chrift is therefore back, to Evidence his willingnefs, that none fhould Perifh, 2 *Pet.* 3. 9. so is he purposed to Wait untill his Precious ones be Ready; as he could not Destroy the *Sodomites*, till *Lot* was come to *Zoar*, *Gen.* 19. 22. so will he now do for his Servants fake, *Isa.* 65. 8. But if his Jewels were all made up, such would not then be faulted for his ftaying: Till when, Chrift's Spirit in them (whilft they are Praying for his Coming) cannot but Tax them, as being the Caufe, why he yet cannot Come: And it will be exceeding fad, if we shall be thus Acceffary to our own and others Mifery.

10. Thus will his Coming be more Comfortable to us, than otherwife can be expected. Chrift in his People, is the Hope of Glory, as to the Groundednefs of such an Hope, *Col.* 1. 27. and is its fweetnefs alfo, fince all Delight arifeth from the Union or Conjunction of things fuitable each to other. They who are fully Ready, will have the cleareft fight of all that Glory; the fineft Tafte of that Provifion, and deepeft fhare in all the other Priviledges of that Difpenfation. Such in whom Love (or Grace) is Perfected, will then have Boldnefs, in that Day of Judgment; becaufe as He now is, fo They are in this World, 1 *John* 4. 17. Whereas that Day will be Confounding unto others, *Amos* 5. 18. who then will be afraid, *Isa.* 33. 14. (as Naked *Adam* was, *Gen.* 3. 10.) and therefore call upon the Hills to Cover them, *Luke* 23. 30. at leaft-wife much afhamed, becaufe they have not kept their Garments, *Rev.* 16. 15.

11. Elfe will it be (at leaft) unto our Lofs, fo far as Chrift will then be fain to Drefs us, or to make up (by his laft Inftantaneous Change) wherein our felves were carelefly Defective. 'Tis true indeed, Chrift will have all his People Ready then, becaufe Himfelf will Cloath them with His Change of Raiment, *Zech.* 3. 4. yet doth it concern them to be Doing what they can, fince their Reward will then be fuited to their own Labour, 1 *Cor.* 3. 8. Saints will then Differ each from other, in point of Glory, *Luke* 12. 44. as at Chrift's Perfonal Coming, 1 *Cor.* 15. 41, 42. which Difference will arife from hence, becaufe fome will have Laboured more, in getting Ready, whilft others have been fleeping, *Luke* 12. 40. 43, 44. The Fuller our felf-cloathing is at prefent, the more Gold Lace fhall we Then have from him, whofe Recompence will be according unto works, *Rev.* 2. 23. although fuch works will then be Changed by Himfelf; but leaft unto their Lofs who are Moft Ready Now.

12. Thus fhall we (at Prefent) have the Comfort of our being Ready,

Ready, as it is in it self considered, and with Respect unto our selves. It is with Spiritual Garments, as with Bodily: Which are no: satisfying (unto Curious Virgins) till All be on; nor Easie, untill the whole be closely Girt upon us with that Girdle of Truth, *Eph.* 6. 14. If that meer Moralist could say, *What lack I yet*, *Mat.* 19. 20. much more is *Paul* forgetful of that Behind, till that Before is also added, *Phil.* 3. 13. Yea, Graces (also) are Odoriferous, *Cant.* 4. 14. and every of a Christian's Garments smell like *Lebanon*, v. 11. whose sweet Perfume doth therefore Multiply together with them. And since this getting Ready is our Main work, we cannot be too soon at Rest, when we shall have nothing else to do, but either to Depart in Peace, or to Go in with Christ unto the Marriage.

13. Thus will Christ's present Tarrying be less Burdensome by far: Or, we shall be thus better able to wait for his Appearing; and therefore is waiting joyned with Compleat Adorning, 1 *Cor.* 1. 7. This Wedding-Garment will supply the Bridegroom's place, as being the Quintessence of that Comforter, which Christ hath sent for such a Purpose, *John* 14. 16. The want of Priviledge is least Oppressing unto these, who are most Busied about their Duty. Grace is a sweet Companion in Christ's Absence, as are that Woman's Children unto her, whose Husband is from home: Since as the Father was to be seen in Christ, *John* 14. 9. so Grace is Christ's (Refreshing) Image, *Col.* 3. 10. as Children Represent their Earthly Father, unto the Comfort of their solitary Mother. Yea, Grace will therefore satisfie, in such a case; because it is the Creature's Will resign'd to God.

14. Thus shall we also keep Awake, whilst others slumber. Undressing and Nodding oft times go Together; but never was Virgin known (I think) to Nod whilst getting Ready. Infants (indeed) will oft-times sleep while they are Dressed by another; which Active self-adorners are not seen to do. Such are kept waking, for fear of being prickt with Pins, if carelesly put in, more than if heedlesly plucked out. Yea, self-adorning Virgins are so apt to be in Love with their Attire, *Jer.* 2. 32. as not to slumber at such a Time, because of self-beholding and self-pleasing Fancies then at work. Such also are convinced of the Near approaching Day, as Putting on this Armour of Light evinceth, *Rom.* 13. 12. who therefore cannot sleep. And as Activity (in any case) will keep one waking, so more especially in this, for fear of Ruffling that by sleeping, which is now putting on with care.

15. Else shall we not Go with Christ unto the Marriage, as is here plainly signified. As all Things will be Ready then, *Mat.* 22. 4. so must all sorts of Persons be, *v.* 12. and if unsanctified *Israel* might not eat.

eat thofe Quails, *Numb.* 11. 18. much lefs this Marriage Supper. If Spots ought not to be in Ordinary Feafts of Charity among Profeffors, *Jude* 12. much lefs will fuch a Glorious Bride and Bridegroom be Reproached with Unready Guefts. Can we then be too forward at fuch a work? Perfons Invited to fome Curious Feaft, need not be bid to Drefs themfelves apace; efpecially when a fecond Meffenger brings word, that All is Ready: This is our prefent cafe, *Mat.* 22. 4. Remember what lies at ftake, and if we have any Appetite to thofe fore-named Difhes, (which he that Eats not of, will Dye for ever;) fo let us call for Help, and ftand no longer Prating; but on with one thing after another, for fear of being fhut out with Foolifh or unready Virgins.

16. This being Ready is of Neceffary Ufe, with reference unto our Change by Death, which may be fudden; although this Coming of the Bridegroom fhould not prove fo near, as fome may hope it is. Were this a Duty meerly relating to an uncertain time, which Poffibly may not be this Hundred Years, we might be Tempted to Defpife an Exhortation thereunto. But if we Judge that Perfonal Death may be at Hand, this Holy Readinefs will then beftead us; and without which our Diffolution will be fad: But when our Courfe is finifhed, then fhall we be (as *Paul* was) Ready to Depart from hence with Joy, 2 *Tim.* 4. 6, 7. And though we fhould not Live to fee this Second Marriage upon Earth; yet if we Dye in fuch a Ready pofture, we fhall be at a better Feaft in *Abraham*'s Bofom, and with the Lord himfelf, *Phil.* 1. 23. till called from thence unto his far more Glorious Perfonal Marriage.

I fhall Conclude with fome few Spiritual Helps and fuitable Directions, (ftill holding to this Metaphor of getting Ready in a Bodily Refpect,) which are as Followeth.

1. Let us Eye the Beauty of our being thus Adorned. This Garment doth confift of Fineft Linnen, *Rev.* 19. 8. and Cloth of Gold, *Pfal.* 45. 13. befet with Jewels, *Ifa.* 61. 10. and all bran New, *Ifa.* 48. 7. which Virgins are Ambitious of. Thus will our Nakednefs and fhame be covered, *Rev.* 16. 15. this Robe being white and Long, *Rev.* 7. 13. which alfo is exceeding Grave, and therefore was Affected by the *Pharifees*, *Mark* 12. 38. Thence is it, that Saints do Love them moft who are moft Neat: And if a finner doth not Love, yet doth he therefore Envy fuch, becaufe out-fhining him: Yea, fuch are therefore Tempted moft by Satan, to become his Harlots, becaufe of their Excelling Beauty. However, as Chrift will thus be moft Enamoured with us, *Cant.* 7. 1. 6. fo we fhall have moft Comfort in our felves, when thus

Adorned;

The Parable of the Ten Virgins Opened.

Adorned; since Man (as Man) would fain be Fine, though (Naturally) Ignorant of truest Comeliness, *Rom.* 10. 3.

2. Let us consider how Fine the Bridegroom and the Bride will be at such a time, which may provoke our Labouring to be accordingly. Christ will appear in Glory then, *Psal.* 102. 16. who will be ashamed of Unready Virgins, *Mark* 8. 38. but will confess their Name before his Father, *Rev.* 3. 5. whose Garments (Now) are undefiled, *v.* 4. The Bride then also will be Ready, *Rev.* 19. 7. who Now is bid awake, in Order thereunto, *Isa.* 52. 1. and if the Mistress be up, what shame it is that Maids should be Asleep. That Dispensation will abound with Priviledges, the having of which Precious Promises should cause self-cleansing from all kind of Filthiness, 2 *Cor.* 7. 1. Could we but Eye that Recompence of Reward, *Heb.* 11. 26. how would it make us to abound in Duty, 1 *Cor.* 15. 58. and we may blush to think of not being inwardly Cloathed on, so as to suit that Outward Glory, which all the Saints will then have put upon them.

3. Did we but seriously enquire, what of the Night, or what a Clock it is, *Isa.* 21. 11. the Watch-man would inform us how far the Night is spent, and therefore Hasten our Putting on this Armour of Light, *Rom.* 13. 12. Satan would fain perswade us, as did that *Levites* Father-in-Law, that either it is too soon, *Judg.* 19. 8. or else too late, *v.* 9. but as the Door is not yet shut, so no Man knows how soon it may be; which should provoke our making speed. The Virgins have had (already) their first sleep, out of Doubt; and such as have been Throughly wakened, can sleep no more, but are self-dressing; and Sluggards never were more heavy than at present, through Multiplicity of Benign Vapours inviting them to sleep: All which are Probable Signs of Day being not far off, And if the Nearness of our Salvation, much more the shortness of that Time which may be Now behind, wherein to get us Ready before Day break.

4. Let us Observe what Haste poor sinners make to Get them Ready for that Dispensation: whose being fitted to Destruction, *Rom.* 9. 22. (or filling up the Measure of their Sin, *Mat.* 23. 32.) is that for which Christ partly Tarrieth, as *Gen.* 15. 16. That Prince (immediately preceding Christ) is therefore eminently called Wicked and Prophane, *Ezek.* 21. 25, 26, 27. that Interest succeeding the Fourth Beast's Destruction (in the little Horn) is therefore Represented by the other Beasts, which were more Grossely wicked, *Dan.* 7. 11, 12. And the *Assyrian* Party (which is the same) are therefore said to be Consumed Soul and Body, *Isa.* 10. 18. That Vintage Ripens most (as in the Letter) towards the Fall; and is it not a shame, that Wheat should

The Parable of the Ten Virgins Opened.

come Behind? Yea, Real Saints shall Purifie, (at such a time) as Others then wil signally be Wicked, *Dan.* 12. 10.

5. The finest Ornaments are soonest had (with Christ) and at the Cheapest rate; yea other things (for Nought) together with them. Trades men will make him stay who onely comes for Thread, to serve Another with Gold or Silver-lace: and 'tis not Christ's fault but ours, in Case the Spirit be no hid for Asking, *Luke* 11. 9. 13; since he made *Jesus* wait for an Outward Mercy, till that Believing Woman's Faith was first relieved, though she came last, *Mark* 5. 22; 23, 25 Yea, Heaven Embraceth (as it were) us Dwellers upon Earth, or offereth it self in no us freely; whilest Lower good things require Digging, *Job.* 3. 21. which should encourage us to covet earnestly that which is Best. And if we help Christ off with choycer Graces, he will Throw in what is of Lesser value: therefore most spiritual Saints have alway been most universally endued with other vertues; and carefull Practisers of Time-Duties, are not Defective other wayes.

6. Let us Use (or Look our selves in) the Glass; by which the Scriptures are resembled, in order unto our being Compleatly Dress, 2 *Cor.* 3. 18. Mens Words and Actions are some kind of Looking-glass, but mostly falfe: the minding whereof too much, occasions Groundless Self Conceit, 2 *Cor.* 10. 12. But taking heed unto the Word of God, is that by which a Young man's Way is to be Cleansed, *Psal.* 119. 9. We Now must see by That, 1 *Cor.* 13. 12. which though but Dark (compared with one's seeing face to face) yet is it True, *Psal.* 19. 9. and that by which all other Glasses must be tryed, *Isa.* 8. 20. Did we compare our selves more with the Rule, how should we Blush, to see our Shame Reflected, through want of what is requisite unto our being Comely. But let us not goe away, till that be Rectified which is Amiss; else shall we soon forget what manner of men we were, whilest self-beholding in that Glass, *Jam.* 1. 23.

7. Let us not choose to be Alone; which in the state of Innocency was not Good, *Gen.* 2. 18; but is Now Wofull, *Eccl.* 4. 10. The time is coming, when Saints shall Equalize the Angels, *Luke* 20. 36; who are Alluded unto in that Description of those four Beasts (or living Creatures) being full of Eyes Before and Behind, *Rev.* 4. 6, 7, compared with *Ezek.* 1. 10. but till that time, a Friend Behind us may be of necessary use, to rectifie what is amiss upon our Backs. Yea Company (in it self considered) doth much provoke to be more Neat than otherwise; so little know we how to walk, as being alway in the sight of God. Affected Solitariness and spiritual Sluttishness, are mutual Causes each of other; whatever Curiosity may be Pretended unto

8. Let us make Choice of our Companions though; else had we better be Alone, as to our getting Ready. Man is so apt to be as his Companions are, that God himself is said to be so, *Pfal.* 18. 26; so far as his Unchangeablenefs, *Jam.* 1. 17, is capable of Variation. But *Peter* put off his *Gentile* (Genteel) Garb, so soon as some of the Circumcifed Habit came, *Gal.* 2. 12: and thereby did much Harm to Others, *v.* 13: and upon which Account, *Paul* feparated the Believing Gentiles from thofe *Jews, Act.* 19. 9. Some call that Pride, which is the Neweft (though Heavenly) Fathion: and if a Councel were Now call'd among Profeffors, fome kind of fpiritual Sprucenefs in Apparel would be Condemned, as that in Letter was, by the Fifteenth Canon of the Second *Nicene* Councel. Some are Enforced to with-draw; yea Others therefore are Caft out, becaufe they Dare not Touch that Garment which is fpotted with the Flefh: and bleffed is he who doth Prevent fuch kind of Cenfures by his felf-chofen Separation, 2 *Cor.* 6. 17.

9. Let us make hafte in Dying unto Carnal Bravery; So fhall we have more Time and Love for Holy felf-Adorning. Some are fo vainly ftudious of Worldly Fafhions, or fo Conformed thereunto; as that Transforming (Inward) Renovations are neglected; thefe being Inconfiftent, *Rom.* 12. 2. 1 *Tim.* 2. 9; 10. 1 *Pet.* 3. 3 4, 5. Chrift finds no fault, (fave with the Plaintiff) when *Martha* (or the Outward man) complains of *Mary*, for leaving her Alone, in competition with that One thing Needfull, *Luke* 19. 39, 40, 41, 42. Perfons in Love with their own cieled Houfes, are foon Prohibited from Religious Building, *Hag.* 1. 4. and feveral would follow Chrift, if they had Nothing elfe to dee, *Luke* 9. 59. 61. Yea fpiritual Neatnefs is therefore fleighted by fome Profeffors, becaufe Induments of a Moral Nature are fo prized: Therefore *Paul* crieth down thefe Lower Gifts, which hindred thofe Babifh *Corinthians* from what was more Excelling, 1 *Cor.* 14. 19, 20. 22

10. Let us look chiefly To our felves; but let us take heed of Looking Too much At our felves, or Trufting in our apprehended Beauty; which doth Begin with Fornications, *Ezek.* 16. 15. and juftly Ends with being ftripped, *v.* 39. Some are fo bufie in Dreffing Others, as to forget Themfelves; which in a fpiritual Cafe is Paradoxal, *Luke* 6. 42. Others are fo in love with fome Particular thing upon them, as to leave Adding thereunto; and fo that fingle Ornament doth but Increafe

crease their shame, as doth a New Lawn Apron upon a Tattered Gown. Whereas Humility is both the Gloss of every Garment, and that which makes unsatisfied untill the whole be on: yea, alway spying some Defect, and earnestly Desiring help accordingly. Therefore so Few are Ready at this Day, because so Many are in Love with former puttings on; not being able to Forget what is Behind, the sight whereof should onely stirre us up to Perfect that which is so well Begun. Then shall we be Ready to goe with Christ into his Second Temple, when all our Women's Looking-glasses are converted into Lavers, as *Exod.* 38. 8; or when our self-Beholding shall be turned into self-purifying, for which that Laver served.

MATTHEW XXV. 11, 12.

Afterwards came also the Other Virgins, saying, Lord, Lord, Open to us.

And he answered and said, Verily, I say unto you, I know you not.

IN these two Verses, we have the Foolish Virgins signified, as by their *Practice*, so by their *Portion*: with reference to such a Time, viz. the Bridegroom's being Come. From whence the General Observation is, as followeth:

Observ. *Upon the shutting of Christs Door, then will the Foolish Virgins come, desiring to have it Opened: but will be Repulsed, with Christs saying to them, Verily, I say, I know you not.*

Quest. 1. What is the Meaning of these words, *Lord, Lord?*

Answ. 1. *Negatively*: They do not Now crie, *Abba, Father*: whatever formerly they may have done, from a presumptuous pretending unto that Spirit of Adoption by which Saints are Authorized so to speak, *Rom.* 8. 15. But Now they onely say, *Lord, Lord*: to signifie (perhaps) the great Abatement of their (sometime) Confidence. Confident ones (as that word [*carelels*] should be rendred) will then be Troubled, *Isa.* 32. 11. Yea Christ will then Evince their being the Devils Children, as at his first Appearing, *Joh.* 8. 44: and when his Door is shut against them, that very thing will Daunt them. Indeed, how can such call him *Father*, who are in Bondage unto slavish Fear, *Rom.* 8. 15. who seek their Own, in serving him, *Phil.* 2. 20, 21, 22.

and

2. As to the *Affirmative* : the words [*Lord, Lord,*] import,

1. Their full Knowledge of his Person, as both that Title evidenceth, and his Disowning Them (in that regard) in his Reply. Thus did that Angel notifie his being Christ, *Luke* 2. 11. thus *Peter* signified his Knowledge of him, *Mat.* 14. 28: and thus Christ hinted (unto Strangers) who he was, *Mat.* 21. 3. These did not seem to Know him in his suffering State, *Joh.* 1. 10: but Now the Blind shall see out of Obscurity, *Isa.* 29. 18. such Now Refuse to know Him through Deceit, *Jer.* 9. 6. but he will Then cause them to know, he is the Lord, *Jer.* 16. 21. He will be then Easily to be Known, as by those many Crowns upon his Head, *Rev.* 19. 12. so by his Vesture dipt in Blood, *v.* 13. and this Name [*Lord*] upon his Thigh, *v.* 16.

2. Their Knowledge of his being Present there; as this directing of their Speech unto him hinteth. This Dispensation hath its Name from thence, *Ezek.* 48. 35. and it will be so fairly writ thereon, that Foolish Virgins will understand it. His Presence will appear, as by the Onenefs of his Name, *Zech.* 14. 9. So by his People's being Powerfull, 1 *Cor.* 14. 24, 25; together with the putting of all Flesh to silence, *Zech.* 2. 13. Therefore All sorts of persons (then) will be Ambitious of Communion with a *Jew*, *Zech.* 8. 23; and Foolish Virgins (among the rest) will therefore seek unto Himself for Entrance, since Fulness of Joy must needs be in his Presence, *Psal.* 16. 11.

3. Their Owning of his Lordly Power; or that Himself, who solely is *Jehovah*, is the most High over all the Earth; which Then will be Acknowledged, *Psal.* 83. 18. He is the Saints Onely Lord, 1 *Cor.* 8. 6. but Foolish Virgins would not that he should Reign, *Luke* 14. 14. as their Disputing his Command (of Going forth to Meet him) intimateth, until This time, and then they yield, *Mat.* 25. 24. These Now pretend to be his Servants; yea they Now grant him to be Lord of All, with an Emphatical Reduplication; and in Particular, as to his Right of Opening here. And what a Glory will it be to Christ and to his People, when These shall thus submit themselves with silver Speeches, *Psal.* 68. 30.

4. The Earnestness of their Desire to be Admitted; as this Ingemination signifieth. Such will then Crie, as sometimes the Disciples did (when like to Perish) *Master, Master, Luke* 8. 24. Thus some will seek to enter, *Luke* 13. 24. since being Without (at such a time) will argue Men to be Dogs, *Rev.* 22. 15. and likely to Die of Hunger, *Isa.* 65. 13. Whilest there is any Work in hand, Dogs love to slumber,

Isa.

heretofore, and as then denying him to Open, Primarily importeth. Lord! Some of our former Raptures from thy self; some of thy Blessings upon our Endeavours; at least, some Tastings of that Heavenly Gift which formerly had been vouchsafed to us, *Heb.* 6. 4, 5. But this will not be granted, in that Day. Self-seeking Preachers (heretofore) may have been usefull unto Others, *Phil.* 1. 18. but Now, such will be silenced by Christ, *Psal.* 50. 16. who therefore shall not profit the People at all, *Jer.* 23. 32. That Light will then be gathered up into the Sun, as in the first Creation, *Gen.* 1. 16. which formerly was Distributed, *v* 3. And Self-Encompassers with their own Sparks, will then lie down in Sorrow, *Isa.* 50. 11.

2. That rightly constituted Churches would receive them in; together with the Second Temple's Opening unto Others. Lord (will such plead) Admit us to thy Children's Table; let us be under their Inspection; and let us sing thy Praises with them. But that will not be granted neither. Where Christ bears sway, the Childrens Bread shall not be cast to Dogs; since it Ought not to be so, by his Order, *Mat.* 7. 6. And if *John* Baptist's Ministration did Refuse those unrepenting *Pharisees, Mat.* 7. 8; much more will Christ's, *v.* 12. Yea, till the Vials be poured out, this Second Temple will be so filled with Glory, as that no Man (that is, no such as These, as *Rev.* 14. 3.) shall then be able to Enter into it, *Rev.* 15. 8; since none but *Zadocks* Sons shall goe into that Sanctuary, *Ezek.* 44. 15, 16, 17.

3. That Saints (at least) as Saints, would not refuse Communion with them, in Religious Actions of a Common Nature. Lord (will these say) let not thy People turn their back upon us speaking: let them not Grieve to Joyn with us in Prayer: let them account us Christian Brethren still; though not in Church-relation. But neither will This be condescended unto. Christ will then bid, Let them Alone; because Blind Leaders, and not of his Father's Planting, *Mat.* 15. 13, 14. Then will there be a Difference put between *Paul's* praying in the Presence of, and Joyning therein, with others, *Act.* 27. 35. Then also will that Phrase be used, of calling such (onely) Brethren, according to the Flesh, *Rom.* 9. 3. by way of Distinguishing them from *Isaac's* Seed, or Children, *v.* 7.

4. That

4. That Equal sharing (Howsoever), in Outward Blessings may not be denied to them, w o were sometimes wont to have the Greatest Portion. Lord (will such Cry, as *Esau* did) let us be also Blessed by thee, *Gen.* 27. 34. hast thou not Reserved a Blessing for us, *v.* 36? although but one, *v.* 38. But *Esau* (then) will not Prevail, as having Sold away his outward Blessing with his Birth-right; however Confident at such a time, *Mal.* 1. 4. That Fruitful Field will then become a Forest, *Isa.* 32. 15. and it shall Hail thereon, when *Sion*'s City shall be Low, in a Low place, or Fruitful Valley, *v.* 19. Now, they who are shut out of Earth as well as Heaven, must needs be in some kind of Hell; which in Respect of wonted Outwards, will be the Foolish Virgins Portion.

5. That such might not (at least) meet with those Positive Hardships, which Excluded Persons may have cause to fear. Lord (will their Last Petition be) yet let us not be over-hardly used by thy self, or by thy Servants, or by our own Accusing Consciences. But this Request will not be granted. Christ will deny them before his Father, who have Persistingly Denyed Him, by their Departure from his work, *Mat.* 10. 33. Such will be Galled with the Name of Hypocrites, and Workers of Iniquity, *Mat.* 7. 23. leaving their Name for a Curse unto God's Chosen ones, *Isa.* 65. 15. Yea, as such will be Abhor'd by All, so will they have a Gnawing, Never-dying Worm within, (far worse than Death) because they have Transgrest against the Lord, *Isa.* 66. 24.

Quest. 3. What should Encourage these to Hope for Entrance? which both their Coming and their Pleading intimate,

Answ. 1. Because of their being Virgins. Lord (may such plead) we are no Harlots, and must we yet be Numbred with them? We have refused to hold Communion with the Strumpets of our Time; and must we Now be made to do so? We have with-stood Humane Inventions in Religious Worship; and are we now Excluded, with the Beast? But it will then be Answered; you were not (indeed) like those more filthy Swine, yet are you Goats, who therefore Now must be Divided from the Sheep, *Mat.* 25. 32. You were no Down-right *Babylonians*; but being joyned to them is sufficient, *Isa.* 13. 15. Or rather, you had the Name of Virgins, but were Harlots; and Christian *Babylon* must be Destroyed.

2. Because of their Having had Communion with the Wife in former times. Lord (may such Plead) we have been welcom to thy Table, *Luke* 13. 26. and are we now Denyed its Crumbs? Thy Guests (within) have been our Fellows; and must we now be used like Dogs? We

The Parable of the Ten Virgins Opened.

We can produce their Letters Testimonial; and will not that Commendamus help us to our Ancient Fellowship? To which Christ then will Answer, I bad the Tares be let alone untill This time, *Mat.* 13. 30. and though my People failed in your Admission, yet am not I therefore bound to do so; nor They, for time to come, *Ezek.* 44. 9. Nay, you are not the same you were, in point of sometime visibility: However, I now must Judge with Righteousness and Equity, *Isa.* 11. 3, 4.

3. Because of their good Service done for Christ, *Mat.* 7. 22. Such will then Plead, Lord, have we not Heard Thee Teaching in our Streets, *Luke* 13. 26? And was not that sometimes counted worth a Supper, *Mark* 6. 34, 35. 37? *Have we not Prophesied in thy Name*, Mat. 7. 22? And dost not thou say, such Labourers are worthy of their Meat, *Mat.* 10. 10? Yea, *Have we not Cast out Devils in thy Name*, Mat. 7. 23? And wilt thou Cast us out, unto the Devil and his Angels, *Mat.* 25. 41? To which it will be then Replyed, but did you not All this unto your selves, *Zech.* 7. 5. 6? And in a Deceitful way of keeping back your Male, *Mal.* 1. 14? Both as to principal Time-Truths and Duties. You have had your Reward already, *Mat.* 6. 2. and selfish Aims have made your work Iniquity, *Mat.* 7. 23.

4. Because they did go forth (at first) to meet the Bridegroom, *Mat.* 25. 1. Lord (may such plead) we sometimes bore an Open Testimony, hazarding our All in the Maintaining of thy Cause: and doth not Half the work Deserve some Part of Pay? But Christ will then Reply, you did run well, who hindred you, *Gal.* 5. 7? Why did you not so run, as to Obtain, 1 *Cor.* 9. 24? My Cross should daily have been taken up, *Luke* 9. 23. nor was Salvation promised, but to Endurers to the End, *Mat.* 24. 13. You were the more Foolish to Begin, *Luke* 14. 28. yea, I was therefore most Reproached by you Apostates, *Heb.* 6. 6. however, you knew the Law, that all the Backslider's former Righteousness shall be forgotten, *Ezek.* 18. 24.

5. Because their Not going out (the Second time) proceeded from their want of Oyl, *Mat.* 25. 8. Lord (will these say) we had not Light unto this Latter work, and wilt thou Gather where thou hast not Strewed, Mat. 25. 24? Heathens will not be Judged for the Light they Have not, *Rom.* 2. 12. and shall we Virgins be more Hardly dealt with? Our Lamps went out, through lack of Oyl, and therefore must we now be cast out into utter Darkness? But Christ will then Reply, you took no Oyl at first, *Mat.* 25. 3. whose Fault was that? You trusted unto flashy good Affections, though I had told you of the stony Hearers, *Mat.* 13. 20, 21. Nay, the Truth is, you wanted not Light, but

The Parable of the Ten Virgins Opened.

Will; and as it now appeareth by your coming, but too late.

6. Becaufe of what they had more Lately done, or fince the Cry was made. Lord, (will they fay) we prefently Arofe and Trimmed our Lamps, as well as our Companions; and is that nothing worth? VVe came to them for Oyl, but were Repulfed, and muft we now Suffer for their unwillingnefs to help us? Nay, thereupon we went to Buy, as they Advifed us; and was there a Defign upon us in that Counfel? To which it will be Anfwered, You did my work Deceitfully; and that Deferves a Curfe, inftead of VVages, *Jer.* 48.10. You begged coldly at the beft; that Taught my Servants to Deny you, as 2 *King.* 5. 18, 19. Nor did you come to Buy of Me; I know you not, 'tis fo long fince I faw you.

7. Becaufe of their not having yet had a Legal Trial, or due Conviction before a Sentence. Lord (will thefe fay,) Thy Servants Generally have not Born Witnefs (Hitherto) againft us; ask them, and they will not deny it: Nor was the Cafe decided (fully) in our Confciences unto this Day: Shall we now be Condemned (by our Exclufion) before a Trial? Or Excommunicated without a Previous Admonition? But Chrift will Anfwer, You heard the Cry, as your awakening thereupon Evinced: You had the Scriptures, clearing up that Duty, wherein you failed: You alfo had fome Pangs of Confcience, witnefs the Trimming of your Lamps: Therefore you had a Three-fold Admonition, which is one more than Neceffary, *Titus* 3. 10.

8. Becaufe they have Now Got that Oyl (as their Returning intimateth) which heretofore they lacked. Lord (will thefe fay,) we Now are come up to Thy Terms: We Now have Light into that work of Going Forth: And wilt thou not Admit Repenting finners, yea, at what Time foever? But Chrift may Anfwer, Your Common-Prayer-Book hath it [*at what Time foever*] but not the Scripture; nay, I have oft told you, that my Door will not ftand alway Open. Nor have you now got Light into your Duty; but onely wit to fave your Intereft, by falling in with fafe and Gainful Service. And if I fhould forgive you this time alfo, the next Temptation would evince your being ftill the fame, as hath been oft Experimented.

9. Becaufe of what Encouragement they fometimes had to Hope, as to a Real work of Grace upon their Hearts, (and confequently for Admiffion) notwithftanding Leffer Failings. Lord (will thefe fay) Haft thou not fometimes Crowned us with Peculiar Favours? Hath not thy Spirit witneffed with ours, that we were Thine? Yea, had we not the witnefs of water, as well as Blood, of Duty (Excepting this Particular)

ticular) as well as Faith on Thee? And shall this one Blot spoil our former Evidences? But Christ will Answer, I never Warranted your Thus concluding: You spoke Peace to your selves, and Fathered it upon me. I gave you Sixpence, and you thence hoped to be mine Heirs. Time-Duties (also) are that by which all other is to be Tried, *John* 8. 24.

10. Because of some Admitted in, who were as likely as Themselves (or rather more) to be Excluded. Lord (will these say,) There sitteth one, who is too Young, to have Deserved such a Priviledge; let him give Place to us his Seniors: Here comes Another, who hath been formerly an Old *Egyptian*, shall he step in before us *Israelites*? Yea, those Wise Virgins there (our Old Companions) have had but a very little Time, wherein to shew their being Better than our selves; why then are we so hardly dealt with? But Christ will Answer, How Bold are you, thus to Reply, *Rom.* 9. 20. or Bind my Hand, *Mat.* 20. 15? These few Wise Virgins came in Time, so did not you: Those Younger ones have not been Tried, as you have been: However, I have told you, *Mat.* 8. 11, 12. that many shall be Admitted, (yea, some *Egyptians* and *Assyrians*, *Isa.* 19. 23.) when such as you shall be Cast out.

11. Considering the Matter of their Request. Lord (will these say) did we Desire a Dispensation to Transgress, or did we onely beg some outward Mercy, then might we Justly be Repulsed: But we Intreat Communion with thy self, and with thy People; and hast thou not Promised to give thy Spirit (or Spiritual Good things) to them that ask him, *Luke* 11. 13? But Christ will Answer, That Promise is onely made to Children: And Promises are onely sure in Me, 2 *Cor.* 1. : 0. whom they who are without, are therefore Strangers from the Promises, *Eph.* 2. 12. save as the Spirit is Promised unto such as do Return at my Reproof, *Prov.* 1. 23. Nor do you so much desire Communion with my People, as with their Priviledges.

12. Considering the Earnestness of their Desire; which doth evince their being Cordial and Affectionate. Lord (will these say, as sometimes *Job* did to his Friends) Look upon us, for it is evident, if we Lie, *Job* 6. 28. Our Coming, and our Pleading intimate that we are serious: Now, will not our Sighs and Tears Affect thine Heart? Yea, hast thou not Engaged to be found, when searched for, with all our Heart, *Jer.* 29. 13? But Christ will Answer, Not simply upon that Account, save as Men seek me Early also, *Prov.* 8. 17. *Esau* would fain have had the Blessing, and sought it carefully with Tears, but was Rejected,

The Parable of the Ten Virgins Opened. 243

jected, *Heb.* 12. 17. because he came too Late, though with Right Venison, *Gen.* 27. 33.

13. Considering the Manner of their present Supplication. Lord (will these say) we do not offer to Enforce a Passage, but onely stand here knocking at the Door: Nor do we call to others, but do desire of Thee, to be Admitted with thy Leave: Nor do we Claim it as our Right, but Humbly Beg it as a Favour. To which it will be Answered, You know 'tis but a Folly (Now) to be Disorderly, as heretofore, else is your Spirit still the same. The Gates of Hell cannot prevail against this Door, *Mat.* 16. 18. Nor will the present Porters Open without mine Order, *Ezek.* 44. 9. and as your Case will not permit a Claim, so neither will your Conscience suffer it; yea, Interest alone doth make you (in Appearance) Humble.

14. Considering the Ingenuousness of their Profession; imported by that Title [*Lord*] which they Now give to Christ. Lord (will these say,) we Now acknowledge thee to be our Lord: We do profess Subjection to thy Laws: Nor shall we henceforth Disobey thee, onely this once forgive our sin, as *Pharaoh* Pleaded, *Exod.* 10. 17. But Christ will Answer, *Not every one that saith, Lord, Lord, shall enter into this Heavenly Kingdom, but he that doth my Father's Will,* Mat. 7. 21. Nor are you better than your Predecessors, *Rom.* 3. 9. who did but Flatter with their Mouth, *Psal.* 78. 36. and Hasten their Destruction by Hypocrisie, *Isa.* 29. 13, 14. all which befell them for Ensample, 1 *Cor.* 10. 11. However Now, the Door is shut.

15. Considering his Graciousness, whom they have Now to Argue with. Lord (will these say at their Last plea,) we do confess thy Sovereignty; but can't thou not evince that, in a way of Mercy, if thou pleaseth, *Rom.* 9. 18? Is not thy Grace Designed for Supremacy in Gospel-times, *Eph.* 1. 6? And will Christ fall therefrom at Last? How can the shutting of thy Door upon us consist with having no Pleasure in our Death, *Ezek.* 33. 11. or thy Delight in shewing Mercy, *Mic.* 7. 18? But Christ will Answer, My Tarrying for you all this while doth witness the Truth of what you say; but Grace hath had its Time, and I have other Attributes to shew the Glory of. However, the Door is shut; my word is past, which must be Magnified more than Sovereignty, Grace, or any other Syllable of my Name, *Psal.* 138. 2. And therefore Now (in brief) *I know you not.*

Quest. 4. What seemeth to be meant by those words, *Verily I say, I know you not?*

Answ. 1. Negatively; Not but that Christ doth know them, in some sence, unto their sorrow; and which They Now shall know, *Rev.*

2.23. He knoweth *Ephraim*, and *Israel* is not hid from him, *Hos.* 5.3. He knows their Manifold Transgressions, and their Mighty sins, *Amos* 5.12. He knoweth (as a Witness) all their Lying words, which he hath not Commanded them, *Jer.* 29.23. He knows the things that come into their Mind, yea, every one of them, *Zech.* 11. 5. He knoweth their Imagination which they go about, even Now before it comes to pass, *Deut.* 31.21. He knoweth they are *Abraham's* Seed, according to the Flesh, *John* 8.37. but yet he also knows, they have not the Love of God in them, *John* 5.42. whatever shew thereof they seem to make, *Ezek.* 33.31.

II. Affirmatively. He doth not know them in a Comfortable sence;

1. He doth (at least) not fully know them, unto satisfaction; as the *Greek* word there used signifieth, 2 *Cor.* 5.1. and that other word, *Mat.* 7.23. compared with *John* 6.69. which also is the same with this, *Luke* 13. 27. Their Voice is *Jacob's*, but their Hands are *Esau's*; and in that Case Christ will not Bless, as *Isaac* did, without Discerning, or certain knowledge, *Gen.* 27.22,23. He doth not know them, as he did *Abraham*, by having made a Trial of their Holy Fear, *Gen.*22. 12. or by his having ever known a Practice suitable to this Profession. Nor is it to be wondred at, they are so altered (Now) from what they sometimes were, at their first going out; and it is so long since he ever saw them, or hath Heard of them till Now.

2. He doth not know them so, as to allow them, or their Practices: In which sence *Paul* knew not (as it is in the *Greek* and Margin) what he did not allow, *Rom.* 7.15. Reprobate Silver shall Men call them, because the Lord will then Reject them, *Jer.* 6.30. Their best Performances will (then) not be allowed of, but will be called Iniquity, *Mat.* 7.23. Their Persons are unclean by having Touched a Dead Body; therefore so are their Offerings, and every of their other works, *Hag.* 2.13,14. They will be now stayed for insufficiency, when putting up their Supplicate for a Degree in Glory. And how will they Gnash their Teeth, as did those Jews, *Acts* 7.54. when they were called uncircumcised, *v.* 51. while Christ stood Looking on, *v.* 55.

3. He will not know them, so as to Love them: As they who Love not, do not know the Lord, 1 *John* 4.8. or as his Sheep are known by Laying down his Life for them, *John* 10.14,15. He will not have any special favour for them, as for others, who will be in his Books, *Rev.* 3.5. Nay, his Rebuking and Chastising Love (to such) doth seem to end with *Laodicean* Churches, *Rev.* 3.19,20. And whom he doth not Love, he Hateth, as he did *Esau*, *Mal.* 1.3. whose Seed (at such

4. As knowing is oft-times p[ut] for Underftanding. Thus, did not the Difciples know, (as it is in the *Greek*,) that which they did not Underftand, *John* 10. 6. and 12. 16. And thus Chrift will then fay, I hear a found of words, but do not feem to Underftand their Meaning. Themfelves are ftrangers, fo will their Language therefore be. They call me Lord, but with an Hollow Voice, or from the Teeth outwards onely. They bid me Open, but do not fpeak diftinctly; I Underftand them not. Now, as the Believer's Happinefs confifteth in Chrift's knowing what the Spirit Meaneth, *Rom.* 8. 27. So when another's fpeech cannot be Underftood, that needs muft Ufher in a being fcattered, as *Gen.* 11. 7, 8.

5. His Abfolute Difowning of any former Acquaintance with them, as is more plainly fignified, *Mat.* 7. 23. *I Never* knew you. This will Deftroy their fometime Hope of having had a fpecial work of Grace upon them. Chrift's having *Never* known Back-fliders here, and their not having *Ever* known the Lord, 1 *John* 3. 6. are two unanfwerable Arguments to Prove, that none do finally and wholly fall from Gofpel-Grace, And if poor *Cain*'s Countenance fell, upon his Prefent Non-acceptance, *Gen.* 4. 5. much more will Theirs, when All their By-paft Duty is Rejected. And when the whole Houfe comes down, (as having been laid upon a Sandy Bottom) how Great muft be the Fall thereof, *Mat.* 7. 26, 27 ?

6. His being Refolved to Deny them, as was *Nabal*, when begging *David* had that Anfwer, I know not whence you are, 1 *Sam.* 25. 11. juft as Chrift (elfe-where) telleth Thefe, *Luke* 13. 25. 27. Now, if it is faid to have been Roughly fpoken by *Jofeph* to his Brethren, in putting that Queftion, *Whence come ye*, *Gen.* 42. 7? much more thus pofitively to Determine it for fuch a Purpofe. They fometime knew not whence he was, *John* 8. 14. elfe would they have Believed in him: And Now he knows not whence They are; therefore they fhall not be Relieved by him. So that, (in brief,) there will be no Door of hope to fuch, when once this Door is fhut, and their ungrounded Exercife of Hope, will therefore be the more Confounding, *Job.* 6. 20.

7. Thefe words import a Pofitive Sentence, as well as Privative. Thus.

1. By a Direct (or Natural) Confequence. Known unto God are

are all his Works, *Acts* 15. 18. and then whose work are They, whom he Denies the knowledge of? He knoweth who are His, 2 *Tim.* 2. 19. Such then (by Consequence) are the Devil's, whom he knoweth not. His Sheep are known by him, *John* 10. 27. though yet uncalled, *v.* 16. therefore such are not His, (so much as by Election,) whom he knoweth not. His having no Pleasure in Apostates, *Heb.* 10. 38. Implieth Hating; his Not Commanding, *Jer.* 7. 31. Implies Abhorring: Such kind of Negatives are sad Diminutives, Implying more (by far) than is exprest. Thus will his word be Magnified (both unto Saints and Sinners) by its being much surpassed in Performances.

2. By our Observing what doth Accompany these words [*I know you not*] both in this place, and other Parallel Scriptures.

1. With Respect unto the Positive Matter (elsewhere) Added hereunto. 'Tis onely (here) Privatively said, I know you not: But other-where 'tis said, *Depart from me*, Mat. 7. 23. *and into Everlasting Fire, Prepared for the Devil and his Angels*, Mat. 25. 41. Those whom Christ knoweth not, are bid *Depart*; not being suffered to continue (so much as) Begging at his Door: And thus the Hypocrite's Hope shall perish, *Job* 8. 13. Nor must they onely Depart from Christ, but into Everlasting Fire; and who (among Them) shall Dwell with Everlasting Burnings, *Isa.* 33. 14? And if that Fire had onely been Prepared for Them, it might have been Less Hot; but they must Now be fellow-Commoners with the Devils.

2. With reference to the Persons speaking and spoken To; I say to you, This shall be Now Received, not as the Word of Man, but as it is in Truth, the Word of God; which therefore needs must be Effectual, 1 *Thes.* 2. 13. *I, who know All things*, John 21. 17. *Know not you: I, who am Master of the House*, Luke 13. 25. *bid you Depart, v.* 27. *I, who have also the Keys of Hell*, Rev. 1. 18. *bid you Go into everlasting Punishment.* Thus he who formerly was a Lamb, *John* 1. 29. will now roar as a Lion, *Amos* 1. 2. and then, who will not Fear, Amos 3. 8? Nor would his Roaring be so Dreadful, if he had onely now to deal with Beasts: But I thus say to you, who have been Virgins, in Communion with the Wise, full of Good works, *&c.* this breeds the gnawing Worm.

3. Considering the Manner of Christ's speaking this.

1. With an Angry Appellation, *Depart ye Cursed*, Mat. 25. 41. *Workers of Iniquity*, Mat. 7. 23. If he and they might Part in Love, it would be less Afflicting; but he will now speak to them in his wrath, *Psal.* 2. 5. and which these Titles Evidence. Instead of Owning any Former Duty, he will now call them Workers of Iniquity, as *David* did

The Parable of the Ten Virgins Opened.

did some Professors in his time, when God had heard his Prayer, *Psal.* 6.8. And he who biddeth Saints to Bless their Cursers, and Pray for their Despitefull Users, *Luke* 6.28. will now (Himself) Curse them who seem to Bless him, at least, to Pray unto him. Thus will the Happiest of them be Accursed, *Isa.* 65.20. and this will be the Top-stone of their Sorrow, to be thus persecuted in his Anger, *Lam.* 3. 65, 66.

2. With an Emphatical Asseveration, Ἀμὴν, *Verily*. Which (in relation to his Not Knowing them) denotes the Certainty of his sad Ignorance; and so the same word, *Mat.* 16.28. is Elsewhere rendred, *Of a Truth*, *Luke* 9.27. And with respect unto the Residue of their Sentence, it importeth, Partly, his sad Assenting thereunto, as 1 *Cor.* 14.16. Partly, his wishing it to be so, as *Mat.* 6.13. And in Relation to them Both, the Vehemency of his Spirit in this uttering of his Mind, as *Mat.* 5.26. and 8.10. and 10.15. Thus will there be no room for Questioning the Truth of what is thus Asserted: nor yet for Hope, as to the Reversing of their Sentence; nor yet for standing any longer before this Angry and Protesting Judge.

3. In a way of serious Deliberation; as that [*I say*] importeth, *Mat.* 16.18. *Luke* 7.47. *Job.* 3.3. Words spoke in Haste are apt to be Repented of, *Mat.* 21.29: but Judgment is an Everlasting bottom, *Hos.* 2.19. and *saying* implyeth Judgement. You say, *Lord, Lord*, as if you knew me, but verily I say, I know not you: nor do I speak this Rashly, or in a sudden Passion, or upon fallible Grounds; but upon due Advice and Consultation. Thus doth the Lord bid, Say to your Brethren, *Ammi*, and to your Sisters *Ruhamah*, I own them not, *Hos.* 2.1,2: and thus saith the *Amen*, (to *Laodicean* Churches and Professors,) *I will spew you out*, *Rev.* 3.14, 16. This saying to them (as before,) will Lock and Bolt and Barr the Door for ever.

Quest. 5. Why is Christ so Inexorable at this Time?

Answ. 1. Because it is a day of Judgement, *Rev.* 11.18; though not That Day, 2 *Tim.* 4.8. or the Great Day, *Jude* 6. nor that Great Day of *Jezreel*, *Hos.* 1.11. or of the Literal *Jews* Conversion, *Rev.* 16.14: but yet 'tis somewhat Like them both; a Taste whereof hath been already given, *Rev.* 6.17. *Act.* 2.16.20. Now Wrath and Judgement goe Together; yea, Judgement without Mercy, *Jam.* 2. 13. or Respect of Persons, 1 *Pet.* 1.17. as is to be observed in all former Dispensations of that Nature. When once the Deluge was begun, no Crying out would save the Life of any One, *Gen.* 7... nor was there any Mercy to be shewn, to such as staid in Old *Jerusalem*, at such a time, *Jer.* 21.7. so will it be, with reference to such like Future days of Judgement.

2. Because these Foolish Virgins Case is very Heynous.

1. They are Virgins, or Professors; which sadly Aggravateth Sin and Punishment. Such had drawn nigh to God: and therefore *Nadab* and *Abihu* had no Mercy, *Lev.* 10. 1, 2, 3. Such hath God Known of all the Families of the Earth; and therefore These must signally be Punished, *Amos* 3. 2. such have been Leaders unto others in their Sin, *Mal.* 2. 8. who therefore Now are most severely dealt with, *v.* 9. Little do many think, how much the Garment of their Profession is like to Cost them, if that be tattered or Defiled. Darkness is blackest unto those who lately came from a Lightsome place: and after a Prolonged Summer-season, when it once sets in Rain, Fair-weather is at an End; so will it be with Virgins, as with *Haman*, *Esth.* 6. 13.

2. Their Present failing is not Circumstantial, but very High as to its Matter. That Notion of Religious Circumstances, (if Commanded by the Lord,) hath ever been Erroneous, and the Betrayer of many Souls into Perdition. Thus *Israel* fancyed, their Not Going up to *Canaan* (at such a Time,) was but a Circumstantial failing at the most; as their Resolving on it (Afterwards) evinced, *Numb.* 14. 40. but to their Ruine, *v.* 45. which Failing also kept the rest from Entring into it for Ever, *v.* 30. And thus Complyers with the Man of Sin, have call'd their Failing Circumstantial, which yet hath alway been the Badge of Reprobation, *Rev.* 13. 8. Christ hath no Witnesses save with respect unto Time-Truths and Duties: wherein these Foolish Virgins fail, and so are guilty of Denying him.

3. The Manner of their Sin is more than Ordinarily provoking. They had been oft Reproved to no purpose, and that forerun's remediless Destruction, *Prov.* 29. 1. They had Relapsed a second Time; and Trees twice dead, are pluckt up by the Roots, *Jude* 12. But more Especially they have persisted in their Evil way, untill the End of Christ's intended Patience, or till the Door be shut: and then a Less Transgression is sufficient to make their Plea of none Effect. Let Persons (at this Day) beware of letting slip a present Opportunity, by trusting unto future Resolutions. Those trifling *Israelites* were free (at Last) to marc and Fight, *Deut.* 1. 41: but it was then too Late. The Timelines of Man's Return is as Essentially required to Admission, as the Act it self.

4. These come with too much Confidence: but without being sensible of former failings. They call for Opening, but not for Mercy they mourn for Suffering, but not for Sin: Here is a Prayer, but no Confession. As Nature (in *Paul*) was willing to be Cloth'd upon

The Parable of the Ten Virgins Opened.

but not to be Uncloathed, 2 *Cor.* 5. 4: fo Foolifh Virgins are for a Return, without Repentance. But as *John Baptift* bad, *Repent, Mat.* 3. 2. before he would Admit unto his Miniftration, *v.* 8. juft fo did Chrift, *Mat.* 4. 17. elfe future Zeal is not fufficient, fave as it is Accompanyed with Repentance, *Rev.* 3. 19 And out of their Own mouth will fuch be judged, *Luke* 19. 22. who have maintained this with reference unto Others, and yet Themfelves would have a Difpenfation: which doth evince their being felf-condemned, together with the Righteoufnefs of their Exclufion, or Rejection, *Tit.* 3. 10, 11.

Ufe 1. This Parable cannot fo Properly be Applyed (as it is by fome) unto Chrift's Perfonal Coming; fince there will then be no fuch room for Foolifh Virgins Pleading with him, as Here they doe. Then will the Earth, and All therein be burnt up with Material Fire, 2 *Pet.* 3. 10: excepting fome few, as in the Ark of Old, 1 *Pet.* 3. 20. and None of which will then come Afterwards (as doe thefe Foolifh Virgins) untill Chrift's Reign is Ended, *Rev.* 20; 5. fo that we either muft refer this to fome other coming, or offer violence unto the Proper Meaning of thefe words. Whereas his Coming with the feventh Trumpets founding, will fairly admit of fuch a Parley, and Prefently upon his being come, as is here fignified. Yet I exclude not his Laft comeing (wholly) from a fhare herein, fo far as it is Capable thereof, or without ftraining.

2. Poor Foolifh Virgins will not Come, untill the Door be fhut: but then fuch may be looked for. This will be the righteous Wages of Carnal Prudence: Thus he that feeketh to fave, fhall Loofe, *Mat.* 16. 25. Chrift hath fore-told it here, that none might be Offended, as *Joh.* 16. 1. and therefore will their Cafe be fad who Tarry for the Other Virgins company. This doth confirm mine Old Perfwafion, that few profeffing *Jews* will find this way untill 'it be too Late, *Mat.* 7. 14. But then fuch will Return, with Open Mouths, unto a Door that will be fhut againft them. I fee what Hafte poor Muck-wet Creatures made unto the Ark, when God had once fhut *Noah* in, *Gen.* 7. 16. and how thofe Eight fecured Souls did then Rejoyce, whileft Others were foon wafht away.

3. Thofe may know Chrift, and give him Goodly Words, yea feek to Enter; whom yet He will not Know, nor Open unto. Some kind of Knowledge doth not Edifie, 1 *Cor.* 8. 1. *Dives* in Hell Knew *Abraham*, but not to his Advantage, *Luke* 16. 23. to fhew how far unprofitable Notions may Accompany. Such alfo (then) will be for fmoother Language, not Daring to Infult, as Heretofore; prepare for Flattery, which yet will not Prevail. Yea fuch will be Diffatisfied in their Diftance

stance from the Wiser Virgins, earnestly Desiring to Build with them, as *Ezra* 4. 2. but will be shamefully Repulsed, as they were, *v.* 3. and yet will not be Able (then) to do the Other any Mischief, as of Old, *v.* 4. for fear of that Decree and Curse at such a Time, *Ezra* 6. 8. 11, 12.

4. Christ is not All made up of Mercy, as some poor Creatures fansie; but Can (yea, Will) give Terrible words, and unto Virgins as well as Others. He sometimes was a Patient Lion; but he will be a Roaring Lamb: Yea he was alway for an Intermixture of Threatnings with Encouragements. I am Offended with some mens Humours, who are Afraid to give one Cutting word unto this Rotten-hearted Generation of Professors, and have observed what hath been the fruit of Dawbing with untempered Morter. But this will Aggravate Christ's Rougher speaking at the last: and it will then appear, how far himself is Bound (from the Necessity of his Nature) to be Gracious. Christ onely now Reserveth Anger, *Nah.* 1. 2. which therefore at the Last will turn into the Plague, or when the Vials shall be poured forth, *Rev.* 15. 7, 8.

5. Christ will then have the Last word, in Discourse; as is here signified by their not Replying to his Answer. Thus will himself be Glorified, as was *Job*, when After his words they did not speak Again, *Job* 29. 22. The *Pharisees* were oft wont to Prate, untill Christ put a Question to them concerning his being *David*'s Lord, *Mat.* 22. 45. and then 'tis said, they neither could Answer him, nor durst they Ask him any more Questions, *v.* 46. to signifie how Silencing that God-like Kingly State will be, when it shall be Advanced. The Dispensation (or Appearing) of this King, will be Evinced by the speechlesness of those unworthy ones whom he Reproveth, *Mat.* 22. 11, 12. Errour and Sin may Now be full of words; but Then all Flesh is bid, be silent, *Zech.* 2. 13. yea all the Earth, *Hab.* 2. 20.

MATTHEW XXV. 13.

Watch therefore, for ye know neither the Day, nor the Hour wherein the Son of Man cometh.

IN this Verse, we have an Account of Christ's Design in putting forth this Parable; or of that principal use which he would have us make thereof, *viz.* Our being *Watchfull.* From whence, the General Observation is as followeth;

Observ. *Since we Know not the Day or Hour in which the Son of Man will come, we therefore ought to be upon our Watch.*

Quest. 1. Why doth Christ call himself the *Son of Man*, with reference unto his Coming in these Latter dayes?

Answ. 1. To declare his being still a Man, though now Ascended; and that his Coming *(*at the Last*)* will be in the Humane Nature also. Some would fain have him turn'd into a Spirit; though he that is now Ascended, is also He who first Descended into the Grave, *Eph.* 4. 10. which is not Applicable to the Spirit of Man, *Eccl.* 3. 21. Others will grant him (as a Man) to be Ascended, but not that he will *(so)* Return; and yet 'tis said, He shall *so Come,* and in *like Manner*, as he was seen to goe, *Act.* 1. 11. And though his Coming (in this Parable*)* will mainly be in a Mystical sence; yet will it be the coming of the Son of Man, though not his coming As a Man (or in his Person, till Afterwards *(*save as some Man (or Men) may Represent him Now, as *Hezekiah* did of Old, *Isa.* 32. 1, 2.

2. To shew the Nature of his Kingly Dispensation (at such a time) in point of Visibility and Temporality; which is most Aptly shaddowed out by his (then*)* coming As the Son of Man. His Ecclesiastical and Spiritual Kingdom was set up at first: besides both which he had Another Kingdom Then, though it was not Immediately to Appear, *Luke* 19. 11; which therefore must be Temporal. ' Now that which is meerly Spiritual, is fitlyest resembled by the Soul; as Christ *(* with reference unto his spiritual Kingdom*)* is called the Shepherd of his Peoples Souls, 1 *Pet.* 2. 25. but that which is Temporal, by the Man. Thus *David's* Temporal Rule was over Men, 2 *Sam.* 23. 3. and as Christ (at his Personal coming) is called a Man, *Act.* 17. 31. so with respect

unto the *Assyrians* coming before that time, this Man (*'tis said*) shall be the Peace, *Mic.* 5. 5.

3. To shew the Greatness of his Humility. He was God's Equal upon Earth, *Phil.* 2. 6; and he (as Man) is far above the Angels Now, *Heb.* 1. 13; yet doth he style himself the Son of Man. He will Then have that Name [*the King of Kings*] upon his Thigh, *Rev.* 19. 16; but in his Mouth, the Son of Man, which is a Worm, *Job* 25. 6. Thus was *Ezekiel* oft-times called, to make him Humble; and thus Christ did as often call himself, to shew, that he is so. When *Israel* was come into the Land of *Canaan*, they kept no more the Feast of Tabernacles, (or the Memorial of their former Low Condition,) till *Nehemiah's* time, but Then it was revived, *Neh.* 8. 17. which Dispensation was a Type of this: And when that self-abasing Feast shall Mystically be Observed in these latter dayes, then shall men thereby know, that Verily the Son of Man is come.

4. To hint (perhaps) the Meanness of his First appearing in these Latter dayes; according to the Constant Purport of that Phrase, [*the Son of Man*,] yea with respect to Christ himself, *Heb.* 2. 6. That as Himself, who Truely was the Son of Man, is onely said to have been Like him Afterwards, *Rev.* 1. 13. (he is so Altered (Now) from what he (sometime) was:) so will it be, with reference to his Dispensation. He will (at Last) come, as the Son of Man, *Mat.* 24. 30; because the Whole of his Own Personal Reign will be but Mean, compared with the Father's Kingdom Afterwards, 1 *Cor.* 15. 28. And so may his Precursory coming here, be fitly called, that of the Son of Man, because it will be Mean, compared with his Personal, when he shall Gloriously appear as God, *Tit.* 2. 13. or in the Glory of his Father, *Mat.* 16. 27.

5. To signifie (perhaps) the great Humanity, or Familiarity of his Conversing with the Sons of Men (excepting some) at his Appearing. His Enemies indeed will be then Burnt up round about, *Psal.* 97. 3. but yet his Anger will cease in their Destruction, *Isa.* 10. 25. and he will then Rest in his Love, *Zeph.* 3. 17. He did Approve himself (on Earth) to be the Son of Man, by suffering his Disciples to 'Ask him any thing, *Joh.* 15. 15. to sit with him at Meat, *Joh.* 13. 18.; Yea, by his Rising to Wait on them, *v.* 4, 5. and so will it be Now. Therefore Christ bids his people Ask of him, at such a time, *Isa.* 45. 11: and they shall then sit with him, *Rev.* 3. 21. yea, he will then Rise and Serve them, *Luke* 12. 37. This King of Glory will not be stately; but as Himself at Last, so he Now in his People, will Affably appear to All, or as the Son of Man.

Quest. 2.

The Parable of the Ten Virgins Opened.

Quest. 2. Why is that called the *Coming of Christ*, which yet ('tis thought) will be so long before his Personal or Proper Coming?

Answ. Because of the full Resemblance that is between them, as may be thus made out.

1. With respect unto the Signs of Both. Christ's Personal Coming will be notified by many Signs, both in the Sun, and Moon, and Stars, and Earth, and Sea, and Powers of Heaven, *Luke* 21. 25, 26: so will This Coming be. We have had wonderfull signs of such a Nature (and in the Letter) of Later years; though we Now see them not, *Psalm.* 74. 9. And in the Mystery yet more Abundantly. The Scriptures (fitly answering to the Sun, or Fountain of Created Light) have been extreamly Darkned, as *Mat.* 24. 29; and more especially some Part thereof. And that which Borroweth its Light from thence (or Moonlike Preaching) hath been turn'd into Blood, as *Joel* 2. 31. at least not given her Light, *Mat.* 24. 29. Church-Officers are called Stars, *Rev.* 1. 20; and these have sadly fallen, *Mat.* 24. 29; at least withdrawn their shining, *Joel* 3. 15. The Earth (or Civil State of things) hath oft-times Quaked. The Sea (or Many Waters) denoteth People, *Rev.* 17. 15; whose Waves have roared. The Powers of Heaven also, (or of the Churches) have been shaken.

2. With reference unto the state of things Immediately foregoing Both. *Elijah* must goe before the Coming of that Great and Terrible Day, *Mal.* 4. 5. and such a Messenger must Prepare Christ's way into his Temple, *Mal.* 3. 1 ; something Like unto which our Eyes have seen. Christ's Personal Coming will be ushered in with great Oppressions and all manner of Wickedness, *Mat.* 24. 29 : so will his Present coming be ; by means of Hypocritical Professors first, and the *Assyrian* afterwards, *Isa.* 10. 5, 6. Yet will all sorts of sinners, Then, be Carelefs or secure, 1 *Thess.* 5. 3. so will they Now, both in *Jerusalem*, *Isa.* 32. 9. and in the Isles of *Magog*, *Ezek.* 39. 6. But they will Then be Generally destroyed, 2 *Pet.* 3. 10. so will they Now, as by an Earthquake, Immediately foregoing it, *Rev.* 11. 13, 15.

3. With reference unto the Manner of both these Comings. His Personal coming will be with the Last Trump of all, 1 *Cor.* 15. 52 : and This will be with the Last Trump of seven, *Rev.* 11. 15. That coming will be with a Glorious Train of Saints and Angels, 2 *Thess.* 1. 7. 10. and so will This with a Glorious Change of Church-Members, *Isa.* 4. 3, 4. and Church-Officers, *Zech.* 3. 4, 5. who are oft-times called Angels. That coming will be on a sudden, 1 *Thess.* 5. 3 : and so will This, *Rev.* 3. 3. and 11. 14. That Coming will be with Clouds, *Mat.* 24. 30. and so will This, *Psal.* 97. 2. both in the Letter and

Mystery.

Mystery. That Coming will be with a shout, 1 Thes.4.16. and wailing, Rev. 1.7. just so will This, with reference unto a Diverse sort of Persons then, Rev. 11. 17, 18. and 18, 19, 20.

4. VVith reference to the Effects (and Principal Designed Ends) of both. He will [Then] raise the Dead, John 5. 28, 29. So will he [Now] Revive his VVork, Hab. 3. 2. and People, Isa. 26. 19. as to their Joy, Psal. 85. 6. He will [Then] Reign, and all his Servants with him, Rev. 20. 4. So will he [Now] Rev. 11. 15. 17. before his Ancients Gloriously, Isa. 24. 23. He will [Then] Judge the Quick and Dead at his Appearing, or at his Kingdom, 2 Tim. 4. 1. So will he Now, Rev. 11. 18. He will then Bind the Devil, Rev. 20. 2. and Satan will be Rebuked by him Now, Zech. 3. 2. whose wrath (a little before) will therefore be the Greater, as of Old, Rev. 12. 12. That Personal Coming will bring Rest unto the Saints, 2 Thes. 1. 7. and so will This, Isa. 10. 27. and 33. 20.

5. VVith reference to what will follow both a long while after their Beginning. Christ's Personal Reign will be a Thousand Years, Rev. 20. 4. and This Dominion is (in some Respect) for Ever, or Everlasting, Dan. 7. 27. That Coming will Establish All, in their Respective present states, Rev. 22. 11. and so will This, as to the Generality of Old Professors, viz. the VVise and Foolish Virgins, Dan. 12. 10. But Satan will be Loosed Then at Last, Rev. 20. 7, 8. So will he Now, as is Apparent from his being Bound (a little after) for a longer Time, Rev. 20. 2. And as there will be [Then] a further Resurrection, Rev. 20. 12. so will the Literal Jews be Now Converted, Rev. 16. 12. or Raised from the Dead, Rom. 11. 15. And as Christ's Personal Kingdom [then] will be given up unto the Father, 1 Cor. 15. 24. So will the Saints Dominion [Now] be given up unto the Son.

6. With reference unto the signal Property of both, viz. the Concealment of that very Time, wherein they will begin: which (in Relation to them Both) is here asserted, and other-where, Psal. 74. 9. Mat. 24. 36. 42. Mark 13. 33. 35. 52. This leadeth me to the Next Enquiry.

Quest. 3. What is the Meaning of these words, *Ye know not the Day or Hour?*

Answ. 1. It cannot be Denied, but that the Apostles themselves are Primarily intended (here) by that word, *Ye*, whom Christ Directeth this speech unto, in Answer to their fore-going Questions, Mat. 24. 3. Now, these Apostles were very Ignorant, in that particular yea, notwithstanding what Christ had Newly said: As is apparent both from his Present Affirmation of it Here, and from their Question afterwards, implying their sudden Expectation of it, Acts 1. 6. Whose being

being Ignorant thereof at such a Time, may yet consist with their more clearly knowing it afterwards, and Others also, or since *John* had his Revelations, and the Spirit's giving forth, *John* 16.13. yet were These (in Their Day) concerned to Watch, though onely with Respect unto the Near approaching Ruine of *Jerusalem*, which was an Emblem of Christ's Coming, which *John* Lived to see, John 21.22. and which are therefore intermingled, both in the Disciples Question, and Christ's Answer, *Luke* 21.7.12.20.24,25.27.32.

2. By this word [*Ye*] may be intended the Generality of Disciples afterwards, as is Evinced by Christ's saying, John 13.10. *Ye are clean*, (that is, Generally) but not All, that is, excepting *Judas* in Particular. And so this may import the General Ignorance (of such a Mystery) among Professors in following times, which yet may be consistent with a Clearer Discovery thereof to some Particular Persons; and more especially towards the End. Thus none of the Wicked (at such a time) shall Understand, *Dan.* 12.10. but all the Vision will be (to such) a sealed Book, *Isa* 29.11. so that no Man or Counsellor will Answer a word, *Isa.* 41.28. But yet the Wise shall Understand, *Dan* 12.10. and there will be some First (or Chief one) with Good Tiding of that Kind, *Isa.* 21.27.

3. This may be Universally Interpreted: and so, No Man doth Know.

1. When Christ's Personal Coming will be, nor yet the Angels, *Mat.* 24.35. neither the Son of Man himself, *Mark* 13.32. Which Personal Coming is not wholly (here) to be Excluded; and so that sometime is applyed to the whole, or both, *Mat.* 27.44. which yet is onely Meant, with reference unto the one, *Luke* 23.39. And so there may (perhaps) be some more full Discovery, (though it be little Understood) as to Christ's Coming with the Seventh Trumpet's Sounding; because there is a seeming Series of Mystical Numbers (in the Scripture) continued beyond that time, or till the Jews Conversion, as some conceive. But after which time, (*viz.* the literal Jews Conversion) no Sober Persons do Pretend to any such kind of Mystical Numbers, till Christ himself shall Come in Person.

2. Yet neither is that former Coming known by any Man.

1. In Respect of Punctuality, *viz.* the very Day and Hour, as is here Expressed; and wherein (possibly) the Emphasis may lye. *Israel's* Deliverance out of *Egypt* was fulfilled unto a Day, *Exod.* 12. 41. whereas their coming out of *Babylon*, is onely said to be in such a Year, 2 *Chron.* 36.21,22. And therefore Gentile-Saints may not Expect to know the very Day of their Redemption out of *Babylon* in
the

The Parable of the Ten Virgins Opened.

the Myſtery, (much leſs out of *Aſſyria* Afterwards) ſince this would not be granted to the Jews of Old, who yet are firſt, in point of Outward Priviledges, *Rom.* 3. 1, 2. But as the *Aſſyrian's* Fall was ſignified (as ſome conceive) within the Compaſs of a Year, 2 *Kings* 19. 29. and which fell out that very Night, *v.* 35. So Time will ſhew the Meaning of thoſe Ten Prophetical Days allotted unto Satan, *Rev.* 2. 10. whoſe Name is never mentioned in a Revelation ſence, but either before the *Babyloniſh* Beaſt came up, *Rev.* 12. 9. or after the Return of that Captivity, *Zech.* 3. 1, 2.

2. Yet will I alſo grant, that no Man knoweth Certainly, (as οἴδατε here uſed ſignifies,) the Moneth or Year, (nor poſſibly a longer time) with reference unto This Coming of the Bridegroom here. King *David's* Diſpenſation was a Type of Chriſt's, *Amos* 9. 11. and though he Knew, or did Believe, that he ſhould ſee the Goodneſs of the Lod (in that Reſpect) before his Death, *Pſal.* 27. 13. yet did he not certainly know the very Year of his Advancement; elſe would he not have fled to *Achiſh*, 1 *Sam.* 27. 2. When *Saul's* Deſtruction was to come in little more than one Year after, *v.* 7. compared with *Chap.* 29. 1. 11. and *Chap.* 31. 1. And thus, not any Man doth know how long; that is to ſay, not as a Prophet, *Pſal.* 74. 9. or in a way of certain and Infallible Knowledge.

Queſt. 4. How cometh This to be ſo great a Secret?

Anſw. 1. Becauſe none certainly doth know where to Begin the Man of Sin's firſt Riſe: Elſe might we certainly know the Ending of his Forty two Moneths, or thoſe One Thouſand two hundred and ſixty Days, *Rev.* 11. 2, 3. and conſequently might give a better Gheſs, as to Chriſt's Coming with the Seventh Trumpet. But the Captivity of Myſtical *Babylon* (therein) Anwereth unto that of Old, which was to continue Seventy Years for certain; yet no Man certainly knew where to begin; elſe would not *Daniel* have been to ſeek ſo Near its End, *Dan.* 9. 1, 2, 3. I am perſwaded the Man of Sin was up, when Marriage was firſt Prohibited, 1 *Tim.* 4. 1. 3. with 2 *Theſ.* 2. 3. which was about the Year Three Hundred and Ninety; and ſo his Forty two Moneths muſt be Expired ſome Years ago: And after which the Earthquake cometh, which uſhereth in the Seventh Trumpet, *Rev.* 11. 13, 14, 15. But few may (yet) be of my Perſwaſion; nor do I pretend unto Infallibility.

2. Becauſe few can Agree who are the Witneſſes, and what their Aſcending intimateth; much leſs do any know for Certain, how long the following Earthquake may continue. I do Believe, the Witneſſes are a very ſmall Number among Profeſſors, who have been Faithful unto

unto THE Truth of such a Time: But most suppose them to be Magistrates and Ministers; though I conceive not how Magistrates (as such) are capable of having Prophesied in a Sack cloath-state. I do believe, the Witnesses Ascending doth import their being Taken out of sight, and their Receiving of a Kingdom, which yet is not immediately to appear, as in Relation to Christ's Ascending, *Luke* 19. 11, 12. But most suppose it to intend their visible Advancement in the World; the failing whereof (at such a late Expected time) hath cast them back again into the Wilderness. However, I dare not pretend to any certain knowledge, as to the Duration of the Earthquake; nor do I know any Man that Doth or May.

3. Because the Dispensation of the Man of Sin is full of Darkness; which therefore is fitly Measured by the Moon or Moneths, *Rev.* 11. 2. with reference unto its Moon-like Light at best. And though Christ's Witnesses have alway had sufficient Light, as to the Testimony of their Day; yet as Professors have Relapsed into such a Spirit again, so have they been (therewith) Benighted, as to their former seeming Light. This is our Case at present. How Evident (of late Years) was our being Near to *Sion*: But being overtaken with a *Babylonish* Mist, we know not (Generally) where we are. And they who daily with their Light, in point of Duty (as the most of Professors have lately done) are justly Blinded or Benighted, as to the Matter of their Peace and Priviledges, *John* 7. 28. *Luke* 19. 42.

4. Because the Generality have no mind to search the Scriptures, nor yet to Ponder what is thence Offered for their Help, in some more difficult cases. *Daniel* understood by Books the Number of the Years of his Captivity, *Dan.* 9. 2. and Prophets (of Old) were wont to search what manner of Time the Spirit of Christ in them did signifie, 1 *Pet.* 1. 10, 11. and thus is Knowledge to be gained, *Prov.* 2. 3, 4, 5. But as there is no fore-telling Prophet toward the End, *Psal.* 74. 9. so neither are there many searching ones: Yea, Ancient Priests (at such a time) before their being laid aside, Reject that Knowledge, for lack of which the People are Destroyed, *Hos.* 4. 6. And as an Hotter Climate disposeth People to be slothful, as in *Sodom*, *Ezek.* 16. 49. so *Israel* in *Egypt* cannot Hearken to Redemption signified, untill they see it, *Exod.* 6. 9.

5. Because the state of things (a little before the End) will be so likely (in an Eye of Reason) to Continue still. Thus was it with *David* in his Time, 1 *Sam.* 27. 1. and so with *Israel* in their Captivity, *Ezek.* 37. 11. as well as *Babylon*, both in the Letter, *Isa.* 47. 8. and Mystery,

Myſtery, *Rev.* 18.7,8. Faith ſees that Promiſe Beſt in Darkeſt Times, becauſe Chriſt Cometh with the Clouds, *Mat.* 24. 30. but Faith will not be found on Earth at ſuch a time, and upon that Account, *Luke* 18. 7, 8. This will Occaſion ſome to ſcoff (in theſe laſt days) at ſuch a Promiſe, for ſince the Fathers fell aſleep, all things (ſay they) continue as they were, 2 *Pet.* 3. 3, 4. and they who grant the Promiſe in the General, will therefore yet ſay to the Laſt, the Time is not yet come, as thoſe of Old, *Hag.* 1. 2.

6. Becauſe the Lord hath Purpoſed, this very Time ſhall not be certainly known by any Man, as is here ſignified; which leadeth to the Next Queſtion.

Queſt. 5. Why hath the Lord ſo Ordered it, as that No Man ſhall Know that Day?

Anſw. 1. To ſhew his Sovereignty, by keeping ſomewhat Secret to Himſelf. His Secret (in the General) is with the Righteous, *Prov.* 3. 32. who are (All of them) Privy Counſellors, Compared with the World, *John* 15. 15. and ſome of his Saints have more Peculiar Secrets hinted to them, *Dan.* 2. 19. theſe are his private Cabal: But as all unrevealed Secrets belong unto the Lord alone, *Deut.* 29. 29. and as ſome of his Judgments are unſearchable, *Rom.* 11. 33. ſo are ſome other things kept ſecret by him till ſuch a Time, *Rom.* 16. 25,26. Thus *Manoah* might not Know that Angels Name, *Judg.* 13. 18. and good *Eliſha* had ſomething Hid from him, 2 *Kings* 4. 27. nor was it for thoſe Apoſtles to Know the Time and Seaſon, which the Father hath put in his own Power, *viz.* this Reſtauration, *Acts* 1. 6, 7.

2. That ſo Chriſt's Coming in theſe Latter Days might Eminently Anſwer unto its being a Type or Sign of his own Perſonal Coming at the laſt. This ſeemeth to be that Sign of the Son of Man, *Mat.* 24. 30. Now, Signs muſt Anſwer unto what is thereby ſignified; and Anſwering in a Chief Reſpect (ſuch as This is) doth hint the Eminency of ſuch a Sign. Therefore *Melchiſedec* was the Higheſt Type of Chriſt, becauſe he was moſt like the Son of God, in that peculiar and moſt ſignal point of Everlaſtingneſs, *Heb.* 7. 1. 3. Some other Diſpenſation (as that of *Babylon*'s Fall, *Iſa.* 13. 10. 13.) might Reſemble Chriſt's Laſt Coming, in ſeveral other Reſpects, *Luke* 21. 25. but Abſolute Secrecy as to the Time, is Eminently reſerved for this Diſpenſation, as being its peculiar Sign.

3. To Exerciſe a Spirit of Enquiry in his moſt Inlightned ones: As God will be Enquired of, with reference unto the Matter of Redemption, *Ezek.* 36. 37. ſo with Reſpect unto the Time thereof, 1 *Pet.* 1. 11. as being of Special uſe, *Jer.* 8. 7. Thus Chriſt oft ſpake in Parables,

bles, to make his Disciples the more Inquisitive, and to bring Hidden Matters before this Altar, 1 *Kings* 8. 31. Those do Mistake his Drift, who argue from a Secrecy, unto their being bound from searching into it, save when that search is absolutely Forbidden, as *Judg.* 13. 18. *Johns Revelations* are full of Mysteries; yet Blessed is he who Reads that Book, *Rev.* 1. 3. Thus are we taught to Aim at that Perfection, which yet is unattainable, at least not Actually (or Already) apprehended, *Phil.* 3. 11, 12.

4. Else that (Immediately foregoing) Hour of Temptation, would be no Trial in comparison; which yet it is Intended for, *Rev.* 3. 10, 11. It is there call'd an *Hour*, to keep from sinking: but yet that Hour, is the same with those *Ten Dayes*, *Rev.* 2. 10. to make it Trying. In case, Late Persecutions should Now Expire, the Certain foreknowledge of so short a Time would have Prevented (probably) that which its being Hidden hath Experimented. But *Abraham's* being Ignorant, how long he might have been without his *Isaac*, was that which Tempted him unto the height, *Gen.* 22. 1. 12. though he was onely Exercised with a meer Affrightment, and but of three dayes Continuance, *v.* 4. and this made way for that Affectionate Blessing afterwards, in way of seeming Righteousness, *v.* 15, 16, 17, 18.

5. Else would not Others be secure, as they must be, at such a Time, *Luke* 21. 35; but in the sight of any Bird, the Net is spread in vain, *Prov.* 1. 17. some cannot Dig, *Luke* 16. 3. as they must doe for Hidden Treasures, *Prov.* 2. 4. yea they are Glad of such a Plea for Slothfulness, who therefore Justly meet with Parables, *Mat.* 13. 13. But with respect unto self-preservation, no good man of the House would suffer it to be broken through, in case he Knew what Hour the Thief would come, *Luke* 12. 39. Now if this Day had Clearly been Revealed in the Scripture, it then might have been Known, unto the Cherishing of a sleighty Spirit in some, untill the last preceding Minute, whom Christ will not so Gratifie; and therefore *John* wondred, who had forewarned such, as to His Day, *Mat.* 3. 7.

6. Else would none Watch; as Christ here signifies: whereof more Afterwards.

Quest. Why is the Day (here) set before the Hour ? Since in a way of Accurate and more Emphatical Speech, it might have run, *Ye know not the Hour, nor yet the Day*; or not some longer time, before that very Hour ?

Ans. 1. To Check (perhaps) that over-much Curiosity (or Exactness) in Discourse, which may be too much the matter of some men's Care; the Want of which in others is oft-times Childishly carped at; and (in

Themselves) is sinfully Afflicting. Too much of some Men's Time is spent in Starching, which is one Argument of their Effeminacy: and as such are too much Admired; so others are therefore tempted to be silent, because they are not Men of Words, *Exod.* 4. 10. or cannot speak so Well as others, *v.* 14. But though one may seek after Acceptable Words, *Eccl.* 12. 10. Yet *Paul* was not for Curiosity in that respect, 1 *Cor.* 2. 1. whose Speech was therefore Contemptible, 2 *Cor.* 10. 10. nor doth the Spirit of Christ keep unto Grammar-Rules, in many places of Scripture, as when the Nominative Case is oft put Absolute in the *Greek*, *Rev.* 2, 26. and 3. 12. 21.

2. Yet may This Order of the Words be most Emphatical and most Proper.

1. Though we take the word [*Hour*] here, as being Less (by farr) than that word [*Day*] or in the strictest sence imaginable, as *Mat.* 8. 13. and 9. 22. and *Mat.* 20. 6. *Luke* 12. 12. and 24. 33. *Joh.* 4. 52. And so [*an Hour*] may import, the very great suddenness of Christ's Appearing, unto an *Hour*, as well as Day; which addeth Force unto the present Exhortation. His Personal Coming will not be Known, untill that very Moment, 1 *Cor.* 15. 52. nor yet this other Coming, untill the Day, no nor untill its very Hour; which should provoke our being Watchfull. Had we a Day to turn us in, some might presume they should get Ready in a few Hours time: but when they hear, his Coming will not be Known untill that very Hour of its Beginning, those must be sadly Desperate, who do put off that weighty work, untill this Nick of time.

2. If we interpret this word [*Hour*] here, as it is Elsewhere plainly meant,

1. For a sett Appointed Time. Thus did Christ eat the Passover (with his Disciples) when the Hour was come, *Luke* 22. 14, 15; or when the Even was come, *Mat.* 26. 20. which was the set Appointed time, according to the Law, *Deut.* 16. 6. This addes an Emphasis unto the Object of our Ignorance, and Force unto the present Exhortation to be Watchfull; since we Know not the Day, nor the Appointed time, in which the Lord will come. This Coming of Christ (in the latter dayes) is every way Determined or Appointed; both as to the Thing it self, *Zeph.* 3. 8. and as to the very Time thereof, *Hab.* 2. 3. which is of that fore-named use. It is Appointed; therefore it Must be; yea it must therefore be at such a Time: which since we Know not, we had need to VVatch, because it certainly will prove according to Appointment, *Exod.* 9. 5, 6.

2. For

The Parable of the Ten Virgins Opened.

2. For some more signal Time, in point of Terrour. Thus was Christ's Dreadfull Passion call'd an Hour, which he desired (if Possible) might Pass from him, *Mark* 14. 35. or that he might be saved from it, *Joh.* 12. 27. This sence of the word is of the like Import with that before, *viz.* That we had need to VVatch, because we neither know the Day (in point of Time,) nor yet the Dreadfull Nature of it, or that Fatal Hour in which the Lord will Come. VVho would have thought, the God of Love could ever have been so Angry with the whole Creation, *Gen.* 7. 22. especially considering the First Occasion, *Gen.* 6. 2. 7? VVho would have thought, that Christ's first Coming would have proved so Fatal to the *Jews*, *Mal.* 1. 11. No more is This Day Known; therefore in stead of Censuring the Declarers of it, let us VVatch.

3. For some far longer time, than either a Day or Moneth. Thus is the same Greek word (sometime) translated [*Time or Season*] in the general, *Joh.* 16. 2. *Philem.* 15. and it is Elsewhere put for (*certain Years*,) as those Ten Dayes, *Rev.* 2. 10. are called an Hour, *Rev.* 3. 10: yea, it is sometime put to signifie an Age or Dispensation, as when *John* saith, His was the last Time or Hour, (as in the Greek it is) 1 *Joh.* 2. 18. And in this sence, (or as the word (*Hour*) is put for (*certain years*) this Order of the words (here used) is both Proper and Emphatical. If men could be Assured, when this would be, as to some Tolerable space of Time before-hand, they might be tempted thence to Trifle, till Towards the End thereof; but since we know not Certainly, the Day or Year (untill which Time it will not be) we had need VVatch.

Quest. 7. But is it not then unsafe, (at least Imprudent) for any man to hint the possible Nearness of this Time, which is Designed for so great a secret?

Answ. 1. VVe are not Ordinarily so apt to Antedate, as to put far away the Evil-day, *Am.* 6. 3. such as this is: and the Delaying whereof is that which men are commonly most subject unto, *Mat.* 24. 48. and is therefore said to be the Character of Evil Servants. And if I must Needs fall, let me fall rather forwards, (in a Doubtfull Case at least) which is less Dangerous of the Two, as in the Letter, so in the Mystery. And as to Prudence, Christ witnessed on her behalf (and to her Praise) who came Afore-hand with a Memorial of his Resurrection, such as the Anoynting (or Embalming) of his Body was, *Mark* 14. 8. Nor doth it so much favour of worldly Wisdom, to be too forward in a Witness of this Nature, (which is so cross to carnal Interest,) as to hang Back, till Providence hath put the matter out of all Dispute.

2. I.

The Parable of the Ten Virgins Opened.

2. I see no Danger at all in Early Apprehensions of this kind, when they are Duely bounded. Those were Presumptuous, who would Goe up and Fight (at such a time,) directly Cross to an Express Command, *Deut.* 1. 43. but when the Scripture doth not forbid it, we then may safely Hope unto the End of Plausible grounds: especially, if matters of Practice (urged unto) are mainly founded on more substanstantial bottoms. Let any man evince the Interfering of my sober Expectations with the Scripture, and I shall then cease therefrom: but else, the Lord takes pleasure in his Peoples Hope, *Psal.* 147. 11. Nor have I exhorted unto any Present Practice, save what doth seem to be a Duty, how far soever we may be from the Bridegrooms coming.

3. Yet is it Therefore meet we should be very sober in our Conjectures of this Nature: since No man Certainly doth Know how long (at least) the Bridegroom may yet Tarry. And this may partly be intended here; especially since being Sober, is elsewhere joyned with being Watchfull; and in relation to This Coming of our Lord, 1 *Thess* 5. 4, 6. 1 *Pet.* 4. 7. The Nearer he is at Hand, the more should all men Know our Moderation, *Phil.* 4. 5. and more especially with reference unto that Time, which he hath locked up in his own Cabinet. This I doe here declare to be the Rule by which my former Application (of this Parable unto our Present time) is to be judged of; and that I have not pretended to Infallibility.

4. Enquiries (with Sobriety) into this Hidden Mystery, are no where Blamed, but Encouraged, as being of use, with reference unto these latter dayes. Indeed the Primitive Christians were forbid to think, Christ's Proper Coming was Then at Hand, before the Man of Sin was up, 2 *Thess.* 2. 2, 3. but Now the Reason of that Prohibition is Removed. Yea we are bid to Argue from such evident Signs, as to the Drawing Near of our Redemption, *Luke* 21. 8. and there is an Increase of Knowledge Promised unto the Runners to and fro, at such a Time, *Dan.* 12. 4. nor is there any Danger hinted, save with respect to men's Delaying it, *Mat.* 24. 48. Nor will it Repent us, if kept Awake, though by Discoursing as Men, or with Mistakes.

5. Christ's chief Design, in bidding us to VVatch, (because No man doth know that Day and Hour,) is to Provoke our being in a Present Readiness, and to prevent our putting that Time off, or at some further Distance. This is Apparent, both from his Explanation of it Otherwhere, *Luke* 12. 40. and from the Reason of this Present Exhortation, *viz.* the foolish (unprepared) Virgins sad Experience here, who therefore Perish, because of their Presuming upon longer time. So that
Christ's

The Parable of the Ten Virgins Opened. 263

Chrift's Principal Meaning is, *Ye know not [how soon] that Day will come, and therefore ye have need to Watch.* From whence it followeth, that fuch do utterly miftake Chrift's Drift and their own Intereft, who are more fearful of being Hafty, than of Lingring, as to their Sober Expectations of this kind.

Queſt. 8. Wherein confifts this work of Watching? To which I Anfwer.

Anſw. 1. Negatively; Not in that which is Competible unto Foolifh Virgins; fince we are therefore bid to watch, becaufe of their fad Portion from the Lord at fuch a time; and notwithftanding what they had Done or Were. Now, thefe poor Foolifh Virgins ftood (for ought we Read) unto their former Practice, of Going forth (at firft) to Meet the Bridegroom: Therefore one may not watch, and yet be no Back-flider, unto fuch an Height; or not turn back again to that which hath been formerly Declared againft as Antichriftian. Nay, Thefe had fometime been in Fellowfhip with the V Vife; who therefore (doubtlefsly) were pretty Blamelefs in their Lives, found in the Faith (or Main, fo called) and very converfant about Religious Duties: Therefore one may continue Praying, Preaching, Hearing, *&c.* and yet not watch. Nay, Thefe are onely Taxed here, for not Going out the Second time, through lack of Oyl; which (when Awakened) they would have Borrowed, and went to Buy it: Therefore one may not watch, and yet be wakened; yea, very Trim as to ones Lamp or good Affections, nay (in Appearance) willing and Defirous to be Compleat.

2. So much as to the Negative. But then Affirmatively; this watching doth confift in fomewhat elfe, Relating to the Manner and Matter of our Duty.

1. Firft, to the Manner of it; and fo it doth confift in being alway ftudious or intent, with reference unto the VVork or Duty which God requireth of us. Thus are we bid to watch in Prayer, *Col.* 4. 2. or to Confider what we are about, *Eccl.* 5. 2. which Duty of Prayer is put for All Religious worfhip whatfoever, *Mat.* 21. 13. and *Acts* 16. 13. 16. VVe ought to Rejoyce (at fuch a Time) as if we Rejoyced not, 1 *Cor.* 7. 29, 30. but yet to Hear, without an Heart, fore-runs the coming of threatned Defolation, *Ezek.* 33. 31. 33. Great is the want of Serioufnefs in Spiritual Exercifes; fuch is the force of Innate Vanity, when in Conjunction with Diverting Objects from the Tempter. But as an Holy fixednefs (or doing with our Might) is alway to be Laboured after, fo much more now, or when we feem Haftning into that ftate, wherein there is no further work, *Eccl.* 9. 10. at leaft for Foolifh Virgins.

2. This

The Parable of the Ten Virgins Opened.

2. This Watching doth consist in what Relateth to the Matter of our Duty; and as followeth.

1. In being Ready, or having All our Garments on; which is the Main thing (in the General) intended here. Christ's Coat was of one piece, *John* 19. 23. to signifie (perhaps) his being Drest at once: But we (poor Creatures) must be daily Adding, 2 *Pet.* 1. 5. Graces are called Armour, *Rom.* 13. 12. which doth consist of several pieces, *Eph.* 6. 14, 15, 16, 17. the whole whereof must be put on by us, *v.* 11. whose Life is a continual Warfare, 1 *Tim.* 1. 18. One Open Guard exposeth to a Deadly Wound, and shame may be Discovered by one Naked place; yea, more unto the shame of some, than Total Nakedness is to others. Now, all complain of wanting somewhat, and which they see upon the Backs of others: But yet how Lightly do Professors bear Convictions of their Imperfections, without a Care and Sense becoming their Complaints.

2. In keeping those Garments close about us, which Christ Declareth to be that wherein our Watching doth consist, *Rev.* 16. 15. Thus let us Keep them from being Lost, as Christ kept his Disciples, *John* 17. 12. or that we lose not that which we have wrought, but that we may receive a full Reward, 2 *John* 8. And let us also keep them on our Back, or by our putting them in ure; as Christ is said to keep his Father's sayings, *John* 8. 55. because he did according thereunto: Since nothing will be saved in that Day, save onely our wearing Cloaths, *Mat.* 24. 18. Yea, let us keep them without Spot, *Jude* 23. or, as we are to keep the Scriptures, 1 *Tim.* 6. 14. since such shall walk in white, for they are worthy, *Rev.* 3. 4. Nay, we must keep them also Girt; else flying Garments may be to our shame, *Rev.* 16. 15.

3. In being of a constant Sober Spirit, which is one Branch of Watchfulness, and therefore is indefinitely required of us, together with our being vigilant, 1 *Pet.* 5. 8. Thus is a Bishop to be Vigilant and Sober, 1 *Tim.* 3. 2. and Aged Men, *Titus* 2: 2. yea, Deacons Wives, 1 *Tim.* 3. 11. and every one, 1 *Thes.* 5. 6. which may consist with Hoping to the End, 1 *Pet.* 1. 13. and with Rejoycing, *Phil.* 4. 4, 5. but not with Levity or Excess, 1 *Thes.* 5. 7, 8. Indeed Sobriety is but a Vertue; yet it is so much wanting at this Day, as that a Sober Man is counted Gracious: and Lightness of Spirit in Professors doth Argue both their lack of Grace and Vertue. Some do so far Indulge their Disposition, as to forget the Dispensation they are under, which calls for Gravity, without Dissimulation, or for a Sober Frame, as well as shew.

4. In being careful of what is more peculiarly committed to our Trust. Thus were those bid to Watch, and Keep what had been weighed

to

to them in the way from *Babylon*, till they should be Discharged of it at *Jerusalem*, *Ezra* 8. 24. 25. 26. And thus, all sorts of *Levites* (or Professors) have some things peculiarly Deposited in their Hand, as those of Old, viz. the *Kohathites*, *Numb*. 4. 4. the *Gershonites*, *v.* 28. and *Merarites*, *v.* 33. and in the Keeping whereof their special Watch consisted. Thus was the Gospel of Uncircumcision (by way of Eminency) committed unto *Paul*, *Gal.* 2. 7. as was his Form of sound words to *Timothy*, 2 *Tim.* 1. 13, 14. who also must commit them unto other Faithful Men, 2 *Tim.* 2. 2. And thus more Eminently Inlightned ones should Watch and Keep that which they are Betrusted with, or bear the Iniquity of their Priest-hood, in case of any failure, *Numb*. 18. 1.

5. In our Improving present Opportunities for Service, while they are continued. Thus *Timothy* was bid to Watch, 2 *Tim.* 4. 5. or to be instant in his work of Preaching, *v.* 2. because the Time was coming, when they would not endure sound Doctrine, *v.* 3. but be turned into Fables, *v.* 4. Thus ought we to Observe (our selves and Others) as to the Season of an Exhortation, or when the Heart is most Prepared for Impression. The Wild Asse hath her Moneth, wherein she may be found, *Jer.* 2. 24. and therefore *Paul* staid so long at *Ephesus*, because so great and so effectual a Door was Opened unto him, 1 *Cor.* 16. 8, 9. Some may Resolve to follow Christ hereafter, *Luke* 9. 61. but by to Morrow the Heart may possibly be hardned, *Heb.* 3. 13. or that Door may be shut, which Now stands Open.

6. In lying at Catch, for any the least Advantage tending to promote a Good Design: As Wicked Men are said to watch the Righteous, *Psal.* 37. 32. and as the Jews did Christ, that so they might Accuse him, *Mark* 3. 2. If Men did Hunger after Righteousness, *Mat.* 5. 6. how would they watch, as doth a Leopard for his Prey, who tarrieth not untill it cometh to his Den, but ventureth thence unto the City, Catching at him that first comes out, *Jer.* 5. 6.! This Lying in wait is Lawful, and a Duty; but little practised by those, who Turn upon the Beds, as doth the Door upon his Hinges, *Prov.* 26. 14. or in a Passive way, as if Conjured into a Narrow Circle. And if Men were as much afraid of Sin, as Suffering, they would then catch at Light for Duty, as *Benhadad*'s Servants did at *Ahab*'s words, for Mercy, 1 *King*. 20. 33.

7. In standing fast, as to the Truths of Christ, whatever Hardships may be met with in that way. Thus were those bid to watch, and to stand fast, 1 *Cor.* 16. 13. as he was bid to watch, and to endure Afflictions, 2 *Tim.* 4. 5. to intimate wherein this watching doth consist.

Back-sliders are no Watchers; however such may Talk (as some do) in their sleep: Nor they who are so very Tender, (or sensible of Cold) to what they sometimes were. It is a Night with us at present; and greatest chilness (or Afflicting Cold) is wont to be at Break of Day: Therefore let us in this sence watch; And let us stand fast, not Reel-ing to and fro, which is the posture of Men half asleep: And let us hold fast that which we have, since aptness to let things fall, is that by which a slumberer is to be known from others.

8. In being careful to Preserve the Life of what is Dying; and more especially in all Momentous Cases. When any one is very Weak, the Friends of such are wont to Watch; in which regard, the *Sardians* are bid to watch, and strengthen the things which did remain, being Rea-dy to Die, *Rev.* 3. 2. as other things were Dead before, *v.* 1. This is the Case of Many in our Days; who seem to have been Typified by those of Old. Some are quite Dead, as to their Zeal, their Confi-dence, their seeming Life and Power: And other things (which yet Remain) are Ready to die, *viz.* their Hope, their Form of Godliness, and Moral Honesty; who therefore had need to Watch. Yea, there is not an Heart (or House) wherein some Good thing is not very weak; which therefore calls for strengthning: and therein lieth our being Watchful.

9. In minding what God doth say; as *Habakkuk* Resolved to watch and see what God would say unto him, *Hab.* 2. 1. and with Respect to such a time, or when the Enemy doth Possess what was not Theirs, *Hab.* 1. 6. Indeed, we cannot well Hear, unless we Watch, 1 *Kings* 18. 27. at least, not some more still (or whispering) voice, in which the Lord is Mostly present, 1 *Kings* 19. 12, 13. Thus are we to Hear what Christ hath said unto the Churches, Relating to these Latter days, *Rev.* 3. 22. how some of them were Threatned (at the first) if they did not Repent, *Rev.* 2. 5. 7. how others were Discovered (after-wards) to be meer Formalists. *Rev.* 3. 1. 6. and how (at Last) Christ is Resolved to spew them out, for their luke-warmness, *Rev.* 3. 16. 22. Thus are we to Hear his Crying Voice unto the City, *Mic.* 6. 9. and what he will speak at the last, *Psal.* 85. 8.

10. In being able to tell the Time, or What of the Night, which is the peculiar work of Watch-men, *Isa.* 21. 11. and wherein *Paul* pre-sumed those Believers were Acquainted, *Rom.* 13. 11. 13. And if Philosophers should not wonder, (as one of them vainly Boasted,) much less should Christians be at a Total Loss, in this regard; since Pro-vidence compared with the Scripture, is like a Dial shone upon, in case our Eyes were Open, *Luke* 24. 25. 27. But few have Knowledge

of

of the Times, 1 *Chron.* 12. 32. though to their shame who do pretend to that All-guiding Spirit of Christ, *John* 16. 13. since (by a Natural Instinct) the Stork in Heaven knoweth her Appointed time, *Jer* 8. 7. But let us watch, in this regard; since Ignorance (in that Respect) is very Dangerous, *Luke* 19. 42. and a sad Judgment, *Isa.* 29. 10. if not wilful, 2 *Pet.* 3. 5.

11. In our Defending others; at least-wise by fore-warning them of what is Notified unto us; and more especially, those whom the Lord hath (by his Providence) Committed to our Care: Thus hath a City its Appointed Watch-men, *Cant.* 3. 3. and more especially in times of Danger, who then are to Declare that which they see, *Isa.* 21. 6. though such cannot be alway Positive, 2 *Sam.* 18. 27. 2 *Kings* 9. 17, 20. Some, under a pretence of looking to Themselves, care not what doth become of others: As if the Command of Saving our selves and others, 1 *Tim.* 4. 16. were not Divine and self-consistent. Others are so afraid of being shamed with a false Alarm, as that they have not Heart to speak at all, *Jonah* 4. 2. which yet is Ordinary in a VVatch-man. Others put off this work to some Peculiar ones: as if a *Cain* were not his Brother's Keeper, *Gen.* 4. 9. or a *Samaritan* were not a Neighbour, *Luke* 10. 36.

12. In being (our selves) aware of Dangers, and suitably provided for them, before we are surprized with them. Thus are those bid to watch the way, *Nah.* 2. 1. and those Disciples to VVatch and Pray, for fear of entring into Temptation, *Mat.* 26. 41. So those *Ephesian* Elders were bid to VVatch, *Acts* 20. 21. with reference unto Wolves without, *v.* 29. and Perverse Speakers from Themselves, *v.* 30. Those are no VVatchers who are Offended with too Early *Items*; who are afraid of being up too soon, who have their Oyl to Buy, when so much of the present Night is spent. Without Dispute this is here plainly meant, as is Apparent, both from the following and fore-going words: Thus therefore let us watch; and with Respect to Spiritual and Eternal Dangers, more than Temporal.

13. In being Eminently careful, as to the Duties and Temptations which Relate to such a Time; in which regard the Porter is bid to watch, *Mark* 13. 34. and all the Disciples, for fear of entring into Temptation, *Mark* 14. 38. This leadeth us to that which followeth.

Quest. 9. What are those special Duties, with reference unto which we are to VVatch at such a Time?

Answ. The Principal Duties of such a Time, Relate unto All sorts of Persons.

I. Unto Sinners, both in the VVorld and *Sion*; and more especially, those

those whom Christ will Then call unto his Bar, as having been his signal Enemies, *Luke* 19. 27. Their Duty is, to get Delivered from their Adversary, in the VVay, before his sitting as a Judge, *Luke* 12. 58: as *Shimei* therefore came to meet provoked *David*, the First of all the House of *Joseph*, 2 *Sam.* 19. 20. and thereby get some present Pardon, *v.* 23. Fury is not in God; therefore let such make Peace with him, and they shall do so, *Isa.* 27. 4, 5. How unexpectedly was *Nineveh* Reprieved, upon the self-humbling of that *Assyrian* King, *Jonah* 3. 10? So doth God promise to build such up among his People, could they but learn his Peoples VVayes, *Jer.* 12. 16. And if *Jerusalem* could but Repent, her seeming Sentence *Jer.* 21. 10. should be Reversed, *Jer.* 22. 4: and therefore, *O Jerusalem wash thine Heart from Wickedness, that so thou maist be saved*, Jer. 4. 14. Think upon this, you bloody Persecutors, sad Apostates, base Complyers, and sleighty Unbelievers; this is the great work incumbent upon you, which must be Now done, or (perhaps) Never.

II. Unto Saints; which are, as followeth, Expressely required at such a time.

1. In making our Election sure; which is the Great work of Time, 2 *Pet.* 1. 10; and more especially at such a time. Men in a Fire, are Firstly carefull to save their Evidences: now since This Day will be with Burning and fewel of Fire, *Isa.* 9. 5. take heed your Evidences be not Burnt. Foundations (then) will be Discovered to the Neck, *Hab.* 3. 13: and therefore Hypocrites will then be Known by their Excessive Fear, *Isa.* 33. 14; and Others, by their holy Confidence, at Christ's Appearing, 1 *Joh.* 2. 28. See therefore to the Ground you Build upon, and bring your Marks unto the Touch-stone; not taking upon Trust; nor Trusting to what might suffice, as to being held Communion with; since Goats will Now be set Aside, *Mat.* 25. 32. which yet were Clean, for Sacrifice, and Food, or Saint-Communion Acts of Old.

2. Let us Occupy those Talents which Christ hath betrusted us with for such a Purpose, *Luke* 19. 13. Each one hath put into his hand, according to his several Ability, *Mat.* 25. 15. and an Exact Account whereof is to be made at such a Time, *Luke* 19. 15; who therefore had need to VVatch. Some want Ability, as to some Kind of Talents; and Others, as to the same Degree, for that, which (in respect of Kind) is Equally communicated unto all. Thus are the Saints betrusted with peculiar Priviledges; yea, every Sinner with some kind of Talent; though Gradually Differing (both of them) each from other: and suitable whereunto, must be their Reckoning. Men must be accountable

for

The Parable of the Ten Virgins Opened.

for their sweet Illapses, Crosses, Opportunities for Duty, Helps therein, and Outward Mercies; what they have Gained thereby; whose Duty it therefore is to Trade therewith; and towards the End especially.

3. Let us be much in Prayer, that we may not Enter into Temptation, *Mark* 14. 38. but be accounted Worthy to Escape, and stand before the Son of Man, *Luke* 21. 36. Now one may be said to Enter into Temptation, when something is that way done, although not to the Height thereof; when sinfull Motions are Parlyed with, or Satan is heard in a plain Case: When foiled Temptations are not pursued, but suffered to Rise again: When Opposite Duty is not duely prized; and when we are not Deeply Humbled for a former Fall: In which regard, Prayer is of special securing use, as it doth bring the Soul into God's Over-awing Presence; as it enlivens other helps; and as it is the likelyest way to be Instructed and Assisted from the Lord. Onely we must therein be Upright, Earnest, Persevering, and not Idle Beggars, but free to Work.

4. What manner of Persons ought we to be, as to All Godliness and Holy Conversation, 2 *Pet.* 3. 11; so as to be found of Christ in Peace, and without Spot or Blame, *v.* 14? Christ will Then come, and his Reward with him, *Isa.* 40. 10 : therefore let us now ply our Work apace; and let us not make light of Idle words, which then must be Accounted for, *Mat.* 12. 36. Each Talent (well Improved) will gain a City, in that Day, *Luke* 19. 17: and little do many think how small a matter will be sufficient to Burn This World, as was to Drown the Other. How forcible (to make us Accurate) would be the constant Expectation of a Dying Hour, and the last Trumpets sounding unto Judgement? And with what Chearfulness doth a Tenant hear his Landlord Knock, whose Rent is Ready, and not to Borrow at such a time?

5. Say not, A Confederacy with Threatning *Ashur*, *Isa.* 8. 12; whose Fall, *Isa.* 31. 8. immediately ushereth in Christ's Dispensation, *Isa.* 32. 1. Some will Confederate with him for Mischief to God's Hidden Ones, *Psal.* 83. 4, 5, 8. and others (in *Jerusalem*) through slavish Fear, directly cross to a Divine Command. And therefore *Hezekiah* would not give him Pledges, *Isa.* 36. 8; although he was not for Provoking Answers, *v.* 21. and thereupon was fortified from the Lord, *Isa.* 37. 6, 7. What Shame and Horrour will then surprize those unrepenting *Israelites*, who have gone down for help to *Egypt*, *Isa.* 31. 1. or to this King with Presents, *Isa.* 57. 9? 'Tis very Probable, that *Shebna* was of this Confederacy, who sometimes had the Key of *David*'s House, but there-

therefore forfeited his Place unto *Eliakim*, *Isa.* 22. 21; before that Siege was raised, 2 *Kings* 18. 18.

6. Come out of *Babylon*; as all Gods People are bid to do, *Rev.* 18. 4. and more. especially at such a Time. Now *Babylon* is to be Known; Partly, by her being very Tender and unacquainted with others Hardships, *Isa.* 47. 1, 2. Partly by her abounding with worldly Great ones, 2 *Kings* 25. 28; and men of greatest Note for Wisdom, *Dan.* 2. 12: Partly, by making a God of *Succoth-benoth*, or Tents of Daughters, 2 *King.* 17. 30; *viz.* the Numerousness of their Party, though onely made up of Women: Partly, by her most cruel Persecutions, *Jer.* 50. 17. and unnatural Oppressions, *Isa.* 14. 20: and Partly, by her Incorrigibleness, *Jer.* 51. 9. This *Babylon* is to be left, *Jer.* 51. 45. and all the Temple-Vessels to be carried thence, which have been there Abused, as was of Old; since Every one found There (it such a time) will be cut off, *Isa.* 13. 15.

7. Forsake not the Assembling of your selves Together, and so much the more, as this Day seemeth to Approach, *Heb.* 10. 25. Those are no Watchers, (especially in these latter dayes,) who are for meeting Asunder, through fear of suffering for so clear a Duty. Thus let us therefore VVatch, in case fresh Persecution should arise, as hath oft done in former times, and after some Respite given. And as men would be kept Awake in that respect, so let them take heed of Trusting in their Former Duty; much more, of pleading for a former Failing, or making light thereof; which is most likely to betray us into fresh Temptations. Yea, let us Adde mutual Exhortations unto other Means, whereby to counterpoise the Practice or Manner of some Others, with reference hereunto, as is there further signified, *Heb.* 10. 25.

8. Let us be Moderate in our Affections, with reference unto Creature-comforts; and more Especially, as the Time grows short, or as the Fashion of This world is seen to pass Away, 1 *Cor.* 7. 29, 30, 31. VVhich word translated [*Fashion*] doth signifie the Out side Cloathing of a thing or person, thus Christ was found in [*Fashion*] as a Man, *Phil.* 2. 8. when he was cloathed with our Nature: so will the Present VVorld be changed (as a Vesture) at his Coming, *Psal.* 102. 25. And that word [*short*] is thought to be a Metaphor taken from a piece of Cloth, whose very End is onely left unrolled up: Or rather it doth import, that Time is Now put into its VVinding-sheet; and so the same Greek VVord is rendred, *Acts* 5. 6. Therefore 'tis Time to take our Affections Off from that, which is Now Dead, and Ready to be Buried.

9. Let us then Flee, out of *Judæa*, into the Mountains, *Mat.* 4. 16. and much more out of Old *Jerusalem*, at such a time, on pain of Death, *Jer.* 21. 9, 10, 11. 'Tis something strange, that it should Ever be a Duty to goe into *Babylon*; but yet 'tis True, as *Babylon* denotes Confusion, (or Going forth out of the City, into the Field,) and There shall *Sion* be Delivered, *Mic.* 4. 10. Thus are the Lord's Pric ls (or Eminent Saints) commanded to VVeep between the Porch and Altar, at such a time, *Joel* 2. 17; which necessarily implyeth, their being Come out of that former Temple, wherein they had been wont to Minister. VVhich fleeing to the Mountains doth fitly suit with Meeting Christ in the Air at last, 1 *Thess.* 4. 17; es being a Middle-state, between the Earth and Heaven; or their being Covered in the shadow of his Hand, till he shall Plant the Heavens, and lay the Foundations of the Earth afresh, *Isa.* 51. 16.

10. Remember *Lot*'s wife, saith Christ himself, with reference unto his Coming, *Luke* 17. 30. 32. whom we are to Remember, as to her Sin and Punishment, together with the Circumstances which relate unto them both. Her Sin was Looking Back (to *Sodom*) or Behind her, *Gen.* 19. 26. contrary to God's Express Command, *v.* 17. which Looking Back unfitteth for an Interest in his Kingdom, *Luke* 9. 62. Her Punishment was, her being therefore turn'd into a Pillar of Salt, *Gen.* 19. 26. which Salt doth seem to be a Part of *Sodom*'s Judgement, *Deut.* 29. 23. *Lot* onely was spoken to in that Command, *Gen.* 19. 17; yet his VVife perished for Disobeying it: therefore take heed of Limiting Commands to those whom they were onely first given forth unto. She also Died without Mercy, although she was the VVife of Righteous *Lot*: therefore Trust no: to Carnal Priviledges. And though she had Come out of *Sodom*, yet did she Perish by the Way, for having an Affection thereunto, or Looking back Behind her.

11. Touch ro Unclean thing; but be ye Clean, who bear the Vessels of the Lord, *Isa.* 52. 11. By which word [*Vessels*] are meant, those Gospel-Truths which have been carryed into *Babylon*: the Bearers whereof (from thence) are Priests and *Levites*, *Ezra* 8. 30. who typified Gospel-Saints, 1 *Pet.* 2. 9: and *Touching* denotes Communion, 2 *Cor.* 6. 14, 17. Thus are we to study, wherein the Purity of Communion doth consist; or what it is that makes Unclean (according to the Mystical Import of *Moses* his Law,) by its being Touched. And let us not be made to think, this Separation is unlawfull, if made by a Lesser Number, or a Particular person; in case the VVhole (or Greater Number) be so Unclean; since the Command is Universal, the Reason is the same for every Part as for the Whole; nor have Particular per-

Sons stuck thereat, 2 *Chron.* 11. 14. 16. *Joſh.* 24. 15. but were Required thus to do, *Jer.* 15. 19. with an Encouragement from the Lord, 2 *Cor.* 6. 18. and without Danger, *Iſa.* 52. 12.

12. If we have escaped out of *Babylon*, let us take heed of standing still on this side that which is our Resting place, *Jer.* 51. 50. The same word (in the *Hebrew*) is applied to *Leah*'s leaving off to Bear, *Gen.* 29. 35. and to the staying of that Widow's Oyl, 2 *Kings* 4. 6. and *Joaſh* his smiting at the Third stroak, 2 *Kings* 13. 18. and *Job*'s Friends being silenced, *Job* 32. 16. and the Sea's ceasing from her Raging, *Jonah* 1. 15. all which clear up the Meaning of it. Thus let us not stand, as to our fresh Conceptions, Multiplying, smiting Answers, and Holy Zeal or Raging: Since *Babylon*'s Plagues may else be apt to over-take us; and if we stand (in such a Case) we possibly may go no further, and so fall short of *Sion*, which is as far from *Babylon*, as four Moneths Journeying can well Accomplish, *Ezra* 7. 9. Let us not therefore talk of Houses yet, but onely Tents.

13. Remember to keep no silence, ye that make mention of the Lord; and give him no Rest, till he Establish, and till he make *Jeruſalem* a Praise in the Earth, *Iſa.* 62. 6, 7. VVhen Christ's Dominion is set up, *Pſal.* 72. 8. and when the whole Earth is filled with his G'ory, *v.* 19. then will the prayers of *David* (the Son of *Jeſſe*) End, *v.* 20. but till that time, they will (they ought to) be Continued, and for the Hastening of that Dispensation. That Day of Salvation will be a time for Praises, *Iſa.* 12. 4. therefore this Hour (immediately foregoing it) should be the Hour of Prayer. And though God needeth not to be Remembred of his Covenant, *Pſal.* 111. 5. yet will he be Enquired of for This, *Ezek.* 36. 37. and therefore let us pray for This; and as we find the Time Approaching, as he did, *Dan.* 9. 2, 3.

14. Mind well the Signs of our Redemption drawing Near, and let us suitably be Affected, *Luke* 21. 28. Signs are no insignificant or idle things, which none but *Phariſees* are Ignorant of, *Mat.* 16. 3. and All but Carnal *Iſraelites* will Believe them, *Numb.* 14. 11. And if some do so Magnifie their own Invented Sign of the Cross, much more should we esteem that sign of Mercy, which is of God's own giving, as *Iſa.* 7. 14. Now, we have had Many Signs and Wonders in our days; which shew the Nearness of Christ's Name, *Pſal.* 75. 1. (upon the multiplying whereof, God doth conclude his People will Believe, *Exod.* 4. 8. though without Signs they will not, *John* 4. 48. But yet (alas) how soon are These forgot? *Pſal.* 78. 42, 43. which is Accompanied with Turning back, *v.* 57. and therefore had need to be Remembred.

15. As

15. As they that have wrought God's Judgment, are to seek Righteousness; so are the Meek bid to seek Meekness, in this Day; wherein it may be such will be Hid, *Zeph.* 2. 3. Which Meekness (to be sought by Meek ones) doth denote subduedness of Spirit to the will of God, in case Afflicting Dispensations be continued; and Hearts established with Patience, because his Coming draweth nigh, *James* 5. 8. We know not certainly how long those signs may go before his very Coming; therefore let us Rejoyce with Trembling, and wait upon the Lord, *Zeph.* 3.8. Himself will (Now) soon Plead our Cause; therefore let not our Passion rise. But we must look to meet with fiery intermixtures afterwards, *Rev.* 15. 2. therefore get store of Meekness.

16. Since God will Now bring Evil upon All, let not Great things be sought for by us for our selves; but let us count it a sufficient Portion, if Life be given us for a prey, *Jer.* 45. 5. In case the City be Low in a Low place, *Isa.* 32. 19. then Blessed are they that sow beside all Waters, *v.* 20. or such as have a Spirit suited to their Dispensation. It is Absurd, (as well as sinful) to look for *Canaan* in the Wilderness. How Childishly do many wonder at their present short Allowance, both in Respect of Temporals and Spirituals. Let Milk and Butter satisfie us in that day, *Isa.* 7. 21, 22. and that we may Trust in the Name of God, though without any Light, *Isa.* 50. 10. or that our Life and Soul are kept together: since we must be like him, *Rom.* 8. 29. who entred into Paradise in a Cloud, *Mat.* 27. 46. *Luke* 23. 43.

17. Let us Account the Bridegroom's Tarrying, or the Long-suffering of our Lord, to be Salvation, 2 *Pet.* 3. 15. It is Design'd (by Him) to be so; and it may easily be perceived (by us) to be of such a saving Nature, both in Respect to our selves and others. If He is unwilling that any should perish, and therefore slackneth, 2 *Pet.* 3. 9. shall we so far indulge our Personal satisfaction, as to wish harm (by our Impetuousness) to an Elected Brother? Nay, if we seriously Observe our own unfitness, we shall have cause to say, that his Long-suffering is our Salvation. The vilest Spirits of Old, and they who therefore justly perished, were of a Murmuring Disposition, for our warning, 1 *Cor.* 10. 10, 11. whereas self-dressing watchers know how to improve that saving Respite to their Gain, at his Appearing.

18. *Remember the Lord afar off, and let* Jerusalem *come into mind,* Jer. 51. 50. It chears the wearied Traveller's Heart when he can see his Journeys end. Look upon *Sion*, as thine Eyes shall see her in due time, *Isa.* 33. 20. The Exercise of this believing Prospect, is both a Priviledge and a Duty. VVe walk by Faith, and not by sight, 2 *Cor.*

5, 7. therefore we cannot Move without Believing. But if the Prodigal's Father Ran, upon the fight of him, when he was yet a Great way off, *Luke* 15. 20. how will our Affections be enlivened by the fight of Chrift, though at fome Diftance. Then will our Tears be wiped away, *Ifa.* 25. 8. and our Blind eyes be opened, *Ifa.* 35. 5. then will our Labours be Rewarded, *Ifa.* 40. 10 and all our Loffes Recompenfed, *Ifa.* 61. 7. Thus let us comfort our felves and others, 1 *Thef.* 4. 18.

19. *Prepare to Meet thy God, O Ifrael*, Amos 4. 12. with reference unto the Terror of his work at fuch a time. The Hearing whereof made *Habakkuk* to quiver, *Hab.* 3. 16. *For who fhall Live, when God doth this*, Numb. 24. 23? Few know the Nature of thofe Clouds, in which the Son of Man will Come: *And who fhall ftand when he Appeareth*, Mal. 3. 2? Something will be, which fhall make finners (then) to be afraid, *Ifa.* 33. 14. who are not frighted with meerly Spiritual Judgments: And Saints themfelves have need to Tremble in themselves, as they would Reft in fuch a Day, *Hab.* 3. 16. Prepare for Rifling, in the Letter, *Zech.* 14. 2. and for the trying of your work by Myftical Fire at the leaft; and therefore take heed of Building with Stubble, Hay, or Wood, which then will Burn, 1 *Cor.* 3. 12, 13.

20. *Take up a Lamentation,* (faith God unto his Prophet, at fuch a time of dreadful Judgment, (*for Tyrus,* Ezek. 27. 2. *For Pharaoh*, Ezek. 32. 2. *And for the Princes of Ifrael,* Ezek. 19. 1. For finners of all forts, and more efpecially for Foolifh Virgins or Profeffors. Their Cafe will Then be very fad, 1 *Pet.* 4. 17, 18. which therefore is the Matter of a Lafting Lamentation, *Ezek.* 19. 17. Nor do they Lament Themfelves, who therefore fhould be wept over by us, as Ignorant. Old *Jerufalem* was by Chrift, *Luke* 19. 41, 42. And it was time for *Jeremy* to be pained at his very Heart for thofe, *Jer.* 4. 19. whom (in a while after) he he was forbid to pray for, *Jer.* 7. 16. Thus let thofe (of the Separation) keep the Paffeover for All the Children of the Captivity, as *Ezra* 6. 20, 21. Mourning for thofe who Ignorantly Defire the Haftening of that Dreadful Day, *Amos* 5. 18.

21. *Go through, go through the Gates ; prepare you the way of the People: Caft up, Caft up the High-way; Gather out the ftones, lift up a Standard for the People*, Ifa. 62. 10. All which implieth,

1. Our fetting an Example unto others, by Going through the Gates before them. This Practical fpeaking is likely to be moft Effectual, 2 *Thef.* 3. 7. wherein Chrift differed, *John* 13. 15. from the *Pharifees*, Mat. 23. 3. This is a fpecial Duty, and Indifpenfably required of us, though very Difficult, as the Reduplication [*Go forth, go forth*] importeth. Thus are we to Remove, and be as the He-Goats before the

Flock

Flock, Jer. 50. 8. saying, *Let us go speedily, I will go also. Zech.* 8.21.

2. Our calling upon others to go with us, or at least to follow us; which is the import of Lifting up a Standard for the People, which therefore is joyned-elfe-where with Publishing, Jer. 50. 2. and Blowing of the Trumpet, Jer. 51. 27. at which time all the Dwellers upon Earth are bid to See and Hear, *Isa.* 18. 3. Persons disposed to slumber, cannot endure to hear a Trumpet sound: But tell them, you are Souldiers, and must Obey the Orders of your General, the Lord of Hosts; and they had better be Awakened with your Trumpet, than with His. You Kill us, said those, when kept Awake in the Sweating Sickness; but had they not been so, they had Dyed indeed. Let us be therefore Crying in their Ears, *All Flesh is Grass*, as we are bid to do, *Isa.* 40. 6. at such a Time, *v.* 10. or shewing the Vanity of all their Glory.

3. Preparing their way, by casting the High-way up, and (as it is in the *Hebrew*) stoning it from stones. Which Casting up (with speed, as the Ingemination hinteth) denotes the making of a Causey, for their dryer passage in those Lower Grounds: And stoning imports the making of it firm and smooth, or without stumbling-blocks, as *Isa.* 57. 14. Thus let us prepare the way for others, not putting any stumbling-block in their way, *Rom.* 14. 13. but Raising it up in their esteem, and Comforting them with the sight of our way and Doings, *Ezek.* 14. 22, 23. Our in-offensive Zeal for Christ, and wise deportment towards others, will much Invite their Coming out of *Babylon*, who else may be affrighted back again. Which yet doth not imply our Daubing with untempered Mortar, but dealing plainly in a prudent way; removing the Matter of just Offence, and Paving their way with solid and substantial Grounds.

Quest. 10. What are the Temptations, with reference unto which we are to Watch, at such a Time?

Answ. These Time-Temptations are either more Gross, or more Refined. Grosser Temptations are as followeth.

1. Blaspheming. Some in the Last Days will be Blasphemers, 2 *Tim.* 3. 1, 2. pretending to be Jews, who are of Satan's Synagogue, *Rev.* 2. 9. Opposing and Blaspheming the Truths of such a Time, *Acts* 18. 6. from an Invidious Spirit, *Acts* 13. 45. Blaspheming the Holy Ghost, by calling that Spirit unclean, *Mark* 3. 29, 30. As peccant Humours (in length of Time) of turn into the Plague; so may Corruptions putrifie (at last) into Blaspheming: And though I will not positively say, who are Now guilty of that sin; yet do I fear its being incident unto these Latter Days, as Christ's first Appearing from the

the Digesting Heat of that Approaching Sun. And it is partly to be known by an Habitual Evil speaking of Time-Truths, against sufficient Light, and without sense or Reformation to the Last.

2. Mocking and scoffing at This Day of Christ. *There will be Mockers in the Last time*, Jude 18. *And Scoffers at the promise of his Coming*, 2 Pet. 3. 3, 4. which is first to be known, or in a special manner to be taken Notice of, as 2 *Pet.* 1. 20. The Reason whereof is, present visible Improbability of such a Dispensation, and walking after their own Lusts; both which will (Then) be in their Prime, and will breed Scoffers. Which will appear, in saying, *Let him make speed*, Isa. 5. 19. and in a Boyish way of Jeering that Opinion, as the *Greek* word Translated [*Scoffers, or Mockers*] intimateth, as some did Christ himself a little before his being Glorified, by Mocking Gestures, *Mat.* 27. 29. Insulting words, *Mark* 15. 31, 32. and scornful Actions, *Mat.* 27. 29, 30. *But be not Mockers, lest your Bands be made strong*, Isa. 28. 22. *Hear this, ye scornful Men*, v. 14.

3. Smiting of Fellow-Servants, *Mat.* 24. 49. and dealing Hardly with them after a promise of doing otherwise, *Jer.* 34. 15, 16. In which regard, Professors are forbid to Grudge, or make each other Groan, for fear of being Condemned, because the Judge standeth before the Door, *James* 5. 9. and Sufferers are therefore bidden to be Patient, *v.* 8. implying the Prevalency of this Temptation at such a time. Thus Faithful Prophets must look for smiting, *Jer.* 20. 2. and others for being Cast out with Hatred by their Brethren, *Isa.* 66. 5. and Manifold Defamations upon known false Reports, *Jer.* 20. 10. But let such know, that slanderously Reported *Paul* was (in the *Greek*) Blasphemed, *Rom.* 3. 8. and let them mind that Persecuted Prophets Prayer, *Jer.* 11. 20. and smiting *Pashur*'s Portion, *Jer.* 20. 2, 4.

4. Sensuality; or Eating, Drinking, Marrying, Trading, and nothing else, *Luke* 17. 26, 27, 28, 30. Yea, Drinking Wine in Bowls, *Amos* 6. 6. and Feasting it in a time of Mourning, *Isa.* 22. 12, 13. Declining Age is Naturally prone to this Temptation, craving the Creature so much the more, when it is threatned with its parting, *Isa.* 22. 13. And Old Men stoop not more (Earthward) in the Letter than in the Mystery, and in a Moral sense. But as this is a Sign of Dotage, (or being Children a second time, who are for nothing else but Eating;) so is it the ready way to be surprized, *Mat.* 24. 49, 50. and Abhorred of the Lord, *Amos* 6. 8. without Forgiveness, *Isa.* 22. 14. This hath abounded in our Days; which is one sign of the Son of Man, *Luke* 17. 30. and of their going Captive with the first, *Amos* 6. 7. who have been at ease in *Sion*, *v.* 1. as well as in *Samaria*.

5. Falling

The Parable of the Ten Virgins Opened.

5. Falling from Heaven, (or from an High Profession;) as Stars will doe at such a time, *Mat.* 24. 29; profaning the Covenant of their Fathers, *Mal.* 2. 10. and dealing Treacherously with the Wife of their Youth, *v.* 14. This have our Eyes beheld; and not in a Trivial matter, or in some Less Degrees; but Many have fallen from Heaven unto the Earth, as *Rev.* 20. 4; yea some to Hell, *Isa.* 57. 9; and some of Understanding also, as *Dan.* 11. 35. Fallen Man is subject to this Falling-Sickness, and more especially toward the Fall, or in these Latter dayes; since Christ is set for the Fall of Many in *Israel*, *Luke* 2. 34. But if one falling from a Window (three Stories high) was taken up Dead, *Act.* 20. 9; what hopes of Life can be conceived of him, who is seen falling down from Heaven unto the Earth?

6. Aptness to be Deceived by false Christs and Prophets, *Mat.* 24. 24. Prophets are noted for their Predictions; as Christ was, for the Newness of his Doctrine, *Mark* 1. 27. both which will [Then] be so far Counterfeited (by shewing great Signs and Wonders,) as to Deceive many, *Mark* 13. 6; and if it were possible, the very Elect, *Mat.* 24. 24. which argueth that Deceiving to be Fundamental. How grossly Erroneous were the *Sadduces* in Christ's time, *Mat.* 22. 23; and yet Co-ordinate with the Priests and Pharisees, or One of those Three principal Shepherds, *Zech.* 11. 8: and as there Never was a Spring without its Frogs and Vermin, so have all greater Revolutions had Old Errours first, on purpose to make New (following) Light Offensive. But as those Locusts did not Hurt the Sealed Number, *Rev.* 9. 4; so neither shall the Elect be Now seduced, *Mark* 13. 22.

7. Oppression of the Poor and Needy; whereof Declining *Israel* is accused Deeply. Thus *Ephraim* loved to Oppress, *Hos.* 12. 7; which *Ashdod* and *Egypt* are bid, Behold, *Am.* 3. 9: Yea *Judah* also did Oppress the Stranger wrongfully, *Ezr.* 22. 29. and her Poor Servants, *Jer.* 34. 16. a little before her Ruine, *v.* 21. Which Poorer sort are Mean as to the World, and small in Number, (in which sence *Gideon*'s Family is called Poor, *Judg.* 6. 15.) and These are most apt to be Opprest by sordid Worldlings, whilest Others of an Higher Rank are let alone. Thus solitary Christ, *Mat.* 26. 56. was Hated to the Death, *v.* 59. by Those, who durst not give the Baptist an ill word, his Party was so Numerous, *Mat.* 21. 26. But as these Poor are chiefly Fed by Christ at such a time, *Zech.* 11. 7. and know his VVord, *v.* 11. so will he Arise or Come, for their Oppression and their Sighing, *Psal.* 12. 5.

8. Formality in Religion, (or Form of Godliness without its Power,) is that by which the last Times are to be known, *2 Tim.* 3. 1. 5.

Thus

Thus typical *Sardis* had (at such a time,) a Name to live, and nothing else, *Rev.* 3. 1 : and others are Taxed for their putting God off with a Corrupted thing, *Mal.* 1. 14. and snuffing at it too, *v.* 13. It is observed, that Aged persons are nothing o Zealous in their Religion, as when Youths; which holdeth true, with reference unto Old *Jerusalem*'s Professors. But such are therefore to be Turned from, 2 *Tim.* 3. 5: nor will the Lord Accept the r worth ess Sacrifice, *Mal.* 1. 14. but will turn to the Gentiles, *v.* 11 : yea if such do not lay this Sin to Heart, their very Blessings shall be Cursed, *Mal.* 2. 2; and their whole Sacrifice counted Dung, together with their Persons, *v.* 3.

9. A very great want of Moral Honesty. Some will be Traytors then, 2 *Tim.* 3. 4 ; and false Accusers, *v,* 3 : Others will Dally with their Light, 2 *Pet.* 3. 5 ; and be abominably Partial in the Law, *Mal.* 2. 9 ; turning the Scriptures into a Nose of VVax, to serve their carnal Interest. Thus will God lead Backsliders forth with workers of Iniquity, *Psal.* 125. 5. on purpose to abate their Pride and Insolency. *Gentiles* and *Jews* will little Differ at such a time, *Rom.* 3. 9. that none might quarrel with their being taken in upon a New Account, *v.* 23. VVhy should not Gentiles be admitted (if Repenting) when Old professing *Jews* are thus Degenerated? Yea Christ will then unmask those wicked Hypocrites, who Lie and Rail, and will not understand, and yet Pretend unto their being Gods Temple, *Jerem.* 7. 9. 14, 15.

10. Impudent self-justifying. Thus were those typical *Pharisees*, They (by way of Eminency and Distinction,) who Justified Themselves before Men, *Luke* 16. 15; not by the real Acquisition of a Righteous Quality, as *Rev.* 22. 11. in the Greek ; but by a bold Pronouncing of that Sentence upon themselves. And thus it is fore-told with reference unto the Latter dayes, (if *Malachy*'s Prophecy be not, To us, a naked History,) that Priests and People Then will plead, *Wherein have we despised thee*, Mal. 1. 6 ? *Wherein have we polluted thee*, v. 7 ? *Wherein have we wearied him*, Mal. 2. 17 ? *Wherein have we robbed thee*, Mal. 3. 8 ? *Wherein shall we return*, v. 7 ? 'As if the Lord himself had falsly charged them. Thus in the Last dayes, 2 *Tim.* 3. 1. men will be Boasters, Proud, Blasphemers, *v,* 3 ; o apt to Justifie themselves, though in a way of Blaspheming God. Age in Profession, and Darkness of the Time, plausible Pretences, and Multitude of Companions, together with their High Esteem, produce this Impudence: but He will then be their Judge, who Knows their Hearts, *Luke* 16. 15. *Rev.* 2. 23.

11. Dis.

not Confider or Regard. At least, God's Hand therein is not taken notice of; but onely the hand of Man, or the Matter of such a Providence; and so the Specialty of a Design is little thought upon. But therefore Captivity is Denounced, *Isa.* 5. 12; enough to make All look about them, before 'tis put in Execution.

12. Resolvedness in an Evil way; Partly from being formerly Engaged in it, *Jer.* 2. 25; partly from Hopes of further Benefit, *Isa.* 57. 10; and partly from a Desperate stoutness of Spirit, without any Reason rendred, *Jer.* 18. 12. Old Trees will sooner Break than Bow; and when the Heart is Touch'd with *Mammon*, it will stand pointing to that Load-stone: Yea Sin is fallen Man's Byas, whose Wheeling Influence (upon his Motion) is most Prevailing, towards the End, as in the Letter. Though some may be kept from Returning, by their false Teachers, and superstitious Fears, and plausible Arguments or seeming Scripture grounds. But if men *will* not walk in that good way, *Jer.* 6. 16. nor hearken to the Trumpet's Sound, *v.* 17. Others are bid to hear their Sentence, *v.* 18.

13. Calling one Contrary by the Other's Name; both as to God's Providences, and mens Moral Actions, *Isa.* 5. 20: And thus in plainer Cases too; or from Affected (at least-wise self-contracted, rather than simple) Ignorance. Thus some Bless God, when prospering in a sinfull way, *Zech.* 11. 5: and Others call that a Judgement, and are Offended with it, which is a Mercy, *Mat.* 2. 3. and 15. 12; calling that Evil, which is a Truth, 1 *Kings* 22. 8. And as to Moral Actions; when Ignorance is called Light, and Disobedience by the Name of Duty.; and when the Bitter root of Sin is called Sweet, that is to say, *Pleasant, Psal.* 119. 103: Comforting, *Eccl.* 5. 12. and Strengthning, *Neh.* 8. 10. This is a wofull sad Temptation, *Isa.* 5. 20: exposing unto all manner of Sin and Suffering; since it is worse than Intermingling Good with Evil; yea worse than Bodily Blindness (which doth not think Darkness to be Light) or a bodily Distempered Taste, which never counts Bitter things Sweet, as is by some observed: and as it argueth a Reprobate Mind, *Rom.* 1. 28. so is it near of Kin unto that Sin against the Holy Ghost, *Mark* 3. 29. 30.

14. Un-

The Parable of the Ten Virgins Opened.

14. Unreasonable self-conceit, and High Pretensions. Pride goeth before Destruction, both as its Cause and Symptom, *Prov.* 16. 18: which therefore is more to be Lamented, than to be Wondred at, with reference unto Dying Old *Jerusalem.* Tell some men of their Sin, they will Deride you, as those did Christ, *Luke* 16. 14. a little before their being Cut off, *Zech.* 11. 8. Tell Others of their hastning Downfall; they say, *Is not the Lord among us ? no Evil can come upon us,* Mic. 3. 11. a little before their being Plowed up, *v.* 12. Bid *Laodicean* Churches, Buy your Gold, *Rev.* 3. 18. they'l tell you, they have need of Nothing, *v.* 17. a little before their being spewed out, *v.* 16. Thus while the true Children of Light are made to walk in Darkness, others will warm themselves with sparks of their Own kindling, but shall lye down in sorrow, *Isa.* 50. 10, 11.

These are those Grosser Time-temptations; The more Refined are as followeth.

1. Affections without Judgement, or Lamps without Oyl in Vessels. This is Predominant in Foolish Virgins as to the Main ; and incident unto the Wise, in some Degree: both which have therefore need to VVatch, in that regard. Old men and Children abound with such Affections ; which therefore had need to be taken notice of, as men would shun the Casualties, both of this Fall, and of the next Spring. Affections raised Above one's Judgement, are like the Speakers Voice above his Spirit; exceeding Prejudicial to the Matter in point of VVorth, as well as Acceptation. And yet, we therefore have so many Staggerers, because they are as it were Drunk with over-strong Affections; which therefore men have need to VVatch against. Onely take heed of sinfull subtle Moderation, under a Pretence of Fearing to be Injudicious: but let our Zeal be under the Command of Knowledge, and let that Knowledge be pursued, then let us be as Hot as Fire.

2. Aptness to Boast of what is Carnal: as being Wise, or men of Parts, *Jer.* 9. 23. and *Abraham*'s Children, or professors, *Joh.* 8. 39. full of Religious Duties, *Luke* 18. 11, 12. and having the Name of Temples, *Jer.* 7. 4. Thence do some boast so of the Spirit : meerly because of their many words: especially if Florid and Affectionate, though such Affections may be meerly Natural, if not Enforced. VVhereas the Spirit in Prayer is to be Known by something which cannot be uttered, *Rom.* 8. 26 : and so, in Speaking, by speaking in a way of Demonstration, 1 *Cor.* 2. 4 : and of Revealing the Deep things of God, *v.* 10. which are not Known by the VVorld, *v.* 7, 8. nor yet Received, *v.* 14. Nor is the Spirit (in any) to be Judged of, but by the
spiritual

The Parable of the Ten Virgins Opened.

Spiritual Man; *v.* 15. *John* must Decrease, as Christ gets up; but Lower things are never more Affected by us, than just upon their being ready to Die. Declining Age (as in the Letter, so in the Mystery) hath least of Substance in it; which therefore most Delighteth in Toys and Circumstances, as being most like unto it self. But it is Weakly done, to Glory in that Flesh, which as it was but Grass at best, so is it (Now) sure to Wither, *Isa.* 40. 6, 7, 8. Instead of founding shining Brass, God is Now bringing Gold, *Isa.* 60. 17. which *Laodiceans* have need to Buy, *Rev.* 3. 18. since other things will Burn.

3. Spiritual Decays, to what have sometimes been. Thus Typical *Ephesus* (at such a time) is charged with Leaving her first Love, *Rev.* 2. 4. and *Sardis* lay at the point of Death, *Rev.* 3. 2. and *Laodicea* was worse than Cold, *Rev.* 3. 15. Men truly Gracious, are alway Growing, *Psal.* 92. 12, 14. but Nature hath its stint, and thenceforth Lives upon its former stock, which therefore needs must waste. This is the more Dangerous, because it stealeth upon Souls and Bodies by Degrees; and not so violently, as in a fit of down-right sickness. And though Gray Hairs can talk of a Consumptive state, (as in a Spiritual case some others do,) yet are they apt to let it Grow upon them, without Resistance. But this alone had need to make us sick, for fear of being spewed out by him, *Rev.* 3. 16. who turneth not unto his Vomit.

4. Lothness to be Transplanted, though for the Better. As all the *Pharisees* stuck fast to *Moses*, *John* 9. 28. So, few (if any) of *John*'s Disciples followed Christ, though by that means they entred not into his Heavenly Kingdom, *Mat.* 11, 11. Nature would fain be cloath'd upon, but not uncloath'd, 2 *Cor.* 5. 4. but none save Fools do look, that what is sown should ever quicken, except it Die, 1 *Cor.* 15. 36. Most think Conversion to be done at once, which yet is a continued Act, as *Peter* found, *Luke* 22. 32. and without which being born again, professing *Nicodemus* might not see the Kingdom of God, *John* 3. 3. it being with Grace, as with the Growing Wheat, which first appeareth like unto Grass, but doth Exchange (in Time) that Lower Blade for something Higher, *viz.* the Ear; and without which it is concluded to be Grass indeed, or little better. Thus are some Accessary to their Spiritual Leanness, by their not following Christ into his Greener Pastures: 'And as Men would facilitate their Removal with him, so let them take heed of Rooting deeper into other things than into him, which is a Vanity more common than Discerned.

5. A proneness to be too much in Love with out-side fairness, so as to Marry others (in the Mystery) on that Account; as did the Sons of God with those Fair Daughters of Men, *Gen.* 6. 2. a little before the Flood,

which

which Answereth unto this Coming of the Son of Man, *Mat.* 24. 38, 39. Which out-side Fairness doth import what is the first *Adam*'s Lustre, which is to have its due, but not to be a Rival with the Second, in point of Conjugal (or Highest) Love. Yet thus did the Disciples Gaze upon those Goodly Buildings, which in a while were laid aside, *Mat.* 24. 1, 2. Such kind of Beauty must be expected then, as in the Face of some Consumptive Persons, a little before their Change; and wherewith many will be Ensnared. But let the Admirers of Parts and Moral Vertues know, and bear in mind, what brought the Deluge.

6. Aptness to be secure, and not to know, till Sufferings come. This will be the World's Temptation, to be sure; yea, Christ saw need to bid his own take heed of promising too quick a Period to their Tribulation, *Mark* 13. 8, 9. I should be glad, if *Sion* might be Delivered, without any further pain; but since she hath not yet brought forth, we may conclude, her Last Pangs will be sharpest. 'Tis true indeed, when Vermin once begin to Run (as some do at this Day already) that is one sign the House is Falling; but on the other side, when Eaves are seen to drop, long after a shower, it is an usual Symptom of more Rain behind, because it Argueth the Air to be still very moist; and some particular Droppings (of a Persecuting Spirit) are still continued. However, National Distresses must come at Last, *Luke* 21. 25. or after-Persecutions, *v.* 12. therefore let us Prepare for further Sufferings.

7. Depending too much (in ways of Duty) upon Encouragements. Satan did sometimes put the Question, *Doth Job fear God for Nought*, Job 1. 9? but with Respect to Satan's Dispensation in these Latter Days, the Lord himself doth Ask, *Who is there even among you* (Professors) *that would shut the Doors for Nought*, Mal. 1. 10? Yea, when the Proud are Happy, and wicked workers are set up, the un-rewarded keepers of Gods Ordinances count his Service vain, *Mal.* 3. 14, 15. Old Labourers are apt to Murmure, in case they have not more than Ordinary Pay, *Mat.* 20. 11. much more, when these are made to work, and others onely seem to have the Wages. But as a Mercenary Spirit is not Filial, *Phil.* 2. 20, 21, 22. So Discontent (on that Account) is the Companion of most worthless Duty, *Isa.* 58. 3, 4, 5. wherein God hath no Pleasure, *Mal.* 1. 10. and the Fore-runner of such Men's being laid aside, *v.* 11.

8. Humane Traditions in Matters of Religious Worship. We Read of Old Wives Fables, 1 *Tim.* 4. 7. and Jewish Fables and Commandments of Men, *Titus* 1. 14. to signifie, what Old Professors (in their declining state) are subject to. And when Christ was about to Change that present Dispensation, the *Pharisees* are chiefly Noted for their own Tra-

The Parable of the Ten Virgins Opened.

Traditions, by which the Commands of God were made of none effect, *Mat.* 15.6. And which Traditions were their underftanding the Scripture, according to the Judgment of their Ancients, right or wrong, *Mat.* 5.43. their preffing outward wafhing, (or Baptifms, as in the *Greek*,) as Neceffary to go Before Communion, *Mark* 7.4. And felf-impofed Faftings, wherein the Difciples of *John* agreed with them, *Mark* 2. 18. fuch like Traditions of a more Refined Nature (for which there alfo is fome Colour from the Scripture, as then was) are to be watch'd againft.

9. Mif-underftanding the Manner of Chrifts Coming in his Kingdom, as if it would be with Obfervation, or of a ftinted Nature, or without Interruption; all which Miftakes Chrift cleareth up at large, *Luke* 17. 20, 21, 22, 23, 24. It will not be with Obfervation, as many will be apt to Fanfie, *Luke* 17. 20. That is to fay, it will not be with any Ignoble kind of fecret lying in wait, or Plotting in an unworthy way; as the fame *Greek* word is oit-times ufed, *Luke* 6.7. and 14.1. and 20. 20. *Acts* 9. 24. therefore let no Men of a Private, Paffionate, or Revengeful Spirit look to Profper, in their pretending to Advance that Kingly Difpenfation; no more than did the Jew fh or Religious Robbers, *Dan.* 11. 14. Since *Sion* muft be Redeemed with Righteoufnefs, *Ifa.* 1. 27. which is not wrought by the wrath of Man, *James* 1. 20. and as an Humorous Perfonal Reformation, is nothing like unto a True Converfion. Nor will this Kingdom Come, with any kind of Heathenifh or Superftitious Obfervation, fuch as the Jews or Gentiles ufed, with Refpect unto their Days, and Monethes, and Times, and Years, *Gal.* 4. 10. where the fame *Greek* word is alfo rendred, *Ye Obferve*. That is to fay, this Kingdom will not Come, with outward fhew, or Childifh Pomp; fo as to Occafion faying, *Lo Here, Lo There*; this Kingdom being of an Inward Nature, or within us, *Luke* 17. 21. as is Chrift's Spiritual Kingdom alfo, *Rom.* 10. 8. to fhew the Inwardnefs of its Nature, and Not its being (then) in thofe *Pharifees*, *Luke* 17. 21. no more than was that word of Faith (at fuch a time) in *Ifrael*, *Deut.* 30. 14. In fuch a Manner will Chrift's Kingdom Come; not in a way of Worldly ftate, but of true Holinefs and Righteoufnefs, or Inward Glory, more than of Outward Greatnefs, *Pfal.* 45. 13. wherein his Spiritual and Temporal Kingdom will Agree, at firft efpecially. Its Coming alfo will be felf-diffufive, not Limited unto (although beginning in) fome little Corner; but will be a the Lightning, out of the one part under Heaven, unto the other, *Luke* 17. 24. Such was the fpeedy felf-extending Nature of his Spiritual Kingdom in the World, *Rom.* 10. 18. Such is its Nature in a particular

Soul

Soul, Extending to the whole Man, Body, Soul, and Spirit, 1 *Thef.* 5. 23. fuch alfo will be the Nature of his Temporal Kingdom, *Pfal.* 72. 8. Therefore Chrift biddeth his Difciples not to follow (or go after) thofe who are of a poor Narrow Spirit, *Luke* 17.23. Confining h's Work or Difpenfation to fome Leffer Compafs; as Partial Reformifts do, in a Spiritual and Ecclefiaftical fence, and others in a Civil or Political, as did thofe Jews of Old unto *Judea*: Since the whole of his Government is endlefsly increafing, *Ifa.* 9. 7. though firft heard of in *Bethlehem Ephrata*, *Pfal.* 132. 6. the leaft among *Judah*'s Thoufands, *Mic.* 5. 2. Nor will that Kingdom be without its Interruption, as Chrift there fignifieth, *Luke* 17. 22., by his Difciples defiring (in vain) to fee one of his Days, who was Then with them. So will it be, with reference unto his Temporal Kingdom, (which hath been formerly proved at large ;) as in Relation to his Spiritual : In which Regard, Souls muft look for a frefh Converfion, upon fome Greater Fall or Revolution, *Acts* 3. 19. The not Underftanding whereof made his Difciples to Rebuke the Bringers of Little Children to him, *Luke* 18. 15. and is the Caufe why others cannot Enter into his Kingdom, *v.* 17. which doth confift of none but fuch, *v.* 16. Therefore let not us (or the Churches) be Offended with this Interruption, and that Renovation.

10. Forgetfulnefs of Old Diftinguifhing Mercies from the Lord. Thus, with Refpect unto the Latter Days, profeffing Jews are Taxed for their faying unto God, *Wherein ?* when he had told them of his former Love, *Mal.* 1. 2. which he re-minds them of, in Competition with their Brother *Efau*, whom he had Hated, and laid his Mountains wafte, *Mal.* 1. 2, 3. Thus *Edom*, in the Myftery (or *Ifrael*'s Elder Brother, according to the Flefh) hath been quite laid afide, of later Years : yet have not the Men of *Judah* walked worthy of their being fuffered to continue ftill. And whereas *Edom* will (at fuch a time) hope for the Return of his Captivity. God will throw down his Buildings, *Mal.* 1. 4 and will be Magnified from the Border of *Ifrael*, *v.* 5. or from fome outskirts of thefe Jews, as that word [*Border*] intimateth, *Ezek,* 11. 11. although the Generality of This People alfo (Now) would foon be laid fide, *v.* 11. and partly, becaufe they (virtually) had forgot this great Difcriminative Favour.

11. Wifhing for the Day of Chrift, without Confidering the Nature of it. Some will Defire it's being haftened, in a way of fcoffing, *Ifa.* 5. 19. but others, fimply, though to no End, fave their own forrow, *Amos* 5. 18. And yet, who is there at this day (among Profeffors) but feeketh it, and is Delighted in its Expectation ? Like thofe of

of Old, *Mal* 3. 1. who yet could not Abide it, nor stand therein, *v.* 2. The Reason is, because All Hope to wear some of that Bridegroom's Favours, as did the Jews, *Mat.* 20. 21. and the *Samaritans* also, *John* 4. 25. but Dream not of his fiery Baptism, *Mat.* 20. 22. In which regard, that Prophet did not desire the woful Day, *Jer.* 17. 16. when others said, *v.* 15. *Let it Come Now*: No more should we, if seriously considering, *How many Virgins then will be Defloured*, Zech. 14. 2. and how much Loss the saved ones will then Meet with, besides Affrightment, *Zech.* 13. 9.

12. A mighty proneness to Impose upon, Observe, and Censure others more than our selves; and to deal thus with some more than with others, in a sinful way. Old Age is more for Talk, than Actions; as were the *Pharisees*, *Mat.* 23. 3. who never thought another's Burden Heavy enough, *v.* 4. And they who mind their own Work least, are apt to be most busic in Observing others, so as to spye their very Motes, *Mat.* 7. 3. which is the Labour of Idle Persons. Yea, Christ and his Disciples (who least Deserved it) had sharpest Censures, and most Observing Eyes; (as Harmless *Jeremy* had from his *Jerusalem*, Jer. 15. 10. Yea, Evil for Good, *Jer.* 18. 20.) while *Herod's* Incest, and their own gross Enormities were over-looked. But as this did evince their being Hypocrites in Christ's Opinion; so is it but a Folly Now, to think of Hiding inward sleightiness by Liveless Testimonies, and being Dis-satisfied with another's Low Attainments, more than our own. It is a slye Temptation this, since Conscience is pleased with Reproving sin or Pressing Duty; and Pride is for that Magisterial Act, with reference unto another: Yea, under this Painted Tomb (of Verbal Declamations) the Old Man's Rottenness lyes undiscovered, *Mat.* 23. 27, 28. Next unto Heartless self-condemning, this Formal witnessing unto the Height of Sin and Duty in another, is one of the saddest Dying Groans (or Symptoms of a Near approaching Change) among Professors at this Day.

13. Mis-apprehending the Voice of Providence; as to its Principal and Proper Meaning. Thus, as the Enemies of *Sion* will not understand God's Thoughts and Counsel, in bringing them against her, to their own Destruction, *Mic.* 4. 11, 12, 13. So neither will some in *Sion* know, wherefore he doth Those things unto them; as is Apparent from their putting that Question to the Prophet, *Jer.* 6. 10. wherein they are more Ignorant than some of other Nations, *Jer.* 22. 8, 9. Such will impute the *Assyrian's* Coming, unto the Grosser Wickedness of those among them: Whereas God chiefly sendeth him against the Hypocrites, *Isa.* 10. 5, 6. Such will Arraign, ('tis like) that Persecuting *Persian* or
Assyrian.

Aſſyrian Spirit, as by whoſe means their following Judgments came: But God tells them, it hath been by Their Means, *Mal.* 1.9. becauſe of their Complying with the *Perſian* Prohibition, *Hag.* 1.9. And when Deliverance cometh, ſuch will be apt to ſhare its Meritorious Cauſe among Themſelves: Which yet, next to the Lord's own Name, *Ezek.* 36.22. is Attributed to a Little Remnant, *Iſa.* 1.9. a Tenth or Holy Seed, *Iſa.* 6.13. and ſingle Cluſter upon a Withered Vine, *Iſa.* 65.8. The Man of Wiſdom will ſee God's Name, *Mic.* 6.9. and Prudent ones ſhall Underſtand, *Hoſ.* 14.9. but none of the Wicked, *Dan.* 12, 20. which is a ſore Temptation.

14. Miſtaking the Predominant Duty of ſuch a Time, as did Five of thoſe Spies to One, when in the Wilderneſs, *Numb.* 14.30. and but Three Hundred in *David*'s Time did ſeem to know what *Iſrael* ought to do, 1 *Chron.* 12.32. And with Reſpect unto the Day of *Jacob*'s Trouble, ſome Ask (as being Ignorant) what God would have them do, *Mic.* 6.6? Gheſſing at ſeveral things, (as Thouſands of Rams, Ten Thouſand Rivers of Oyl; yea, their Firſt-born, *v.* 7.) which in their Eye were of the Greateſt Value; and yet All wrong, *v.* 8. though ſuch had Meant according to their Proffer, which yet is Queſtionable. Thus at this Day, ſome count a Witneſs againſt the Papiſts; others againſt the Prelates, others againſt the Hearing of Conformiſts, *&c.* to be the Principal Duty of this preſent Time, with reference unto which, they Nobly proffer the Sacrificing of Ten Thouſand Lives. But if our Going out of Old *Jeruſalem* be a preſent Duty, *Mic.* 4.30. that ſeemeth (Now) to be Predominant, as being of a Later Date, moſt Rarely Practiſed, and moſt Oppoſed by Profeſſors, by which Time-Truths are to be known, when Groſſer Worldly Perſecutions are ſuſpended, as they Now are. The not Underſtanding of which things (belonging to our Peace) was that which made Chriſt Weep over Old *Jeruſalem*, *Luke* 19.41, 42.

15. Aptneſs in ſome, (who ſtill Continue in Dying Old *Jeruſalem*) to Bleſs themſelves in ſuch a worthleſs Portion, and Deeply to Cenſure others, (although the Son of Man's own Brethren) as being far from God, (Compared with themſelves) becauſe of their having Gone out of that Wicked City, *Ezek.* 11.15. before thoſe other; although God's Glory was then Removed out of the Temple, *Ezek.* 10.19. All which befell a little before *Jeruſalem*'s Sacking, *Ezek.* 12.11. Something like unto which, doth Uſher in Chriſt's Coming in theſe Latter Days, *Zech.* 14.2, 3. One of the Chief among which Vapourers, *Ezek.* 11.1. was ſtruck with ſudden Death, *v.* 13. to ſignifie the Doom of all his Fellows, *v.* 10. who did Encourage the reſt to Build, preſuming that Day was

not

not yet Near, *v.* 2, 3. and who did therefore thus Bless themselves and Censure others, *v.* 15. Thus will some Boast of their Abiding in that state, from whence God's Glory is Departed; and Curse their Choiser Brethren, for being in *Babylon*, or Confusion: wherein yet God will be (unto these Censured ones) a little Sanctuary, *Ezek.* 11. 16. and will give Them (in his due time) the Land of *Israel*, *v.* 17. when their Deriders will be sadly Recompensed, whose present Worship is called Detestable and Abominable, *v.* 21.

16. Lingring too long in Spiritual *Sodom*, as sometimes *Lot* did, *Gen.* 19. 16. whose Day was Typical of that wherein the Son of Man will be Revealed, *Luke* 17. 28, 29, 30. The Reason of whose Lingring then (perhaps) might be his casting about to save some of his better stuff; like unto which will be the Temptation of some others in this day of Christ, *Luke* 17. 31, 32. Thus will some (Then) Go forth at Last, as *Lot* and his Family did, but not at the first bidding, *Gen.* 19. 15. till some Good Angels lay hold upon them, and Bring them out, *v.* 16. Or it is very probable, *Lot's* Daughters Lingred for their New Betrothed Husbands, *Gen.* 19. 14. their Mother for them, and so *Lot* for them All: Thus Prejudicial (unto a Spiritual Quickness) are Bad Examples; and Natural or Carnal Friends. But as he is an unwise Son, who stayeth long in the place of Breaking forth, *Hof.* 13. 13. So let such Lingerers bear in mind, how hardly *Lot* was saved, *Gen.* 19. 23, 24. more for the sake of *Abraham*, than for his own, *v* 29. upon strict Terms, *v.* 17. not having Faith sufficient for his Duty, *v.* 18. nor yet security in his own choice, *v.* 30. and now his Lingring Wife perished in the way, *v.* 26. whilst he and his Daughters Lived in a Cave, *v.* 30. unto their own perpetual shame, *v.* 36. and *Israel's* being vexed afterwards with their Incestuous Off-spring, *v.* 37, 38. with *Zeph.* 2. 8, 9, 10.

17. Enquiring the Mind of God with Idols in Heart, and stumbling-blocks of Iniquity before ones Face. Thus did some of the Jewish Elders, *Ezek.* 14. 1. 3. who were then carried into *Babylon*; as is apparent, from their Coming to this Prophet, *v.* 1. and sitting probably in *Ezekiel's* House, as *Ezek.* 8. 1. who then was in *Chaldea*, *Ezek.* 1. 3. though sometimes (Visionally) in *Jerusalem*, *Ezek.* 11. 1. but Now was brought (in Vision) back again into *Chaldea*, *v.* 24. So that these Hypocritical Enquirers were Persons carried out of Old *Jerusalem*, before the rest, as some may be whose Hearts are not sincere. Which Idols in their Heart (when they did thus Enquire of God) might be, partly, their being Resolved (Before hand) what to Believe; *viz.* what *Hananiah* and such false Prophets said, out of their own Hearts,

Ezek.

Ezek. 13. 2. and boldly Fathered it upon God, *v.* 7. which therefore was fitly called an Idol, *Ezek.* 14. 3.

18. Aptness to Question God's Design of Laying Old *Jerusalem* quite aside: which seemeth to be hinted by the probable matter of their Enquiry before-mentioned, *Ezek.* 14. 1. and as may be collected from God's following Answer, *viz.* Whether *Jerusalem* was wholly Now to be laid VVaste; (as *Jeremy* and this Prophet had declared;) or whether themselves should not be suddenly brought out of *Babylon* back again to Old *Jerusalem*, as *Hananiah* had foretold, *Jer.* 28, 1, 2, 3, 4: so loth are some to leave their ancient Temple altogether, till they shall see it quite Demolished. With reference unto which, God tells the Residue of those in *Babylon*, *Ezek.* 14. 22. that Old *Jerusalem*'s Ruines must goe on, though *Noah*, *Daniel* and *Job* were in it, *Ezek.* 14. 14. 18, 20 ; and her Inhabitants must be cut off, *v.* 21 ; excepting a Remnant, who shall come unto these in *Babylon*, and Comfort them (with the sight of their Wayes and Doings) concerning Old *Jerusalem*'s Just Destruction, *v.* 22, 23. VVhich staggering at the Present state of things, was that which *John* and his Disciples laboured under, when the Preparatory or Destructive part of Christ's Administration (answering to that of *Babylon*) was Begun : as is Apparent from their asking, *Art thou He? Mat.* 11. 3. The Reason of which Doubting was, *John*'s being Now cast into Prison, *Mat.* 11. 2 ; who Formerly had VVitnessed unto that Truth, *Joh.* 1. 29. but was Now at some Kind of Loss ; whom therefore Christ then call'd a Reed, that was shaken with the VVind, *Mat.* 11. 7 ; and by which Character *John* and his Followers (at such a time) are to be Known. And from Christ's Answer may be gathered, how scrupling Baptists may be satisfied, that Christ is He, in case that Gospel is Now preached (onely) to the Poorer sort ; and if the Blind and Lame, and Leapers, and Deaf and Dead (among them) be strangely wrought upon, *Mat.* 11. 4, 5 ; which argueth his Over-turning Dispensation to be Now on foot, according to the Scriptures, *Isa.* 61. 1. and 35. 6.

19. Unsteadiness in that (upon a fresh Temptation) which hath been Manfully Returned unto, or Begun. This was their Case of Old ; who did Begin to build the Temple, or Open VVorship, *Ezra* 4. 1. till the *Assyrian* spirit in that Day, *v.* 2. prevailed so far as to prohibit them, and whereupon that VVork did cease, *v.* 24. Yea, when they did Return thereunto, *Ezra* 5. 2. upon *Zachary*'s and *Haggai*'s prophesying, *v.* 1. before the Prohibition was Reversed, *v.* 3. yet they did fall off again, (upon that fresh Discouragement, *v.* 3, 4.) as may be gathered from those Prophets writings, although it be not Expressly mentioned.

ceuariny intertes then having again Denied (upon some item Temptation) from that work, which had been at the firſt Begun, and which more Lately was Returned to; unto the making of them all unclean, and the Reviving of their former Judgements, *Hag.* 1. 9. and Loſs of all their former Labour, or making the Temple's Foundation to Commence from their laſt Twenty fourth Day, *Hag.* 2. 18. in which they Laſtingly did firſt Return unto this Work; and from which time, their Adverſaries could not make them ceaſe, *Ezra* 5. 5. And though my ſelf am ſatisfied, that This hath been Already in Our dayes, ſufficiently to make unclean; yet Now a little time may ſhew, Whether that freſh Deſiſting be not (by ſome) to be Repeated: and if it be, then let thoſe Three forenamed Motives be remembred by us, to Prevent our falling under that Temptation, in caſe freſh Perſecution ſhall ariſe.

20. Shortneſs of Spirit; or being unable to Hold pace with Chriſt, unto the End of his deſigned Journey. It is with ſome Men, as with Poſt-horſes, who have their Stages, beyond which they will not be made to goe, with ſwitch or ſpur, and ſo their Rider is neceſſitated to take other. This is foretold at large, (with reference unto the Latter dayes,) by that remarkable Viſion concerning ſeveral Horſes, of divers Colours, by which their ſpirit or mettle is commonly judged of, *Zech.* 6. 2, 3. and as they were Types of divers Spirits, *v.* 5. The firſt of which Horſes are of a Red colour, *v.* 2. which is a Natural ſymptom of their being Waſhy in the Letter: and ſuitably whereunto, we read of Nothing Done by that firſt Spirit or ſort of Horſes. The ſecond are Black, *Zech.* 6. 2; which is a far Better Colour in the Letter: The third are White, *v.* 3. which alſo Excells the Red; and ſuitably whereunto, theſe Black and White are ſaid to Go forth into the North (one After the other) *v.* 6. and to Accompliſh what they went about, in that Particular Northern Quarter, *v.* 8. The Fourth and laſt ſort of Horſes, are the Griſled and the Bay, *Zech.* 6. 3. whoſe Colours do evince their being of the Fineſt Mettle, that is, compared with the Former Three: though of theſe Two, the Bay is Beſt. Which Griſled and Bay, do ſeem to have been ſometimes Joyn'd together, in One Chariot at the Firſt, *Zech.* 6. 3. but at the Laſt they part, as is

Pp apparent

apparent, *v.* 6, 7. which sheweth them to be of Differing Spirits between Themselves, as well as with respect to all the former. Onely the Grisled (or Dapple-gray) being Better than the Black or White, goe forth unto the South, *Zech.* 6. 6. or Nearer to the Sun; though These are also satisfied with their respective single quarter. Whereas the Bay (whose Colour is the Best of All,) are said to goe forth, and seek to goe, that they might walk To and Fro, through the Earth; who are Bid so to doe, and they Doe so, *Zech.* 6. 7. Thus will some spirits Quickly Tire, and Doe Nothing: Others may Gradually Excell and be of use; but yet are Limited to some one Quarter: whereas the Largest spirited ones (Alone) will carry Christ (in his Triumphing Chariot,) and Accompany him Throughout his Progress. But scarcely One of Five, (as in that Vision,) or onely Two of Twelve, (as other where,) will evidence their being of that Other Spirit, by following him thus Fully, *Num.* 14. 24. though None but such will enter *Canaan*, *v.* 30. which is a fair Warning unto All, *Heb.* 4. 1. *Mat.* 24. 13.

21. Aptness to be Offended with Christ, as at his first Appearing; and upon such Accounts. Thus will some be Offended with him, as were the *Jews*, when *Herod* was so, *Mat.* 2. 2, 3. fearing lest the Offerded *Romans* would therefore Take away their Place and Nation, *Joh.* 11. 48. Others, because of his being Counted *Joseph's* son, *Mat.* 13. 55, 57.; as some are at this Day, who onely see the Hand of Man (but not of God,) in what hath come to pass in Later years, answering unto Christs Birth or first Production. Others, because Humane Traditions are not Observed, but sharply Taxed; as were the *Pharisees*, *Mat.* 15. 2, 3. 12.; and some in these our dayes, who cannot bear a being Contradicted by a Differing Practice, much less to be dealt Plainly with. Others, because of some more High or spiritual Doctrine, as were the *Capernaites*, *Joh.* 6. 58. 61. and Many at this Day, who are Offended with the Hearing of any Other Manna than what their Fathers have been wont to eat. Others, because of Persecution; which maketh Many to be Offended, *Mat.* 24. 9, 10: and in particular, unrooted Flashy Hearers, *Mat.* 13. 20, 21; Yea *John* himself, when he is once become a Prisoner, *Mat.* 11. 2, 3. 6; nay and Christ's own Disciples too, *Mat.* 26. 31. however Confident they Never would be so, *v.* 33, 35; Thus will Christ be for an Offence to both the Houses of *Israel*, *Isa.* 8. 14: but as, Wo be to him by whom Offences come, so Wo be to the World because thereof, *Mat.* 18. 7; and Blessed is the Non-offended one, *Mat.* 11. 6.

22. Contentment with Lesser Duties, in the Neglect of Greater. Thus did the *Pharisees* tythe their Mint and Annise and Cummin; *Mat.* 23. 23.

The Parable of the Ten Virgins Opened.

23. 23. and Rue and all manner of Herbs, or Trivial things, *Luke* 11. 42; accounting This to be the Tythe of All they did poſſeſs, *Luke* 18. 12. who therefore ſaid, *Wherein?* when God impeached them of Robbing him, *viz.* in his more Principal Tythes and Offerings, *Mal.* 3. 8. at leaſt they did Omit the Exerciſe of Judgement and Mercy, and Faith, *Mat.* 23. 23; or Judgement and the Love of God, *Luke* 11. 42; which in Obedience unto God, they ſhould have done Each toward Other, in more Weighty caſes. Thus did thoſe Daily offer upon their Altar, *Hag.* 2. 14. to ſalve the Neglect of Temple-work; which yet was Greater: and thus is Active Duty Multiplyed, to gain thereby a being Diſpenſed with from that which is of a Paſſive Nature: Yea thus ſome boaſt of being Charitable unto Other Sufferers, as did the *Phariſees* of Building the Martyrs Tombs, *Mat.* 24. 29; who yet Themſelves did Perſecute the Preſent Truth, and thereby evidenced their being thoſe Former Perſecutors Children, *v.* 31, 32. becauſe they Owned them as Fathers, (whom they ſhould have Diſowned,) and Did Accordingly: But if the Leaſt omiſſion (Juſtified) doth make men Leaſt in Chriſt's account, *Mat.* 5. 19; much more with reference unto VVeightier matters, ſuch as Time-truths and Duties are; and by which Rule, men have been Alway (Chiefly) to be Known, as to the Viſibility of their ſpiritual State, in point of being Reprobated, *Rev.* 17. 8. or Elected, *v.* 14.

23. Imperfect Reformation, or ſelf-Purifying, from contracted Guilt. Thus Old *Jeruſalem* is likened to a Pot, whoſe ſcum was in it ſtill, though boyled up by fiery Diſpenſations, but yet not Gone out of it; which cauſeth her being Brought out, without the ſaving of any One piece by caſting Lots, *Ezek.* 24. 6: that being the Land that was Not Cleanſed, nor Rained upon (or Waſhed) in the Day of Indignation, *Ezek.* 22. 24. which made the Lord to gather them in his Anger into his Fire, and there to leave them, *v.* 20. What Carefulneſs, ſelf-clearing, Indignation, Fear, Deſire, Zeal, Revenge, doth Godly ſorrow work, 2 *Cor.* 7. 11? but ſelf-Abaſing Exerciſes are ſoon thought to be ſufficient, eſpecially by thoſe who have moſt need to Multiply them. Thence are ſuch moſt Impatient, if not Immediately Reſtored to Communion-acts: whereas that True returning Prodigal thought himſelf No More worthy to be called a Son, *Luke* 15. 21. But if a Fathers ſpitting calls for ſeven Dayes Shame, much more doth ſelf-contracted Leproſie; and 'tis a Mercy to be Then Received in again, *Numb.* 12. 14. ſo long muſt ſelf-polluters Purge Themſelves before their Offerings will be Accepted, *Ezek.* 43. 26, 27: therefore God calls for Mourning Apart at ſuch a time, *Zech.* 12. 12: nor may (perhaps) that

work be throughly Ever done, if not at First, *Ezek.* 24. 13.

24. Aptness in some to beg a Liberty of Resting in the Plains, or somewhat short of where the Lord would have them be. Christ biddeth (in the Day of Old *Jerusalem*) to flee into the Mountains, *Mat.* 24. 16 : such also was his Order unto *Lot, Gen.* 19. 17. in *Sodom*'s Day, which answereth unto Christ's. But *Lot* then said, Not so my Lord, *Gen.* 19. 18; I cannot scape unto the Mountain, *v.* 19 ; let me continue (at some Distance) in the Plain, at *Zoar* ; v. 20. and which was sadly granted, *v.* 21. Thus some would be content to leave a wicked *Sodom,* (especially when Forced thence;) but fain would have some other City or Capacity to goe into, fearing some Evil in the Mountain ; as if Christ had forgotten to consult for their Accommodation. These may have their Desire granted, as *Lot* had his; but mind what followed, for our Admonition. *Lot* had no lasting satisfaction in his saucy Choice, but went at last into the Mountain, *Gen.* 19. 30. through slavish fear. Nor had he Wit or Will to goe thence to his Unkle *Abraham,* who lived not far off, *Gen.* 19. 27 ; but dwelt there in a Cave, half Buried whilest Alive, with his two Daughters, *v.* 30. unto the Rotting of his Name to all Posterity, *v.* 36, 37, 38. Let those mind this who will Dispute the Case with Christ, as to their being in the Open Field, which they Must come into at length, and upon dolefull Disadvantages, *viz.* Unquietness, and being left Alone, if not an Afterfalling into *Sodom*'s Sin ; yea possibly to be there Judged, in the Borders of their Land, *Zech.* 12. 11.

25. Trusting to one's Own strength (or Resolution) in a Trying Hour. In which regard, the Mighty man (at such a Time) is warned, Not to Glory in his Might, *Jer.* 9. 23. And as a fuller Evidence hereof, let us Observe, the sad self confidence of *Peter* and the Rest, *Mat.* 26. 25. upon Christ's telling them, *v.* 31. they All should be (That Night) Offended because of Him. Thus doth the *Assyrians* coming (into *Immanuel*'s Land,) occasion *Judah*'s looking to their Armour, *Isa.* 22. 8. and making up their own Breaches, *v.* 9, 10. and being supplyed with store of Waters, *v.* 9, 10 : who then are Jocund, *v.* 13. as being Confident, although such look not unto God, *v.* 11. But Christ bad those to Watch and Pray, *Mat.* 26. 41 ; whose heels were soon struck up, by standing thus upon their Tip-toes, *v.* 26. for Our Admonition, lest We be also Tempted. -

26. Distrusting God, and his Provision, because of its being Contemptible in an Eye of Sense and Carnal Reason. This was their Case of Old, who did Refuse the Waters of *Shiloah,* that went softly, *Isa.* 8. 6; and as there was therefore Joy (as it is in the *Hebrew*) in their

Ad-

The Parable of the Ten Virgins Opened.

Adverfaries, (fuppofing it an Eafie thing, to Take *Jerufalem* which was fo weakly Fortified,) fo did the Men of *Judah* flight that Mean Provifion, and rather chofe Affociating with *Affyrians*, unto their Ruine, *v.* 7, 8, 9. The Main of which Confederacy (in thefe our Days) may have been made already; but to prevent its further poffible degree, at leaft continuance; its being Now Mentioned, may be of Ufe. Which *Shiloah*, or *Siloah*, Neh. 3. 15. (the fame with *Siloam*, John 9. 7.) was a fmall Rivulet, arifing from the foot of *Sion*, *David*'s City, *Neh.* 3. 15. and therefore had a fpecial Inftituted Virtue in it, (on Occafions,) as to Reftore that Blind Mans fight, John 9. 7. fo to fecure Thefe at fuch a time, in Competition with unfanctified or unlawful Means. And fo the Lord hath fent, (as *Siloam* doth fignifie, John 9. 7.) fufficient means for our Security, in time of Danger, (fuch as are fitting ftill, *Ifa.* 30. 7. and making him our Dread, *Ifa.* 8. 13, 14.) which yet are apt to be Refufed (at fuch a time) by unbelieving Jews, though to their Ruine, who do Perfift therein.

27. A making Light of Time-Temptations, and counting Duties of that Nature to be meerly Circumftantial. Chrift's deareft ones are little ones, *Mat.* 18. 6. and his Meat Offering was Green Ears of Corn, *Lev.* 2. 14. fuch are Time-Truths and Duties; which therefore Man makes leaft Account of. This made the *Pharifees* to flight Believing, that Chrift was He; becaufe they counted Faith on the *Meffiah* (in the General) to be the Subftance; and that other but a Circumftance. If *Ifrael* (in the Wildernefs) had known, that not going up to *Canaan* (at fuch a time) had been fo Great a fin, *Deut.* 1. 32, 35. they would not (certainly) have made fo Light thereof; nor of their Tarrying in Old *Jerufalem* afterwards, *Jer.* 21. 8, 9. The Reafon of whofe fleightinefs in that Regard, might be, (as at this day it is,) becaufe they had the Law Compleatly given before; which though it fpake of thefe Time-truths to come, John 5. 46. yet did they place the Main of Faith and Duty, in that which Commonly was Known and Practifed of Old: through which Miftake, they Died in their fins, *Numb.* 14. 32. Jer. 21 9. John 8. 24. and wherein no true Saints (in their Refpective Ages) finally Mifcarried, but thereby were Diftinguifhed from Others.

28. Hard thoughts of God, becaufe of his Severity at fuch a time: As in thofe Jews of Old, who did evince it, by calling that Word [*a Burden*] which *Jeremy* uttered againft *Jerufalem*, Jer. 23. 33. the ufing of which Phrafe is fadly Threatned, *v.* 38, 39. and by their calling of his ways Unequal, *Ezek.* 33. 17. for his being fo Exact, *v.* 10. and not regarding their former Duty, *v.* 12, 13. and by their Mourning one towards another (in a Pining way) for what the Lord had done.

done to Old *Jerusalem*, though stoutness of Spirit would not let them (at the first) to do so Openly, *Ezek.* 24. 22, 23. and by their solemn Fasting afterwards for many Years together, *Zech.* 8. 19. *viz.* in the Fourth Moneth, because the City was Then Taken, *Jer.* 52. 6. and in the Fifth Moneth, because the Temple was Then Burnt, *Jer.* 52. 12, 13. and in the Seventh Moneth, because of *Gedaliah*'s being Then slain, *Jer.* 41.1,2. and in the Tenth Moneth, because the City Then was first Besieged, *Jer.* 52.4. Thus do some count it very hard, that such a particular failing is so taken Notice of; and not their Manifold Service otherways: Who therefore Fret and Pine away through Inward Grief and Vexing; yea, therefore have such their Fasts, as had the *Pharisees* and *John*'s Disciples, because Old things went then to wrack, and wherein Christ's Disciples could not joyn, *Mat.* 9. 14, 15. But let such know, it is Their way that is unequal, *Ezek.* 33. 17. according unto which the Lord will Judge Them, for thus Charging Him, *v.* 20. since he had given them Timely warning, *v.* 11. and was yet willing to forgive, *v.* 18. in case they Timely did Return, before his Door was shut.

29. Despondency at least, or want of Due Composure; because of the Bridegroom's Tarrying, and Tryals still continuing, if not Increasing. *Joshua* himself, when in that Typical Valley of *Achor*, did sadly Wish, that he had been Content to Dwell on *Jordan*'s other side, *Josh.* 7.7. At such a Time poor *David* also did Conclude, that he should perish by the Hand of *Saul*, 1 *Sam.* 27. 1. And *Hezekiah* thought (in the *Assyrian*'s Day,) that *Sion* would go nigh to Die in Travail, *Isa.* 37.3. Derided *Jeremy* was self-suspended, if not silenced, *Jer.* 20.7, 8, 9. and those in *Babylon* gave up themselves for Hopeless, *Ezek.* 37. 11. fearing their Heightned swelling Expectations would prove at last a false Conception, *Isa.* 26. 17, 18. or Groundless Trusting, *Luke* 24. 21. Thus will not Faith (at such a Time) be found on Earth, *Luke* 18. 8. which shews what All (the very Best) have need to Watch against. And as a Motive thereunto, it else will sadly signifie, since all these fainting Holy ones were in the Issue Over-comers, and whose Reviving Cordials (prescribed by the Lord himself,) are therefore Registred to be Our Helps.

30. Excessive Fear, when that Day cometh. Then will the Nations be Distressed, and their Hearts failing them for Fear, *Luke* 21. 25, 26. Then will the *Babylonians* Faces be as Flames, *Isa.* 13. 8. the sinners in *Sion* also will be then afraid, *Isa.* 33. 14. Yea, *Moses* then had much ado to make God's *Israel* stand, they were so Fearful, *Exod.* 14. 10. 13. Then will be the Compleating of that Earthquake, *Rev.* 11.

11. 13. at which the People Generally will flee, *Zech.* 14. 5. Yea: God will then Roar out of *Sion,* and shake the Heavens as well as Earth, *Joel* 3. 16. which needs must Terrifie. But yet the Saints Amazing Fear (at such a Time) will be their sin, because They are Then bid to Look up, and Lift up their Heads, *Luke* 21. 28. Yea, want of Confidence (in such a Day) will Evidence their not Abiding in him, 1 *John* 2. 28. who will Then be his People's Hope and strength, *Joel* 3. 16. And he that would Rest in that Day of Trouble, must Tremble Now, *Hab.* 3. 16. and Pray, that God would not be Then a Terror to him, *Jer.* 17. 17. and put Iniquity far away, so shall he not Fear, *Job* 11. 14, 15.

31. Unwillingness in some to own that Hand of God upon them, which they will then Feel, but not Acknowledge. Thus when his Hand is Lifted up, some will not see: *Isa.* 26. 11. nor lay to Heart their Sin or Punishment, *Jer.* 12. 11. Yea, when the Lord shall take from Old *Jerusalem*'s Adherents, their Strength, the Joy of their Glory, the Desire of their Eyes, and that whereupon they set their minds, their Sons and Daughters, *Ezek.* 24. 25. yet will they not Mourn nor Weep, save in a more secret way, *v.* 23. nor go Bare-headed, as *Lev.* 10. 6. or bare-footed, as 2 *Sam.* 15. 30. nor with a covered Lip, as *Mic.* 3. 7. nor eat the Bread of Men, as *Jer.* 16. 7. all which were Signs of Mourning. But let such know, they shall be made to see, unto their shame (at last) and sorrow, *Isa.* 26. 11. Yea, therefore the whole Land shall be made Desolate, *Jer.* 12. 11. from one End of it to the other, *v.* 12. and they shall therefore Pine away (through inward Mourning and Vexation) for their Iniquities, *Ezek.* 24. 25.

32. The Painting of an Harlots Face, and calling her (then) a Spouse of Christ. Thus were the *Pharisees* (in Christ's Day) like unto Whited Sepulchres; as full of Inward Rottenness as ever, onely New Whited with an Out-side Beauty, *Mat.* 23. 27, 28. Thus were the Generality of Professors (then) like to an House Swept and Garnished, but Empty still, *Mat.* 12. 44. and sadlier Re-possessed afterwards than ever, *v.* 45. Thus also was their Temple (lately) Beautified with Goodly Buildings, wherewith Christ's own Disciples were Enamoured, *Mark* 13. 1. *q. d.* Must we now leave this stately Temple? Which yet was (then) a Den of Thieves more than before, *Mat.* 21. 13. and near its utter Dissolution, *Mark* 13. 2. Yea, thus we Read of *Jezebel, Rev.* 2. 20. (with reference unto these Latter days) Resembling that self-painting Harlot, 2 *Kings* 9. 30. who did (Now) call her self a Prophetess, *Rev.* 2. 20. and is Described by her Teaching and Seducing Christ's Servants, to Eat things Sacrificed

unto

unto Idols, *Rev.* 2. 20. or to make light of that for which God doth pronounce Professors to be unclean, as *Hag.* 2. 14. They who are Now of such a Spirit, are justly to be called the *Jezebels* of this Present Day; whatever Paint they have upon their Faces, or by what Name soever they are called. And as a warning unto such (in these our days) let them consider (before it be too late) how sadly *Jezebel* is Threatned there, *Rev.* 2. 22. together with her Friends, *v.* 20 and Children, *v.* 23.

33. Aptness in some (in the *Assyrian*'s day) to go down into *Egypt*, to get Relieved from Threatning *Ashur*; as is fore-told at large in *Isaiah*'s 30*th*. and 31*th*. Chapters. Which *Egypt* was the Old House of Bondage to God's *Israel*; and fitly Answereth (in these Latter Days) unto some former Persecuting Interest, which some may seek to curry Favour with, to save them from a Later and more Cruel Adversary. Thus did some Trust on *Egypt*, in the days of *Hezekiah*, or else the *Assyrian* lied, 2 *Kings* 18. 24. and in the days of *Zedekiah*, to be sure; by means of which *Egyptians* (then) the *Babylonians* Siege was raised for a while, *Jer.* 37. 5. but came again, and sackt *Jerusalem*, *v.* 8. Thus in the *Assyrian*'s day, *Isa.* 30. 31. some will go down to *Egypt*, *v.* 2. and will not be with-held by any means, *v.* 9, 10, 11. though sitting still (in that regard) would be their strength, *v.* 7. and safety, *v.* 13, 14. But those *Egyptians* Help will prove in vain, *Isa.* 30. 3. 7. because they are but Flesh, *Isa.* 31. 3. and were sought unto in God's stead, *v.* 1. Yea, contrary to an Old express Command, *Deut.* 17. 16. therefore both he that Helpeth, and is Holpen, shall fall down together, *Isa.* 31. 3. and Flee, one Thousand of them, at the Rebuke of one, *Isa.* 30. 17. Whereas, they who then Trust in God, shall be Defended by him, *Isa.* 31. 4, 5. and they shall see the *Assyrian* beaten down by God's own voice, *Isa.* 30. 31. and his Young Men shall be Discomfited, *Isa.* 31. 8. his Princes also shall be afraid because of the Ensign, *v.* 9. Yea, some (who have escaped Old Jerusalem's Plagues) will chuse going into *Egypt* still (through causeless Fear) rather than to continue in *Judea*. This was their Case of Old, *Jer.* 41. 17, 18. because the *Ammonites* had Hired *Ishmael* to Murder *Gedaliah*, *Jer.* 40. 14. through his own Folly, *v.* 16. wherein the *Chaldeans* had no Hand. Thus when *Jerusalem* is Sacked in these Latter dayes, some may Impute the Plotting of Malignant *Ammonites* (against them still) to their Abiding in that state of Desolation: Yea, notwithstanding God's Command, and Promise to Deliver them, as *Jer.* 42. 11. whom they Dissemblingly Enquired of, *v.* 20. and solemnly protested a Comporting with, *v.* 5, 6. So prone are Carnal *Israelites* to be in Love with

Egypt

The Parable of the Ten Virgins Opened. 297

Egypt still, (their Ancient state, and where their Heart hath Alway been, in times of Trial;) as having never yet been truly Humbled for their Old Abominations, *Jer.* 44. 10. But as a Warning unto others in our Days, let us consider, their Growing sin, *Jer.* 44. 16, 17. and Threatned Judgments, *Jer.* 42. 18.

34. Despising the Day of small Beginnings. Thus did the Jews, when they first Built the Second Temple, *Ezra* 4. 12. something like unto which our Eyes have seen, of Later Years, or with Respect unto *John Baptist*'s Dispensation in our days. Yea, when that Temple-work Revived afterwards, those did still Labour of that Old Distemper, as seemeth to be hinted, *Hag.* 2. 3. and *Zech.* 4. 10. because this Second Temple had not that Gold and Silver, *Hag.* 2. 8. which was in *Solomon*'s; nor was this made (like That) of Hewen stones, but onely Rolling ones, *Ezra* 5. 8. as in the Margin and Original; nor had This any Priest with *Urim* and with *Thummim*, *Ezra* 2. 63. (or such who did pretend to Absolute Infallibility) as had the first. But let them who thus Labour (being Tempted) know, that Christ was (at the first) a Child; so will his Kingdom be: And those were Unbelievers, who for that Reason did Despise him, *Isa.* 53. 1, 2, 3. and that This work is in his Hand, who will Compleat it, unto their Joy, *Zech.* 4. 10. and will not fail or be Discouraged, *Isa.* 42. 4. till he had made the Second Temple Greatest, *Hag.* 2. 9.

35. Not Knowing Christ, at his Appearing in these Latter days, no more than did the World, at his first Birth, *John* 1. 10. nor his Disciples, at his Resurrection, *Luke* 24. 37. Among the Many Thousands of the Seventh Trumpet's Hearers, how Blessed will that People be, (and therefore but a few) who know that Joyful sound, *Psal.* 89. 15. when Christ shall Come as King, *v.* 18. and *Rev.* 11. 15! Some took *John Baptist* to be Christ, *John* 1. 20. Others took Christ to have been *John*, *Mat.* 16. 14. So may some (in our days) Confound the Bridegroom and his Harbinger; and so not know the Proper Name of such a Dispensation, through self-contracted (if not wilful) Ignorance. And which Mistake will not be Trivial; since they (and they alone) who know the Joyful sound, shall walk, O Lord, in the Light of thy Countenance, *Psal.* 89. 15. in thy Name shall they Joy, and be Exalted in thy Righteousness, *v.* 16. Whereas Mistakers (in that regard) can neither look to share in those peculiar Priviledges, nor yet to Understand their special Duty, which is Depending upon Knowledge of the Times, *1 Chron.* 12. 32.

36. Deferring that Day, through Unbelief; or being too much in Love with Present things. Thus some will not Believe for Joy, as

Luke

298   *The Parable of the Ten Virgins Opened.*

Luke 24. 41. Others (for Anguish) will not Hearken, as *Exod.* 6. 9. and others because of visible Improbabilities, as being too Marvellous in such a day, *Zech.* 8. 6. This will betray some into Sensuality, *Mat.* 24. 48. others will therefore say, *Come, Let us Build,* Ezek. 11. 3. and others, that Visions (or Discourses) of that Nature, are to no Effect, *Ezek.* 12, 22, 23. But this Delaying it, (though ouely in one's Heart) is said to be the Character of an Evil Servant, *Mat.* 24. 48. and one of those, *Ezek.* 11. 1. who said, *It is not Near*, *v.* 3. was therefore struck with sudden Death, *v.* 13. Yea, this Deferring of it, is quite contrary to Christ's Design, in this whole Parable and other Scriptures; which therefore had need be watch'd against, as that which is the Bane of watching in the General.

37. Groundless Presuming upon Mercy, to the last. Thus Old *Jerusalem*'s Inhabitants were apt to Fansie, that the *Chaldeans* should depart, *Jer.* 37. 9. because they had with-drawn a while, through fear of *Pharaoh*'s Army, *v.* 5. and would have had the Prophet to Comply with them, *v.* 3. Thus in all probability, those Ante-deluvian Sons of God, *Gen.* 6. 2. did Hope, they should not All be Wash'd away, according to the Rigour of that Sentence, *v.* 7, else would they not have so Neglected Hastening into that Ark; the like Figure whereunto (in point of saving us in such a Day) is Now Christ's Baptism or Dispensation, and our being gathered up into it, 1 *Pet.* 3. 20, 21. Distinct from *John's*, as at Christ's first Appearing, *Mat.* 3. 11. and as is hinted in that 1 *Pet.* 3. 21, Yea, when *Jerusalem* was laid waste, yet the Inhabiters of those wastes presumed they should Inherit them, because of their being Many, and *Abraham*'s Children, *Ezek.* 33. 24. though of the same Spirit with those Before, *v.* 25, 26. who therefore were alike Destroyed, *v.* 27. And thus will Foolish Virgins Hope, that so many Persons and Professors of their Parts and Gifts, and seeming Graces, will not be wholly laid aside, untill the Door shut upon them will Decide the Controversie. This is that Great Temptation, with reference unto which, Christ biddeth All to Watch at such a time.

38. Aptness to call in Question the Exercise of God's Disposing Providence, in such an Absolute Confused state of things. Foundations being out of Course, *Psal.* 82. 5. what can the Righteous do, *Psal.* 11. 3? Yea, therefore some will say, *Where is the God of* Judgment, Mal. 2. 17? The Earth will then be without Form, and void, the Heavens also will have no Light, Jer. 4. 23. as in the *Chaos*, at the first, *Gen.* 1. 2. which needs must have Astonish'd *Adam*, if he had Then been Made; much more his Fallen Posterity, who will be Now in Being.

                                                                    But

The Parable of the Ten Virgins Opened. 299

But though God is no Author of Confusion in a Moral sence, 1 *Cor.* 14. 33. yet doth he own his being the Creator of Afflicting Darknefs, *Ifa.* 45. 7. who alfo can improve all manner of Darknefs and Confufion, to Aggravate the Lufter of his following Light and Order, as in the firft Creation. Yea, thofe are Weariers of him (and therefore will be foon caft off,) who do thence Argue, his being Abfent, as well as They, who therefore fay, *He is Delighted in Evil Doers*, Mal. 2. 17.

39. Eminent Profeffors (or fuch as *Joſhua* the High-Prieft was) will then be apt to be Refifted (yea, to be Overcome, without Chrift's Help) by Satan, *Zech.* 3. 1,2. or under Satan's Difpenfation, in a Revelation fence, *Rev.* 2. 10. which Anfwereth to that time in *Zechary*. The Matter of which Conteft, Relateth to the Body of *Mofes*, as is more plainly fignified, Jude 9. where this very Form of words [*The Lord Rebuke thee*] is quoted hence. Nor need we ftick at his being called [*Michael*] in *Jude*, who is here [*Called the Lord.*] Zech. 3. 2. fince Chrift is granted to be meant, by that word *Michael*, *Rev.* 12. 7. as Mr. *Brightman* there confeffeth, although he doth Diftinguifh them, *Dan.* 12. 1. However, Chrift might fpeak this in *Zech.* 3. 2. and *Michael* (or a Created Angel, Employed by Chrift in this Conteft) might fpeak the fame words afterwards, as *Jude* Relateth. And fo, by [*Mofes his Body*] is meant his Miniftration ; which *Joſhua* (then) was Tempted to keep up in Rigour, or elfe to lay it quite afide: As he was a Tye of others in thefe Latter Days, Comparing Times with Times.

Firft, *Joſhua* might be Tempted to keep that Miniftration up in Rigour, as to the Tabernacle-ftate (in *Mofes* his Time) in Competition with the Prefent Temple; becaufe the Building of this Latter (*viz.* the Temple) was Now Prohibited, and therefore Perillous. Thus have fome Argued of Later times, (or fince the Prohibition iffued forth) that a Lefs Solemn, and more Private Worfhip (fuch as that in the Tabernacle in the Days of *Mofes*) was more Agreeable unto their Prefent Wildernefs-condition, than what is of an Open Temple-Nature. Yea, fome are Tempted to Obferve *Mofes* his Seventh-day-Sabbaths, and other Ordinances, upon this Account.

Or, Secondly, *Joſhua* might then be Tempted to lay that Inftituted Miniftration quite afide, becaufe of Troubles in the Keeping of it up: Pretending its having been Abolifhed in *Babylon*. And thus fome may be Now Tempted to conceive, that Gofpel-Inftitutions are no more to be Regarded, as having been carried into *Babylon*, and not to be Reftored again.

But *Joſhua* Overcame, in that Conteft; and Chrift will give an Effectual

Effectual Rebuke to Satan, on the behalf of such, as he then did; which is good News to Them, but sad to Others, who are in bondage unto that Temptation; since the Neglect of typical Temple-worship (then) was so severely witnessed against; and since the Reviving of *Moses* his Authority (Now) is so directly cross unto a Gospel-rule, *Rom* 7. 4. 7; and since the Restauration of Gospel-Institutions (after the full Return of *Babylon*'s Captivity in the Mystery) is so Expressly signified, *Rev.* 11. 19. and in a Way of full Agreement with that in the Letter of Old. And Presently upon the Rebuking of which Temptation, *Zech.* 3. 2. *Joshua* was cloath'd with Change of Raiment, *v.* 4. and had a Promise of Presiding in Christ's House, and Walking with those who then stood by, *v.* 7. *viz.* the Angels, *v.* 5.

40. A Stealing of the Word of God (by some) each from his Neighbour; as in the Day of Old *Jerusalem*, *Jer.* 23. 30. which VVord of God (in all probability) was, that VVord which *Jeremy* had there declared (a little before) concerning the VVhirlwind of God, that was gone forth in Fury, to fall upon the Head of that wicked Generation, *Jer.* 23. 19. and not to Return, untill the thoughts of his Heart were Executed and Performed, *v.* 20. This VVord the Devil (in his Instruments) endeavoureth to Steal (or Catch away) from others, as *Mat.* 13. 19: Partly, by making a Derision of his Message, *Jer.* 20. 8. and loading his Person with false Reports, *v.* 10. that People might not Hear him, as *Joh.* 10. 20: and Partly by substituting their False VVord instead of his, *Jer.* 23. 25. with utmost Confidence, *v.* 31. on purpose to make the People Forget the Other, *v.* 27; yea (possibly) offering to Prove their Own false Prophecy, (concerning *Babylon*'s being then to be Broken, as *Hananiah* did Assert, *Jer.* 28. 2.) from *Jeremy*'s own words against *Elam*, *Jer.* 49. 35. in the Beginning of *Zedekiah*'s Reign, *v.* 34. since *Elam* then was under *Babylon*, as some doe (very Probably) conceive. But as this sort of Stealers are Sacrilegious, *Rom.* 2. 22. so doth the Lord declare himself to be Against them, *Jer.* 23. 30: and as, if he be For us, VVho then can be Against us, *Rom.* 8. 31? so if he be Against a man, who Can, who VVill, who Dare be For him? Yea, 'tis Expressly said, with reference to such a Time, that as there will be Stealers then, so will a flying Curse pursue them, and Cut them off, with their whole House, *Zech.* 5. 3, 4.

41. The having of some men's Persons too much in Admiration. Thus were the *Pharisees* (at such a time) in High Esteem, *Luk* 16. 15. among those men by whom Christ was Despised, *Isa.* 53. 3. And as unworthy. *Shebna* (in the *Assyrian*'s Day) was Steward in *David*'s House

House, *Isa.* 22. 15. 21, 22; so Christ himself did suffer *Judas* to be his Steward, *Job.* 13. 29. a little before the setting up of his Own Ministration, who therefore Doubtlessely was most Esteemed by his Fellowes. Thus some make bold to Linger (at this day) in spiritual *Sodom*, because of Righteous *Lot's* Example, *Gen.* 19. 16. and will Dispute Escaping to the Mountains, because *Lot* did so, *v.* 17. 18; especially considering his Gracious words then uttered, *v.* 19. and God's Acceptance of him, *v.* 21. but not his Portion afterwards, *v.* 30. 36. Yea thus some argue from the General Faith and Practice of Professors, unto the Warrant of Believing as they doe; and Daring others to Condemn so many Holy ones. But though God knoweth who are His, 2 *Tim.* 2. 19. and how to Deliver the Godly in such Cases, 2 *Pet.* 2. 9; yet is it Desperately Presumptuous, to set Our good Opinion of any Person, in competition with Christ's Command, and so to honour Them more than Him, 1 *Sam.* 2. 29; which is the ready way to Perish, *v.* 30, 31. 35.

42. Aptness to fansie its being a Duty to be meerly Passive, and not Active, in a way of self-delivery out of *Babylon*. Thus have some pleaded, the Time was not yet come for Temple-work, *Hag.* 1. 2; because the Law of Man was still in Force, *Ezra* 4. 21. although directly Cross to God's Command, *Ezra* 6. 14: till they had almost quite undone themselves, both as to Temporals, *Hag.* 1. 9. and Spirituals, *Hag.* 2. 14. And thus, some Dare not stirre out of a Present (though Corrupted) state, till Providence doth Force them out; as those of Old, whom therefore God bad to Deliver Themselves, *Zech.* 2. 7; which leaveth Others (at this day) without Excuse. It is a Scruple (this) against the very Law of Nature; since every living Infant (in the Womb) is some way Active to its own Production; and therefore *Ephraim* had not the Wit of an unborn Child, for staying so long, till fetched out, *Hos.* 13. 13. which is a sad sign the Child is Dead. But *Jeremy* went forth of *Jerusalem*, to separate himself from thence, and in the Midst of all the People, *Jer.* 37. 12; till he was Forcibly brought back again, and put in Prison, *v.* 13, 14, 15. which others cannot truely say, they are, as to their tarrying in their ancient Temples, and Active Complyance with unrighteous Laws.

43. Aptness in some to Murmure, because of Others Equal Pay (for One Hours labour) with Themselves, on whom the Heat and Burden of the Day had fallen; as Christ Expressely signifieth, with reference unto his Day, *Mat.* 20. 11, 12: much more in case these Later labourers shall have All, as seemeth to be intimated, *v.* 16. and as the *Gentiles* were to have, in competition with the *Jews*, *Mat.* 6, 11, 12.

Thus

The Parable of the Ten Virgins Opened.

Thus might *Abiathar* take it ill, that he, who First came unto *David* in his Low Condition, 1 *Sam.* 22. 20. was afterwards made to give place to *Zadok*, 1 *Chron.* 24. 3. who came not in till *David* was come to *Hebron*, 1 *Chron.* 12. 23. 28. especially when *Zadock* (in the Issue) was High-Priest Alone, 1 *Kings* 2. 27. 35; and wherein *Zadock* was a Type, with reference unto these Latter dayes, *Ezek.* 44. 13, 15. Thus also *John*'s Disciples did Repine, to see their Master's Successor Preferr'd before him, *Joh.* 3. 25, 26. and so will some of Christ's Disciples doe, (upon a like occasion, to be looked for) in case they be not well laid in with Self denyal against that sore Temptation; since First and Last must Counter-march in such a Day, and wherein (partly) will appear his Glory, *Mat.* 20. 15, 16.

44. Withstanding Christ, at least by Praying (Peremptorily) Against that which the Lord hath signified to be his Purpose. Indeed, there was a Time, when God sought for a man to stand in Old *Jerusalem*'s Gap, *Jer.* 5. 1. and Then might *Jeremy* have safely Prayed for that People, whom afterwards the Lord Prohibited, *Jer.* 7. 16. We know not what to pray for, as we Ought, save as the Spirit helpeth us therein, *Rom.* 8. 26. according to the Will of God, 1 *Joh.* 5. 14. There is a Time for Silence, *Eccl.* 3. 7; and much of Prudence doth appear in being silent at some time, *Am.* 5. 13. with reference unto our Deprecating an Afflicting Providence, *Am.* 6. 10. Thus *Abraham* Prayed for *Sodom*, but within Compass, *Gen.* 18. 32; because he knew what God would doe, *v.* 17. and therefore *Jeremy* (in such a Case) did onely Threaten those, *Jer.* 37. 6, 7, 8. who did Request his Praying for them, *v.* 3. And though *Isaiah* (in the *Assyrian*'s Day) Pray'd for *Jerusalem*, 2 *Chron.* 32. 20. as it did shadow out Christ's Kingly Interest; yea though some are Commanded (then) to Pray for sparing Mercy, *Joel* 2. 17. yet did the Lord Reveal (at such a time) that sin which then was unto Death, *Isa.* 22. 14. and which should not be Prayed for, 1 *Joh.* 5. 16. the Knowledge whereof is a Peculiar Gift, by which those of that Other Spirit have been Distinguished from the Generality.

45. Reproaching those of the Separation, as favouring of Carnality and Worldly Ease, compared with those who still Continue in their former State. Thus did the *Pharisees* and *John*'s Disciples censure Christ and his, because These Fasted not, as did the Other, *Mat.* 9. 14. And thus some may upbraid withdrawers from them, as having Eased themselves of many Burdens, which They still bear. Thus, if *John* be Austere, he hath a Devil, *Mat.* 11. 18. if Christ be otherwise, he is Licentious, *v.* 19. but Wisdom is Justified of her Children. And yet as Christ's Disciples

The Parable of the Ten Virgins Opened.

Disciples Could not Fast (at such a time,) as did the Other, because of their Different Apprehensions about the Present Dispensation, *Mat.* 9. 15: so neither could the Other (Truely) count themselves more Heavy Laden; considering what Christ and his Disciples met with for their separating from the *Pharisees*, far worse than what the Other groaned under. And as it argueth Little Zeal for Duty, to count it Burdensome, *Mal.* 1. 13. so God Accepted not their self-imposed, Soul-afflicting Exercises, in a *Babylonish* State, *Zech.* 7. 3 5: much more will Christ soon reckon with those, who thus Reproach his Peoples Duty with that Disgracefull name of Carnal Liberty.

THus have I now finished the Explication of these words. It onely Remaineth, to conclude the whole (both of this Verse and Parable) with a few words of Exhortation, to be Watchful in the General, or with respect to Every of those forementioned Particulars. In order whereunto, these following Motives may be of use.

Motive 1. This work of Watching, is incumbent upon All, *Mark* 13. 37. which Virgins therefore have no cause to think much at. All are not Bound (as some may be) to Watch for Others, *Heb.* 13. 17: but Every man is bid to prove Himself, 2 *Cor.* 13. 5. and his Own work, *Gal.* 6. 4. or to work out his Own Salvation, *Phil.* 2. 12. Those are Soul-damningly Presumptuous, who Trust unto Another's watching for their Souls, and therefore sleep themselves; as in a Bodily case: since Every self-neglective Soul shall Die in his Iniquity, together with his Carelefs Watchman, *Ezek.* 33. 8. Now if Professors should do more than Others, *Mat.* 5. 47; will such fail in a Common Duty? No Servant will refuse the doing of what his Master may expect from Others; and Virgins do Profess themselves to be Christ's most Obedient and Proper Servants; whose being such, is to be Evidenced by their Watching, *Luke* 12. 37. and VVaiting for him, *vers.* 36.

2. Saints have their Name from hence; who therefore (Eminently) are called, VVatchers, as well as makers of Decrees, *Dan.* 4. 17. VVhich Holy ones may be so termed there, Partly with reference unto Others; but Chiefly with respect unto Themselves. Thus was *Ezekiel* made a VVatchman to his fellow-Captives, *Ezek.* 33. 7: but to keep Others Vineyards, and not one's Own, is that which Spouses may confess with shame, *Cant.* 1. 6. And if a spiritual sleeper (in the General) is called Dead, *Eph.* 5. 14. much more a slumbring Virgin or Professor, who hath his Name from VVatching. Therefore Christ said.

said to *Peter*; *Simon, Sleepest Thou*, Mark 14. 37? as being worse in Him (because of his Profession) than in some other. And as None can be Waking, in case the Watchers be Asleep: So He must look to Suffer more than all the rest, for his Names-sake, *Mark* 13. 34.

3. How vigilant are sinners in their Evil way; who cannot sleep till they have done some Mischief, *Prov.* 4. 16. Yea, who are most awake (or Active) in the Night, and who are therefore waiting for the Twilight, *Job* 24. 15! Now, if it be a shame for Men (in what is useful) to be Inferiour unto Brutes, *Isa.* 1. 3. or Birds, *Jer.* 8. 7. or Creeping things, *Prov.* 6. 6. much more for Saints to be out-stript by Sinners in their Respective Watching; Especially since Saints themselves have sometimes been (as sinners are) exceeding Vigilant, in a sinful way; whose Change (by Grace) doth not Diminish (but rather add unto) their Circumspection, although with reference unto a Changed Object. In which regard, Believing *Paul* did Persecute still (as in the *Greek*) or follow after that Truth in Love unto it, *Phil.* 3. 12. which he had formerly Persecuted Others for, in way of Hatred, *v.* 6.

4. Others are watching for our Halting, and therefore we have need to take heed to our ways. How was Christ watched by the *Pharisees*, *Mark* 3. 2. and *Jeremy* by his Familiars, *Jer.* 20. 10. and *David* by his Observers, which made him Pray for being Led in a plain Path, *Psal.* 27. 11! Which being so Narrowly Observed by others, may prove our great Advantage; it being so Natural to be Remiss, if winked at by Fellow-Creatures. Yea, some must look to be Enticed, as *Jeremy* was, *Jer.* 20. 10. on purpose to make a Breach upon our Principles, whereby to be Revenged of us, for a Differing Practice or Profession. In which regard, Christ biddeth his Disciples to be wise as Serpents, and to Beware of Men, who watch for something by which to Colour over their Designed Mischief, *Mat.* 10. 16, 17. Those of the Separation have been alway Censured for their over-strictness; but if the least Mote be to be seen upon them, it will be put into their Eye; who therefore have need to Watch and Keep their Garments.

5. Be therefore *Vigilant, because your Adversary the Devil, as a Roaring Lion, walketh about, seeking whom he may Devour*, 1 Pet. 5. 8. And as this was his Practice alway, so more especially, must *Joshua* look to be Resisted by him at This Day, which Answereth unto that of Old, *Zech.* 3. 1. He can apply Temptations suitable to our Tempers; yea, he can shrewdly Ghess at our Inclining thereunto, and so Pursue them in their fittest Season. And what would not he give, to have his Will (next unto *Christ*, *Mat.* 4. 9.) upon some Christians, 2 *Cor.* 12. 7? He knoweth who is likeliest to be his Greatest Adversary; whom

The Parable of the Ten Virgins Opened.

whom he would therefore win, or weaken by some Fall: Yea, were it onely to prevent their Near approaching Crown, whom he doth therefore stronglieſt Tempt at ſuch a Time, as in that Caſe of *Joſhua*, *Zech*. 3. 1, 5. He alſo hath Devices on both hands, or under a moſt fair Pretence, 2 *Cor*. 2. 11. by which he will get an Advantage, in caſe we be not very Vigilant, wherein it is a ſhame to be out-ſtripped by him.

6. Chriſt alſo is called a Watcher, *Dan*. 4. 13. which is there plainly meant of Him; as by his being ſingularly (there) ſpoken of; ſo by that Work it ſelf, *v*. 14. which Primarily belongeth unto Him, although his People ſhare with him, both in that Work and Name, *v*. 17. who is ſo called, partly, becauſe he Watcheth (or Keepeth) his Vineyard Day and Night, *Iſa*. 27. 3. for he that Keepeth *Iſrael* doth not ſlumber, *Pſal*. 121. 3. and if he watcheth them, ſhall not They watch Themſelves? Yea, he (as Man) did ſometimes watch, in ſuch an Hour of Temptation, to ſet us an Example, *Mat*. 26. 38. *And could ye not Watch with Me*? ſaid he to his Diſciples, *v*. 40. He alſo (as Mediator) watcheth ſtill, and Prayeth for his *Peters*, *Luke* 22. 32. which ſhould provoke Their joyning with him in that Work, *v*. 46. as *Joſhua* was to Fight whilſt *Moſes* was at Prayer, *Exod*. 17. 9. though *Iſrael* Prevailed upon *Moſes* his Account, *v*. 11. as if Chriſt doth not Keep, the Watch-man waketh but in vain, *Pſal*. 127. 1. yet ſhould we therefore work, becauſe God worketh in us, *Phil*. 2. 12, 13.

7. As watching is incumbent upon All, *Mark* 13. 37. and in All Things, 2 *Tim*. 4. 5. ſo at All Times, *Luke* 21. 36. which therefore ought not to be wondred at, if Now required; but ſhould be more attended to, on that Account. In which regard, it may be ſaid of watchfulneſs, as it is ſaid of Holineſs, 1 *John* 2. 6. and Brotherly Love, *v*. 9, 10. which is not any New Command, *v*. 7. ſave with Reſpect unto a Circumſtantial Variation, *v*. 8. as Legal Duty is Now turned into Evangelical; and as our watching (in the General,) is Now Commanded in Relation to the Duties and Temptations of ſuch a Particular Time. Now, when Chriſt putteth (upon his) none other Burden, ſave what they have already; he ſignifieth it as a Motive to Hold faſt that which they have, untill his Coming, *Rev*. 2. 24, 25. And if Obedience be our Centre, as we draw Nearer to its End, ſo will our Motion be the quicker, as is to be Obſerved in a falling Arrow. And if Men very Aged, (or drawing nigh unto their Diſſolution) are alſo moſt Awake, or apt to Riſe up at the voice of an Early Bird, *Eccl*. 12. 4. it will be to Their ſhame, who are moſt Heavy Headed, in a Spiritual ſence, a little before their dropping into the Grave.

8. Sleep

8. Sleep is so Natural, (as in the Letter) and pleasing to the Flesh, especially unto some, which is another Motive to be Watchful. In Moral cases (to be sure) we may conclude that to be Excellent which Nature (at least Corrupted Nature) is averse unto: And such is Spiritual Vigilancy. The Old Man is so called, partly, because of Drousiness; and if the first *Adam*'s sinless Nature was apt to sleep, *Gen.* 2.21. as being of an Earthly Make, *v.*7. much more doth sin dispose thereunto, and more especially in this Moral sence. And though some cannot sleep (as others do) or sin to such an Height, yet do All Love to slumber, or Dally with Temptations of a sinful Nature. And as Men of a more Feeble Spirit, and Cold Complexion, and Grosser Bodies, are most Heavy-headed, in the Letter; so let those look about them, in the Mystery, whose strength is gone, whose Love is Cold, and who are most encompassed with this World's Fatness. Nor ever had the Tempter such Advantages (as Now) in point of Watchlesness, it being Now so Universal; which yet should stir up others to be Singular.

9. Some (at this Day) have need to watch, because they are so much Alone; as did the *Psalmist*, upon that Account, *Psal.* 102. 7. He that will be (as Sparrows are) upon the House-top, must look (in Times of Danger) to be Alone: And wo be unto him, whose solitariness (at such a Time) and sleepiness are in Conjunction. These are Dividing Times, wherein we therefore should be gathered up (so much the more) into our selves, and into self-defending Circumspection. Those are poor Creatures, and have Nought to Lose, who can sleep in a solitary Cottage; which is the case of several Now, who have been wont to Live in Families. Let scattered ones improve this Consideration in a self-rouzing way; whom Providence hath Now constrained to be Watchful, and which may prove a great Advantage. Now is the Watchmens Day of Visitation, *Mic.* 7.4. wherein Old Shepherds shall be made to cease from Feeding the Flock of God, *Ezek.* 34. 10. onely Lambs Feeding alone are in great Danger, *Hos.* 4. 16. who therefore had need to watch themselves, as they would not become the roaring Lions Prey, 1 *Pet.* 5. 8.

10. The Spiritual Nature of Chiefest Duties and Temptations, doth call for Watching, at the Highest Rate. The very first Principle of Gospel-Duty is self-denial, *Mat.* 16. 24. a Failure wherein, is so far from being Censured by the Generality, that Men will Praise thee, when thou dost Well unto thy self, *Psal.* 49. 18. Yea, Conscience also is un-acquainted with Holy Curiosities, or Time-concernments; which therefore may be over-looked without any inward Check, save as we are under Conscience, unto Christ. Grosser Temptations are like
Swords

Swords or Spears, which being more Obvious, may therefore be more Easily avoyded: but Time-temptations are like Arrows; more out of sight, which are more Dangerous, and by which *Saul* (for all his Shield, 2 *Sam*. 1. 21.) was Deadly wounded, 1 *Sam*. 31. 3. Now as we are to *Watch* in Prayer, *Col.* 4. 2. becaufe that Duty is moſt fpiritual; fo have Saints need to be Compleatly armed, *Eph*. 6. 11. becaufe they Wreſtle not with Fleſh and Blood, but fpiritual Wickedneſs in High Places, *v.* 12.

11. It elſe will evidence our being Poor; ſince the Rich man's Abundance will not fuffer him to ſleep, *Eccl*. 5. 12. Worldly Poor men ſleep moſt fecurely; and fpiritual Sleepers may be concluded Poor, as are unarmed Travellers in Thieviſh wayes. Sinners are either Really poor, (as to what Souls are fubject to be Robbed of;) or elſe ſuch know not the Worth of what they have, elſe would they be more Watchfull. Their Portion is in this Life onely, *Pfal*. 17. 14; who cannot Reſt, if That be hazarded, *Ifa*. 30. 15: but matters of a fpiritual nature are Another's (*viz.* the Saints Own, *Luke* 16. 12.) which therefore Sinners care not to fecure. As where the Treafure is, there will the Heart be alfo, *Luke* 12. 34; fo when the Heart is in a ſlumbring Frame, 'tis from the Want of fpiritual Treafure. VVhereas, they who have Moſt of Grace and Joy, are alway fearfull leſt they ſhould Lofe it; who therefore keep a conſtant VVatch, becaufe they Know the VVorth of ſuch Commodities, and their continual Danger.

12. *In cafe I fin*, (faith *Job* to God) *Thou Markeſt me*, Job 10. 14. *Thou lookeſt Narrowly to All my paths*, Job 13. 27; *Doſt thou not Watch over my Sin*, Job 14. 16? And if it be fo, then *Job* and we had need to VVatch Againſt it. 'Tis true, God Marketh Iniquity (in his People) with a Forgiving Eye; but that Forgivenefs worketh Fear, *Pfal*. 130. 3, 4: yea his very Marking it, doth make them VVatch againſt it, *Pfal*. 44. 20, 21. And with refpect unto thefe Latter dayes, God reprefents himfelf as one that Hearkeneth, *Jer*. 8. 6. *Mal*. 3. 16; which ſhould Oblige us to be very Circumfpect, ſince he doth know the things that come into our Mind, *Ezek*. 11. 5. and which is ſignified (there) with reference to ſuch a Time. Thus Chriſt came down (from Heaven) in *Sodom*'s Day, to know the Certainty of what he heard, *Gen*. 18. 20, 21; becaufe he Then was come to Judge upon the Cafe; as he Now will, *Rev*. 11. 18. Now when poor Creatures ſtand before the Judge, how VVatchfull are they, (as All at This day had need be) for fear of Aggravating their final fentence!

13. Let us not be lefs *watchfull* in a Spiritual Cafe, than in a Bodily

dily; or with respect unto an Earthly Interest. Men (of a sober Spirit) will not Play with Edged tools: and Sin is VVounding, *Jer.* 30. 14: the Thought of Foolishness is (also) Sin, *Prov.* 24. 9. therefore take heed of Dallying with such Temptations. How do men also *watch* for worldly Gain; though many to little purpose, *Psal.* 127. 2: now Duty is Enriching, *Prov.* 8. 18: nor will that labour be in vain, 1 *Cor.* 15. 58: therefore take heed of letting slip such Opportunities. Shall we be Circumspect, whilest in the sight of Men, (for fear of losing our Esteem with them,) and not much more before the Lord? What is the Body, to the Soul? or Time, compared with Eternity? or Reputation, to our being saved? spiritual unwatchfulness proceeds from Atheism in its Spring, and runneth at the last into its Ocean.

14. 'Tis but an Hour of Temptation, this, which Now is come upon us. *Rev.* 3. 10: and can ye not Watch One Hour, *Mat.* 26. 40? Yea, This may Possibly be the Last Hour of our Present day; and if the shortness of Time should make us *weep* as though we *wept* not, 1 *Cor.* 7. 29. 30; let it then make us *watch*, (in competition with complaining) as though we watched not. The time may Now be very near, when either we shall *watch* no more (if Dying in the Lord;) or not be so Extreamly Tempted, as we Now are. Though *watchfulness* will be a Duty to the End, yet may the Labour of that Duty be Abated together with the Overcomers being made (within a while) a Pillar in Gods Temple, *Rev.* 3. 12. Nor do I doubt, but that conflicting *Joshua* may be (e're long) Relieved with greater Strength, as 2 *Cor.* 12. 9. or Less Temptations, as *Zech.* 3. 1, 2. I dare not set the time; nor is it our Duty to Depend thereon: yet should it Encourage us to keep *Waking*, since our Salvation Now is Nearer every day than other, as is argued, *Rom.* 13. 11.

15. Let us consider, of how great Consequence it is, to *Watch*; and as Continually, so Now especially.

1. Such will be most Dignified by Christ, at his Appearing; for he will then make them sit down to meat, and Gird himself, and will come forth and serve them, *Luke* 12. 37. *Watching* and *Standing* goe together, *Isa.* 21. 8. which Standing is a weary posture, and therefore such shall Then sit down; yea Christ will then set them, or make them sit. *Watching* and *Fasting* goe together, 2 *Cor.* 6. 5. yea want of Sleep requireth Meat, instead of Nourishing Rest: therefore these VVatchers shall sit down to Meat. Such also have approved themselves to be his Servants, by their VVatching, or VVaiting for him, *Luke* 12. 36. therefore he Now will be Their Servant, which Masters are not wont to be. They have been *waiting* with their Loyns Girt, *Luke* 12. 35. 36.

The Parable of the Ten Virgins Opened. 309

to keep themselves from being VVeary: and therefore he will Gird himself. And though their watching hath been most *within*, yet he will then come forth and serve them. Yea such shall be made Rulers over All, *Luke* 12. 44.

2. Such do Enjoy themselves (at Present) with the Best Advantage, (as in the Letter) both in Relation to Themselves and Others. Persons Awake, can Hear, and See, and have their other Senses better exercised, than if Asleep: so in the Mystery. Such are not Deluded with idle Dreams themselves; and Pity others who Laugh more Heartily, but in their Sleep. Beauty is chiefly seated in the Eye, *Cant.* 4. 9. which none but Watchers can keep Open: nor can any other prevent their being shamed several wayes, *Rev.* 16. 15. Such can perceive the Tempter at a Distance; and quickly clear themselves of that Pollution which resteth upon Others till they *wake*. And though Sleep in the Letter is Refreshing, yet in a Spiritual sence, those are most Cheary who are most Awake. Yea such are also in the best Capacity of being helpfull unto Others.

3. Such will be Forwardest to See and Know and Open unto Christ when he shall be revealed. Those had the first Tydings of Christs Birth, who were then keeping Watch over their Flock by Night, *Luke* 2. 8,9. as if Christ had been onely born for them, *v.* 11. The VVatchmen upon Mount *Ephraim* are First heard to crie, *Arise and let us goe up to Sion, Jer.* 31. 6: and *Sion's* Watchmen shall lift up the Voice with Singing, for they shall see Eye to Eye, *Isa.* 52. 8. If *Mary* had not been up before Day-break, *Luke* 24. 1. she had not seen her Lord so soon, *Joh.* 20. 1. 8: and Early Sights of such a Nature, will countervail the want of Sleep sufficiently. Such also will Immediately Open to him, *Luke* 12. 36. since Readiness consists in Watching: and if it be a Priviledge to be *In* Christ First, *Rom.* 16. 7. by way of Trusting, *Eph.* 1. 13. then to be First *with* him; which is reserved for the *watchfull* Ones.

4. Such will be less Affrighted (as in the Letter) with that Noyse, wherewith the Old Heavens must pass away, when Christ doth come, 2 *Pet.* 3. 10. How did that Jaylour Tremble, when he was Frighted out of his Sleep with that tremendous Earthquake, and its Consequents, *Act.* 16. 26,27,29; who else would not have been so much Amazed; nor Others Now, (at such a like Earthquake in the Mystery,) but for their having been Asleep. Sleep makes secure; Security preventeth Expectation; and unexpected Troubles are Transporting: thence are the Sinners in *Sion* so Afraid (at such a time) becaufe surprized, *Isa.* 33. 14; and that surprizal is the Fruit of slumbring. Whereas Awakened ones are in the constant Exercise both of their Sense and Reason;

or like an Army Training in the Field, who therefore are not so Affrightingly alarmed, as when Asleep in their respective Quarters. The Holiest ones in former times, have been least Terrified with those Revolutions which have betrayed Others into Ensnaring Fears, by reason of their unwatchfulness.

5. Such are most likely to Escape; since Watchers are counted *worthy*, in that regard, *Luke* 21. 36. The Centinel (with Men) is in the Front of Danger from an Enemy; but Christ bids, save the *Watchman*, as having delivered his *own* soul at least, *Ezek.* 33. 9. Yea Christ will not Come (as an Adversary) upon Watchers; who onely threatens his Coming as a Thief, in case men do not watch, *Rev.* 3. 3 : nor could the Devil much infest us, if we did Fire at him when he first appeareth, *Jam.* 4. 7. However, *watchers* are best able to defend themselves; whilest sleeping Crocodiles are apt to be destroyed by an *Egyptian* Rat. Next unto Death Sleep is the greatest Leveller; or that which maketh All to be Alike : Yea *waking* Infants are more self-relieving than a slumbring Giant. If some had not been fast Asleep, the Enemy had not sown his Tares, *Mat.* 13. 25 ; nor had she lost her Living Child, 1 *King.* 3. 20. nor *Sisera* his Life, *Judg.* 4. 21 ; nor *Sampson* both his Hair and Eyes, Judg. 16. 19. 21 ; nor would the good man's House be Broken through, if he had watched, *Luke* 12. 39.

6. Such will be in the best Capacity to entertain whatever may befall, in way of Tryal. Sleep maketh Tender; but Watchers are more Hardy; and Holiest ones have alway been the bravest sufferers. A waiting servant (well Employ'd) cares not how soon his Master cometh, but Ecchoeth presently unto his Knock. Such are Aware of what is coming; and being Provided for Tribulations, that sort of Guests are not so troublesome as if they had been unexpected. Christ dreaded not the Devils coming, because he could find Nothing in him, for he had been Obedient, *Joh.* 14. 30, 31 : and he whose Course is finished in such a way, need not be frighted with the News of his Departure, 2 *Tim.* 4. 6, 7. None know's how soon that Day may come, *Zech.* 14. 2. and Then, wo be to spiritual sleepers, who possibly may be Awakened with a Sword or Pistoll, and be run through before they can Repent. However, we daily hear of some or other struck with suddain Death; whose Case may be our Own ; and Blessed then is he that watcheth and is Ready.

I shall conclude this Exhortation to be Watchfull, with some few Helps; which are, as followeth.

Helps: 1. Let us be throughly Wakened out of a Present Sleep : 'tis but a folly (else) to talk of future Watching. Sleep in a Moral

sence

fence, is called Death, *Eph.* 5. 14. and Watching is an Act of one Alive; till Men be therefore Quickned by Awaking, they cannot mind this work of Watching. Such also must be throughly wakened; else will they quickly sleep again, when once the startling Rouzer is withdrawn, *Mat.* 26. 13. Now, all will readily confess their having been Asleep, of Later Times; But if they be more sleightily Awakened, they will soon Nod again. Overly Convictions, and Gentle self-reprovings are wont to end in sad Relapses; nor is he to be Trusted for the Future, who is not deeply sensible of former Failings. Men un-convinced cannot watch, because they are Asleep: And Men not duly Humbled (for their sin) will sleep again, because They are not Throughly wakened. Make your awakening sure, one way or other, as you would not be over-taken with a Second Sleep.

2. Take heed of being Alone, in way of sinful Choice, which is a woful Disadvantage, *Eccl.* 4. 10. but get into some kind of Body; and which is Competible unto scattered ones: Disperled ones cannot be in an Instituted Body strictly taken; but such may be Together, as those Disciples were, before the Spirits pouring out, *Luke* 24. 33. and which is an Awakening Help. Such may Pray each with other, as They did, *Acts* 1. 14. if Prayer be not some way hindred, 1 *Pet.* 3. 7. and Prayer is an Awakening Exercise, which therefore is oft joyned with VVatching, 1 *Pet.* 4. 7. *Luke* 21. 36. *Col.* 4. 2. *Eph.* 6. 18. Such also may speak oft one to another, as *Mal.* 3. 16. and by that means may keep each other waking: Yea, where that Body is, there will the Eagles be, in way of Feeding, *Luke* 17. 37. and seldom do Men sleep whilst they are Eating. Nay, Fellow-Captives may watch over one another, as *Ezekiel* did, though in a Larger fence, *Ezek.* 33. 7. and Exercise some kind of Common Censures, which needs must be Awakening.

3. Make Choice of your Companions though; else had one better be Alone: since sleep is as Infectious as the Plague, and in a Spiritual fence more Dangerous. In case Two lie Together, they have Heat, *Eccl.* 4. 11. supposing them both to be Alive; but else a dead Log (in Bed) is not so Cold as a Dead Body is. I am perswaded, some find it an Advantage to them, (at least no Loss) to be Discharged of their Old Companions; and not without sufficient cause, which is the Present Case. If you would know the Newest Fashion, then go to the Professors of this Generation: But whither shall one go to find a Savoury Spirit, a Spirit savouring what is of God? Let one begin to tell a story, (or start some Idle Curiosity; and then he may have Talk enough: but serious Communications shut Men's Mouths, if not their Eyes. *Jo-seph*

seph in *Pharaoh's* Court, *Gen.* 42. 15. and *Peter* in the High-Priest's Hall, *Mat.* 26. 72. had quickly Learn'd their Late Companions Language: Yea, *Barnabas* was thereby much in Danger, *Gal.* 2. 13.

4. As Men would not be over-come with sleep, so let them take heed of slumbring, the Latter of which is but an In-let to the Former; as all the Virgins have Experienced, *Mat.* 25. 5. *Eve* was Beguiled, by her Parleying with the Serpent, *Gen.* 3. 1, 2. and fell in Love with the Forbidden Fruit, by Looking on it, *v.* 6. therefore *Job* made a Covenant with his Eyes, *Job* 31. 1. One stick will drop out after another, in case the Binder be Relaxed; and therefore we should rather wedge more in, 2 *Pet.* 1. 5. since our best Duty (like Green Wood) is apt to shrink, and so to slacken. A Tender Conscience is a precious Mercy, and a great preservative; whilst others of a Bolder Spirit, are oft-times caught before they are aware. The Nearer that Duty is, the better is its Beauty seen: But sin's Deformity is best discerned at a Distance, or when it is quite out of sight, as to a Carnal Eye. When once a Virgin hath lost her shame, the Tempter grows thereby more Impudent; and sinful Dallyings will enfeeble Holy Bashfulness, which being Lost, the Soul lies open to more Gross Temptations.

5. Take heed of shutting out the Light, since Darkness doth Invite to slumber. When Persons have a mind to sleep, they shut their Eyes, and draw the Curtains close; since Light (though but Reflected by a Glass) would keep them waking. Thence sinners are so fast asleep, because they are the Children of the Night; which Children of the Day are not so wont to be, 1 *Thes.* 5. 5, 6, 7. Yea, thence it is, that Day-time is oft turned into Night; and Children of the Day will sleep, in such a Case; who therefore should take heed of that Temptation. They who Rebel against the Light, are such who also will commit the works of Darkness, *Job* 24. 13, 14. There are Two greater Moral Lights (as well as Natural) *viz.* that of the First and Second *Adam*; both which are Lovingly to be received, and with Respect unto their fresh Appearances. Though Nature's Light is but like that of the Moon, the letting in whereof doth not so much disturb the Sleeper, as doth that of the Sun; thence may one sleep, and yet be Morally Obedient: And Mid-day Light is most Awakening; therefore take heed of shutting out more High Discoveries.

6. Take heed of being in some kind of Posture which doth betray into a slumbring Disposition; as in the Letter, so in the Mystery. As sitting (in a Bodily Respect) exposeth unto sleeping, in the Letter: So doth the want of being well Employed, in a Mystical sence. Sleepers are therefore bidden to Arise, and to be Going, *Mat.* 26. 46. that

being

The Parable of the Ten Virgins Opened.

being likeliest to keep them waking. And the more Spiritual that any Duty is, the more are sleep-inviting postures to be shunned: Therefore we do not Reed of Sitting in that Duty of Prayer (save in that private Soliloquy, 2 *Sam.* 7. 18.) but either Standing or Kneeling; which is upon Record for our Instruction, save where good Reason warranteth some other Posture. However Sitting, in the Mystery (or any kind of Idleness whatever,) doth very much prejudice one's being watchful. Persons (in Bed together) quickly Talk themselves asleep; but if another's being up at work, doth keep us waking, much more if we our selves are so in Action.

7. As Drunkenness and sleep are joyned together, 1 *Thes.* 5. 7. so is Sobriety and Watching, 1 *Pet.* 4. 7. with reference to their Respective Influence. Full fed *Uriah* slept at *David*'s Door, 2 *Sam.* 11. 8. And he that Tarryeth at the Wine, *Prov.* 23. 30. will fall asleep upon a Mast, v. 34. So will Professors do, when growing sensual, as to their Bodily or Spiritual Diet. 'Tis not Men's Using of this World, but their Abusing it, which is forbidden, 1 *Cor.* 7. 31. as Men are not Distempered by their having great store of Wine and Meat before them, but by their taking in too much thereof into themselves. I never yet saw too Liberal Feeders upon Creature-comforts to be the choicest Christians: Nor can it be Expected; since Love (in an intense degree) cannot be fixed upon the Father and the World at once, 1 *John* 2. 15. Yea, they who are too Dainty toothed, in a Spiritual sence, (or who take more than is their share of Spiritual Comforts) have been Observed to be less Watchful than some others, who take what is convenient for them, and no more.

8. The want of Due Rest Occasions Drouziness, when one should Watch and be at Work. The Cares of this Life are over-charging, as well as Surfeiting; both which Occasion sleeping, and so Christ's Day doth come upon Men unawares, *Luke* 21. 34. God teacheth his the Vanity of Distracting Care, and so he giveth his Beloved Rest, *Psal.* 127. 2. Yea, he so keepeth them Awake in Spiritual Exercises, Whereas self-over-setting Workers all the week, are usually the greatest Lords-day sleepers; and they who will be Rich, cannot avoid Temptations of a Sinful Nature, 1 *Tim.* 6. 9. As Worldliness hath overcome Professors, so have they let their Duty Fall, which (whilst they were Awake, and not so Earthly minded) was held fast, 2 *Tim.* 4. 10. So let your Hands be Exercised with the World, as that your Hearts may (through Believing) be at Rest; else will you Nod in better Exercises. Yea, they who cannot mind their Duty, without sollicitousness about Events, or being too busie in what concerns another, are thereby oft betrayed into slumbring, for want of Rest in its due Time and Place.

9. They

9. They who are Heavy-headed (and would keep Awake) must not be apt to be Offended with a Friendly Nip, or being Jostled, and sometimes Prickt or Trod upon; at least-wise Touched, and more shrilly spoken to. Some are too Proud to be Reproved; and others too self-loving to Offend them: Thence is the Generality so fast asleep, till Christ himself doth come, or send to waken them. Some must be vexed, before they will unfold their sluggish Arms; and let them Fight with their Awakeners for a while, rather than sleep the sleep of Death. Christ tred upon the People's Toes, till some cryed out, *He had a Devil*, John 10. 20. and *Peter* prickt his Hearers to the Heart, who then Awakened, and called him Brother, *Acts* 2. 37. whom formerly they had Abused, *v.* 13. When apt to be Offended with some Rougher handling, let every one consider there may be much of God in such a Portion, and in a way of Mercy to mine heavy-headed Soul. I could sing Requiem's (as well as others) or smoother things, and thereby gain poor Children's Love: But let me rather Rouze them with a Faithful Testimony, than Rock and Flatter them into a Sleep.

10. Offer some kind of Holy Violence unto your selves; as in such cases (in the Letter) Men are wont to do; not onely by standing up, but shaking off an Heavy Disposition. True Godly Sorrow worketh Indignation, 2 *Cor.* 7. 11. and when a Man is vexed with his sin unto a self-abhorring, *Job* 42. 6. his Eye is Opened, *v.* 5. and will not readily shut again. Chase in upon your Hearts some Rouzing Terrors, as well as Comforts; so will you keep your selves Awake, and Others too, 2 *Cor.* 5. 8, 9, 10, 11. I have Observed, where some lye Napping Now, in whom the Old Man hath prevailed to a self-indulging; or who have been afraid of giving him one Angry word. Did we first (alway) speak unto our selves, and Labour to make Convictions Powerful upon our Consciences, it would Awaken them, which else will sleep the more securely, because of sleightiness in serious Matters. This some can Recommend, as *Eliphas* did his Counsel unto *Job*; *Loe, we have searched it, and so it is; hear it, and know Thou it, for thy Good,* Job 5. 27.

11. Busie your selves with something of a Curious and stirring Nature: Else Ordinary work may not prevent a Spiritual Nodding. Persons Engaged in some Deep Discourse, (which calls for study, and stirreth up Affections,) are not so apt to Talk themselves asleep, as others are. Coldness in Arguing for the Truth, (proceeding from Indifferency) is very prejudicial unto Zeal in Practice: whereas a Lively Advocate doth Heat himself, and thereby is the more Inflamed with Love unto his Cause, 1 *Cor.* 9. 26, 27. There are deep things of God, 1 *Cor.* 2. 10. and Mysteries of the Kingdom, *Mat.* 13. 11. which he who rightly

The Parable of the Ten Virgins Opened.

studieth, is not so likely to come short in Lesser Matters. *Paul* Laboured to attain the Resurrection of the Dead, *Phil.* 3.11. that kept him waking; whilst he that Fancieth his being laid in sufficiently, will say, *Soul, take thine Ease,* Luke 12.18,19. They who care not for Going on, *Heb.* 6.1. may fall Asleep; yea, quite away, *v.* 6. because of Resting in Old Received things, *v.* 1,2. or that which is short of Perfection: which Therefore *Paul* Resolved to take heed of, if God permitted, *v.* 3,4.

12. Take heed of Worldly sorrow, which made the Disciples sleep, *Luke* 22.45. Now, let the Cause be what it will, immoderate sorrow becometh Worldly, and that works Death, 2 *Cor.* 7.10. which sinful sleep is oft-times called. *Job's* Grief was very Great, *Job* 2.13. and that betray'd him into a sinful Passion, *Job* 3.1. and *Baruch* Fainted in his sighing, *Jer.* 45.3. that made him seek great things at such a Time, *v.* 4,5. And they who (in the Creatures presence) can Rejoyce, as if they had Rejoyced not, will also (in its Absence) Weep accordingly; and by that means be kept awake. *Jonah* was therefore Angry, *Jonah* 4.9. (with reference unto his withering Gourd,) *because he had been so Exceeding Glad whilst it continued, *v.* 6. who thereupon did sinfully wish for Death, *v.* 8. and Justified it before the Lord himself, *v.* 9. Yea, they who do inordinately Delight in Choiser Priviledges, (such as Christ's Bodily Presence was with his Disciples,) may soon Ditt up their Eyes with such a kind of dirty Tears, as some do Now, because he Tarrieth: which also holdeth True, with reference to any Priviledges whatsoever.

13. Labour to be more Spiritual; since in Relation to this work of Watching, the Spirit is willing, but the Flesh is weak, *Mat.* 26.41. Angels are Spirits, *Heb.* 1.7. who therefore do not sleep, but alway Behold the Face of God, *Mat.* 18.10. so will it be with Saints, (both in a Natural and Moral sence) as they grow more like unto Heavenly Angels. The first *Adam's* utmost is called Flesh, *Mat.* 16.17. and Legal things are termed Carnal, *Heb.* 9.10. Yea, so are also Babes in Christ, 1 *Cor.* 3.1. and these are weak, or likeliest to fail in Spiritual Watching. Nature skills not of Instituted Duty, nor yet a Legal Spirit, of what is Evangelical; both which are therefore apt to fail, in those Respective cases: And Babes (in Christ) are very prone to sleep and fall, as Children, in the Letter are. The Cry is Now, *All Flesh is withering Grass, and all the Goodliness thereof is as a fading Flower; but the Word of our God shall stand for ever,* Isa. 40.6,7,8. and by which Word is meant what is of a Proper Gospel-Nature, 1 *Pet.* 1.24,25. and therefore, as Men would stand in such a day, (or as they would not fall asleep,) so let them Labour to be Spiritual and Evangelical.

14. Get.

14. Get well Acquainted with the Time, which being known, is much awakening, *Rom.* 13. 11. and inability to Discern its signs, is that by which an Hypocrite is to be known, *Mat.* 16. 3. And though we should be sober, (in point of Peremptory setting such a time,) yet let us take heed of saying, *the Lord Delays his Coming,* Mat. 24. 48. considering what sinful Temptations that will Expose unto, *v.* 49. Most talk of some great Revolution near at hand; which if they seriously did believe, it would awaken them into a suitable watching. Would some Men Beautifie their Old defiled Temples with such goodly stones, did they fore-see their being soon to be demolished, *Mark* 13. 1, 2? Or did they look (e're long) for New Created Heavens, *Isa.* 65. 17? Would others fill their Houses with such dear-bought gain, did they believe their being Rifled, now within a while, *Zech.* 14. 2? Would others dally with their gross Temptations, were they aware, how soon all sinners now may perish by the Sword, *Amos* 9. 10? I am not positive, as to the very Time; but such a study might keep men waking: and though Grace turneth upon Golden hinges, or Nobler Motives than Mercenary Hope, or slavish Fear, yet may these help to prick us out of sleeping. And this indeed is Christ's own Motive here, to make us watch, because we know not how soon he may Thus come, in these our Days.

15. Let us be much in Prayer, which Duty we are bid to watch unto, 1 *Pet.* 4. 7. and to be Conversant about, together with our watching, as we wou'd not be led into Temptation, *Mark* 14. 28. Prayer carrieth a Soul into Christ's Presence; and whilst he was with his Disciples, he would not suffer them to sleep, at least not long. And if He doth not keep, the Watchman waketh but in vain, *Psal.* 127. 1. therefore let us engage him (by our Prayer) to watch over us, as he Obligeth us (by his Command) to watch our selves. But let us also watch unto Prayer in this regard, not Tempting him, (by our neglect) who will take no Man's work out of his hand, and who will not Relieve an Idle Beggar. Thus let us Watch and Pray, and Pray and Watch; this is to be at work with Both our Hands, which is the likeliest way to Overcome.

Thus have I now done with this whole Parable, which hath Occasioned my walking in untrodden-paths, and wherein some may possibly have stumbled; whom I would onely wish to Weigh the Premises, before they do reject them. And having now born my Testimony, I shall endeavour to stand upon my Watch, and see what I shall Answer, when I am Reproved: Submitting all my Sober Apprehensions unto Clearer Light, and Providential Determinations in God's Valley of Decision.

THE .*END*.

www.ingramcontent.com/pod-product-compliance
Lightning Source LLC
Chambersburg PA
CBHW030755230426
43667CB00007B/980